RUSSIAN
VOICES

RUSSIAN VOICES

Tony Parker

An Owl Book

HENRY HOLT AND COMPANY

NEW YORK

Library of Congress Cataloging-in-Publication Data
Parker, Tony.
Russian voices / Tony Parker. — 1st Owl book ed.
      p.   cm.
"An Owl book."
1. Soviet Union — Politics and government — 1985-   2. Soviet Union
— Social life and customs — 1970-   3. Interviews — Soviet Union.
4. Russians — Interviews.   I. Title.
DK288.P37   1992   91-44521
947.085 — dc20   CIP

ISBN 0-8050-1978-2

First Owl Book / American Edition — 1992

Printed in the United States of America
Recognizing the importance of preserving
the written word, Henry Holt and Company, Inc.,
by policy, prints all of its first editions
on acid-free paper. ∞

10   9   8   7   6   5   4   3   2   1

'vertical poem' from *Complete Poems 1910-1962*
by e e cummings is reproduced by permission of Grafton Books,
a division of HarperCollins Publishers Ltd.
'The Red Wheelbarrow' from *Collected Poems*
by William Carlos Williams is reproduced
by permission of Carcanet Press Ltd.

For
Galina Fadeyeva
assistant, interpreter and friend
with love and gratitude

Contents

Introduction

Most of the individuals to whom I first mentioned the idea that I had of trying to put together a book of tape-recorded conversations with a small cross-section of contemporary Russian people were doubtful if it would be feasible. I was myself. Only four years ago in their admirable *Citizens' Diplomacy: A Handbook on Anglo-Russian Initiatives* (Merlin Press, 1986) Claire Ryle and Jim Garrison had written: 'Almost all Westerners wanting to undertake projects with Soviet citizens want to do so independently. It is hard for us to appreciate the extent to which official permission is necessary in the Soviet Union. So uncertainty is the inevitable ingredient of any pioneer undertaking. Perseverance, and a commitment involving not months but years, is necessary.'

Apart from the unfailing encouragement of three people – my editor David Godwin, my agent Gill Coleridge, and particularly Barbara Laird of East-West Reach – the advice I received from everyone else, including seven different organisations who claimed to have special expertise in Anglo-Russian relationships, was that (a) the Russian authorities were very unlikely to allow me to go where I liked and talk to whom I wished without close supervision, (b) it would take so long, because of Russian bureaucracy, to get all the necessary visas and permits, that by the time they'd been obtained I should be too elderly and infirm to carry even the lightest of tape recorders, and (c) most Russians would be unfriendly and suspicious towards someone from the West, and unwilling to talk to him because of fear of the consequences. There was going to be too what seemed the insuperable obstacle of my not speaking Russian; and for me to learn to do so with anything even approaching the degree of fluency required would take several years of intensive effort.

However, many of these doubts and reservations were dispelled between 11 a.m. and midday on a Tuesday morning in January by Vladimir Stabnikov of the Union of Soviet Writers, when I went to see him in his office in Moscow, and ask him his advice. He said he thought the idea was an interesting one, and he couldn't see any reason why it couldn't be done: the Union of Writers would be happy to send me an invitation to come to Russia as often as I liked, and stay for as long as I wished. They would attend to all the form-filling and application-making on my behalf; and in addition they would provide me with accommodation, interviewing and sec-retarial facilities, a personal assistant and researcher, two interpreters and, whenever I wished to make use of them, a car and a driver. There were no conditions or restrictions; but perhaps at some unspecified future date reciprocal facilities could be offered to a Russian writer who might want to try and do something similar in England? Meantime, if I could give an approximate idea of when I would like to start . . .? When would be convenient, I enquired? Mr Stabnikov thought for a moment: Well probably any time after Thursday of the following week, he said.

During a period of just over a year, I went to Moscow five times: twice for a week, once for a fortnight, once for a month and once for three months, making a total of five months in all. In sequence, the seasons I was there were summer, autumn, winter and spring. I talked freely and at length with 141 people, tape-recording inter-views totalling 230 hours. No one was at any time reluctant or unwilling to talk to me, although a few people in official positions took what seemed an inordinate length of time to arrange appoint-ments. On each such occasion I felt it was due to procedural inefficiency and bureaucratic inertia, and nothing more: it was no worse than the same kind of thing which sometimes occurs in government or official departments in England.

But there were anyway very few instances of it, because most of my interviews were with individuals who represented no one but themselves. And among these ordinary everyday citizens of Moscow, men and women, young and old, there was no hesitation at all about meeting with a foreigner. On the contrary, almost everyone exuded warmth and friendliness, extended immediate hospitality, introduced me to their families and friends, and talked and talked and talked. To have someone from the West in their home, most of them for the first time ever, to ply him with food and drink, to tell him about themselves and their lives, and ask him about his own, seemed for nearly all of them to be a uniquely enjoyable occasion; and one which, despite the language barrier, brought a flood of offers of future hospitality and accommodation for me, my wife, our children, our grandchildren and, if quarantine regulations permitted it, our dogs.

The language problem, although never entirely satisfactorily solved, proved to be not as difficult as expected. In all, I used six different interpreters, three women and three men: two of them were provided by the Union of Writers and the other four were private contacts I made while I was there, whose existence the Union never knew about. A surprisingly large number of Russians speak English: in some cases fluently, in others well, and in yet others with sufficient ability to be perfectly understandable. They make up about half of those with whom there are interviews; where people spoke through an interpreter, the symbol * appears after their name. The interpreters were all skilful translators, and we worked out a system of self-effacement which they rigorously put into practice: it involved their always sitting slightly behind the person I was talking to, avoiding any eye-contact with them, using a low-pitched unobtrusive monotone and, except on the very rare occasions when it was unavoidable, never discussing until after the recording was finished any questions about the speaker's precise meanings.

A few, but only a very few, of the people I talked with – usually those who were in some official capacity or other – were introduced to me through the Union of Writers. But most were found independently or at my request by my assistant Galina Fadeyeva, or through the other interpreters, and many as a result of contacts made beforehand in England. A large number also were friends of friends of people I talked to while I was there. Helpful and co-operative though they were always ready to be, I avoided the Union of Writers ever knowing too much about where I was or who I was talking to. This involved some amount of being dropped off at street corners rather than specific addresses by car drivers, and finding my own way back again on the Metro, which was probably mostly unnecessary.

But this was because some of the people I went to see specifically asked me to do it, and not to bring an interpreter: if one was going to be required, they would ask one of their friends. There is still a residual fear among some Russians, not unreasonably, about 'the authorities' knowing exactly who they are and what they are saying. It is for this reason, and again at their request, that I have changed and to some extent Anglicised most of the names of those I interviewed. As one person explained it: 'Now we can say what we like – but by two years from now, if your book is published in Russia, it could be that it had not been wise to say it.'

I most deeply hope that that will not be true.

T P

1 Men I

Kolya Kolyavich, plumber

Yuri Averbakh, international chess grandmaster

Viktor Endrobkin, freelance journalist

Konstantin Dolyich, musician

Yevni Tarin, unemployed

Nikolai Serov, 'blue'

Kolya Kolyavich,
plumber*

A powerfully built man in a thick sweater and newly pressed blue denims, he sat slumped back on a chair in the unfurnished kitchen of an empty apartment on the twentieth floor of a tower block. Fair-haired, rough-voiced, at first seemingly resentful of everybody and everything. He smoked continuously.

– Why you should wish to talk to a person like me is something that has not been explained to me. I have been told you wish to meet all kinds of people who live in Moscow today – to write a book, about what I do not know. Why should someone from the foreign country of Great Britain wish to talk with me? About my work, about my housing conditions, about what? I do not know anything about politics and the present situation, I have no views upon that, so what is it you want? It has been explained to me by my bosses that they picked me out, and I had their permission to meet you here in this apartment in the building where I work and which will be empty until tomorrow. I do not know why they picked me out. Then after that this man here who is your interpreter, he came to explain it again to me. After his explanation it is even more difficult still for me to understand what you want. Yes, it is true I was told on both occasions it was to be my own free choice whether I wanted to talk with you or not. So I will tell you I do not want to do it, but I am here only because I wish to try to discover the reason for it. Also just a little, to speak frankly, because if your bosses say they want you to do something, then most times it will be to your benefit to do so. At least then it cannot be put against your name as a black mark that you would not do it. Such things are very important in Moscow, if you do not already know that.

No I am not a Muscovite, I come from the Kalinin region. I came here five years ago to find work, which is why I am now a maintenance plumber on this housing estate. It is not a very good job or highly regarded, or one which has much prestige to it, but it was all I could find. Already now I am thirty, and only to have got this far in life at my age – well no one could say it was a great achievement. I work for the management of the plant which produces the hot water and central heating for all the apartment blocks here in Area 11 of Housing Estate 17. I say it is not a highly regarded job because it is true: it is not, and nor is it a well paid one. Its only advantage is that it provides an apartment for myself and my wife, or rather the share of a two-roomed apartment where there already lives a divorced woman with her eight-year-old son. It has two bedrooms, one for her and her son and the other for my wife and myself, and we share the kitchen and bathroom and toilet facilities. It is on the twelfth floor of the block over there which you can see from that window. When we were given it, we were told that if my work as a maintenance plumber was satisfactory for ten years, then my wife and I would qualify for an apartment on our own.

The woman we share with, she is a nice person and her son is a good boy and not noisy. We are all friendly together; but obviously at the end of the day when I come home and I am tired, or if I am working on the night shift and wish to sleep in the daytime, then we would sooner have a place to live which is our own. The sound of the television from their room where her son is watching it, or equally I am sure for them the noise if I wish to put on some rock music on my record player – well, all such things make for difficulties. Fortunately my wife and I are very compatible with each other, but there are many cases one hears of where marriages do not last, because of such cramped conditions that the husband and wife live together in.

To tell you of my wife, well she is a person like myself who comes from a small town in the Kalinin region, which was where we first met each other. I had been in the Army for my two-year period of service, and I then had a number of occupations such as working in a steel factory, in a construction plant, and at one time briefly as a carpenter on a building site. I found it difficult to settle down to any of them because I am not a skilled person and I do not have such things as proficiency certificates in any subject. My wife, before she was my wife she could do typing and office work generally, and she also has a head for figures and can operate such things as large calculating machines for example. But we neither of us liked the town that we lived in, and if we were to marry as we wanted to, the only place we could have lived was in the apartment with her mother which we did not wish to do. That was the reason for our decision to come to Moscow. I had been told there was plenty of work here, and many jobs which also included the opportunity for accommodation. But you know one hears these things, and instead of being cautious one hastily takes a decision, and that was how it was with us. Afterwards you regret it.

Since we came five years ago, my wife has done better at finding work for herself than I have done. She earns a bigger wage and has shorter working hours and better working conditions. This is not a good position for a man to be in, it does not make him very proud of himself. But I do not see any prospect of change in the near future. I think though if we were to return to the situation we were in when we first married, we would probably take the same decision again. There is no real chance of a good life for anyone except here in Moscow. Here there is always the possibility an unexpected opportunity may occur, and the future take a turn for the better. Outside Moscow, in the small provincial towns, there is nothing at all, and no chance of anything like that ever happening.

What you ask is correct, there are many times when I feel I have made a mistake to come to Moscow, yes. I hope this does not offend your interpreter that I should say this, but many Moscow people are not at all friendly or good-natured towards people such as myself. I do not mean to be impolite about it, but they give you the impression if you do not come from Moscow, then you must be in some ways an inferior kind of person. They tell you you belong back in the place you have come from, because everything about you is wrong: your manners, your clothing, the way you eat your food, everything. Because there are shortages in the shops, they think it is your fault, you are taking goods they should have first. It is not possible for you to live and work here unless you have a residence permit, but when you have such a permit and have every right to be here, I think they should accept that. Just the other day I was instructed to go to an apartment to mend a toilet that was leaking; and the woman whose apartment it was – well I was the third person who had been sent to do the repair and yet still the toilet was leaking. She said to me angrily 'Oh all you peasant men are no good, why cannot we have proper workmen to do these things for us, who know their job?' All the other men I work with, they are all themselves Muscovites, so it was they who had done the bad workmanship, not me. This does not make me contented in my work, to be spoken to like that.

Other things that I do not like with my work? I will tell you exactly, and then you will know. The first is that it is not skilled work, and when I am doing it I am doing nothing that allows me in any way to improve myself and learn things which would allow me to move up to a better job. As it is, it is mostly such matters as closing leaks in pipes and wrapping them in strips of waterproof material. And climbing into holes in the ground, which are dirty and sometimes even filthy and small. Or I have to sit for hours by a pumping machine that is old and noisy, to test it and ensure it is functioning properly, for so long that my head is splitting and my eyes are running. I do work like this for twelve hours at a time on one day, then I have twelve hours off, then twelve hours working again: so it is always sometimes in the night and sometimes in the day. In total I should work for 168 hours a month and be allowed one complete rest-day a week, but this rarely happens because if a job is not finished, you have to finish it, because you are always told there are not enough relief workers to take your place.

The busiest time is of course like now in the summer, because it is when the central heating is switched off. This is the time for the principal maintenance work to be done. It is also the time when you would prefer it if you were walking in the evening in the park with your wife, or going on a boat trip on the river. You would much sooner be doing one of those activities instead of crawling in tunnels underneath buildings, I assure you. And at times it can be hazardous also: this mark here on my hand is where I was severely scalded, from there all the way up to my shoulder here. It was last year: a heating pipe of boiling water burst as I was working on it.

So you see altogether it is not a good life, and I do not like it.

There are very many things that I regret. The first is that I was not a good student at school: I did not work at my lessons, but preferred to play football with my friends, or ride bicycles and sit around and talk. If I had paid more attention to my teachers, I think now I would be a more clever person with more opportunities to better myself. I can see my wife's example of that, in how it is with her because she took advantage of her schooling. It is often so when you are young: you do not take the opportunities, and they pass, and then when you are older you realise they will not come again.

Another such important occasion which I see now, was when I went into the Army to do my two years' service. During that period one thing that I learned was how to drive a truck. At the end of two years they offered me to remain in the Army for a further period of five years' service. Instead I declined. I see now that if I had not, I might well have become an experienced truck driver, and I would then have had security and regular work. Who knows, perhaps even the opportunity following that of being a truck driver in civilian life. That is a job with good pay I believe. When they have war films on television, I see the supply columns of trucks going along, and although of course they look now to be very old-fashioned vehicles, it seems to me it would not have been such a bad occupation to follow.

Well that is my story, I think there is nothing else I can tell you about myself. To tell you the truth I have surprised myself that I found so much to talk about. At the beginning I thought I would find nothing to say, so it has been an unusual experience for me. I would like to give you my best respects and good wishes. Let us shake hands.

Yuri Averbakh,
international chess grandmaster

The sitting-room of his apartment was large and comfortably furnished, one wall of it entirely taken up with long rows of jacketed new books in glass-fronted bookcases, and another with open display shelves with carefully arranged French porcelain, Maori carvings, water-colour miniatures, silver trophies, rows of tape cassettes of Vivaldi and Mozart and Brahms and Beethoven, inscribed photographs in silver frames and a telephone answering machine. Tall, distinguished-looking, grey-haired: he wore a dark business suit and white shirt, and a plain dark red tie. Smiling and gracious, he bowed courteously as he shook hands. He was sixty-seven.

– Do please sit down. I have ready for us on the table here some tea. It is English tea, Earl Grey, but if you do not like that please say so because I have other kinds. Help yourself to sugar if you wish, and milk also. These biscuits were made by my wife, and she sends her apologies that she cannot be here to greet you this afternoon, as she has a meeting with a friend. She will not be returning until this evening, so we have as much time to talk as you wish. Allow me to pour your tea. So what do you think of our Moscow summer then, is it as warm as this sometimes in England?

Indeed yes, this is a most pleasant district where we live, it is called the Lenin District: you would not think it was central to the city, because it is very quiet and leafy, with many trees and it is surrounded from the Moscow River on three sides. Perhaps as you came you passed the Lenin Sports Stadium? It is the biggest sporting arena of Moscow. I go sometimes to watch football: last year for instance there was a gala occasion with many famous players from all over the world, a match for the benefit of our great goalkeeper Lev Yashin who had been captain of the Soviet football team for many years. Alas, he has died now. In the game there played Franz Beckenbauer from Germany, your Bobby Charlton from England, Eusebio of Portugal and many others. It was wonderful to see. When I was a younger man I was very much interested in football, but not so much now because my mind is filled with so many other things.

Today my main occupation is to edit two magazines. One is called *Chess in USSR* and the name of the other one is just *Bulletin*. It is for foreign distribution to grandmasters, and has in it all the world's up-to-date results and information. This I have been doing now for twenty-seven years, a long time I think. Well, before that I was just an ordinary professional chess player you know.

I do not think you have the position of professional chess player in England as we have in the Soviet Union. Here if you are a promising young player you can make application to the State that you should have a stipend, and if you pass examinations to show you are good enough, you then receive sufficient money that allows you to do nothing else but study and play chess. In return you have the obligation to teach chess to younger players, to play for Soviet teams in matches around the world, and also to go to other countries to play in exhibitions.

At first for me as young man there was big problem. I had become interested in chess from my early age, six or seven years perhaps: my father and my uncle were both good players, and I watched them and played with them and read many chess books and magazines. By the time I had come to fifteen, I was champion of USSR for schoolboys, which meant by then I was already quite good player. But I was student at a technical institute and it seemed I was also promising to become good scientist. So I had to make the choice, because you cannot play chess only in tournaments that are in your vacation time. Well if I was right or wrong I do not know, but my choice was chess, and that has been my life ever since. After I was twenty I became first of all champion of Moscow, then I became grandmaster, and in I think 1953 I played as candidate for the world championship, when I came then Number Ten. Two years later after that I played for championship of the USSR in tournament which included Korchnoi, Petrosian, Geller and Flohr; and two years later in same contest again, when the result for me was tie with Taimanov and Spassky. In the play-off for the title I came Number Two. At other times around those years I was sometimes fourth, sometimes sixth and again sometimes second. So you could say I was good player but not the very outstanding one of all in the world. Who at that time was? Well, do you know the story about Isaac Stern the violinist? One day somebody said to him what was his opinion of David Oistrach, and he said: 'Undoubtedly, he is the second best violin player in the world.' And then this person was asking him 'So who then is the best player in the world?' and Isaac Stern said 'Ah, there are so many.' Does that answer your question for you?

Great players, it is very hard to say, you know? For one thing, it depends so much on who else there is around at the time. There may be very many other good players, or only a few. I think it is for example bad luck for Karpov that he is playing in the same time as Kasparov. If there were no Kasparov, I think Karpov would be the undisputed champion of the world. But no, it is Kasparov: and this means too that Kasparov must be exceptionally fine player, if he is champion when Karpov also is playing. It is said of him that he is the greatest chess player the world has ever seen. I do not know: perhaps – perhaps – it is just correct, how shall one tell? It is my opinion the four greatest players of all time have been Kasparov, Karpov, Fischer and Botvinnik.

Let me get for you from the bookcase there this book. It has only been just published here in USSR, and not yet I think in your country. It is called, I will translate it for you, *Warriors of the Mind*. It is analysis by English grandmaster and Canadian professor of mathematics, with a computer: they have analysed ten thousand results of all games played by total of sixty-four champions in the last 150 years. The reason for sixty-four is one for each square of a chessboard. They have very complicated points system, every win and every loss by whom against whom: and at the end they have produced list which ranks in order each one of all of them over all time. The order they have, it is exactly the same as mine that I gave you. Kasparov, Karpov, Fischer and Botvinnik – so naturally I approve of it, I think it is very good book indeed. Well yes I am in it: here, a little above the middle, they have ranked me Number Twenty-Five ever in the world, which is very flattering to me of course and gives me great pride. I think perhaps before long there will be an edition of this book in England, and then you may read it.

I should say though that I think it has faults. Well no, perhaps not faults is the word, because it is things you cannot measure in any way with a computer. It is how much the modern game has progressed from what it used to be. The early great players – Morphy, Lasker, Capablanca and so on – they did not have the huge mass of games behind them to be analysed and for them to study and learn from. Another thing is it is all much higher standard now, and all play now too so many times. When I played it used to be in one year about forty or fifty games: now Kasparov and Karpov and the others, they play a hundred games a year, perhaps more. They play, study, play, study, and so it goes on all the time like that.

There is one other point too that it was impossible to take in account for this book. It is at each match, how did player feel? Was one a little sick perhaps, or with a cold or an ache in his head? I played only three times in my lifetime against Botvinnik; he was my idol, as he was to many young chess players then: all wanted to imitate him because he had iron logic and great strength. But you know, in all the games I was disappointed, because he was not at his best and I could beat him. Another great player, Fischer, when I played him he was at his peak nearly; we met only once in international tournament, and we had a draw. This pleased me because he was a very great player and could be sometimes brilliant one. He was a nice person. Kasparov and Karpov, I have never played them in competition, I am too old. But I could not even at my very best I think achieve with either of them even a draw. It would take ten lions to confront either of those young men. But someone will come, someone will come: you are at your peak only between age thirty and forty mentally and physically, for you need of course great stamina.

This is what I do not have now. It says of me in the book that my best quality as player was my energy, which I think was right. My biggest fault? Well it is interesting you ask me that. This book does not say it because I think you cannot estimate it, it is only the person

himself who really knows. I will tell you: let me try to say it like
this. When you are player, if you lose it is big shock for you every
time. It is much more than unhappiness, it is deep distress. But
when you win, you should experience as compensation very great
joy, it surges up from inside of you like this. If you do not have that
feeling, then you cannot be truly great player. And I am sorry to
say, I do not know why it was but I never myself had that feeling. I
liked to play and I liked to win; but never once did I have joy from
winning. Pain and sadness when I lost yes, but when I won joy was
not there.

It was because I knew I did not have that necessary thing that I
retired from playing soon after I was forty, and began to edit
magazines and write books on chess instead. Now that is something
that does give me joy, to have written books: I do not know exactly
how many, but they have been translated into many languages and
published all over the world. They occupy all of that shelf, all of the
one underneath it, and you see even now a half of the third one too.
I like to write little books, small books that are easy for people to
read, and my subject I specialise in is end-games. The last two I
have done are the ones at the end, you see how I mean by small? So
far they are published here in Russia only, with half a million copies
of each of them printed.

One day perhaps I would like to write a very big book: not so
much about chess but about all places in the world I have been to to
teach and play matches, and where I give exhibitions of simultaneous
play. That is when there is a hall, each player with his board sits
along the walls facing inward, and the Grand Master walks round the
hall making a move in turn on each board. When you come round
again to your opponent, he has made his answering move, you
make your next one, and so on. The largest number of opponents I
have played against in this way all at once was in New Zealand:
there were eighty players I think. But it is only exhibition, you
know? I have been of course also to Australia, USA, Canada, Great
Britain, France, Spain, once even to the island of Curaçao. Chess is
like music: you can play music and be understood anywhere in the
world, and it is the same with chess also. In every country its rules
are the same and the board and the pieces, so if you wish to play
with someone there is no need for you to speak any word of each

other's language, you may just sit down and play. It is a very wonderful passport: there have been grandmasters who travelled the world knowing only their own words, but I liked to learn a little of the language where I was if I could.

In Soviet Union it has always been a privileged position if you were in USSR chess team. Even at the worst years of restrictions on travel, we could go still almost anywhere, and as you see I have many souvenirs. Even my English teabags. May I offer you another cup?

Warriors of the Mind: A Quest for the Supreme Genius of the Chess Board by Raymond Keene and Nathan Divinsky is now published in England by Hardinge Simpole.

Viktor Endrobkin,

freelance journalist

The old-fashioned low block of apartments where he lived was built round the sides of a small square of rough ground: there were a few thin and tired-looking lime trees in it, and at each corner entrance-tunnels led in to the outside staircases.

He sat in an armchair near the open window: a plump man in glasses, going bald, and wearing rumpled blue cotton trousers and a white T-shirt with a coloured stencil of palm trees on the front over the words 'Fame City, Miami'. Near him an electric fan swung from side to side, rattling.

– Hell hotter still today than yesterday huh? They said that was twenny-nine, what's that in Fahrenheit, eighty-two, eighty-four? Doesn't suit me the heat, everyone's lethargic, Russians like the winter best, your brain comes alive and you think clearer. Say, do you think I have an American accent, how does my English sound to a Britisher? A lot of people think I'm an American guy when we meet because of the way I talk. You see I was born in New York and lived there till I was eight, so that's where I picked it up.

I'm not American in fact: I have what you might say was an international biography. My father was Russian and my mother was French. He was an *émigré*, he was taken to the US of A by his parents in 1921 when he was around fourteen or fifteen. To make a long story short he was a Belorussian, people used to call them White Russians, and when Belorussia became a constituent republic of the USSR he and a lot of others fled to America. He had what was called a Nansen passport, d'you know what that is? Well Nansen was a Norwegian Arctic explorer and after the 1914–18 war he did a lot of relief work for the League of Nations in Russia, and got special passports for those who wanted to leave. He won the Nobel Peace Prize, and my father always used to say he owed his life to him.

My father was a film technician, and a good one: he went to Hollywood and worked himself up to a pretty important position in one of the big studios there. He did pretty good until a few years after the finish of World War II, then the Cold War began and relationships between America and Russia got bad and then went on from there to even worse. There was all that business of the McCarthy UnAmerican Activities witch-hunts: it concentrated on Hollywood. And my father, he was told he couldn't any longer hold a high-up position like he did because he wasn't an American citizen and he didn't have an American passport.

He was pretty furious about that, after he'd lived and worked in the US for so long. But by then he had quite an international reputation in the film world, so he thought he'd take his wife and family and live in France where she'd got lots of relatives. She'd kept her French citizenship so she was OK, but the French wouldn't give him a visa. My mother could go and me and my brother, but not my father. For a long time he couldn't find out the reason for it, but eventually he somehow discovered the Americans had told the French he was a suspected Communist. All this stuff made him very angry indeed, and he said OK then he'd go back to his country of birth, the USSR. But even that wasn't easy to do: first we had a spell in Poland, then lived a while in East Germany until the end of '52 when we were finally admitted and came here to Moscow.

As a young man my ambition was to become a film director at first. But when I went to school and university, I found I'd quite a facility for languages, and I got very interested too in ancient Asian history, particularly Vietnamese and Chinese. When I say ancient I mean from around say the beginning of the tenth century. To study it of course you need to be able to read texts and manuscripts. So languagewise although I guess my first language is Russian, I speak as well French which is my mother's language. After that, because of my childhood upbringing in America, I'm pretty fluent in English or American, whichever; then I have some Polish, some German and some Vietnamese. I can't speak it but I can read ancient Chinese in the form some people call Mandarin: only with a dictionary though, I can't read it without one. You know the joke? If you speak a lot of languages you're a polyglot, if you speak two languages you're bilingual, and if you only speak one language you must be an American.

Well as far as nationality's concerned, what I feel I am depends basically I guess on which country I'm in. In America I've felt American, in France French, Germany German and so on: like I said, an international biography. I have a Russian wife, and my daughter certainly thinks of herself all the time as Russian. But I could go and live and work in France or the USA tomorrow with no problems at all, and settle down living in either of them. I've made the conscious choice though to make my life here as a true blue Russian. Maybe I ought to say true red Russian, right?

That doesn't mean I don't from time to time wonder whether it was the right decision. In many ways life's not easy here, I don't mean just in the way of shortages of material comforts either. I write articles for Russian magazines, French magazines, American magazines, and a good number of others world-wide. They're usually on matters that have what might be called historical or cultural or philological backgrounds, but naturally you have to make contemporary references and make comments sometimes of a social or political nature. There's more freedom than there was, but in the past I've had to take a lot of censorship which annoyed me, and I made it plain it did. I've never been heavily persecuted because I'm not important enough, but I've never liked working with the feeling all the time that maybe something you're writing isn't going to be allowed to be sent abroad. There's still a lingering suspicion in some places that I might be a kind of deep-cover agent for the USA; and I guess if I went there to work, there'd be the same notion there that I ought to be kept an eye on in case I was spying for the USSR.

I find that very distasteful you know, to work as a writer in a country where you don't have the freedom to say and write exactly what you want. You feel too that what extended freedoms there now are might suddenly be taken away again, almost overnight. In my heart I'm convinced that the system we have here, socialism, despite all its negative points it's still the most fair one in the world for the largest number of people. Not for me personally, I'd probably be better off in the West; but for the ordinary common person, I do think it's the best there is. We've bureaucracy and privilege, but what country in the world doesn't? Our standard of life isn't high if you compare it with yours or the French or Americans. But compare it with that of Africans and Asians and Central and South Americans and Chinese – more than half the population of the world – and for ordinary people, it's pretty high. We have only a few wealthy people, but not many. A Party high-up, he has a nice apartment, perhaps a dacha in the country though it's not usually anything splendid, a slightly larger car, he can maybe shop at the hard-currency shops, and that's about it. It's not a lot. One important thing, which I think is very important indeed, is his son won't ever be let inherit either his wealth or his position. If he gets anywhere in life it'll be on his own merit, not on who he is or who his father was. You have people in the West, who from the moment they're born, it's known their lives will be privileged: what schools they go to, how much money they have, which professions they can have good positions in, everything. In the West if you don't have money you're handicapped as soon as your life begins. If you do or rather if your parents do, you can get better schooling, better medical care, better housing if you marry, and better care when you're old, to list only a few. It's not so here.

We have certain basic rights, and they're free. Education, health care all through your life even if its standard often could be better, the right to housing and employment, to being looked after when you're old. All these provisions are enshrined in our laws. Some people behave illegally and like in the West again, try to benefit themselves in various ways: but the point is their activities are illegal, and they can be and are prosecuted if they're caught. We don't have the unrestricted freedom you have in the West to take advantage of other people, to do better for yourself at other people's expense. Sure we have faults and failings, we have monsters like Stalin: no one'd deny he was a monster. But also there is everywhere a kind of a fundamental caring by everybody for everybody, a feeling that that's right, that's how life should be, particularly since it's the only one there is.

It's a mistake for the West to judge us from their point of view, and think of us as a whole lot of suppressed individuals trying to break free. We're not, we don't want to break free so we can rip off other people. Another big thing they misjudge is they think we want things which most people actually don't, and that most Russian people don't even particularly care about. An example would be our system of having internal passports: if you want to go from one place to another some distance away, you need a passport to do it. It's only my opinion, but I'd say maybe as many as ninety-five per cent of the population doesn't care one way or the other about that: they don't want to travel long journeys very often anyway. If they live in Murmansk, why would they ever in their lives want to go to Odessa or Vladivostok? To visit relatives, it's usually claimed. The fact is they don't have relatives in those places, they're literally foreign countries far away: they'd have no wish to go there even if they could. I read a book once about a small town in the middle of the USA in Kansas: it said most of the people who lived there, if something happened outside their town, somewhere else in Kansas say, they weren't greatly interested, it was no concern of theirs. If it happened where the government was, in Washington, well that had even less do to with them; and if it happened outside of America altogether, well they most often hadn't even heard of the country it happened in. It's just exactly like that here in the USSR. To someone in Mongolia, what they read about or hear about in say Odessa, well where the hell's Odessa, is it in Africa or where? It's maybe five thousand miles away, London almost to Tokyo, something like that.

Most of the population of the Soviet Union, the most important things they want in life are a decent place to live, decent food and clothing, education and medical care. They remember how things were for their parents and grandparents, who were poor and illiterate, and they look around and see how life is now for them, what tremendous progress there's been in raising basic standards for such a vast population. Later on, maybe they'll start thinking about how important travelling around is, seeing the rest of their own country and maybe even a bit of the outside world. In ten years or fifteen or twenty: and when they do they'll start agitating about it. But I don't think so yet awhile.

Heh my gosh, is that the time, I'm supposed to meet a guy at four. I'll walk across the yard with you.

★

As we crossed the ground towards one of the entrances, he paused for a moment at one of the empty benches under the trees.

– Let's sit here for a minute, there's something else: only I prefer to say it in the open, not in a room with ceiling and walls. Inside, you mentioned you'd like to meet someone who worked for the KGB, did I have any idea how you go about it? Let me tell you something: you already have. Not a full-time person: but all the time, wherever you are, whoever you meet, say chambermaids in a hotel, people you have conversation with in a café some place, workers in an office – it's a fairly safe bet in every group of five or six people you come across, one of them'll be in the business of passing information to the KGB. Not for money, maybe usually for their own protection: they're already being leaned on themselves about something they've done wrong, or even they're just building up a sort of bank credit in case sometime they're in trouble in the future. Thought you'd be interested to know that.

Been nice talking to you.

Konstantin Dolyich,
musician*

One small room of his apartment had been set aside as his practice-room: it was almost entirely taken up by a grand piano. There were books, cassettes and records everywhere on shelving round the walls, and there was a small armchair, a music stand, and a low table with sheet music and a metronome on it. He had thick dark curly hair, a smiling friendly face, and wore horn-rimmed spectacles. While he talked he perched on the music stool with his feet up on it and his arms round his knees.

– I am not, you know, a very great or famous musician: I am no more than an ordinary working musician who is lucky to have a contract with one of our biggest symphony orchestras. Under the terms of it I am also able to take short-term engagements with other orchestras if it can be conveniently arranged. This means that I can say truly that for almost now twenty years, I have never been out of work. I have been able to earn my living without cease and by doing the thing I most enjoy, which is to play music. I can therefore say that in every way I am a truly happy man. I do not want to be, I have never wanted to be, the celebrated soloist on whom there falls all the time the spotlight of famousness: I like to be competent, of high standard, and the member of a team. Besides, I do not know of many special opportunities for performers of my kind, or any great music that has been written for virtuosi of the instrument which I play, which is the double-bass. In our time I know only of the famous conductor Koussevitzky who was in this category.

How I came to take this as my instrument is I think something of a lucky story, which began when I was sixteen. My family is in no way musical at all: not my father, my mother or my sister, and there was no interest in it in our home. I was not a very talented pupil in any subject at school, and I had no idea in my mind of any kind about my future. The only direction in which I could see that I might go was to have work of some kind in a factory perhaps; I did not think even that I would be accepted into the Army when my conscription time came, as my eyesight was poor.

It happened sometimes in the afternoons, when I was coming home from school, that I would take a path which went behind one of the apartment blocks near where we lived: and from the open window of one of the first-floor apartments there that I passed, I could sometimes hear someone playing a piano, and perhaps sometimes a gramophone recording of a piano concerto. Always there were sounds I loved to stand and listen to, even if I had no idea what the music was or by which composer: I would become quite lost in the beauty of it.

One day the man who was the occupant of the apartment saw from his window that I was listening, and he came out to me and offered me to go into his home and sit there to listen in comfort for a while. His wife, who made me welcome and gave me tea and some little cakes, she had also seen me from the window on other occasions, she said, and told her husband they must invite me inside when they next saw me. They were both musicians, but not on a professional level: the man had been the one who sometimes had been playing the piano I heard, and the woman liked to play the flute. So this strange friendship developed for a little while: a youth, and a much older man and his wife. On one occasion each week on my way home from school I would visit them, they would play for me to listen to, and we would talk. I could not read music; but sometimes when I played a few notes on the piano, which I learned how to do by watching, they said I had what is called a natural ear: I should go to learn music they said, because it would always give me great pleasure all through my life.

If I may express it in this way, very quickly music seemed to become a second language to me. It is not easy to describe how it was, but my thoughts and my feelings began to come more and more to me as music, and in only a short time I had a great desire that I wanted to study to learn how to play an instrument. I thought in terms of the piano only: that was the one I had access to when I went to the apartment of my friends, and so it seemed to be the natural one for me to want to play. I decided therefore that I was going to put all my energies into learning it, and asked my friend if he would give me some lessons, which he did.

When you are young, I think it is very often that your ambition for something is more than your understanding of your capabilities, or lack of them. It was so in my case, for in a very short time nothing would deter me from making application to the Conservatoire that I should be accepted there as a student of the piano. I laugh now at my belief that they would even consider to have me, it is so absurd. To begin with, if you are going to make a career as a concert pianist, sixteen is at least twice the age or even more at which you should start. There are so many brilliant musicians here in the Soviet Union, young pianists even of the ages of six, seven, eight or nine, that you would have to be an outstanding genius almost at any age to match them. In recent years for example, Evgeni Kissin who is still a young boy, already he was giving performances before audiences all round the world by the time he was twelve.

I do not know how it was that I was even considered for audition at the Conservatoire, because there are so many who wish to go there. I think it was perhaps as a favour to the man who gave me the lessons: I think he knew someone there. However it was, I was given a day and a time to go, and when I got there I played a little on the piano in front of four or five teachers. Of course what else could I expect, they thanked me and then said unfortunately I was too old to begin studies and it was not possible for them to offer me a place. At once, only because I had heard my friend's wife play the flute, I asked would they consider me instead to be a student of a wind instrument. But again they said they were sorry, but no.

I had built up my youthful hopes so high, and I recall how disappointed I was to have my dreams shattered in this way. I walked around in the Conservatoire for a while, because it seemed to me such a wonderful place, so full of music that it was coming even from its walls. I knew I would never be there again, and I wanted to soak in the atmosphere of it. I walked along every corridor I came to, and I was very sad and unhappy and cast down.

As I was going up one of the big staircases a man stopped me, a man who was coming down. I did not recognise him, but he had been one of the examiners who had listened to my playing. He must have seen from my face how sad I was, and he stopped to talk to me: he told me every year thousands of applicants from all over the Soviet Union were unsuccessful, and I should try not to be too much disappointed. Then, perhaps because I had so quickly asked if I could be considered for something else after being told I had failed, he enquired if I had had any thoughts of studying some other instrument, say one of the violin family. No I had not I said, I had never given it any thought whatever. So then he asked would I be interested to study to play the double-bass. I was completely puzzled by his question, and he could see it I am sure. At my expression on my face, he said to me simply 'Come with me' and took me by the arm along a corridor, where he opened the door to one of the classrooms.

Inside it, a big room, there were four or five students playing the double-bass under the instruction of their tutor. And I was astounded. Because you see, until then the only time I had ever seen someone play a double-bass had been in jazz programmes which I watched sometimes on television; and they had always used both their hands and made the rhythm noise on it. Thrum-thrum, thrum-thrum, thrum-thrum like this. But these people, they were playing the instrument with bows, and bringing from it such a wonderful deep sound. The man told me to sit for a while at the back of the room and listen; then later he came back again, and took me out in the corridor and he enquired of me what I thought.

I told him it had been something which had opened my eyes, I had never known the double-bass could be like that, and it would give me the greatest pleasure if I could study how to play such a beautiful instrument. The words truly reflected my feelings. And that is how it came about for me: I was accepted as a student, and I had five years of study, and every day of my life since then has been one filled with pleasure. I like still to play the piano, and a little sometimes on the cello; but the double-bass is the love of my life. I have been fortunate in attaining a high standard of playing it, to the extent that I am offered more work than I can perform. So my life has so far been one not just of good fortune, but of great satisfaction also.

I am now forty-four, my father has died, my sister is married, and I live here with my mother. All day long when I am not playing I am practising: this has to be so for any professional, an athlete even, you have to keep yourself in the highest condition in both your health and your head. I have travelled extensively with my present orchestra and with others, and at certain times I am able to play too with a small chamber-music group, which gives me much pleasure also. It is hard to say which has been my greatest experience, because there have been so many. But if you press me to choose one, then I would say I think it was perhaps the occasion when I played in Berlin with an orchestra a few years ago, where I took part in a performance of Brahms' Second Symphony under the great conductor Herbert von Karajan. We had altogether with him six rehearsals before the performance, which will indicate to you the kind of perfectionist he was. He must in his life have conducted that symphony fifty or perhaps even a hundred times, yet for our performance it was as fresh and as beautiful as if he had only just discovered and fallen in love with it. He would ask in rehearsal the most demanding tasks of every single one of his players or groups of players; but never once did it evoke any protest, he could inspire in every single player a determination to give him what he wanted. It did not matter how difficult and tiring it was, he would repeat every bar time after time until he was satisfied with it. I think he left a kind of magical impression on every player who experienced working under his direction: he inspired this desire to seek a higher standard than you had ever thought yourself capable of.

It is a quality I think cannot ever be explained. It happens quite often as a player in a famous orchestra, to have a new and perhaps well-known conductor come to stand before you to make the first rehearsal. From the beginning, from the very first gesture he makes, every player knows if he is going to draw from them a good performance or not. If you know he will not, you feel disappointed, you were hoping it was going to be something new. I have never met a single player once, of any instrument, who has said he experienced such a feeling as disappointment, if he played under von Karajan.

I have no wishes for my future except to continue as I am. It is not realised always, I think, that the quality a musician must have above all if he is with a famous orchestra, is stamina: travelling, touring, rehearsing, playing, they all make great demands. So long as you are healthy enough, you accept them and enjoy them, and then you can have the fulfilment and satisfaction of living the beautiful life of music.

Yevni Tarin,
unemployed

A small undernourished man of thirty-seven with thinning hair and a pencil moustache, he sat on the park bench late one afternoon with his shoulders hunched, one hand deep in his anorak pocket and the other holding a cigarette in his fingertips, cupping it in the palm of his hand.

– How do you say in English, 'I have had break-up'? What do you say, 'break-up' or 'break-down'? Of the nerves, yes. You understand? I am not having a well life, I think you call it 'a bad case for treatment', I read that in a book once, an English book. It means some person who does not fit well into his society. This is my position here in Moscow in Russian society. The authorities would regard me if I came in their hands as a person to be corrected into a certain way so he fits with other people in society. This is why I asked you do not bring an interpreter. Interpreters have connections with authority, they could report I should be thrown away.

No, I do not mean I have done something criminal: it is nothing I would be put in prison for, or I do not think so. It is something I have not made enquiries about, mm? I make a little joke for you, yes? It would be a joke also to say that in England, I have not enquiried if what I am doing is something to put me in prison for? Because it might be they say Yes it is, thank you for telling us, now come along and we put you in prison. It is a nice joke, you think so, good, thank you.

Well, what I am doing, it is nothing serious at all. It is only that I have no papers. So because I have no papers I am not permitted to reside in Moscow: I do not have a Moscow residence permit, that is all it is. If they catch me I think all that they do to me is to say I must go out thirty kilometres beyond Moscow and must not come back. It is possible they would do only that, but not put me into prison because it is a trivial thing.

What I do for a living? Well this is another thing I think you also have an English phrase for. I am what you call 'a jack of all trades', is that right? I read such a phrase in a book also. Most of all I think what I am is a writer of poetry: that is my opinion, but alas it is not the opinion of editors of magazines I send my poems to, or of people who are in charge of our publishing houses.

I even at one time tried the occupation of married man: but this also was no success, my wife and I we have divorced. Our marriage lasted for two years and then it ended. I have a daughter by my wife who is now seven perhaps or eight, but I have not seen her for five years. She lives with her mother in the city of – well perhaps it is better I do not say the name of the city: it is where I come from, where I am registered as resident, and so where I would be sent back to you see. I will say it is in the south. It is in Armenia in fact. But I would sooner be here in Moscow than there. Why? Because there is more opportunity in Moscow: opportunity for things to do, places to live with my friends, everything. Opportunities for opportunities, if you understand me, can one say that? I am on the look-out always for opportunities. One day the correct one for me will come along and then life will be better.

But I should say this definitely to you I think, it is something I would like please for you to understand clearly. It is that I am not interested in political opportunities: I am not a politician, I do not take part in political activity of any kind whatever. I would like to make it clear that I am not in any way against the State. I think politics is a curse of our time. It is necessary always to make this clear to people you talk to, especially when you do not know who they are. They may be members of some organisation or other, and so they may feel they should report you to the authorities. Not the Party no, I do not think a member of the Communist Party would even begin to talk to me in the first place. I am thinking instead of the new parties which we are having now: we call them informal organisations, some of them will not even register themselves. They wish to get rid of the Jews, or to send the Azerbaijanis back to

Azerbaijan or the Armenians back to Armenia and so on. So you see why I am thinking as I am thinking.

Also there is one more thing to make clear. I do not take part in political activity and so the State has nothing to fear from me; and I do not take part in criminal activity, so the ordinary citizen has nothing to fear from me. I do not carry a gun in my pocket – as you see my pocket would be too small anyway. I do not set fire to people's doors to their apartments, and I am not the Mafia or a drug smuggler. Oh yes there is much of this kind of crime now in Moscow. The English phrase is 'crime wave' is that correct? Well I am not part of it and I am not responsible for it. There is nothing I have done that I would come to court for. Do you understand me?

Do I steal? Ah. Well this would depend on what meaning you are putting to the word 'steal'. If there was an old woman on the Metro and she dropped her purse with all her money in it, I would not pick it up and run away. Even if she had not seen she had dropped it, I would pick it up and run after her and give it back to her. I am an honest man. I would not come to your house and steal something from you out of your house. I do not do things like that, never anything of that kind at all. But well let me say for example if I was walking along one day and I saw by the side of the road a shirt or something, or perhaps a pair of shoes, or even some short pieces of wood – if I saw something like that which did not seem to belong to anybody, yes perhaps I might take something under such circum- stances as that. Not for myself you understand, but to sell to one of my friends and have a little money for food and so on.

I remember I was in hospital once – it was not hospital here in Moscow but somewhere else – and there was an old man who said I had taken something of his: I think it was a brush for his hair, something of that sort. I had one like it myself, it was a very ordinary kind of hairbrush you understand: but he said that I had taken it from the cabinet at the side of his bed. There were a hundred hairbrushes of that kind in the hospital, but because my papers were not in order, everyone turned against me and they said 'Yes yes, he took it', 'He is a common thief, throw him away' and things of that nature. I do not like it when people speak like that, so I would not stay any more in the hospital and I went away from it immediately the next day. The doctors did not want me to go or the nurses, they said I had not finished my treatment and it would be harmful for me to leave. Well in fact I do not think it was so, I think I had been there in that hospital too long time anyway. What I had had was treatment for nerves: this was four years ago, and I have not been back in a hospital since that time so I was already cured I think. The treatment? It was nothing, just many different kinds of pills, and sometimes a talk with a psychologist, perhaps once a month only. And something that was called, well I do not know an English word for it: it is when you do work for example like making baskets, or simple toys out of wood and you get a little money for doing it.

Oh yes I am cured now. I used to have bad headache and depressions, but now I do not, not at all. Still, it is difficult for me to concentrate sometimes: but I am working against this myself in my own head. I have some problems, but I think to myself I can solve them if I make a sensible approach to how I should live my life. How? Well it is such things as that I should not take a job for example at a factory, or anywhere where it is always the same hours of work, every day, day after day. I think that would be bad for me. I do not drink so I do not have the need for alcohol. And when I am hungry I have something to eat, and when I am tired I have some sleep. I have many places I can stay, there are a thousand of places where you can sleep in Moscow if you know where they are: no one will come to disturb you there because no one knows they are there, so you are not troubled by drunken people or the militia for example. As for food, well I have many friends who always will give me something; then these friends I will do a favour for in return. I get them some small thing they want, some packets of cigarettes for example.

What will I do in the future? This is something I do not know. Perhaps one day I will write a book do you think? I have had many experiences. Or in a little while I will start going to classes to learn English, so eventually I could get a job as a translator perhaps. No, no, my English is not good enough at all for me to get such a job now. I can say it better than I can read the words of a page, if you understand me. You have to have a very high standard to be translator from a newspaper or a book for example.

I learned it from perhaps when I am eight years of age. All Russian children at school, I think they all begin to learn some English from that age. It is a language I have always liked very much, and when I was younger than now, about fifteen or sixteen, I used to read many English books at school. Always I have done. My favourite writers, they are William Shakespeare, Ernest Hemingway, Agatha Christie and a poet called John Donne. He is a difficult poet for me to understand because I think he is out of this present time. He lived a long time ago yes? And of course I like also the great English poet Lord Byron, as all Russian people do. Every Russian person will tell you they think he is your greatest English writer after William Shakespeare: but for me if I may say so, he is your greatest English writer before William Shakespeare. Perhaps one day I will take my English studies again, to a standard that is higher, and in this way come to a better job for myself. But you see, as I am now, I am what you would call – well I do not know if this is the correct word. What I would say is that I cannot do this because I am a de-societyised person. Is there such a word in English? No? Good, then I have invented one.

It is becoming cold now, I should go. Thank you, I have been very pleased to meet you too.

Nikolai Serov,
'blue'

There was very little space to spare in his tiny room. It had a double divan bed taking up one wall, and arranged round the rest underneath rows of crammed bookshelves were a dining table and chairs, a writing desk, a typewriter and table lamp on another table piled high with papers and magazines, and a stereo record player with twin speakers. In odd spaces there were twenty or more vases and other pieces of pottery, ranging from abstract figures to realistic figurines of Austrian and Dutch *kitsch*.

A diffident and neatly dressed man in his green suit, and open-necked pink shirt and a cravat, he had a carefully trimmed goatee beard and hair cut short without a parting. He talked in a quiet voice, sitting on the edge of the divan with one knee crossed elegantly over the other, supporting himself with his hand.

– I am forty-three years old, and I'm a married man with two children, a boy who's sixteen and a girl of twelve. More correctly I should say I am not now married: I was until two years ago, but then after eighteen years of marriage my wife and I divorced. She lives in the apartment we formerly had together, and where I live here is not far away. I rent this room and the use of the kitchen and bathroom from a friend who owns it. He's an engineer and at present he's in Egypt where he'll be for one year, I think. My wife and I are still good friends: she is a nice woman, and once a week I go to see my children. We have a regular arrangement: on Saturday afternoons she goes out to friends until the early evening, then when she comes back we all have a meal together which I've prepared. If you were to be with us on such an occasion, you would think we were one family always together, and be surprised to learn we're divorced.

The reason we're divorced is my wife refuses to share me with anyone else. She tells me that if there ever comes a time when I wish to go back and be only with her, she would be very happy for us to have a sensible discussion about it and see if there is something we could achieve. I'm sure she means it, but I'm afraid it's something that will now never happen. I live here with my lover: there have been other lovers, and I am sure there will be other lovers yet again. I am what is called in the Soviet Union 'blue'. Your word for it in English is 'gay'. I am an active practising homosexual, and it is against the law in the Soviet Union. It is a criminal offence and therefore I have to live one half of my life as a secret life, and not reveal this fact.

When I first discovered a few years ago I was sexually drawn towards other men, I hoped I might be bisexual, someone attracted both towards men and women. But unfortunately it soon became clear to me I was not. I had never in our marriage been unfaithful with another woman to my wife, so I hoped she would permit me to stay with her but without us having any kind of sexual relation-ship. She wouldn't agree to this, and said she'd share me neither with another woman nor with another man. It was very hurtful to her, I'm sure, that I found men more sexually appealing than she was. She made no suggestion that such sexual activity was in any way abnormal, or something to be despised; but she was quite firm in her attitude that I couldn't continue to live with her and at the same time share a bed with someone else. So that was how we came to part and then finally to be divorced. To my children and to most of our friends who knew my wife and me as a married couple, we've allowed them to assume what is commonly the case, that I've fallen in love with, and am now living with, someone else. This is the impression I've given also to my employers at my work. It is true: but what I don't reveal, and what my wife has promised she will not reveal either, is that this other person is a man.

Very few people indeed are trusted with this information, because it is a fact that if it were to be known, the consequences would be very severe indeed for me, disastrous in fact. In my job, I work for a government department: if it became known I was blue I'd be dismissed instantly, because as I've said, homosexuality is illegal in the Soviet Union, and carries a penalty of as much as five years' imprisonment for those proved to be indulging in it. Of course here, like in many other countries in the world, there are a number of well-known people, especially in such places as the theatre and the world of music, it's known by everyone that they're blue. But I'm afraid that here as in other countries too, the law doesn't seem to operate in their case, and they behave as they wish.

Another thing that would happen to me is I would no longer be able to live in this apartment. The friend I rent it from, who allows me to live here, he works for the same government department as I do, and he wouldn't be permitted to continue to do that.

As you understand, everything in my life has to be very discreet. In fact that's not an accurate word: I ought to say everything has to be kept absolutely secret. At all times and in every way, nothing must be done which would cause anyone I work for or work with even to let the possibility I was homosexual cross their mind. The clothes I'm wearing now, for example, I'd never allow anyone at my place of work to see me dressed like this. I don't think they're effeminate, the colours green and pink worn together please me: but they're strictly for private leisure-wear only. And another worry I have, it's constantly growing, is my voice might betray me. You can never really hear what your own voice sounds like, even if you record it on tape and then play it back to yourself: I've done that on more than one occasion. But I can't help wondering if after five years of living a homosexual life and mixing in all my spare time with homosexuals – well, I begin to wonder if it shows itself in my voice, and I speak with a somewhat effeminate articulation. I make efforts all the time not to speak in such a way in Russian. But does it strike you I do so in any way in English? Well I'm glad to have your assurance of that, thank you for it.

Obviously I don't want to reveal many details of what my occupation and position is. But I'm willing for it to be said that I have, and have had for a number of years now, a fairly high position in a government department which is concerned with the arranging of art exhibitions world-wide. The exhibits are such things as tapestries and what may be termed artefacts, both historical and modern, from different parts of the Soviet Union; and this has involved me for many years in travelling abroad to arrange such exhibitions. I'm not a member of the Party, but my father was, and quite prominently: it's only honest to say, I think, that although he wasn't in any way connected himself with the art world, his position did enable him to introduce me when I was younger to people who could aid my career in this field, which was my only major interest from the time I was at school. I think though it'd also be honest to say that although influence can help you obtain a position, it can't do much to help you make progress upwards, unless you do have the ability to take advantage of the privilege you've been given. In my case I have studied my subject and worked hard in it for years, as well as having some natural flair towards it.

I'm very conscious of the fact that I lead two lives: during the day, if I can use the expression I'm an esteemed and well thought-of government expert in the area of art I specialise in, and receive a certain amount of respect therefore when I travel abroad as a representative of my country. While at night, one may say, in my spare time and at weekends, I'm my real self. And when I'm that, I'm a person who would be cast out from society, looked down on by the very people who put me forward as a person of worth. A homosexual's in every way regarded as someone who's beneath contempt.

To me the irony of the situation is that it's because of my travels, particularly to western European countries, that I first became aware of my nature. For many years in my department my travels were to such places as India and China and Indonesia; then about six years ago I was promoted to a different division, and I travelled instead to Spain, France, Germany, Norway, Holland, Sweden and Denmark. I would of course have liked to go to England, but that opportunity has not yet been given me. When it is I'm sure among other things it'll give me the opportunity to speak better English than I do: so far I've only ever spoken it with European people who aren't themselves English. But that's what you call an aside, I think.

What I'm mainly saying is that it's when I first went to Denmark and to a lesser extent to Holland, that I found the gay scene, or the blue scene, was very open and relaxed. Homosexual relationships between men were accepted as quite normal. This helped me, so to say, to experiment a little in such matters: and my first male lover

was a young Danish man. In Denmark life's very free and easy: you
go where you like, talk about what you like both with women and
with men, and behave as you wish. This is not to say it's in any way
an abandoned or uncivilised way of life, in fact I would say quite the
opposite, it's very polite and civilised.

It's hard for me to explain how discovering, almost in the middle
of my life, that men attracted me more than women – how it came
to me as something which seemed to broaden my outlook and
increase my maturity. The feeling of attraction is in no way different
to the feeling of attraction I had in the past towards a female, and in
particular and for a very long time towards my wife. But there is
one thing: it's only one thing that I've discovered to be different,
and it depresses me that it's so. Perhaps it may be that it'll alter in
time, because it's my hope that it will. It's this: no matter how much
I wish it weren't so, I've discovered that in my homosexual
relationships, I'm very promiscuous. This is something that shocks
me: when I was a practising heterosexual with my wife I was
completely monogamous. I don't know why it should be so, and
it's my hope that one day I will discover a partner with whom I can
settle down into a lasting relationship. I don't believe that sex
matters above everything: so I also want comradeship and the
sharing of life's tribulations, as well as just sharing sexual pleasures
with another person. But so far, and I am speaking of five or six
years already now, my love affairs have always been with young
men, and very much one after another. Some of them have been
very passionate, but always I've known there was something missing
from them, they were going to last at most no more than six
months. I've never yet met a single male lover I could totally share
all my feelings with. And I have to say God knows whether I ever
will.

'Blue'? Do you know, I don't think I can answer that question.
Wait one moment, yes I can, the reason for it's returning to me. I
believe it's this: it comes from a stage or a film production of a play,
which was named *Cabaret*. I saw it some years ago, but I wasn't
myself then aware of my own nature, so I didn't really notice it
much. There's a famous scene in it: an older man, he's an aristocrat
I believe, and he's attracted to a younger man. His name I think was
John, and he was about twenty. The nobleman gives the young man

one of his garments, I recall it was a kind of military decorative jacket, and he gives it him saying he thinks he'll look very good in it. The young man puts it on, the jacket's blue, and the nobleman says to him 'Oh yes you look very fine indeed, blue is definitely your colour.' I believe that's the reason for the name. I am not a very good example for you this evening am I?

2 Women I

Anna Petrova, research technician

Adeleida Fedinskaya, 'babushka'

Katya Chilichkina, beauty queen

Maria Malenkova, housewife

Tamara Pavlova, secretary

Anna Petrova
research technician*

On a hot July afternoon she was strolling in the sunshine in a park along the side of a six-lane carriageway in the centre of Moscow. She had two English setters with her on leads: one an orange belton, the other a tricolour.

A few evenings later she sat at the large, gleamingly polished mahogany table in the sitting-room of her apartment: it was laid with lace mats, cups and saucers, plates and knives and white linen napkins. In the middle of it were four silver dishes of iced buns and freshly baked biscuits. She had dark hair, short and neatly cut, and wore a light green blouse with a brown skirt and bolero jacket. She smiled and made a slight gesture with her hands towards the food.

– Please, as we talk, I hope you will take something to eat. I have made everything myself, yes, it is all for you and your young lady interpreter. Also here on this other table by me there is tea or coffee, whichever you prefer.

First I would like to say it is a great pleasure for me to welcome you to my home, and I shall be delighted to talk with you. I have never before met an English person, so it is very interesting for me. I do not know why you should want to talk with me and about what, but I hope it will be equally of interest to you as it is for me. Please, ask me any questions that you wish and I will do my best to answer them for you. About myself and about my two beautiful dogs? Yes of course, anything at all that you wish. Now to drink, do you prefer to have coffee or tea?

So to begin, I tell you about myself. I am forty-nine years of age, and I work in a technical section of the Information Ministry. We perform quality-control checkings on such manufactured goods as

metal instruments for hospitals and laboratories. It is something I
like to do yes, but you will understand I have been doing it for most
of my working life, and now that I am in middle age, well
sometimes it seems to me to be a little boring. My husband, he is an
engineer and he works at the Ministry of Public Work, to do with
the construction of roads. We have two children, and both of them
are now grown-up: our daughter is twenty-six and she lives in the
Minsk region, where she is married to a scientist teacher. And we
have our son Mischa, he is twenty-three and also married, and he
lives in a small town two hundred kilometres to the south of
Moscow, where he is engaged in supervising transportation of
machinery at a factory.

Well yes, in contemplating it now I think perhaps if I had done
something else in my life I might have preferred it. Most of all I
would have liked it if I had been a musician. But when I was a girl
you see, I would not work hard enough at my piano studies to pass
my examinations. It seemed to me it was all the time that I had to
practise playing the music of Bach, and I did not like his music. Is
there such a phrase that it can be said I overdosed on Bach? Yes?
Well that is what I did, and it turned me away from him for the rest
of my life. Mozart I like, Chopin I like, Rachmaninov, Schumann,
Schubert – all of them yes. But Bach, not at all.

Another thing I would have liked to have done with my life, is
that I would have liked to study to become not a technician as I am,
but a psychologist instead: not a psychologist for human beings but
for animals, to learn about animal behaviour. But I discovered my
interest in this subject when it was much too late in my life to think
of doing such a thing, when I was almost forty. It was at the same
time that I had my first English setter dog, the smaller one who lies
by your feet now and has the white and brown coat. Her name is
Tetti and she is now ten years old. Yes that is exactly correct, her
colour is called 'orange belton', you have the same expression in
England also? That is very interesting. And her son Remi who sits
there in the corner watching and hoping I will give him a little cake
to eat, he has the coat which is white and brown and black, and we
call that 'tricolour'. Yes you also do in England? Oh that is very
good, I think it is perhaps an international language to describe them
is it not?

How did it come to happen that I have English setters which are rarely to be seen in Moscow? Well I will tell you. It is true there are very few of them: so not many people know at all what beautiful animals they are. For me it happened like this. My husband and I went to a party when a man who was his work colleague was to retire; and I do not recollect now how it came about, but someone began to speak of their dog and they produced a photograph of it to show. It was a borzoi I remember. And then it was so strange, because one after the other all the rest of the people began to bring out photographs of their dogs to show. This is something that happens more usually with people's children you will agree, they all show pictures of them; but in this instance everyone was talking and showing photographs of their dogs. One had what is called a Collie dog, one a big Newfoundland, another a St Bernard, an Afghan hound, a Beagle hound which is a hunting dog, and on and on. And you know it seemed to us we were almost the only people there who did not possess a dog of some kind. After a while I looked to see my husband, and he was standing with a lady and gentleman who were showing him pictures, and he gestured like this to me to come to them quickly. He said to me 'Look, look Anna at this most beautiful dog! We ourselves, we absolutely must have such a dog as this.'

It was an English setter, and the lady and gentleman who owned it, they began to tell us what a wonderful and beautiful dog it was – so kind and gentle and affectionate, so well behaved and did not make barking noises all the time; how she was such a companion and loved all people everywhere, and there was not one other dog in the world to compare with her. She and her husband invited us to visit them and meet their dog and see her for ourselves.

So we did, and all she had said was true, and we were totally in love with this kind of dog. She told us of a lady who was breeding them, and in due course we were able to obtain a puppy ourselves. That was Tetti whom we have had now since she was twelve weeks old. All the things the lady had told us about her dog, they were equally true of Tetti, or even more true still, if that is possible. She is the sweetest and kindest of all dogs that have ever been. Also when she was younger and could run freely and swiftly in the forest, she was of so outstanding beauty in motion, your heart would flutter up into your mouth with joy. We have bred with her two times, when she had three puppies on each occasion: and one we have kept which is that one Remi, her son. And he has been so patient while we have been eating, I will give him one cake for himself now. Yes Remi this is for you, you have been so good a dog yes.

And he is very famous too, did you know that? You have not had this film in England which is called *Beam*? It has been so popular here, they have shown it many times in the cinemas and even twice or I think three times now on television too. It is a story which is very sad, and I cry when I think of it even, but I will tell it to you. It concerns a man and his dog, who is his inseparable companion after his divorce from his wife. They wanted to have a perfect dog to play the part in this film, so what sort of a dog did they choose? What else, an English setter of course! No it was not Remi, I am saying that for a joke – Remi looks very much like him only he is younger of course, but the dog in the film was also the same colour, a tricolour.

So to continue for you with the story. One day the man who owns Beam, he falls down with a heart attack on the floor of his apartment, and Beam barks and barks until help comes. An ambulance is sent for to take the man to hospital; but one of the neighbours in the confusion leaves open the door of the apartment, and Beam runs out and searches everywhere to try to find his master. Some of the people he encounters in his search are kind to him, but others I am sorry to say they are not. They shout at him or throw stones at him, and one man even kicks him when he is trying to eat some old meat on the ground near the market. And this is how it goes on: it is so so sad, and poor Beam searches everywhere for his master but cannot find him. And then if you can believe it, it becomes even more sadder than that still. Beam's master recovers from his heart attack, and when he comes out of hospital he too is searching – he is trying to find Beam, and Beam is trying to find him. Sometimes you think they will meet, and they come very close to it, but they do not, it does not happen. Then finally, this is the most terrible part of it, Beam strays on to the railway line and there he gets the bottom part of his foreleg here trapped in some place where the lines switch from one side to the other like this. Trains are constantly coming, and each time you hear one your heart is in your mouth because you think it will kill him. None of them do: but they rush past him at great speed on the next track to him on this side or that. So just when you are thinking then that he might survive, along comes with a van a man whose occupation is to catch stray dogs and take them to be destroyed. And he takes Beam, and that is what happens to him. Oh it is so sad: as I said to you, even to tell it makes the tears come into my eyes.

At the ending, the man finally gives up hope of finding Beam, and he gets for himself another dog. But of course it is not Beam: it is a nice dog, but Beam will never be replaced in his heart. It is a film about kindness and love and fidelity between man and dog, and I think one of the loveliest films that has ever been made. So many people have seen it now, and yet still whenever it is to be shown at some cinemas again, you will always see there long long queues of people waiting for the cinema to open. This is why I made the joke to you that Remi had become famous: because whenever I take him walking with his mother, to the park or anywhere along the street, people see him and they point to him and they say to everyone around them 'Look, look – it's Beam!' So they all smile at him.

In Moscow an English setter is a dog of very great prestige, and very much prized. I think there are not more than perhaps two hundred of them altogether in the whole of Moscow. They have even special quarters for them at the Military Academy, I believe there are about eighteen or twenty of these dogs there. You say 'Whatever use would English setters be in the Army?' Well of course, in that sense no use whatever, of course not: as you say they do not fight or chase people or even growl ever, no. I did not mean they were used in the Army. What it is, you see, is that for the important professional soldier, a colonel or a general for example, if when he is out walking in his uniform and he wants people to notice how splendid he is, he has also an English setter walking by his side with a little chain, in order to perfectly complete the picture of smartness and elegance. You understand? Of course.

But permit me please, may I ask you one question: how is it you are so familiar yourself with such details about these dogs, the names of their colours and their nature and so on? Ah! Ah ha, so now I see, yes, I had been wondering ever since the other day in the park when you first approached me with your interpreter to ask if we could have a talk! You have an English setter yourself, of course, of course! You are obviously then a gentleman of the greatest sensitivity and character! So then I insist: we drink no more of this tea, we have a glass of the special vodka I have here in the cabinet, to toast each other's health! And our beautiful English setter dogs!

Adeleida Fedinskaya,
'babushka'*

A summer evening and she was round the back of the old-fashioned red-brick apartment block where she lived, sitting in the shade on a bench with three other elderly women outside the entrance to one of the stairways. They looked identical: despite the heat they were wearing thick skirts and fastened-up anoraks, with dark woollen scarves knotted round their heads and winter boots on their feet. She was the first to stand in greeting, and offer directions where to find someone who lived in the block.

But a week afterwards in her own apartment at the top of the staircase on the first floor, sitting at the table in the tiny living-room and pouring tea, she could be seen more plainly. A frail elderly woman in a plain dress, with arthritic hands and pale blue eyes, and a lined and wrinkled face. She was of a generation from whom living had exacted the price of making faces look ten years older than they were.

– I am an old woman, a simple old peasant woman of no importance. Of course you may ask me whatever questions you wish, and I will try my hardest to answer them for you; but I am an old person of no education, and also my memory is poor: I forget things or I cannot remember things, and so that makes me sound foolish. I have had a very ordinary life, but I will tell you what I can about it, and then you must decide whether it is interesting or not.

To tell you what I am, I would say I am an old woman who would be called by most people a 'babushka'. This is the word which means the scarf which you tie round your head with the knot under the chin. This is what nearly all old women do such as myself, so the word is also said as meaning an old woman, a grandmother perhaps. And there is another meaning still, that I am a sort of a caretaker as well for the entrance downstairs to this part of the apartment block. So for a description of me, you should make it 'babushka' and then everyone would know what you mean.

I will tell you first my age, which is seventy-eight. I have lived in Moscow since I was a girl of eighteen. I was born in a little village three hundred kilometres to the north, and altogether there were nine children in my family. I had three younger brothers, three older brothers, and two sisters. You will think me very stupid I am sure when I tell you I cannot exactly remember all their names, and I am not sure either which ones were the eldest. We were poor people, my family, country people, what are called peasants. We lived a simple life, my father and mother dug the ground and grew food for us, and we also had a cow and some chickens I remember. All the children had very little schooling, just at the village school. There we learned to read and write but not much else, because as soon as we were old enough we worked on the land with our parents. Or one would go fishing, another trapping, another searching for fruits, or twigs for the fire. Or sometimes it was your turn to help our mother to make soup in a big pot, and so on and things like that.

When I was sixteen my mother died, and then it was my job with my sisters to look after the male members of the family so that they could go to their work. We made all the clothing for them as well: everything, because we had little money to buy things. Sometimes two of us would come on a shopping trip to Moscow for two days, and if we could afford it we would take back a few luxuries such as brightly coloured fabric to make covers for the beds, or perhaps a new lamp to hang over the table where we ate. I liked always to be one of those who came to Moscow: it seemed such a fairyland place to me, with big shops with many different goods on display. When I hear people nowadays who make complaints that there is nothing to buy in the shops, I remember how those same shops looked to me as a peasant girl visiting from the country. I thought they were treasure houses full of so many things I could stand for hour upon hour looking at everything.

I am talking now of a time that was sixty years ago, so I cannot remember my age when I made up my mind I did not want to live with my family in the village any longer, I wanted to come instead to live in Moscow. Did I say I had lived here since I was eighteen? Well then that is probably correct. It seemed to me I would like it better to live in a big city because it was more interesting and exciting; and also that I could earn more money here and send some of it back to my family. So that is what I did, I came here.

I was young and healthy, and even though I had had no schooling, what I did have to offer was strength. So I became a building worker, and at that time, which would be 1930 perhaps, many blocks of apartments were being built. Stalin had ordered there should be living places for everyone, and there was so much building going on it was easy very quickly to get work. I took accommodation in a women workers' hostel, which was a cheap place to live in; and I worked hard and all the time sent as much money home as I could to my family. Sometimes I would go back to them for one day or two, and I never regretted the move I had made to the city. One day my father told me that he was proud of me: and this was an important occasion, because before that I had never been sure if he approved of me leaving or not.

I was an unskilled worker, and did only such ordinary things as carrying bricks and holding up pieces of timber for the carpenters to fix together. It was hard work, and sometimes in the winter the weather was very cold and the snow so thick we were unable to do any work, and so were paid less. But it is the only kind of work I have ever been capable of doing through the whole of my life, and always when you were doing it there were many other young women working with you. So you made friends and it made life much more interesting than it would have been if I had stayed with my family.

That is how it went on and that is how I lived, right up to the time when the Germans invaded our country in 1941 and the Great Patriotic War began. At once there was a call for all men who were able, to go into the Army and fight to defend their country – and for everyone else who could do so to devote all their efforts to whatever work they could do of a civilian kind. Women building workers were formed into labour battalions, and we were immediately in great demand to build shelters for people against air raids, and soon to start to dig trenches for the defence of Moscow because the advance of the German troops towards us was so rapid. As the German Air Force more and more often began to bomb Moscow, there was even more work for us still in trying to clear up the debris afterwards when buildings had been destroyed. And it was often a very sad time, because we had to dig graves for the many people who had been killed.

The German Army was very strong, and they had many tanks and aeroplanes, and it seemed at one stage as though nothing could stop them from entering Moscow. But our brave soldiers finally halted them, though it was only when they were very near. They had come so close that we women of the labour battalion that I was a member of, we had to keep with us at all times a bundle of clothing to take with us in case we had suddenly to be evacuated and taken to another place to avoid capture. There were many brave deeds and many brave actions in the war by both men and women: one of my friends now, she was a nurse and she was on several occasions under fire from the enemy. She still talks little now about those terrible times.

Many millions of our citizens were killed in the war, and among those who lost their lives were three of my brothers who had gone to the Army. Two more of my brothers returned from the fighting in conditions of bad health, and both of them died not very long after the fighting had finished. My father died during the war, as also did my two sisters. So from my family, only one of my brothers and me have survived. As you can see, it is something which is difficult for me to talk of without tears. That such a war could ever be fought again, well it is simply not to be contemplated.

After the war was finished, of course there was much work to do both in rebuilding places which had been damaged, and in making new apartments as homes for those returning from the war. I remained in the labour battalion and we went to many different cities as well as working also in Moscow. It was during this period that I met the man who became my husband when he was discharged from the Army. There was a great shortage of places for people to live, and at first we had only a room in a hostel, which we shared with two other couples. After two years our daughter was born, and life became very hard for us. My husband had been injured in the war, so I had to be the principal bread-winner, and there was always a possibility when you were in a labour battalion that you would be sent to some other place. Fortunately for me I was able to obtain my discharge from it, and join another battalion which was stationed in Moscow permanently. After my assignment to that, when our next task was completed, because I had assisted in it I was given preferential treatment for obtaining accommodation in the apartment block.

It is this one where we are now sitting this evening. Since I was one who helped with the building of this block, this is how I come to have this very place as my home, because I helped to build it with my own hands. Here also now lives my daughter and her little girl. My husband died eight years ago, and my daughter of course is divorced, so they have their home now here with me.

To summarise my life story for you, I would say it can be done with one word. My life has been working, working, working. I have had much grief and sorrow in my life always, from the time when my mother died from fever when I was a young girl. But all the same I have something to show for it perhaps. I will show it to you because I am proud of it. I took it out of the cupboard earlier this evening in preparation for your coming. It is the tunic you see hanging there on the back of the door. Wait for one moment and I will take it down for you. So.

I wear this when there are ceremonial occasions, which when I receive an invitation I sometimes attend. Here pinned to it is my medal, which is awarded to someone who is as I am, a person designated a Veteran of Soviet Labour. And with it I have this framed certificate which was presented to me at the same time, saying I am an Honoured Communist Worker. These are my rewards for my life, and they give me joy and satisfaction as I come near to the end of it. But I think mostly my life has been sad.

Katya Chilichkina,

beauty queen*

She turned the typing chair round and sat astride it, resting her elbows on its back: a long-legged young woman, slender and tall, with slanting brown eyes and her fair hair in a pony tail. She wore red jeans and a crisp white blouse, with a blue chiffon scarf knotted round her neck. From time to time she took off her big pink-framed glasses and nibbled thoughtfully at the ends of the arms while she talked. She smiled often, and laughed at some of the things she said about herself.

– It all began really you know as completely a joke. I had one day a very big row with my boyfriend, and I spent the whole evening in the apartment of my family, crying and feeling sorry for myself. The longer the evening went on and he did not telephone, the more miserable I was. My younger sister Nadia, she is sixteen and three years younger than me, she became very cross with me because I was all the time speaking about my unhappiness, and she was looking at the newspaper. Then suddenly she said 'Katya, there is an announcement here that there is to be the first ever beauty-queen contest in Moscow. It asks you should send a photograph and some details of yourself. Why do you not enter for it, you might win?' My sister she is very pretty, I think she is much better-looking than I am, and I told her she should go in for the competition, not me. And then we began to laugh together about what sort of things we should say about ourselves. We were joking all the time you know, so it cheered me up.

But then the following day I thought to myself, Well why should I not do this? If my boyfriend does not appreciate me other people might do so. So I sent in the photograph to the newspaper with

some information about my age and my schooling and the office
where I was working, and how it was my first job. Altogether I
think there were 1,703 girls who entered this contest; the first thing
I heard was about two weeks later when I was told I had been
selected as one of the final hundred girls. I thought it meant, well,
nothing. Then soon after that I was told again I was chosen now as
one of the thirty-six finalists, and I should appear at the All Union
Central Hall on such and such a date and to be there for three whole
days. There would be many preliminary rounds of different kinds,
until there were only twelve left. And then there would be the final
judging by a panel of journalists and musicians and designers, and
this final was to take place on the evening of the last day, and would
be shown on Moscow television.

Well I had not told my parents or my sister or the people I worked
for that I had entered for this competition, and I knew it would be
necessary that I should tell them now. The people at work, they
were very pleased and said I could take time off, and my sister was
very very excited and said 'You will win Katya, I know you will
win.' But my parents – well I am afraid they were not very pleased
at all when I told them, in particular my father. But my mother
talked with him and in the end they decided to instead drop their
objection. I was very nervous myself as to what would happen in
the three days of the judging, and there were several times I thought
I would withdraw. Some of the things I had been sent a list of that I
should have to do, well I am nineteen only and it was very alarming
for me to face. But my sister all the time talked me out of it,
whenever I told her I was too nervous and couldn't go. And when
the time came, in fact to my surprise I enjoyed the three days very
much.

It was a competition which was based so to say not just on our
looks, but just as importantly what was inside our heads. There
were different parades we took part in, we all had to wear a variety
of different costumes and outfits, and also to appear in turn in front
of a panel of writers and artists who asked each one of us completely
different questions. All the time there was a very big audience, of
about twelve thousand people, all of them of course cheering for
their own favourites. I liked the fashion and parades the best of it:
for one we had to appear in bathing suits and we were allowed to

have no make-up of any kind for that, and only to comb our hair in
a natural way. For another, there was a huge pile of different fabrics
we could choose from, and we had to make ourselves a dress from
a piece we liked – but not by sewing it, only by pulling and folding
it and tucking it in. I made myself something like a fish's skin
wrapped very tightly around me, from a material coloured like
copper, and many people in the audience liked it.

But the most frightening part of all to me was the question session
with the writers and artists. I was asked such a thing as this: 'What
do you think would be going through the mind of an old-fashioned
Party bureaucrat if he was sitting here and seeing the first ever
beauty contest to be held in the Soviet Union?' My answer was to
make it into a joke: I said I thought he would like to come up on to
the stage himself and have his picture taken standing with so many
pretty young ladies of Moscow. Everyone laughed, and nearly all of
the contest was like that, everybody enjoying it and trying to put all
the girls at ease and be relaxed. And it succeeded to be like that:
before very long we were all feeling the same way about it, that it
did not matter who came the first or the second or third, it was just
good to be there.

When the final judging came, first of all I was chosen as the
Number Two. It was a very nice girl of the same age, I think, who
was chosen by the judges to be the first 'Miss Moscow'. They by
the way included Alla Pugachova, who as you know is one of the
very top pop stars of all Russia. But then it was also asked of the
television viewers they should send in their votes for their choice,
and a week later it was announced I had been fortunate enough to
be the top one of that poll. So I could say I am 'joint Miss Moscow',
is that the right expression?

Then it happened just a few months after that, last March in
Helsinki there was a competition among all the beauty queens of
different countries for the title of Miss Europe. I was sent to
represent Russia because the other girl was ill and she was not able
to travel. There were girls from altogether twenty-one different
European countries – England, France, Germany, Spain I think,
Austria, Sweden, Italy and many more. On that occasion to my
great surprise I was the winner also, so this year I am Miss Europe
as well, which of course has never before happened to a Soviet girl.

There have been objections, yes, from many people in different positions, even some of them members of the government, saying such things as that beauty contests are wrong and should not be held. In many ways our country, it is very old-fashioned and puritanical you know: by some people for instance it is considered, they say even immoral, for young women to show themselves in bathing costumes with bare shoulders and bare legs and bare feet unless they are by the side of the sea. The argument they put forward is that there are very many things in life which are much more important than how a pretty girl looks, and at a time when all our country's thoughts and efforts should be concentrated on how to improve the economic position and such things, it is wrong and trivial to have beauty competitions. This is true: in USSR there are hardly any jobs for young people as for example professional models for clothing, because we do not have advertising for them like in the West. There are no such things as schools where you could go to learn to be a fashion model or something of that kind. Modelling is done only by amateurs, we have no professionals.

So the Moscow beauty-queen contest was a big step forward, or a big step backwards perhaps, however the way different people looked at it. My own father, even though he was pleased that I had won the title – well I think still he feels not completely happy about it. But for me it has had a very big effect on my self-confidence and upon my personality: it opens a different horizon for the way I think about my future, and if it would be possible now I would like to be a professional model. At the Miss Europe competition in Helsinki I met there many people, especially from England and France, who had come not to take part in the competition but to help with the arranging of it – and many of these people, they were models themselves and I had not met such people ever before. What was so interesting to me was that they were not all of them young and pretty girls at all, but older women. As their age increased, so that was the sort of modelling they did: a woman of thirty, she would model clothes for thirty-year-old women, or the same at forty-five. And it was not just clothes that they modelled, but many other things too – for example washing machines, or typewriters, or shoes in pictures of just the feet here, where it was not shown what their faces looked like. I had never thought about this; I had thought that if you were a model you could only work for a few years, then you would be too old.

Now just two weeks ago I have been offered for myself an agreement to take a position with a joint venture with a Russian company and an Italian company also, to work as a model for them in advertisements which are to do not with clothes but with computers. These pictures are to be of a young person working with such things and other kinds of similar equipment as well. It is for one year and will give very good experience to me, so as you will imagine I am very happy about it. I may also be able to go to Italy and do pictures for the company there. Most of all for me it will be an opportunity in which I shall work hard and learn many things. And there will certainly be better chances for me to earn much more money than if I stay in the office where I was typist. My father is an engineer and my mother is an invalid, and in our apartment there lives with us also my sister and my grandmother. We are not at all wealthy people, and therefore I think what I will be doing will be earning more money for all of us in the family to live better. There is even the possibility that I should go to work for a few months in this company in Japan. So you see there are good opportunities in many ways for me if my work is satisfactory to people during my year. I have talked with my father about this, and I think he begins to see it is a time of possibilities, and not something that is here only for today. Or well I should say it is not only for this year while I have my title, until the new contest when there is the next girl who is Miss Europe.

I shall try always to keep myself in health and physical fitness because I want very much now to be a very good professional model. And as you become older you know, you realise something that it is very important you should never forget. It is that it was just a matter of good fortune for you that you grew up to have the kind of looks which other people like. And this is not anything you can feel superior about, because you did not work to make yourself so, it was sheer good chance. But if you have been given good fortune of that kind, then it is work: you must work and you must build on it to make a good future for yourself, it is up to you, no one is ever again going to give things to you as easily as that.

I have said to Nadia, and it is true, that without her to make the suggestion I would never have won the competition – and that now next year she also must enter for it. Because it is also true that she is really very much better-looking than I. But no she will not, she says, she likes too much to have a good time and has a new boyfriend every week. And I say to her that it was due to her I went in for the contest but also because my boyfriend had given me up, so as soon as one does that to her, she must follow in the same way. It would be a very surprising thing I think if two sisters were to win such a competition, and I cannot imagine what my father would say about it then.

Maria Malenkova,
housewife*

A slim dark-haired woman with an olive complexion and grey eyes, she wore a brown blouse and tight-fitting black leather trousers. She talked in a quiet voice, from time to time tossing back her head and sweeping her long brown hair away from her face with her hand.

– I would say just now I am nothing, I am not working, so all day I stay at home in my mother's apartment while she is at work. I take my daughter Lydia to school in the morning, she is seven; and then I come home again to the apartment, I do things about the house and cook an evening meal for us, or some sewing such as making a dress for my little girl. I like doing these things, I am happy, it is a period of calm in my life. I have a diploma as a teacher of biology and maybe I will resume the career of teacher again before long, but I really do not know if I want to do that. My life has been until the end of last year how shall I say, turbulent, so it is good for me to have peacefulness and quietness for a few months in my life with people I love such as my mother and Lydia my little girl. I have been you see an exile, and now that I am home again it gives me a good feeling and I like it. I was born and grew up all my life in Moscow, I am true Muscovite, this is where I belong, Moscow is my home.

How I became to be exiled is like this. I am twenty-nine years of age, my parents are divorced and I am the only child they had, before my father went away with another woman when I was six. I do not remember very much what he was like: a nice man I think, but I never saw him again after he had gone. I do not really know what he was like, there is not much I can say to you about him except I regarded him as being on the whole kind. It was hard for my mother of course to earn money to keep us, and we lived with my grandparents, also in Moscow. At school as a student I would say I was average in my lessons.

I went to college to take my diploma and it was my intention that I should be a teacher. But a teacher in what would be so to say further education, in teaching older pupils, I did not want to teach young children in a school. So it was necessary for me to be a student for four years to become qualified to do this.

But when I had done two years of study and was twenty only, I became ill with a serious illness of the chest, and it was necessary for me first to go into a hospital and then to have a long period of recuperation in what is known as a home for convalescence. It was a place which was on the outskirts of Moscow to the north: it was pleasant and the attention you received was good. But for a young person of course it was lonely: I had friends in the city and they used to come and visit me, and so did my mother. But it was a long journey for them to make, and sometimes it would be ten days or two weeks even when I did not see anyone whom I knew except the other patients.

It was the same situation for them of course, and many of them too were lonely as I was. So in that situation as you will understand, the relationships which sometimes form between people can become very intense. It was in that way with me and a young man there who was of the same age: we became very deeply in love with each other, and we had no thought in our heads but that we wanted to be with each other all the time. Our only wish was that we should both be fully recovered from our illnesses, and then as soon as possible after that we should become married.

So it happened in the early summer of that year, in June, that we were both told we could be discharged because we were well enough to carry on with our lives. He was in a different position however to me: I had my mother and grandmother living here in Moscow, whereas for him, his home and his family were in the Irkutsk region of Siberia. Before he became ill he had had a good job there in a managerial capacity at a coal mine, and the position had been promised back to him when he returned. And even if it were to be no longer available, there were many other mines around the town where he lived, so there would be no difficulty for him to obtain well-paid work. But if he did not go back there when we married, but were to stay in Moscow instead – well, what should he do you see, there was no work here for him where he could earn similar pay.

It did not seem under the circumstances there was much we had to discuss about the situation. I was at that stage which sometimes occurs when you are very much in love, you would be willing to go and live on the moon if necessary, or anywhere else so long as you could be with the one you loved. So I announced to my family that I was going to go with this man after our marriage, to live in Irkutsk. It was so far away that if you were to go there by train from here, you would have to make a journey of over a day and a half of travelling.

My relatives and all my friends, well of course they were sad but they understood without hesitation how it was for me. One of them called me the name of 'the brave Decembrist', and soon everyone was calling me that, to tease me. The reason for it – I do not know perhaps as many of the historical details as I should – is that the Decembrists were a group of Army officers who rebelled in December of 1825 against the Tsar Nicholas the First. They had as some of their aims the bringing of democracy to our country, and to abolish serfdom as well. But their rebellion was crushed, and the Tsar banished them for life to Siberia to Irkutsk, and many of the officers when they went there, their wives went with them also. So that is how I was called 'the brave Decembrist', because I was going to live so far away in Siberia with my husband, in exile from Moscow.

We had applied to marry as the end of our stay in the convalescent home came close, but after we were discharged there was still a short period of three weeks or a month for us to wait. My husband returned to his home at once, and I remained in Moscow to arrange formalities with the institute where I had been studying, to allow me to continue as a student by correspondence. He then returned once more for the marriage, and then I went back after that to his home with him. His job had been kept open, and because of his position he had had little difficulty in finding an apartment for us.

I did not know anyone at all in the town where we lived, but I quickly made friends and found my new life very interesting. It was a little hard for me to find a job but I did so eventually. I worked as a manager in one of the maintenance offices on a housing estate. For several months, a year perhaps, we were happy. My husband worked underground, and it was hard and difficult work, but he was well paid. Then I became pregnant and after a year my daughter was born.

I think it was in total seven and a half years that I was there, until our marriage ended and I came back here with my daughter to Moscow. I am afraid I have to say that I think the main cause of the break-up between us was alcohol. Like many people who work in the mines my husband drank a great deal. I myself am completely teetotal because I do not like the taste of any alcohol at all, and so I could not understand how he could drink so much of it. Of course not all miners are alcoholics, but I think he was so much in need of drink that he should have sought some help or treatment of some kind. Unfortunately although he recognised it was a problem for him, he never brought himself to do anything about it. In many ways it was not too hard for me because I had my child, and many friends; but we had quarrels and arguments and other things, and it was not good for our little girl to see her parents behave in this manner. Sometimes I went with her to stay for two or three days away from him: he would always then come after a while and say he was sorry and ask us to go back to our home, which we did. But of course then another situation, or rather the same situation, would arise again, and eventually it came that we applied for divorce.

In our country when you do that, if there is a child there is a hearing in a court. The judge asks questions of the husband and wife and tries to get a satisfactory solution for looking after the child and making the end to the marriage as painless as possible. In such a situation it is often difficult not to begin to make serious allegations, but I did not want to say about my husband's drinking because it might have affected his position at work. I think the judge understood this, because she gave us the divorce without asking too many questions of each of us. She ordered that my husband should pay one-quarter of his salary towards the upbringing of his child, and this he will have to do until she is eighteen: it is taken from his salary by his employers, and sent to me. The divorce was granted within one week of the hearing at the court; we had already agreed amicably between us about the division of our possessions, and so there was little else to do afterwards and I came back to Moscow in November of last year, and now I am to build a new life here. I hope it will be possible for my daughter to go to see her father, perhaps at holiday times when she is a little older. He and I have it as our intention to remain on terms of friendship, for her sake. I hope that we shall, because although we no longer love each other, I think we still have respect between us.

So that is the story of my exile, and I hope I have been able to recount it to you without bitterness. In Siberia it was a time for me of experience and learning about life. There was also there something that occurred which made it very much easier for me to bear the loneliness when my husband and I had separated and were living apart from each other, for the period of the last twelve months when I was in Siberia. It was that I had by then become friendly with another man whom I had met there. He is not a miner and he does not drink, and he is a kind man and my daughter likes him also. He does not have very much education, and he does not have work qualifications that would allow him to make a lot of money. But these things are no guarantee of happiness are they? It is our intention to get married and when we do I will find work also, and I think we shall have a good life together. Our pleasures are the same and they are simple: we like to walk in the country, to go sometimes to the cinema and perhaps even to a disco. I think we are well suited to each other. Although he is fond of my daughter, I think it would be nice for all of us if we also had a child of our own. For myself I would like it, as he would, and I have talked already about it with my daughter and she says she would be glad if she had a brother or a sister. So we shall try to make a nice home, all of us together, and I think it will be good.

I am sure I will be happier living again here in Moscow than in Siberia. This man has said he would like to come to live here, it would be most interesting and exciting for him. He has made a visit twice already, and next month he comes again. It will mean of course that he would leave his family and friends and live far away from them, as I did. I told him what my family used to call me when I went to Siberia, and he laughed: he said that so now, this time it will be him coming to live far away from home, so he is the one who will be the brave Decembrist.

Tamara Pavlova,

secretary

Tall and vivacious in manner, her hair stylishly cut and highlighted, she wore a black mini-skirt and a loosely fitting high-collared white angora sweater. As she talked she stretched out her long legs and looked at her glossy black shoes, turning her feet in towards each other. Her tights were decorated with clusters of tiny white beads.

– You mind if I smoke? One day I will give up, I guess: I am always promising it to myself but then I say you know, Oh what the hell, who cares, life's too short.

So what shall we talk about, what shall I tell you of myself? Anything that I like, yes OK why not? I am happy to do it. You wanted to talk with a modern woman of Moscow today, my friend said, to help you to obtain a picture. She has told you anything about me? No, well then that is good because it means it is up to me entirely to speak as I wish, yes?

So I give you some basic information to begin with OK? My name is Tamara, I am thirty-two and I have a son who is twelve years of age who is called Sasha, and he lives with me and my husband here in this apartment in the Mayanana district of Moscow, which is a modern development of very good flats. It is three years since we have been living here, as soon as they were completed. My husband is a businessman, he works for a French-Russian company to do with the manufacture and importing of military equipment: I do not know much of the details, it does not greatly interest me. He has a good position, he travels a great deal to France and other countries of Europe many times in a year, and he has a good salary.

My own occupation is that I work for an American company in Moscow, it is what is called I think a personal assistant to one of the directors. Additionally I am in charge of the general office where there are twenty-two secretaries, typists and those who work with word processors, telex machines and all the rest. It is a busy office and I have to work hard, and also long hours: sometimes from eight o'clock in the morning until almost the same hour at night. Americans you know, they work much harder than Russians: most of my staff are Russian girls, and they find it hard sometimes to keep up with the pace. We are not used to such hard work in this country, believe me: I think we are lazy and dilatory and not at all well organised, so when we find ourselves having to work as the Americans do, it is a shock. It is good for us of course, but all the same it is new to us and we have to adjust to it.

I speak Russian, English, French not so fluently, and a little German also. I will not be silly and say I think I do not speak very good English, because I know that I do. My English is fluent, yes? I am almost bilingual, and this is because I studied it at school, at university and then after that took it as a special subject in the Pedagogical Institute. I like the language and enjoy to speak it and to practise speaking it, and I have the idea that before long I may leave my office after I have fully learned modern American business methods, and perhaps then work on a freelance basis as an inter-preter, secretary, and translator. There are always many oppor-tunities in Moscow to do work of that kind: for businessmen especially, to interpret for them at conferences, to translate letters and agreements and contracts and so on. You can always get a very good wage for yourself, especially if you are efficient and competent. It would also perhaps give me the opportunity to travel: this is something I would like very much to do, you know? Soon you see my son will be a young man and will start to lead his own life, so I will be free to do what I wish and go where I like.

With my husband, well we are married now in name only, and this is how it has been between us for five years. We do not go to bed together, and we are agreed that we are free to lead our own lives. I am not a promiscuous person, so I have just two lovers – one is a very sweet boy who is much younger than me, he is twenty only, and the other is nearer to my own age but he is married and has two children. He does not wish to leave his wife and I would not want him to do that. I do not wish to marry again, either with him or anyone else. I prefer it to be as I am, free to choose what I do and to go where my fancy takes me. I like to dance and sing, to go to theatres and concerts of classical music, sometimes to a restaurant and have a good meal and some nice wine, and to enjoy myself. But I am not a frivolous person, and most of all I enjoy freedom. It was a very big mistake for me to marry when I was young and have a child. When my son was little, one or two years of age only, I stayed at home for a time, and tried to be a good housewife and mother, and a good wife to my husband. But I can tell you I was not a great success at those things, and life became very unhappy for me. I am a good mistress for a man I think, but not a good wife.

Well I am not a good wife because I cannot comply with the rules as far as our society in Russia today is concerned. I think increasingly more women are not doing so, you know? But there are still very many of the old attitudes. As soon as we married my husband expected that always I should cook for him, clean the house, meet all his sexual needs and be in every way his slave. I do not mean he was physically cruel, because if he had ever showed violence to me I would immediately have taken my son and gone from the house. I mean that in everything in life he expected everything to do with me was second to his wishes. Women nowadays are coming to demand more that marriage should be a partnership, and they want more consideration to be shown for them.

I was not unfaithful to him until we agreed we should go on in our separate ways, but he was I think perhaps to me. Like a lot of women I do not like loneliness you know? With both of my lovers it is not just a sexual partnership I have with them. I enjoy sex and it is good for me and they enjoy it also I think with me; but I like it also that we spend time together, I do not have to spend every moment of my life with my son. There is an English phrase that someone said to me once, that I wanted to have my cake and eat it as well. But I do not think this is so. The older of my two lovers, he has his family and he has me, and I am his cake yes? This I do not mind at all. But with my younger one, well here it is more difficult. He says it does not matter that our ages are so different, he wants still most of all to marry me if I will have him. It is wrong, but sometimes I get angry with him. I telephone him and I say 'What are you doing today?' and he says 'Today like all days I am sitting here waiting for your call.'

I tell him he should find some much younger girl who is nearer to his own age, and should marry her. Because you see I fear I would not at all be the sort of wife he wants. He says he does not want such a person who would cook and keep house for him, but I think he could not help it, it is ingrained in him because he is a Russian man. I think also that I do not love him in the way I should for that: we match well in bed, but there are too many big differences between us in other ways. I enjoy sex with him and he has quickly learned to be different in that way from most Russian men: for most of them it is their own satisfaction only that matters, they do not show consideration for the woman to have satisfaction too. He is a very sweet boy you know, but marriage to him, well I think not. I tell him of the difficulties, that perhaps it may happen when we were married I would want to be once in bed with some other man. And you know he is so young, he says he would make me so happy I would never feel that. It is funny but it is sad also, yes?

I like him, he tries so hard to understand and to satisfy all my wishes you know. I will tell you that perhaps as you know, in Soviet society generally the taking of birth-control precautions is regarded as something entirely for the woman, and if she becomes pregnant then she should have an abortion. This is so even when the man and the woman are married, if they do not want to have more children then abortion is the chosen way. Only very slowly is coming the knowledge of the contraceptive pill. But to use it is not popular. It has one side-effect that if you have what is called a certain kind of I think the word is metabolism, it will cause you to put on weight. It does so for me; and most Russian women do not like taking chemical pills, and I am one of those also. For women the most common birth control to use therefore is the coil. I went to my doctor to ask for this to be fitted, but when she examined me she told me it would not be possible, although I didn't fully understand the reason for it. But to get to the point of what I was going to say about the young boy who is my lover, when I told him this he said he did not ever want me to have an abortion from him. And so always when we make love he uses a condom, and he is very good about this and never fails to do so. Perhaps he is after all one of the younger generation of men who are becoming more responsible and aware. But if we were married, I think still he could change and become like the rest. I do not know: but in all ways that I consider it, I feel sure that marriage to anyone is not something I want again.

With sexual things such as birth control and for example the techniques of love-making, we are still far behind the West I think. You will not find books on any of these subjects in the bookshops, there is still much we must learn about openness and discussion of them, and try to imitate and copy so many of your ways. Other things? Well I have never been to the West, but from what I have read in magazines and seen on television, and talked about with people who have been there – most of all you know, what I think we should learn from you is politeness. Everyone says this who has been there, the thing that they notice so much is the politeness and friendliness of people. They say in shops, in restaurants, hotels, in the streets, almost everywhere people are nice to you. I do not know why it cannot be like that here, why everyone has to be so rude, to shout and quarrel all the time. It is something I do not like. Even in hospitals nurses will be very rude to patients, you know? It is the exceptional waiter in a restaurant, or person in a railway ticket office even, who will smile at you and be polite.

The reason, I think well in my opinion there are two. The first is that in our society we have always been brought up to obey all the tiny little rules and regulations that there are for everything. In a shop you must go in at one door and go out at another, and if you do not then people will shout at you. Everyone must behave in the same way, and everyone joins in condemning a trangressor. And the other reason is that I think here everyone lives under such great strain all the time. They have little privacy anywhere: not in their homes because all apartments are shared sometimes with many others, not when they go to work when they are hustled and jostled on the buses and trams and in the Metro, nor in the shops where there are nothing but queues and queues and queues. There is so much harshness in everyday life, so it is no wonder people are as they are, except with their friends. They live close to anger all the time, it is everywhere around them.

I would very much like to go to the West and see how life is different there. I do not want to emigrate or leave my country, but just to go and see. Perhaps it will not be long now before it becomes easier, not only for me but for everyone; I think we shall not like some of the things we see, but others I am sure we will.

Well it has been nice to meet you too Toni and I hope you will not think I have talked too much!

3 War and Peace

Alex Yeverenko, World War II tank commander

Viktoria Bolova, World War II nurse

Valentin Leminev, Afghan War veteran

Robert Serlov, conscript

Lev Gorolin, conscript

Edik Mamenk, conscript

Alex Yeverenko,
World War II tank commander*

He liked, he said, to walk about a little as he talked, because as he got older his leg became stiff if he sat for too long. He was thin and grey-haired and wore a well-cut dark suit. His voice was level and firm.

– As you will know, the war began for us in June 1941. I first heard the news that the enemy had invaded our country over the radio while I was walking along a corridor in our barracks. There were speakers along the walls: this was a military barracks you understand, and music and news was being broadcast all day. Already I was in the Army: I was nineteen, and I had chosen it for my future career. The barracks I refer to was a training school for officers who were to join tank regiments. This was what I wanted to do, it was my ambition; and at that time I was just half-way through my training course.

I went into a room in the corridor where I knew there would be other students such as myself: they were all sitting at tables in silence listening to the radio, and hoping to learn information of where the main attacks had occurred. No one was expressing surprise: we had all been certain for several months that it was inevitable war was coming sooner or later. I could almost say there was a feeling of something like relief that it had now finally happened, and the uncertainty and waiting were over.

I am sure young men are the same everywhere in the world, and so the main feeling in the air was one of something like excitement: it was eager anticipation you may say, the feeling we were ready for this and now were going to prove ourselves. Like myself none of the others had completed their training; but if war begins war begins, and it is then the soldier's duty to fight with what skill he has and with what weapons he is given. For most of us our graduation was in the nature of three months away, but it now had no importance. The time had come for study to cease and action to begin.

Almost immediately the door of the room opened and one of our senior instructors entered. We all of course stood to our feet: he briefly spoke to us, giving us our orders to collect our clothing and possessions, and then to assemble at a specified point ready for transport to take us to our destination. I remember it occurred to me, I am sure to all the others also, that it was similar in every way to any other day – an officer gave us our instructions and we then carried them out.

The barracks where we were, it was situated in an area near the border of the state of Latvia. We were told the advancing enemy were making rapid progress towards us, because they had struck without warning, so we must proceed towards them with the greatest possible speed. At a certain point tanks would be waiting for us: we were then to form ourselves into a small armoured unit, find the enemy and engage him in battle. Overwhelmingly for all of us there was a sense of excitement: no one felt fear or hesitation, we were ready to do our duty and fulfil the mission we had been given. We were then continuously on the move in our transport lorries for all of that Sunday night, throughout Monday and for Monday night as well. It was not until early on Tuesday morning we reached our destination, and there as we had been told, tanks were waiting for us. We formed ourselves into a battalion, made up of a number of individual groups or units.

Our armoured equipment consisted I am sorry to say of rather old tanks: they were very small and of poor quality, with thin armour and a limited number of guns. Some for example had as their crew only two men with one machine gun: one man was the driver and the other was the machine gunner. My unit consisted of six or seven such vehicles. We had no information as to the direction from which the enemy was advancing, so our only possibility was to set off and look for them along the country roads, and this was what we did.

It was then I had my first sight of war and what it means: for we

were very soon among, coming towards us, a great column of
ordinary peasant people who were fleeing from the advancing
Germans. They were poor, and they had loaded as many of their
possessions as they could on to carts, with the lucky ones those who
had horses to pull them. Those who did not, they had to pile their
things into wheelbarrows or even perambulators, and push them
themselves. There were old men and women, children, infants,
livestock such as goats, sheep, pigs and cows, and all were fleeing
for their lives along this dusty road on the hot summer morning. I
had never before seen such a sight: when you do training exercises
across the countryside from the military academy, of course they do
not arrange for refugees to be included. The sight was astonishing
and greatly sad to me: I had given no thought at all before to what
you may say is the totality of war.

Because the road was soon becoming impassable by reason of the
great number of people, I gave the order for my unit to turn away
from it in the direction of the right, and go across some fields where
all by comparison was calm. But after about a distance I suppose of
some two or three kilometres, there suddenly appeared before us,
coming from within some woods, a large formation of German
tanks and armoured troop carriers, in total about twenty or thirty
vehicles. We were of course completely outnumbered, and in
addition their tanks were larger and heavier than ours, and carried
more guns. It was at that moment you may say that I grew up from
being a boy of nineteen into manhood. The enemy advanced
towards us firing, and it was for me the first moment of realisation
that I was not taking part in a game. I and my men we were all in
great danger, and could at any moment be totally destroyed. I have
no hesitation to say that I was very afraid, and I gave the order at
once that we should turn and flee.

Fortunately the damage the enemy was able to inflict on us was
slight and we escaped without casualties. From that time onwards,
as I'm sure you will know, the whole of the Russian Army
everywhere was in total retreat for several months. It was forced
back almost to the gates of Moscow. There is a memorial on the
outskirts of the city, in the symbolic form of a big anti-tank trap to
mark the nearest point that the enemy reached. It was merely
eighteen kilometres away from where we are here today in your

interpreter's apartment. It used to be wondered for many years why the Germans stopped there to regroup, instead of advancing and taking the city. But it has recently been revealed by former German generals that they were of the opinion Moscow would certainly be heavily fortified, and they must make careful preparation for attack. But Moscow was not heavily fortified: they could have taken it with ease if they had wished.

Then came the winter, which brought us respite from retreat, and in the months that followed the fortunes of war slowly turned to our favour. With the help of our American and British allies we were able to build up our fighting strength: our tanks and armour became stronger, and our weapons were more numerous and effective. It is my opinion, and not just mine alone I may say, that one of the most important of these, and which came in increasing number into production, was something we called 'Katusha'. It was a multiple rocket-launcher, which when it was fired made a strange sound: to some people it reminded them of the distant singing of voices. At that time in the war there was a very popular song of that name, about a girl, so that is how the weapon came to be called it. But of course the greatest of all weapons that we had was the courage and determination of our soldiers. It was this most of all which with our allies' help brought us victory. But you will know that the cost in lives was enormous: over twenty million people of the USSR died, a number which cannot be comprehended.

I took no further part in combat myself after the middle of the year 1943. Tanks of much bigger size were being introduced; some of them were coming from our own factories, and others from America and Great Britain. Eventually there were tanks with crews of five men in each, with two gun turrets and sometimes three or four additional armoured pieces as well. They were giants, and so with the great need for properly trained personnel to operate them, I was sent as instructor to the Military Academy. It then became my turn to teach young officers how to be tank commanders. It was felt that with my long experience of combat and my knowledge of tanks of all kinds, I would be a suitable person for such a position. Many with similarly extensive knowledge had not unfortunately survived the ferocious battles of such campaigns as that of Stalingrad as I did.

Of those who took part in it, I was one of the few fortunate enough to remain alive.

You are correct in suggesting it, yes: I am being a little reluctant in telling this part of my story. The reason is because it is difficult for me to do it without in some way sounding as though I am trying to give an impression of myself as a brave man. As you suggest, I was wounded, in fact on three occasions. Once was when my tank was hit by enemy gunfire: I received thirteen wounds from flying metal in my legs. Another time was when my tank was hit and burst into flames and I was burned. The third time was when my tank was bombed by an aeroplane. Such things are common occurrences in war; they happen to many soldiers, and those who keep their lives as I did are fortunate. I have some medals, yes, campaign medals and such things: but I didn't think them of sufficient interest to bring to our meeting. This was all now many years ago, and to talk about it is only to reproduce old history.

What I did after the war is that I continued my career as tank instructor at the Military Academy until I retired, which is now seventeen years ago. I taught army officers from Cuba, Egypt, India, Indonesia and Iran. Since that time I have lived in Moscow, at first with my wife until her death five years ago and now with my daughter and her husband and their son who is my grandchild.

To conclude for you I would say that I have had an interesting life, but it is not one that could be described as greatly enjoyable. What I mean is that you see as I become older, and the longer time I reflect on these things, I become absolutely sure that no one needs war. To put it simply, it is murder, it is the killing of people. There must be a different way and a better way for all the countries of the world to settle differences, without trying to discover which one can kill more people and cause more destruction. I was affected, I see now clearly, by the fact that I had no youth: I was completely deprived of it by the war and spent all my young years in training and in combat. I was therefore never able to reflect and, if I may say so, to mature. Now I realise this, I say with all my heart 'Let there only be peace.'

Viktoria Bolova
World War II nurse*

A small white-haired woman in a navy blue dress with white piping round the collar and cuffs, she sat in a high-backed chair at the table in the sitting-room of her apartment. Neatly set out in two rows in front of her were ten medals and a small pile of folded papers. Her voice was weak and high.

– Well our name for it in the USSR is the Great Patriotic War; and it began on that terrible Sunday of 22nd of June 1941. I was then a girl of seventeen, an ordinary girl straight from school: my job, my first one, which I had not been doing for long, was at a printing factory. Also I had begun studies when I was at school, and was continuing them in the evenings, to be a nurse. Then the German Army turned on us and invaded our country, and I can remember my feelings when my parents told me it had happened. I could not believe it at first, and then I saw my mother was afraid and so I could. I was afraid also. My father said at once that he was going straight away to join the Army and fight to defend his country: he went that same evening to volunteer at the local meeting hall. I knew I must offer my services also, so I went in the evening to the printing factory, and I found every other girl and woman who worked there had all come to be told what they should do.

The arrangements were in the hands of the members of the Party Committee of the factory's management, and they asked that first all women should make themselves known who had any medical or nursing knowledge. Together there were about thirty of us: our names were taken and we were told to go back to our homes, to return to work the following morning, and wait until further instructions were given. The way the committee organised every-thing, it was almost miraculous: later we heard that many of them did not go to bed for three or even four nights one after another. This must have been so: for within less than one week we were told we would be formed into a special unit and sent at once to a camp north of Moscow to be given our training. We left that same day on the journey.

It was a military camp, and for the first three days we were taught intensively. Not in matters that had anything to do with nursing, but how to handle and shoot with rifles, how to dig with shovels to make trenches and holes in the ground to shelter in, and everything else that was needed to ensure we could take care of ourselves in all combat situations. It was only after that, that we were then shown how to carry stretchers, how to use emergency field dressings and so on.

Then to my great anger, because after all I had gone to take care of our soldiers who were injured, I was stupid and allowed myself to be injured instead. It was I who was the one to be put in hospital and taken care of. The Germans had located the position of our camp and sent aeroplanes to drop bombs on it, and one of them fell near a hut I was sheltering in. Imagine such a foolish thing for me to have happen to me! My injuries were insignificant: some cuts on my leg here and here, and also on my face and my nose injured slightly, but in total it was nothing. In the hospital I was told I would need to stay there only one week; but after four days I went to the commander and told him I could walk, and although my face did not look pretty there had been no damage to my brain, so there was no reason that I should not return to my friends in my unit. He gave his permission for me to go: of course, because if he had not I should have gone without it. After that I then nursed soldiers for the whole of four years, completely to the end of the war. No, excuse me please: it is more correct to say nearly all my time was spent in nursing, but when we were bombed by aeroplanes or fired upon by the enemy, we took our rifles and fought.

In many ways it was a hard time for us, especially in the winter: very cold, a great deal of snow and ice, and mostly we lived in tents or under the shelter of trees. We were giving great care to our brave soldiers who were fighting to save our country; but all the time the enemy were pushing us back and back, until eventually it seemed even Moscow itself would be captured. I remember how in those days sometimes we had so little food, it was so cold and every day we were retreating: all we had left to sustain us was the song we sang in the evening as we crouched together round the small fire we had made to heat some soup for ourselves. Yes I remember it still, I do of course. My voice is perhaps now not so tuneful, so you must forgive me. It goes like this.

> I belong to the military
> And during the nights of darkness
> In front of the Moscow streets with the volunteers
> We know the enemy tries fiercely to conquer us
> But we all stand ready before him
> Covering Moscow with our hearts.

Many many times we sang that song. Then later we were sent to take part in the battle at Stalingrad which lasted for two hundred days, to nurse the soldiers fighting there. They fought a heroic campaign and finally the German Army was overcome, and later it was seen to be that battle which was the turning point of the entire Great Patriotic War. After it the Germans won no more victories, but were themselves driven back everywhere right to the end. I was one of those who had the good fortune to accompany our battalion through the whole of that time. I have here among these papers a printed drawing we were presented with after the war, a sketch map of the route we travelled. Permit me to show it to you. Here you see is Moscow: we came by this route south to Volvograd, which in those days had the name of Stalingrad, then to the west here to Kharkov – it was here I met the soldier who after the war became my husband – then we continued to Kiev, across the Polish border to the liberation of Warsaw here, and on like this to our final stopping place of Berlin. A long journey oh yes, a very long one, and many lives were lost. As for the other papers, well these are identity papers, passes, and these are certificates of description which accompany these medals.

Well altogether as you see there are ten medals. This one was for the anniversary of the Stalingrad campaign which was issued after the war, this is a general medal for the Eastern Front, this one for the Polish campaign, this to mark the liberation of Warsaw, and then these others, well they are for other campaign anniversaries and so on. These two smaller ones, well I hope you will not think I am immodest but they are medals given to me for acts of bravery. You should understand though of course two things: one that there are many thousands of people who have such medals, and the second is that equally there are many thousands who do not have medals but should. It is only that they were unfortunate, whatever act they performed was not noticed and so had no attention drawn to it.

The details of this one, well it is not a nursing medal, it had to do with the putting-out of a fire, a truck carrying supplies of food and I believe some ammunition, which was bombed and became ablaze. I was not in any way the only person to assist in putting out the fire you understand.

And this, well yes this could be described as a nursing medal. I was awarded it after the Stalingrad campaign, and it concerned an incident there which as I have said was one that happened to be noticed, that is all. One of our brave soldiers had been very badly wounded in fighting in the streets of a suburb of the city, and both of his legs had been blown away. Rather in fact one leg had been blown away completely, and the other was later amputated by our surgeons. He was lying in the street and there was a certain amount of machine-gun fire and throwing of grenades, rifle fire and other such things. I was able to run out quickly from a building where we were sheltering, and pick him up and then to run carrying him on my back to bring him to safety. So that was the incident for which I was subsequently awarded this medal.

There is a nice conclusion to the story, which I will tell to you if you would be interested. The soldier, of course I did not know his name or anything about him, and he was immediately taken to hospital afterwards. And I thought he would certainly die, because his injuries were so severe. Well I did not know it, but he survived; and then one day many years later, among with others who had been wounded, he was interviewed for an article in a magazine. In it he said that he had lost his legs in fighting in a certain place on a certain date, but he had no recollection at all of how it had come about. All he could recall was regaining consciousness some days later in a military field hospital. This article in the magazine was read by many people: and among them was a man who did not know him, but had been himself a soldier there in that fighting, and had seen him lying wounded in the street. He wrote to tell him how he had seen a young nurse who was perhaps only 155 centimetres in height[1] and could have weighed no more than fifty kilos[2], and she had run out of a building and lifted him up on to her back and run with him to safety. He wrote he did not know who she was, but he believed she had been awarded a medal for it.

Well, you know, this was twenty years afterwards; but this man who had been wounded, when he learned of this story he began to make enquiries. He wrote to where the records of such medal awards are kept, and asked them was there some person to which it had been given for this incident on this date in this place. So eventually he was led to my address – and imagine, all that time afterwards he wrote to thank me. He lives now in Kiev, but two years ago he made a visit to Moscow with his wife, and they invited me to go to their hotel to meet them. I will tell you what his first words to me were. He looked at me and he said 'But how could *you* carry *me*?' So we had a good talk, and it was a great pleasure for me to meet him. I was sorry my husband was not still alive to meet him also then.

So many others, as I have said to you, they have performed acts of much greater bravery, many of them at the cost of their own lives. Every year here in Moscow we have an annual reunion of the women who were together in that unit of our battalion. And it is a sad occasion always: some have died, and those who remain, mainly we talk of those who were killed with us when they died at our sides. They were so young, and our tears fall.

It is so terrible is war. There was too much suffering during it for anyone to look back on it with feelings other than sadness. You did what you could to tend those who were wounded and in pain, and it made no difference whether they were Russian or German. There were times you held a man in your arms, he was perhaps only merely a boy: you could do nothing for him, you knew he was going to die and he himself knew it too. And he was there, a young

[1] 5′ 1″.
[2] 110 lbs.

man far away from his home and his family, and you were the last person to whom he could say his final words, in perhaps a language you could not understand. And that was how he died.

War is a curse. I believe most of the German people did not want it, and like us they were caught in a situation they did not understand. Since the war I have met German people of my own age, and I know them to be ordinary people just as we are. War must never come again between us, it is too terrible, we must never let it be.

Valentin Leminev,
Afghan War veteran*

He wore a white sports shirt and jeans, and a pair of new white trainers. Sitting on the bench by the side of the school football field, he watched a practice game between two teams of boys with a critical eye, from time to time calling out comments and instructions, then continuing talking again. He was tall, dark-haired, fit and athletic-looking, with a tan.

– I am twenty-six now; I came out from the Army four years ago when I had completed my two years' service. When you received your papers, like everyone else you had it in your mind you might be sent to Afghanistan: in my case it happened after six months only, immediately I had finished basic training. What was different from many others was that I volunteered for Afghanistan, I put forward my name as one who wanted to go. It was because I liked being in the Army and took the training with enthusiasm: I was rewarded as soon as it was over by being made straight away a sergeant. Also I had a group of friends who felt the same as I did: there seemed to be something, I would say perhaps romantic, about the idea of going to fight in Afghanistan, we were eager to have that opportunity. It was a parachute regiment that we belonged to; I do not know if it is the same in your country, but in USSR it is considered in all ways you are an élite among soldiers if you are a parachutist. Everyone when they go to begin their service, everyone of those who like the idea of being in the Army, they ask always can they be put to a parachute regiment. Only a few are chosen.

To have wanted to be a parachutist, to have been accepted for such training and to have completed the training successfully – well, naturally you feel then you wish not to waste your time on performing only exercises, but to do what you have been prepared for, which is to engage in combat and to fight. I have read somewhere, perhaps in a magazine, that also in your army there exists this similar feeling among some soldiers. In their case I believe the place they want to go to is Northern Ireland, because it is the place where they can fight, and there is danger and excitement for them there. It was the same feeling for us, and that is why we volunteered to go to Afghanistan. My girlfriend at the time to whom I was writing, she sent me a letter trying to dissuade me but it was ineffective; and I did not tell my parents I was going, because I thought they would worry greatly about it.

The greatest surprise I had when our troop transport plane landed at the base near Kabul was the terrain. The part of Afghanistan in the mountains to which we were sent the following day, it was like a desert, a vast sandy desert. Not only had I not imagined it would be, but I had never seen such a place anywhere that was like it. I was born and grew up in Moscow where the climate is reasonably temperate; but in that place, the heat during the day was unbelievably extreme, perhaps as high as seventy degrees or eighty degrees centigrade[1]. Then at night it would drop almost to freezing cold. Everything was bare, arid and lifeless: I cannot think of enough words to describe it. I had never in my life experienced tropical conditions: in a mountain jungle there once we saw monkeys and giant snakes, and we were in such conditions for a year.

We were fighting very frequently: at times there was day-after-day action. The guerilla forces who were opposing us fought fiercely, and they were naturally more familiar with the type of country than we were. We suffered great losses of both men and equipment, substantial losses, and myself I was injured with concussion when we came under artillery fire as we were crossing a river in a ravine. I had head injuries and was flown to military hospital, but was back in action after only two weeks. When you are a fighting soldier, your only thought is to get back and join your comrades again, because it seems somehow that you cannot live without the anger of it, and it has become an addiction like a drug.

My feelings about the people we were fighting were simple. To

[1] 158°–176°F.

us they were rebels who were fighting their country's government, and they were causing deaths and injuries to their own people, and destroying their homes and their land. We had been told always in our newspapers and on television that we were there because we were answering a request for assistance from the government of Afghanistan. So we heard and saw nothing that gave us cause to think any more of it than that. Certainly the ordinary people of the country we met, the villagers and peasants who lived in the places where we were fighting, they were always friendly to us. They bartered food with us and never in any way appeared to resent our presence.

Then came the day we heard suddenly that our army was to be withdrawn and we were all to be returned to our own country. As you can imagine, it was a great shock to us and we could not understand why it should be. We had fought in very bad conditions of discomfort, many had been severely injured and many had died. But now we found we were being referred to by other countries in the world as invaders. This was a term we could not believe was being applied to us. There were many angry discussions and arguments among us, which included at times those with officers. We asked to be told what had brought about this situation, because we had not been beaten in battle or anything of that nature, nor had the opposition forces surrendered. They told us only that our government had changed its policy and we were going back to USSR. Well, we were soldiers: and soldiers obey orders whether they understand reasons for them or not.

My personal view now in view of what we have learned and what has been told to us since, is that it would have been better not only if we had withdrawn our forces sooner, but perhaps even if we had never sent those forces there in the first place. I think on reflection it was a senseless war and one that we could never have won. We went there knowing nothing about the terrain, the climate and the conditions we were fighting in; and we knew nothing either about the people, their customs, their religious and political differences, or any of their way of life. Some of my comrades felt if we stayed and were sent more planes and soldiers and supplies, in a short time we could finish the war and make a victory. But I think the only way we could have won was by total destruction of a large part of the country, and killing many hundreds of thousands of its people. That is the only way it could have been achieved. It is true to say a number of fighting soldiers wished to do that, and were bitter that the sacrifices that had been made of their comrades' lives had been for nothing.

It was harder still to bear, when we came back, that we found people here in our own country did not look upon us as returning heroes or anything of that nature. On the contrary, we were regarded as having done something wrong. Indeed we were criticised for having done what we did, in some cases even by our own families and friends. It became so much that large numbers of men suffered psychological effects: as a result of this, clubs and even some hospital clinics were set up to render assistance to them. Associations of those who had fought were formed, so that soldiers who had been in Afghanistan could talk with others who had had the same experience, and who understood one another's feelings.

I belonged to one such club myself, in fact I belong to it still. I go there once a month to meet others, just to talk and listen, and be among former soldiers in Afghanistan. It helps me. About one year ago we learned that in the United States of America there are similar organisations for ex-soldiers who fought in Vietnam. Therefore last November we invited a party of thirty of them to come and visit us. It was what I can say was a most extraordinary occasion: all of us felt, I think Russian and American without exception, that we understood one another better and were closer to one another in our feelings and thoughts than we were with many people of our own countries. We had much common ground between us, and it was remarkable. There are for example instances which are common in both countries, that such ex-soldiers of these two wars feel they can no longer go on living and they commit suicide. It is as extreme for them as that. Or men go to live the lives of hermits, because they cannot fit to our present society as it exists. The most frequent problem we discussed was the feelings we had, in both our countries now, that we were being rejected for having done what at the time we were told was brave and right.

In both our countries too there are still many soldiers who have not returned home, and no one knows what has become of them. They are described just as 'missing in combat'. Some of them it is true they were probably killed; others perhaps were taken prisoner, and are being held possibly as hostages to be used on some future occasion. And others are deserters: we agreed we suspected many such men, from both our armies, simply went away and are now living as the case may be in Afghanistan or Vietnam, perhaps with a girl or woman they have formed a relationship with. We frankly agreed also there were instances of this which applied not only to ordinary soldiers but to officers as well. We had many long discussions through interpreters with the Americans, and I think it may be said truthfully many friendships were formed. We understand that now even American and Russian doctors and psychiatrists are meeting, to discuss and share their knowledge of combat soldiers who have suffered the kind of psychological damage I mentioned. So perhaps who shall know, perhaps in the end some good may come out of the Americans' experience matching with that of our own military's difficulties. And of course it would be better if we could also understand each other in every other way too.

For myself, I did not suffer in my mind to such a similar extent as many others did: I cannot think especially why that should be. I learned certain good things in the Army, such as self-discipline. And I think the responsibility of command and to have to take decisions which other people's lives depended on, that was also of value. But I feel that what I most importantly learned was I think we should no longer keep conscription. Young men should have a choice whether they wish to go to the Army or not. We do not need the size of army which we now have, I am sure of that.

For the future? Well for three years I have been a physical training instructor here, but now I have a new job which I begin next week. It is to be in charge of a youth and sports club for young people, I am to be its director. I shall like this very much, for always when you work with young people you feel you are building for the future. I am married last year, and my wife and I are expecting our first child in two months' time, so this also gives a good feeling to me as well.

Robert Serlov,

*conscript**

Broad-shouldered and stockily built, with short-cropped fair hair, he sat on a small chintz-upholstered sofa in the sitting-room of his parents' first-floor apartment. He smoked one cigarette after another, stubbing them out in an old metal ashtray before they were finished.

– I have just ended my two-year Army service period: one week ago only, so now I get on with the rest of my life. I don't know what I am going to do: I have applied to go to an institute to be a student of electronics, but I think perhaps I may have to wait. So I am beginning to consider what else I may do first. I have a girlfriend and we would like to marry, but it will not be until the future is clearer for me. It is not a good time, when you return from service in the Army: you have had a long period when you have done only what you were told to do. You are obeying orders, not thinking for yourself, having all the decisions about everything made for you. Then you come home and have to continue with your own life. It is a feeling I am waiting for someone to tell me what I should do.

It is not good for a man, that the Army takes his initiative from him. I think to have to serve compulsorily in the Army for everyone is a bad thing, a new law should be passed to bring it to an end. A few years ago you could not even say such a thing, so perhaps it is a progress that now you can. The next step must be that you are allowed to choose whether to go to the Army, or instead do something of more use. I think there are many things young men could do which would be better for the State than to serve in the Army. It is absolutely a waste of time, all it does is to interrupt your life for two years.

Before I went I was student at school. I have to say I was not a
clever pupil, and I was unable to pass examinations. When you are
in that position, you ask yourself why you should bother with
thinking about your future. It has already been decided for you,
your future is to be going to the Army. So you decide you will not
think of your future until after the Army, which is now how I come
to be in my present position. After I am in the Army I am finding it
hard to think of a future for myself. I am repeating myself, and
perhaps this does not make sense to you, what I am trying to say?
Well if you understand it that is good, it is of encouragement to me.
I am sorry to say my parents do not like me to talk like this. But
sometimes it is true that to talk about something is of help to you to
discover your own thoughts, it helps you to make order out of
them.

Now I will tell you about my service in the Army. First you
should know that it happens often, it is more customary than not
that you are sent to a place far from your home, a thousand
kilometres away or more. It is possible also, again it is more
customary than not, that for the two years of your service you will
not be allowed to go home for a period of leave. This is the policy
of making it clear to you there is no point for you to imagine things
should get better after a time. They will not, this is how it is, this is
how it will continue to be, and therefore you should make up your
mind to it.

So it happened to me that I was sent far to the north, to the region
of Archangel near the White Sea: it is not within the Arctic Circle,
but perhaps only four hundred kilometres from it. As you can
imagine the conditions are very severe, with great cold. I had been
told I was to be put with a cavalry regiment. Naturally I thought of
the modern usage of this word, that it would mean a regiment of
tanks. Imagine therefore my surprise when I arrived to find that no
it did not mean tanks: cavalry meant exactly what it said, it meant a
regiment with horses.

This was of course ridiculous for me, I had never had anything to
do with horses in all my life. Is it the same in the Army in your
country? In the Soviet Army it is always that if you have a skill for
something, you may not know what you will be doing, but you
know for certain it will not be that you are utilising that skill. So it

was with me except I did not have a special skill. But I may say definitely that of all the skills I did not have, being a horseman in any way was one of the most prominent. What is more, being as I am a city person, I was actually very frightened of horses and did not like them in any way whatever.

On the first day at the Army camp I was told: 'Look, there is a horse and it is yours entirely at all times. You must teach yourself to ride it and you must look after it in every way.' There was a large number of those horses, and each conscript soldier was given one for himself. I may tell you they were not good horses. Most of them were rejects from riding schools, animals of that kind, or even they were bought cheaply at sales because no farmers wanted them. Some I think had even bred among themselves and in many instances they were truly almost wild horses. There were accidents of course almost constantly: inexperienced men trying to handle animals of this kind, it was inevitable some of them were hurt and so were the animals too.

But so it was, I had no choice. My horse was given to me and from that time onwards we were fastened together. I knew that if I was to avoid injury, there was no alternative for me except to watch what other people did who had already been in the cavalry for some time. So I had to study what they did and try to imitate it: to put it into one word, to practice. This is what I did for one whole year, the first year of my Army service. It is not correct I should praise myself, but it is a fact that at the end of that period I had learned everything without exception. Not only how to look after my horse, to feed it and saddle it and unsaddle it; but I also knew how to ride it in every way, both with saddle or bareback, and to do anything I wished with it. I learned how to ride my horse, how to light cigarettes and smoke while sitting on my horse, how to eat my meals and read letters from my girlfriend while sitting on my horse, and even how to sleep on the ground with my horse. In such weather as we had, of extreme coldness, this was an advantage. I was fortunate that the animal I had was a docile one and of good temperament.

As you can imagine it was difficult for the officers in charge of us to find exercises of a military nature for us to perform. One cannot now think of many circumstances in warfare of such kind as there would be today, in which horses might play some part. We were therefore sent to ride our horses in this direction for several days at a time, making shelter for ourselves in the forest to rest and eat and sleep; then for another few days in that direction, and so on. Men can be told they are lazy and should make themselves tougher, but you cannot do this with horses, especially if they are old and in poor condition. But to be sent out on a long ride was not so arduous for us, because it was the horses who dictated the pace at which we should move and the distance we would travel.

But there did come once an occasion when at last a use could be found for us. A film director from Moscow came, and he was making a film of a historical story in which hundreds of charging horsemen were required for a great battle scene. He had obtained permission by the authorities to use our regiment for this: so for several days we wore old-fashioned uniforms and performed the manoeuvres he required. This operation was of such success that since that time other film directors have followed it: so now the cavalry regiment of the Soviet Army is used for film-making purposes. The film we took part in has been shown on television: I was unable to recognise myself, nevertheless it was of interest to me to see it, even if I was only one horseman among hundreds.

When my year in the cavalry regiment had passed, I was then transferred to serve in a different place, to the south and east, near the city of Sverdlovsk. There is very little I can tell you about this period which is of interest. I was with a construction battalion, which is simply a way of describing a cheap labour force. Soldiers are used everywhere, even in Moscow, for such things as repairing roads and railway lines, digging trenches for draining pipes, clearing land that is to have buildings put on it, and for one hundred other menial tasks for which all that is required is physical labour. This is the consequence of having the system that we do, in which able-bodied young men are required to do this two-year period of service in the Army. When they have got them, the Army then has to try to find ways in which they can be given something to do. I don't know how this is to be resolved in the future: to abolish conscription would be to cause another problem, that of the unemployment of large numbers of young men. Better brains I am sure than mine will be required to find the solution.

It is necessary to say that I think the experience of service in the Army is not a good one for a young man, I believe it is not likely in any way to be of benefit to him. I reflect on my second year of conscription as totally a waste of time. So was the first also, the time I spent at the cavalry regiment. There were some times, but they were few, when I felt warmth and affection for the horse which was in my care, but only for example if I was feeling lonely and far from home. At such times it is possible to experience a feeling an animal is the only real friend that you have. But this did not make me like it greatly, or leave me with a lasting love for horses as a result.

Should you return to Moscow in one year or two years, I hope by that time I shall have been able to find a clearer picture for you of the future for myself. In saying that I remind myself that I have some photographs of the time I was in the cavalry regiment. I requested a friend to take them of me and my horse, in the snow: they are of not very good quality. I have them here in this drawer, it will be my pleasure to show them to you.

Lev Gorolin,
conscript

He said he would prefer no description of him should be given except to say he was twenty-two, and there should be no indication of where he lived. He also said that though his English was not good, he would sooner try to say what he wanted without the presence of an interpreter.

– I am happy to have meeting like this because then I can make criticism things to say about being in Army as I like, and there could be no danger for me if I am asked at the place where I am student why I say such things about Army. You understand it is better now in these days than it used to be, but there are people still at the, well I will say it is an institute, who believe you should not speak out against Army and tell truth of what it is like. Not so much people of my own age you understand, but well I will say teachers, because they belong to old generation. They say all citizens should do his military conscription service, and you are not patriotic if you protest: therefore if you are not patriotic, you should not be allowed to have student place at the institute. So you see it could have something awkward for me; it may not but it could.

I will tell a little more about me first that it is OK that you say. It is two years now I am finished from Army, I am not married, and I am student of English. It is good practice for me to speak it without help. In two years' time I shall finish my studies when I hope to become teacher but I am not sure. I think there are many bad things about our education system, I do not know that I would be happy to work with it.

I will say at once immediately I think Army is poor organisation. I think it is terrible thing, most completely I think it is waste of time. I do not know why it exists in such numbers, and why it is necessary all men should serve in it at period in their lifes when they are young they should have to enjoy. It is not good for them, and also it is not good thing for Army either, to have people who do not want to be there and are so to say malcontented at idea.

Always you are put far from your home. For me, I was situated in Siberia near to the border with Mongolia, which is a distance of six thousand kilometres away; I was there clerk in the barrack stores department. It was work of great boringness, all day long sitting at a desk to fill in forms and more forms and more forms. There was no point of it: all I wanted was for time to pass and for me to come home. I sometimes now imagine what I know to be true: it is this, that when it came that day and I could come home, as I stepped out from my place another man came forward immediately and sat into my seat. He went on filling of forms, and then after his time ended another man, and so it goes still now up to this day.

This boringness was bad and I disliked it there was no doubt; but it was nothing compared to many other things worse which could happen. There were harmful things, very brutal things all the time, and you saw that they happened day after day. But you could not take an action, you could not say anything in protest, so you turned away your eyes. I would say behaviour of nearly every person who was soldier was either rough and coarse and brutal, or was like that of those like myself who saw these things but did not step forward to condemn them for fear of what would fall upon themselves.

You feel, how shall I say it, that terrible things is happening to you in your head: in your brain, in your heart and in your soul. Companionship and compassion, you have thrown these things away from you, you do not allow them any longer to exist in you, and you wonder if you will remain like it afterwards for ever. If it has made imprint on you which will never be removed, this is what you ask yourself. It is difficult to try to explain it for someone who has not had such experience, how you must feel when you are all the time so close to so many terrible things. Some of them even if I could speak of them and had the words for describing, I would not. Constantly, for everyone, there is humiliation. Cruelty, beatings, things of disgust that one person who is human should do to another. These are things that when you come to think of them, you cannot believe them, you think they must have been in your dreams.

In my opinion which I have reached only because I had such experience, and since then opportunity for thought – my opinion because of system of military service for every young men that we have, is what happens in Army is inevitable: it is that all worst elements should rise to the top. I speak now not of the officers: they are professional soldiers and could therefore be removed from their positions and lose entirely their careers. It is the lower order of soldiers, those ones especially who have some small rank or position above the rest of the conscript people, these are the ones that are bad.

Some of these men are tough and brutal peasant people, with great crudeness in the way they live in their ordinary lives even before they are in Army. They can be so cruel and unkind because to them that is their ordinary life: I think it can be said of such people they know no other knowledge of things. But these are not the ones I am talking of, because they should be pitied and forgiven. No, much worse are those who come from the cities and towns, and have more sophisticated ways. They are in fact criminal elements; there are such in every population, and would be criminal elements wherever they are. In towns and cities they devote themselves only to criminal activities, and so they behave in the same way exactly when they come into Army.

They are bad men: all their lives are devoted to selfishness and obtaining what they want for themselves at expense of other people. I speak not of property only or something like that: I speak of position and power. They are never going to be officers or Army leaders, they have no wish to be: like all other conscript soldiers, most of all what they wish is to be away from Army and back in the places they come from, making more of a luxury life for themselves than is possible where they are. But while they are there in Army, they make it certain that without their activities coming to the attention of the people of higher command, they will make their lifes easy and comfortable for themselves if it is possible. To do this they will lie, they will cheat and they will steal: but much more badly, they will terrorise everyone round them into satisfying their wishes and obeying what they say.

They do not do this single-handed you understand. They could not, it would not be possible that one man on his own should terrorise one hundred fifty two hundred people, which is what the number is in the section building where they reign. No, they form themselves with perhaps six seven others, who are of similar natures and of same inclination, into a gang. Then they recruit also as their helpers say ten twelve perhaps or even as many as twenty minor helpers, assistants perhaps should be the word. They recruit them for such matters as the beatings-up of people who have not obeyed them, or have offended them in some way.

These original six or seven principals, they are not friends: they could be described as coalitions, whose only purpose in common is to prey on others for their own benefit, and they do this with success. What gives them their success is there is no one brave enough, or foolish enough, to oppose them. Sometimes new conscript comes, and after he has suffered and discovered what this situation is, he says he will make complaint to officers. When that happens, immediately he is advised by other soldiers he should not do such a thing, for he will be putting even his life in danger. But if he is again brave, or again foolish, and continues to insist he is going to do this, well then shortly he will receive visit from so-called 'master criminals' themselves. They will soon persuade him such an action as he is contemplating will not be to his benefit.

I could tell you also other things about these people. I do not wish to dwell on them, but I will say as you can imagine they involve such things as drug-taking and dealing in supplies of drugs, their sexual satisfactions and how they force others into giving them to them, and other matters I should prefer you should not ask me to talk in details about. It is sufficient I think that I say that before I went to Army as conscript, I thought of myself as young man with a certain knowledge of the world and its ways. But when I did go, I found I had been living it might be said in something which until then had been rather an innocent fairy tale.

To end what I say, there is question I would like to ask of all people, and it is as follows. If you are good citizen and you are proud of your country, you should be proud of your country's army. You should have confidence to know it is to defend you and your family and your friends, and all citizens of your country. But if you want it to be such organisation, how can you let it be not in the hands, as we are led to believe, of true dedicated patriotic soldiers, but in power of such brutes and barbarians as I have been speaking of? What they do to those who are supposed to be their fellow countrymen is beyond what can be imagined. So what they would do to the people of another country? If such circumstances arose that they should be there – well it cannot even be thought about.

There is one further thing to say if I may be permitted. It is something very important that happened to me when I was in Army. Before that time I had no Christian belief; but when I found myself so far away from my home and my family, I do not know the reason for it but sometimes I prayed. Not that I could escape or be released from the situation, which so many others were in besides myself: but only that I would have strength to not become a brutal person myself, who would think only of his own advantage and with no concern for others. I do not know how this happened, but in times of greatest wretchedness I felt God was listening, and he would help me find strength I was asking for. I truly believe he did, and I have remained with this belief inside me. It has been said, I have heard many people say this, that going to Army makes a boy into a man. It was in my case of some difference: going to Army made a man into a Christian.

Edik Mamenk,

conscript

Of medium height, with thin and unkempt hair, he wore wire-rimmed glasses and spoke in a soft thoughtful voice, sitting on the small balcony of the apartment block where he lived. Smoking, he turned his cigarette packet round and round all the time in his fingers.

– My mother she does not like it that I smoke cigarette inside, so we come out here if you do not mind.

Well I am twenty years in age and I am student at the university for the subjects of biology and chemistry. I began to be student there two months ago and it will be for five years. Then what I will do I do not know, but I think perhaps I will try to be a teacher of biology. Before I came to the university I was in the Army from the age of nineteen, and before that I was not an employed person. I ended my school at sixteen, I did one or two small things sometimes to earn some money, but mostly not. I was living with friends outside Moscow in the woods, or in the winter in old wooden houses that you can find in the country everywhere, dachas that no one comes to at the part of the year when it is too cold.

We were peace people. There were twenty to thirty, about half and half male and female, and we did not want to live in the city in the kind of life there is here, motor cars and everyone running about for work and money. We grew own vegetables, we had hens for the eggs, we made bread and such things like that, and everything that we had to eat was natural: fruits, nuts, but no meat. I think the word for it is how you say vegetarian. It was a good way to live, and to us the important thing was to do no harm to any person or to any living thing.

It has always been the law of our country that young men have to go to the Army, in what is called national service conscription. There are two times of the year when the main numbers of people are going in the draft, in the spring and in the autumn. So some days in these periods we came here to the centre of Moscow, and we made protest demonstration, holding up signs we had written saying not everyone should have to go to the Army. There should be free choice and a change to the law to allow so to say 'objection of conscience'. We would walk a little in the street together, and talk with people and ask them to sign a declaration, a petition for it.

It was decided by all of us one day when it was Saturday, that instead of walking in the street we would sit down in the square by Komsomol Railway Station. This we did, and we were not expecting anything because at all times before the militia had only looked to us as we walked, but they did not do anything. But then this day when we were sitting in Komsomol Square, suddenly many cars with militia arrived, and they told us we must not sit but get up and walk. We told them No we did not wish to do this. The militia told us to go away and not make such demonstration: we still would not, so they brought two large militia vans and told us to get into them. They took us to the militia station and ordered us to give our names and addresses and show them our papers. Those who could not do this or would not do this, they kept them there, but the others they were allowed to go.

When they saw my papers they saw I was of age to be in the Army, and I had a paper telling me where I should go to report. I had not gone, and it was three months before that day that I should have done it. So at the militia station they said they would keep me until soldiers came for me. After two days this is what happened: soldiers came, and they took me to the city of Kiev in the Ukraine, and from there to the south-east, another five hundred kilometres perhaps, to a town where there was Army barracks.

At that place I was ordered to put on soldier uniform and then to attend on the parade ground. I said I was pacifist and I would not do this, so I was put into a cell. I was kept alone for several hours, then a group of twenty soldiers came to take me out to the parade ground, and I was given a beating: punching and kicking to my face and body, and hitting me with the wooden parts, the butts of rifles.

This was in daylight and in full view, to show to the other soldiers what happens when someone does not obey orders. I am sorry I have to say this but it is true: the soldiers who were beating me were most of them the same age or a little older than me. They all went on punching me and kicking me without restraint until they were ordered to stop. It continued until I was unconscious, when I was then returned to the cell.

I was kept there I think it was for two days: sometimes I was given a little food and some water. I was told also that when it was considered I had recovered enough, I would be given another beating if I again refused to put on the uniform that was lying there in the cell for me. Sometimes someone came to see if I was yet wearing it, but always they found I was not.

Then came an officer one morning, and he told to me this was my final opportunity: if I did not put on the uniform at that time when he was there, he would have to give the order for me to be beaten once more. He said the only future for me was one of continual beating until I obeyed. I told him I did not agree not to follow my principles: I was pacifist, and I would not wear uniform of the Army or accept to be trained as a soldier. The officer was himself only a young man, and of course he was a professional soldier; but he seemed to have feelings and be a thinking person. He said to me that this was the law of our country, and he could not allow me to break it, it was his duty to enforce it. But he added he would give me a little more time to consider it, two hours perhaps and then he would return.

When he did so, I was still as I think you say brick wall: I told him No, however many beatings they gave I would not put on uniform. He said then that he had made arrangement: which was that if I would agree to it, I would be put to work only in the kitchen of the feeding hall, where I would not have to wear soldier uniform but only the white apron and cap of the cooks. We discussed this and he talked quietly with me, he did not shout at me or try to order me. Eventually I said very well I would agree to this, so the overall of cook was brought and I put it on. For my sleeping at night I was put into a small hut with some other men who I thought were also cooks. They were not: they were those who had been in trouble for not following orders for other reasons, for example such as drunkenness or fighting. None of them was pacifist like me, so this was a very awkward situation because there was much fighting between them. They thought I was there for the same reason as they, and they wanted me to join in.

I had gratitude for the officer who had made the arrangement for me to be cook, but in a few days it was no longer happening. I was not cook for all hours all the time; so when I was not on duty as cook I had to attend lectures. In these, officers instructed us about warfare, and said such things as we must be proud to be part of our country's army, and what a good fighting army it was, and other things like that. At first I sat silent, but before long I began to speak and say that what the officers were telling was untrue. I tried to start discussion in the classroom, with everyone to say in turn what they really thought. This was something that was not popular with the officers, so I was taken out of the classroom and put once more into the cell, and told I could not be cook any more. Then I was told again to wear the soldier uniform but still I would not: so once more came beatings, each one a few days then another one.

I did not know what to do. At first I thought to try to escape, to run away. But I was many thousand kilometres from Moscow and my home and friends, and I knew it would not be possible. I remembered soon something that I did know also, that the only people who did not have to serve in the Army were those who were ill. They were either physically in their body ill, or they had bad mental disturbance. I began to act in ways I thought would show I was in this condition: but a doctor who was of the Army came to see me, and gave it as his opinion I was only pretending. This of course was true. Then I knew I would have to do something to give more serious impression, so I one morning took a razor and slashed at my wrists. As you see, here are the marks still, here on this one and here on this. I knew it was dangerous and I could injure myself fatally, but fortunately that did not happen. I was taken by army ambulance at once to hospital, which was a psychiatric hospital for suicide people, it did not belong to the Army.

I was given treatment with pills and many talks with a number of doctors and psychiatrists. Most times I was asked by them why I had tried to kill myself, was it because I was in Army and I wanted to be free of it? Sometimes I said yes that was the reason, sometimes

I said it was not. I think I was presenting them with a big problem about what they should do with me. From my talk and my behaviour it was eventually decided by them I should be diagnosed as schizophrenic, and this was done. They gave me more treatment with pills but I did not take them as I should, because I wanted myself to remain aware of the situation as much as possible. It was that it could happen they would say I was made completely cured and was to be put back to the Army again. Finally they considered this would not happen, or not so that it would safely continue to be that I was no more going to be suicidal. So at last a certificate was given that I was unfit for military service on mental grounds, and I was discharged to come home.

I do not know how to answer the question why I am pacifist. All I can say is that I am Christian, and I have inside me the feeling that if you are true Christian, then you have to be pacifist. Jesus Christ was pacifist, he said that the cheek should be turned and there should only be the way of peace. You have to be brave and say that no matter what happens to you, and what pain people may inflict on you for it, you will not fight or take part in wars, and you will not change your belief that it is wrong for people to do that.

My mother is also a believer of this, and has given me books to read since I was a young man, about the men of peace in history throughout the world. These have influenced me to think as I do. When I was living with the peace people, we had many talks and discussions of the subject. Some of them but not all of them were like I am, Christian; others were not, and just believed in peaceful life. I think such ideas as these are beginning to spread now in our country amongst young people, and they will bring up their children to think in the same way. USSR considers itself to be great military power, equal with USA; but I think this not the way to be, and we must do all we can to change it.

If it is something you would like, I have two friends who are older than me, they are peace people and they would talk with you. It can be arranged I am sure.

4 Health

Vladislav Margolis, surgeon

Nina Pevlovskaya, nurse

Zorina Korganova, general practitioner

Germani Shirokov, psychotherapist

Aina Ambrumova, professor of psychiatry

Fyodor Petyavin, Red Cross & Red Crescent

Vladislav Margolis,
surgeon*

Tall and heavily built, with an expansively genial manner, he wore a pale blue cotton operating gown and a tight-fitting cap of the same colour perched on top of his curly greying hair. His brown eyes were deep-set, his voice lively and sharp. He chain-smoked.

– Well I am pleased to see you in my hospital, I like people of all kinds to come and visit us, not just our patients. I do not know if it is the same in other countries with medical matters, but in the USSR those in the medical profession in hospitals mix always only with patients or with others in the same profession as themselves. It cuts them off from the outside world, gives us the impression this huge place is all there is to life, you know how I mean?

I must not pretend I do not like my hospital of course. It is one of the largest and most modern of all Moscow hospitals, with 1,600 beds. It was completed only a few years ago – in fact it is not yet totally completed. Those blocks of flats you can see through my office window behind me are also part of our complex: they are accommodation for members of the staff, and even now some of them are not yet finished. We do not treat our staff with enough concern, I think.

My own position here is that of Chief Surgeon of the hospital: I am in charge of three departments and I have forty doctors working under me. They are all of course qualified, but this is a teaching hospital so I am also responsible for a further number of student doctors and their programme of lectures and practical work. Although I act as a consultant to other doctors and surgeons here, I still do some practical work too, and I perform three or four major operations a week.

My own special interest, well it is in the subject of abdominal surgery. I find it by far the most interesting surgery to perform. Let me think for a moment why I do. Yes: I think it is because in recent years much surgery has now become a matter of following a set pattern after diagnosis with our marvellous new technology. But in stomach surgery it is not like that: when you begin an operation you are often not at all certain what you are going to find. You can use exploratory methods initially and be helped by such things as X-rays, or endoscopy, or nowadays ultrasound. But finally you still have to guess what is wrong and precisely where, and take the responsibility of following through your decision when you operate. So it is not only a machine who is doing the thinking, but a human being too. There is a mystery to it which I find intriguing; no, perhaps mystery is not a descriptive enough word, it is like going on a voyage of discovery. A patient may be brought, and there is an amount of uncertainty in the cause of his condition. Sometimes in an emergency, he may be unconscious and unable to tell you anything that will assist you, and you will have no previous history to guide you. A perforated stomach ulcer, well that is obvious from the patient's condition: but as to its exact position, you have to make your guess and hope your experience has led you to the correct one.

I speak of course not only just of my own work. Other doctors and surgeons will discuss a case very thoroughly between themselves before taking action – and then they will come to me, saying what they have decided to do, and how, and why they have decided to do it. They ask me my opinion about it, if you like to say it this way, to test their theories. And so this too presents me with interesting problems each day. Some of the younger doctors now, it is very good to hear their reasons, indeed to learn their whole way of thinking. Often you know, it is much more modern and up to date than my own, which after all was learned in the old days. So it is good for me to hear it, and good for them to learn what might be described as the conventional view – and most importantly of all, we hope it is good for the patient, whose cure is what we are all working together to try to achieve.

I do not come from a medical family, no. This is not a tradition in the USSR as I believe it is in some other countries. My father was a railway engineer, and I think he was surprised to have a son who did not want to achieve the same heights of prestige as that. But even if that attitude has still not changed in many places, all the same some others of my own family now are doctors. My wife is and my daughter is; and my granddaughter has started saying recently she too wishes to become a doctor. At the moment she is only five years of age though, so perhaps later she will change her mind.

How I became a doctor myself, well that is rather an ironic story. It happened because when I was a student at Moscow University, I intended to become a journalist and perhaps too a playwright, a dramatist: writing was a subject which I liked very much. But I was prevented from completing my course by Stalin. I do not mean him personally of course, because we did not know each other. Had we done so, had I come to his personal notice that is, then I think undoubtedly even worse would have happened to me than what did. I certainly would not be sitting here talking with you today. Stalin you see, well at the time I am speaking of he was engaged in a campaign against people whom he referred to as 'Cosmopolitans'. That was the word he used, and he used it to mean Jews. He became more and more anti-Semitic as time went on; it is a common thing in history of course that the Jews have been blamed for almost every misfortune which has ever befallen anyone.

So he was against Jews, and soon it came to be to such an extent that people, who in my opinion should have known better, in institutes of learning started to consider whether there might not be certain areas of study where Jews should not be encouraged. Journalism was one of them: gradually it came to be thought that if they were encouraged in it, Jews might begin to influence and perhaps even gain control of the media. So difficulties were created for students, obstacles put in the way, programmes of study refused on the grounds that there were too many students, and other things like that. Before long it became obvious to me and two or three of my student friends who were also Jewish, that we were not going to have a very bright future. Instead of our prospects depending on the quality of our work as students, they would be influenced by who we knew who would offer us promises of work, or at least a trial. And these obviously were becoming rapidly fewer.

I had one good friend, who was a member of the university's teaching faculty; so he suggested to me that I should change direction. Additionally he said he thought he could help me to become accepted as a medical student. So that was what I did, I changed from one faculty to the other; and eventually after eight years' study I became a doctor. Yet I still enjoy writing, and take what opportunities I can to do it – not only with articles in medical journals, but also by writing books or contributing to them. I am not at all modest about my achievements either: let me show you this one for example. It is a collection of essays on different aspects of the subject of abdominal surgery, by leading practitioners of it. I edited all their contributions, and made some of my own, and this work is now I may say the standard textbook on the subject. I think it will remain so for many years. This other one here with it is also the standard textbook for its subject. This one I wrote entirely myself. It is called *Vagotomy in the Treatment of Duodenal Ulcer.* As I expect you will know, vagotomy is to do with the cutting of the nerves of the stomach, and as you can see this book is very nicely produced with very many excellent photographic illustrations in colour. I like to hold the book in my hands like this, I am very pleased with it. I have plans to write other books also; and who knows, perhaps one day even to produce one which is not on a medical subject at all. About what? My friend, I do not know.

I strongly have the feeling that if I had not been Jewish, I would have achieved far more than I have in my life. I do not mean only in writing either, I mean also in medicine: I think I would have gone further. Towards the end of his life Stalin also began a campaign against doctors. He persuaded himself and many others that doctors were enemies of the people, and there were a number of trials of eminent figures in the medical profession, for what were called 'activities against the State'. And as for Jewish doctors – well, they were even more looked upon with suspicion than most. Heads of hospital departments and clinics were appointed on a basis not of their medical knowledge or competence, but on the basis of their Party status. This greatly lowered the general level of competence in hospitals, because these people in their turn appointed to the staff poor doctors so long as they too were Party members. I am sure this held me back in my career.

Perhaps it may surprise you when I say that the effects of what happened in that period – well, they have still not vanished. Anti-Semitism is growing once more in the Soviet Union. You may have heard – if you have not done so yet, I am sure you certainly will – of the society which is called 'Pamyat'? It is a word which means memory. Pamyat has come into being, its members will tell you, to help preserve what they call the true historical past of our country. They perform many activities in many fields – in the restoration of old and historical buildings for example, that is one of their activities. They call for the preservation of old traditions and old culture. Well, they may feel such things are very necessary and important, and few would disagree with them. But there is a strong element in it which pushes the idea that much of what has been lost is because of the activities of the Jews. They say for instance the Revolution was Jewish-inspired, that Lenin himself was not a Jew but he was surrounded and greatly influenced by many who were. And some members of Pamyat of course are very eager to deny it is an anti-Semitic front. Well, the organisation has not yet achieved much power or influence; but it is growing, there is no question, and this is most worrying.

I am sorry to say this, but I think anti-Semitism exists also to a great degree in the medical profession. You will find very few Jews, indeed you may not find any at all, for example, who are in high positions in the Soviet Academy of Medical Science, and this is but one illustration. And of course, as it was in Hitler's Germany, this means that in medicine there is great lack of exploitation of talent, because Jews feel uneasy in it and unsure of how far they will be able to progress.

To take a more general view, I think if I may I should also like to emphasise to you that from what I understand in my reading of journals and newspapers, it can be said that rightly or wrongly, the profession of medicine is more patient-oriented in the USSR than in the West. By this I mean I understand that in the West, medicine is usually a very lucrative profession for the practitioner, and that most doctors have a great deal of prestige in the eyes of the public, whether or not they are good practitioners. It is possible, I understand, that in the West there can be very successful doctors: this means not in terms of their skill, but according to what fees they can earn and how much money they can make. Well in the Soviet

Union it is not like that. A patient is not primarily regarded, or in fact not even at all regarded, as a source of income. It is only one or two doctors here at most who are rich. But in Western countries I think there are only one or two who are not.

In the United States of America too, I believe, medical treatment is very expensive and it is not uncommon for someone not to have treatment because they cannot afford to. To someone in our country, whether they are the doctor or the patient, this is very difficult to understand: the only concern is what the patient needs, not how much or how little money they have. I do not deny of course that in some hospitals the standards of comfort and treatment after surgery may be low, and minor improvements to these can in some cases be bought. But medical treatment actually itself, whether it is surgical or some other kind – well, the quality of this cannot be purchased. It is given to the best extent available, as of right, to everyone. This is as it should be, I am sure.

Nina Pevlovskaya
nurse*

Small and slightly built, she wore her dark hair drawn back from her face and fastened behind her head in a plait which reached down her back to her waist. Most of the time as she talked she looked down at her fingers, or glanced round the half-empty hospital canteen as though embarrassed someone she knew might see her.

– I will do my best to talk with you about myself, but it is not something I have done before so you must forgive me if I seem nervous. I am the sort of person who is happiest to talk with others in a group: others who work here as I do as a nurse and about the hospital and such matters as concern us all. I hope you understand me and do not think me rude. Because I do not have a husband or a boyfriend I am especially shy when I am talking with a man. When Vladislav Roskovich Margolis asked me to talk with you I said I would not be able to do it. He said I should try, and so that is why I am here. But I think though he could have found some better person, who would be more helpful to you, and I do not know why he asked me, I really do not. He and I, we do not work together often, and if we did he would know I am a shy person and do not find it easy to talk. I see him perhaps only once each week, when there is perhaps a case which has been referred to him. Then I am at ease to talk to him about medical matters, and I tell him my opinions straightly, so perhaps that is why he has misjudged me.

To tell you first something about myself, I will say that I have worked at this hospital for eight years; I am thirty-three years of age, and I came here to live and work in Moscow when I was twenty-five. Until that time I had been working in a hospital in the town of Minsk where I was born; the reason for me coming to

Moscow was that I had hopes at that time of becoming a doctor. I had already by then been working and hoping to do that for six years since I left college when I was nineteen. Someone at the hospital where I was working told me I would stand a better chance of progressing from nurse to doctor in Moscow than in Minsk.

I think the fact of the matter however is that really I was not good enough as a candidate. I had always had the idea and ambition to be a doctor since I was at school, because I have a cousin who is a physician and he would often tell me about his work and how much he liked it. But when I did the examinations for a place in medical school, I was not successful to enter it. My cousin advised me instead then to become first a nurse, and after a few years of doing that, try again with the examinations. Again I failed I am sorry to say. His final advice was that which I have said already, to come here to Moscow and try in that way yet once more. But I have to say I think it is not his advice which is at fault, but my own capabilities: if I cannot have succeeded to enter medical school by the age which I am now, then I begin to feel it is late in life for me to start a new branch of my career. I think I will remain a nurse, and continue to do what I do now. I enjoy it well enough, I am not unhappy with it at all: but I have a little ambition inside me still, and perhaps one day the opportunity might come in some way. I am happy to be as good at my work as I can, and there is nothing else that I would sooner do than this.

Here I am the senior nurse, or I should say one of them to be correct, in the emergency admissions department, or what might be called I think in some hospitals the casualty department. I like this sort of work: you never know what is going to happen next and what sort of a medical condition each new patient you have to deal with may have. So there is always variety, you could almost say excitement. Someone might come who has been badly injured in a motor-car accident, then a sick and unconscious person who has collapsed in the street, and no one knows what is the matter with them. Then perhaps immediately at the same time, all within a few minutes, may come as well a mother with her child who has swallowed something which might be poisonous, and a person who has been severely wounded in a fight, and together also with them shall we say someone who is having a heart attack, and yet another person who you are not sure whether they are staggering and unable to speak because they have a medical condition, or if it is merely that they are severely drunk. It goes on like this all the time, so you can see why it is so interesting, because together with the doctors you have to try and make quick preliminary diagnosis and a decision what should be done with them.

I have been in the department for three years. Before that I was in charge of the nurses in the operating theatre for one year, and for one year before that I was working as a nurse on the ward where we treated chest and heart cases. All of them I enjoyed, but in each case the work was different, and so also was my degree of involvement in it. On the chest and heart ward, in most instances what was being done was carrying out the plan of treatment which had already been decided in advance by the patient's doctor or surgeon. It was work which enabled you in many cases to build up a relationship with the patient, but I found it at times a little boring, because there was only limited opportunity to use personal medical initiative and skills.

In the operating theatre, well there was more chance there for responsibility, but of course a great deal of what you did was under the instruction of the surgeon who was operating. It was how shall I say, very mechanical and often repetitive: there was standard procedure for most operations, and you merely carry it out according to the individual surgeon's wishes. The only variety came from them, from the surgeons themselves, in the way they worked. But even at the base of it, they are of course all doing the same thing, although when you watched them and listened to them, often you would find it hard to believe.

There are so many different ways they have, you know? One will like all the instruments laid out just so like this, with the same spaces in between and always in sight; but for another they have to be here and here always, and like this. One surgeon will ask that everyone in the operating theatre remains totally silent while she is working, and say not more than one word whenever it is necessary to speak. Another, well he has to be talking the whole of the time, he cannot work unless he does, and it might be to you and everyone else, or it might be to himself. Some, always they are very confident: sometimes you feel they may be like that not because they are conceited that their work is good, but because it is necessary for them to have this feeling to support them. Others, well they seem somehow a little nervous, they perspire and such things. It is interesting to watch this, but of course they are only very small variations such as you could get from any very skilled persons anywhere. The work is the same, only the personality of the practitioner different.

None of it compares for interest for me every minute such as one finds in the emergency admissions department. I think it is the best and most responsible work of all, and each day I look forward to the next new thing which is going to happen and surprise me. I like to think, as every nurse does, that whatever it is she is ready for it and will know what is the best thing to be done for the patient. This is the reason why I – excuse me – the reason why I said to you that I would not ever like to do anything else, because it is never boring and is always satisfying. Oh please again excuse me, I am sorry that I yawn in this way, it is because last night I was working until late because of the good weather we are having this year. It is exceptional you know in our summer for it to be as light until long past eleven o'clock as it was last night. It is a very strange summer for us indeed this year.

No I was not working here at the hospital, of course not, it would be a funny hospital I think if its hours of work depended on the daylight. No, it is that at present I have another job also, as well as my work here. The big block of apartments that are not finished yet, on the other side of the park, that is where I work when I am not on duty here. It is nothing unusual, I am working there at present in the evenings and at the weekends as a builder's labourer. What do I do? Well I mix plaster for the plasterer and take it up ladders in buckets to where he works, or I carry planks of wood for the carpenters or bricks for the brickmen: whatever is required, and needs physical effort but not skill – well then, I do that.

You see, when I first came to Moscow eight years ago to this hospital, I was living in its hostel for nurses. It was quite pleasant but a little old-fashioned, and also like all hostels it had rules and regulations which were irritating if one lived there. It was never your own home, even if it meant I could live with friends among the colleagues I work with. Three years ago it was announced new blocks of apartments were to be built on the other side of the park, and there would be one for the nurses and others who worked at this hospital. There was unexpected delay before the actual building began; and then last year it was said that those who helped in any capacity at all to construct it, they would be given special priority when apartments in it came to be allocated. There are not many, as you can imagine, which are for one person only; but I have seen some of those which have already been completed, and they are especially nice, with balconies facing the afternoon sun and every modern facility. So immediately I went and asked if I could be employed in my spare time, and have my name put on the list to be allocated one, and I was very happy that the building managers agreed.

What spare time I have from my job here, well I do not go out very much to parties and things like that, so I am happy to work on the buildings instead. It can be often quite hard physical work, but sometimes I am surprised to discover I actually enjoy it. Last winter at weekends, often it was a hard time because the weather was very cold indeed. But always if it is like that, you have the knowledge that what you are doing, before very long it will result that you have your own nice little apartment, with everything new. Then for all the time afterwards in your life you can sit back in it and relax, and say to yourself you have got such a home of your own at last because you have worked for it. Sometimes when I am on night work at the hospital here, if I feel not too tired afterwards I go and do extra work on the site: there is a system that for each hour you work, you get an allocation of points towards your own eventual time of occupancy. It is becoming very near now for me, perhaps even it might be by the end of this year, so this gives me a feeling of great excitement. I may not look to be so, but I am physically quite a strong person; also I think I am a little determined towards something that I have made up my mind to do. So I shall survive happily I think, and be still young enough to have many years' pleasure in the results.

Some of my friends, they tease me. They ask me what will I do if just as I am at last about to occupy my apartment, suddenly I meet a man who wants to marry me and so we apply for a two-roomed apartment instead. What will you feel, they say, if after all your hard work it happens that in the end someone else gets your nice little modern apartment? Well, I think if she is another nurse, I will not be too unhappy with that. But anyway, where should I meet such a man to marry me? He will perhaps be brought into the emergency department unconscious after an accident, and I will help to save his life and he will be so grateful he will carry me off when he has recovered, and marry me? Well I think it is not very likely somehow you know?

I was not as shy as I had thought I might be in talking to you. I have enjoyed our conversation thank you.

Zorina Korganova,

general practitioner*

A stocky, dark-haired woman of forty-five, she wore a green tweed jacket and skirt, a plain white blouse and low-heeled shoes. Sitting at the living-room table in her apartment she sipped occasionally at a cup of instant coffee, talking rapidly and smoking incessantly.

– My philosophy as a doctor is the one I learned from my father. He said that a physician's work consisted of three things: to cure, to ameliorate, and to comfort. By this he meant if a patient was sick, to try to make him better; if that was not possible, to try to make his condition more bearable for him; and finally, when that could no longer be continued, to give support and courage to continue through his illness until his life concluded.

He was not a doctor, my father, but it was his influence more than anyone else's which caused me to choose the profession of medicine. I loved him very dearly, and he died when I was seventeen and he himself was still young, only fifty. He was a teacher at an institute of mechanical engineering, but also he was a great reader. Particularly he admired the works of Anton Chekhov, who was a writer with a high regard for doctors, shown very frequently in particular in his short stories. My father's attitude came from him: he said many times to me that being a doctor was a noble occupation, one which he wished he had studied to follow himself when he was younger. That was his view of doctors, even though in our country it was not then, and still is not, very highly regarded as a profession and it is not a well-paid one.

Well you know I think the reason for it is that since the Revolution it has been the government's belief that a doctor is not much more than a mechanic who services a piece of machinery called the human body: he is not in any way a producer of things which are of benefit to the community. He is not a true member of the proletariat, so only in a few cases, if you are right at the top of the tree in surgery for instance, can you earn a high salary. Never if you are only an ordinary general practitioner such as myself: you are not of special value, you are not productive, and you do not have the status or importance of a coal miner or train driver. I am not sure that I do not perhaps myself agree with that. But argument about my relative importance and place in society, well in fact it does not greatly interest me you know. I am a doctor because I wish to be a doctor and have always wished to be one. That is all that matters in life for me.

Soon after my father's death I was successful while I was still at school in passing the necessary examinations to enter as a student to a medical institute, where I studied for a little under ten years before finally becoming qualified and obtained my physician's diploma. However hard the work was, and although the grant I was given as a medical student was small, my determination to become a doctor never changed. It was increased in fact when my mother also died four years after my father. She too was comparatively young, fifty-two or fifty-three, and I think if both of them had had when they were ill better and more skilled medical attention, they could have lived longer. So that belief influenced me too, it made me determined to try to do better for patients when I was able to practise myself.

Sometimes it is difficult for me to remember that somewhere in the period in my life as a student, I also had time to fall in love, to marry, to have a child and then in a few years to become divorced. How I managed to find time to do it I cannot now imagine. My son is now eighteen years of age, a student who is just about to enter university himself, to study languages. Until recently, for a short time he was at what is called preliminary vocational medical school: it was for the intention of discovering if he too wanted to become a doctor or not. He has discovered, he says, that he most definitely does not want to. I do not know exactly what he means, but he says he knows now he is not at all the sort of person who has so much love for humanity that he will devote his life to caring for it. But whatever he means, I am sure it is good he has found it out for himself. I think it shows even at such a young age, he is quite a mature person to have reached his own conclusion.

Even when I was at my loneliest and unhappiest as a student, deserted by my husband and with a small baby to take care of in addition to working at my studies, I myself you see never had such feelings. It would have been easier for me, I think, if I had: perhaps then I would have turned to some better way of making a living. It may sound strange for it to be said, but I felt I had almost a duty to my father, to follow in the career that would have given him pleasure and pride to know I was doing it. Does that sound foolish to you?

But this is all not very interesting for you to hear about I think. I will continue now instead with a description for you of my work, which could be taken as that of any average general practitioner in a big city of the Soviet Union. So, I will say first that like nearly all such doctors, I work in a polyclinic which serves a certain area of the city. In the one which I am at, there are a total of fourteen doctors and perhaps twenty nurses and others: in a way it is like a small general hospital. Some of the doctors are specialists in different areas of treatment such as gynaecology, obstetrics, maternity and heart illness; two of them are surgeons who perform minor operations. The other physicians and myself work as a team in referrals and discussions, and in general we work with two kinds of patient – those who come to the polyclinic for attention, and those who are too ill or too old to come, and whom we visit in their homes.

One half of the time each of us works at the clinic seeing patients, and the other half is visiting. We try to arrange our schedules so that one week half the doctors work in the morning at the clinic and do their visiting in the afternoon, then the following week it is the other half. Our schedule includes time off for each doctor, and time on emergency call. I am sure like all schedules everywhere, even in most other occupations, the description of it makes it sound quite a little better than it turns out to be in practice. There is an appointment system for patients, and of course this also does not work as smoothly as we would like it to. One silly problem we have is we are a nation of full-time queuers. Whatever time their appointment is, many patients arrive at eight in the morning and insist to queue, perhaps even until half-past ten. Once when I asked a patient if she had an appointment for the following week, she said 'Yes I have an appointment, I will come early and wait for it.'

The total number of patients we see, well it is difficult to give you an exact number. I think the average for a doctor would be to see perhaps fifteen patients at the clinic shall we say in the morning, and then perhaps a slightly fewer number of twelve in visits to their homes in the afternoon. So this would give an average of seventy-five in one week at the clinic, plus another fifty at their homes. Sometimes of course it is the same patient that you have to see several times during one or two weeks, so it cannot properly be estimated how many patients there are altogether. Also we have several thousand who are registered with us on the basis of which district they live in. In this instance it is not possible to give an accurate figure of the number, because some people who are registered with us are not often ill and we may not see them from one year to the next; others we see very many times because of their need. But one fact there is, is that there are not enough doctors to provide as much health care as is needed. This is because not sufficient people are attracted to the profession, because of the low wages I have spoken of that are paid at all levels in it.

I would say on the whole that services in medicine for Soviet citizens are good in most instances. But of course you can find examples of instances where they are not. It is good that it can now happen that magazines and newspapers will print articles which are very critical of certain hospitals they name, which have low standards. I read one recently which described a maternity hospital where the nurses would not bring a patient clean sheets or other things unless the patient would give them money. Such things are scandalous and it is right they should be written about; but a solution would be, in my opinion, for nurses to be better paid so that they do not need to resort to such supplements to their income. Also the managerial control of that hospital should be better, to ensure practices of that kind lead to dismissal. This opinion is one that most doctors I know would give you.

And there is noticeable now, I am afraid, what I and many others regard as an unfortunate trend which is increasing in medical care. It is in this area of paying for additional things, and not getting them if you don't. One of the most unfortunate developments is a new law we have which permits the establishing of what are called 'co-operatives'. People may start as a group together small businesses which they run for their own profit. Perhaps there can be no disagreement that people should have the right to do this for example if they are selling goods such as food, or starting a restaurant, or even some kind of business on a larger scale. But what I think is wrong is that now also doctors are permitted to do it – not for treatment they give at the clinics, but with the home-visiting side of their work. Doctors are permitted now to make a charge for this if they form such a co-operative as I have described. If you pay, there is no question that you will get better or different treatment, you will not. But a doctor will come to your home more readily or more quickly, that is all. As the patients who most often are in need of being visited at home are nearly always the elderly ones, they are the ones on whom this burden of having to find extra money falls, when they are in need. I do not agree this should be allowed, nor I am glad to say do any of the other doctors at our clinic, and so we do not follow this practice. Trading in health is wrong, surely.

Another thing about it also is that it is in this area – the care of the elderly and infirm – that our health system operates at its poorest level. It is because there is a long Soviet tradition – you may almost say it is part of the Russian character – that old people should be looked after by members of their own families. It is a principle which is a good one, and in most cases it is satisfactory. But there is a growing number of elderly people who no longer have family members near at hand to care for them, and there is only one word for what happens to them in big cities such as Moscow: in one word, it is neglect. Some small voluntary organisations, I believe, most of them connected with churches, such as one which is called 'Misericordia', are trying to bring into being a system which will seek out and help such people. My feeling is that there is a great need not only for proper study of this problem, but it must quickly be followed by extensive action. I would like to think that if you return to Moscow at some future time, say perhaps in five years at the most, you will find there have been improvements in this. It is one part of the Soviet health system that we cannot hold up our heads about.

Germani Shirokov,

psychotherapist

A small slim man in his mid-forties, wearing glasses and going bald, he wore a dark suit and a white shirt, and sat in an armchair in his apartment without his shoes on, his feet curled up underneath him. His manner was quiet and serious, but he smiled often and talked in an easy friendly way about himself and his work.

– Well you are polite to say my English is good, and I will do my best in it for you. It is a language I like to speak and to hear, and I am always glad to have the opportunity to practise it. I hear it spoken as a rule only on the radio, but I like to listen to the BBC World Service so that my ear remains accustomed to the sound of it. But as for speaking it, well as a rule the only opportunity I have for that is with one of my colleagues: she has visited England and can speak much better than I can. However, let us see how we proceed, but tell me please if I do not express myself clearly enough for you.

I am a director of one of the hospitals which is part of what is called the Moscow Crisis Intervention Centre. This is a network of out-patient and in-patient clinics which exist specially for treatment of patients who are depressed and in some cases suicidal, but who are not suffering from mental illness. If I may put it in such a way, it is for neurotic but not psychotic patients – they are those suffering from mental illness, and they need treatment of a different kind. We have a total of twenty-three such centres in Moscow: some are departments of hospitals, where patients can stay for a time while they have treatment, and others are out-patient centres for people to visit on a daily basis. At the hospital where I work, I and each of my colleagues has a case-load of one hundred to one hundred fifty patients who we see on a regular basis.

As well as this I work for an organisation called 'The Telephone of Trust'. This is a counselling service by telephone. Its number appears on the first page of every telephone directory, and it is displayed in all ordinary medical clinics and pharmacy shops in the city. Also its number and information about the service it offers is broadcast regularly in short announcements on television and radio.

The Telephone of Trust is for any person at all who has pain either here in the heart or in the head. If they have a personal problem of any kind which makes them sad and unhappy, they may telephone the number at any hour of the day or night, every day of the year because it is never closed. They can talk without giving information about themselves, not even their name if they do not wish to, to a qualified medical doctor or psychotherapist. Those of us who give our work to it – I do not exactly know how many but it is a large number – are on duty for twelve hours at a time, followed by three days when we are not. We have a rota system: it is work which makes great demands on you, and we do not feel it is good for someone to be involved in it for a consecutively longer period than this as well as your ordinary work as a therapist. In one year the number receives in the region of twelve thousand new calls; the average number of calls made by each person is five, so as you will see it is a very busy telephone number, in great demand, and with many lines for calls to come in on.

We estimate that in an average of five telephone calls, each caller will have received sufficient assistance with his problem or her problem to be able to deal with it, will have decided that we can be of no help at all, or will have gained sufficient insight into themselves and the need to seek help for their problem, that they should come for further consultation and treatment at one of the service's clinics. We offer that they should do so, but of course choice has to be for them.

The treatment we give for such patients is almost that of psycho-therapy. Perhaps not even that, but what instead may be more correctly described as psychotherapeutic listening. In a textbook which was written by the great Professor Ambrumova she said 'The

less psychotherapy there is in psychotherapy, the better the psychotherapy will be.' Sometimes when a patient comes to our clinic we
give for a short time a mild dose of tranquilliser or anti-depressant,
but we do not like really to use drugs. We prefer to treat by
individual sessions with therapists or analysts, group therapy or so
on. We try to make the clinics as comfortable and bright and
welcoming as possible, and encourage people to feel they can have
confidence in us, and therefore through that regain confidence in
themselves. Advice is something we never give to anyone: instead
we encourage them to talk about their problem, explore their
feelings about it, and view it from as many different angles as
possible. We try to work out with their own strength what is their
own best solution for themselves. If I may say it in this way, we try
not to take away the problem from them, but help them to withstand
its pain and to find, if it is possible, their own solution for it. If they
wish, we can provide for them as part of their treatment a place
where they can retreat for up to a few days into solitude, to think
more about their situation and alternative solutions. This might
almost be said, I think, to be self-treatment – the patient as doctor
for his own ills, rather than the patient as someone dependent for
cure on others. I hope you will understand what I am trying to
describe; but I am hampered from doing it because of my poor use
of your language.

Like all others who work in the clinics and centres, I am a qualified
medical doctor who has also taken a further two years' training in
the subjects of psychology and psychiatry when deciding to work in
that area. In my case, the speciality I have is in the problems of
marital conflict, in the love and hate relationship between males and
females whose marriage is broken or is breaking down. If it has
caused severe problem, to the point that they try to take their own
life, then they could be referred to me to try to help them. The first
thing I must do then is to try to remove the inclination towards
killing themself. Only when they feel that is no longer the solution
for them, it is only then that we can begin to work towards finding
some other way. The problem in many marriage cases will still
remain, because another person is involved in the creating of it.
Then the most you can hope is that the patient will come to accept
the reality of what the situation is. You try to help them to find

strength in themselves to go on living in that situation and not regarding killing themself as a way out.

Yes certainly I will give you an example of a case I have treated of this kind. I will tell you of two recent ones. In one I have so far achieved very little, and in the other – well it is too early I think to say this finally, but its prognosis is more hopeful.

The first concerns a woman teacher of thirty-two, a very handsome young woman who lives in Moscow with her husband who is an Army officer, and their two sons aged nine years and three years. They had a small but comfortable apartment which was provided for them by the Army, because of her husband's position. Three or four months ago her husband met another lady who he decided he liked to be with better than his wife. Although this must have been difficult to do, and I have no idea how he achieved it, he managed to find further accommodation for them to live together. He gave his wife no money at all for herself and the two children to go on living on. Then in a very short time, only a few days, it was discovered she was living in Army accommodation but without her officer husband. This was against regulations, and it was a very cruel situation, but she was told she must leave the apartment.

Naturally she became very upset and depressed at this prospect: she therefore made an attempt to end her life by taking some kind of poison. From the hospital where she was taken she was referred to the clinic I am at, and there she became my patient. It was not possible for her to continue any kind of discussion with me about her husband: always she became almost hysterical, and I did not feel we could make much progress in our talks unless she could exercise control over herself to some degree. I therefore – as I now see quite mistakenly – prescribed for her, as an in-patient, a mild tranquilliser in the form of tablets. When she took them, in a very short time indeed she became much calmer and more controlled. She is an intelligent woman, and she said she realised she had probably lost her husband completely. But she told me for the sake of their children she would like to talk briefly with him, to see if some arrangements could be made about such matters as finance. It was my estimation that if they could meet together at the clinic and talk about the matter, it would probably help her to take the first step towards facing her situation. This was another and even more serious mistake on my part. I arranged for him to come: he too had seemed a reasonable person in phone conversation, and I am sure he was. But their meeting together on their own was absolutely a disaster. It resulted only in a furious quarrel, and at the end of it her husband walked out. The deeply distressed patient immediately swallowed the whole quantity of the drugs I had given her, and had to be taken into a special care unit to have them pumped out from her stomach.

So you see this can only be described as very bad handling of a case on my part. I think the reason was that I was much too hasty in my judgement of the patient herself, and had not discussed her feelings for a long enough time with her. And also of course I had tried to cover up the depth and strength of them with drugs. Now it is obvious she will have to remain an in-patient for several weeks; her children have had to be accommodated in residential care, and I feel there is nothing in this case at all that so far I can congratulate myself about.

The other instance – well this is a not-unusual sort of case, and I have I think handled it better. It concerns a woman of forty-five who has recently become a widow, is childless, and who learned two weeks ago that she was going to lose her job. She has been for more than twenty years in a very responsible position in control of clerical work in the despatch department of a factory, with thirty people working under her. Recently the company she works for has replaced her and her entire department with a computer, which has resulted in a reduction of staff to two persons only. She has no knowledge of computers and other modern methods, and so she has completely lost her position and her status and, to be frank, has very little chance at her age of finding any other position which will carry with it what she most values, which is not the salary she earned but her importance as a person. She made a very severe attempt last week to take her own life, and is now another of my in-patients.

It is difficult, you know, to help such a person find any hope of achieving much of a future at all. But in the talks we have so far had, although she is still very distressed and I think still potentially suicidal, I do not know why it is so but I feel she is at heart a very brave person with much inner strength of character. I have the feeling, I do not know why, that the prognosis for her is better than in the other case I have spoken about.

As you will understand, I find my work interesting and enjoyable. It is important that I should remind myself of my mistakes but not be too downcast about them: after all, doctors are not omnipotent and beyond failings, though many of them like to think they are. So too I am afraid would their patients like them to be. These are things which were said to us many times by Professor Ambrumova – a great and remarkable woman whom you should try to meet if it is at all possible for you while you are in Moscow. She is becoming old now, but I am sure, like me, many of my colleagues would say she has been the greatest inspiration to all of us in our lives and work.

Aina Ambrumova,
professor of psychiatry*

On the wall of her office in the hospital were two large framed photographs: one of Ernest Hemingway and the other, inscribed to her, of Chad Varah. She was a tiny, stout, white-haired elderly lady, gesticulating and talking so rapidly that she was often breathless.

– I am professor of psychiatry, doctor of medical science, and also have qualification as sociologist. I work here within the Ministry of Health of the Soviet Union; this is what we call a suicidological clinic, and it has been my workplace for eighteen years. Now I am old I give more time to teaching than to practice: students come here to study under me, and I give lectures at other hospitals and at the university. I have a very busy life: I like to be busy all the time and I enjoy everything – my work with my patients here, and very very much my talks with young students. Psychology and psychiatry are now becoming once more respectable subjects in the Soviet Union, and I am glad I have remained alive long enough to see it happen. There were some bad and unhappy years in our country in the past, but I think those times are over now.

It was always my dream from the time I was a student myself to be a psychiatrist. I had the choice of studying to become one or to be a student of law, and I am glad I made the choice which I did. It is difficult to explain, but I like it because I think it is not only a science but an art. It is very clever, very intelligent, and those who practise it best I think are delicate and sensitive persons; but it is exact and disciplined also, and it is most satisfying when all these things come together, and you feel you are putting to use every part of your heart and brain. You are dealing so to say with the human soul itself: you cannot cut it open and stitch it together again all in one morning as you can in surgery, so you must feel your way very sensitively and carefully with each patient. This I like.

There is art in knowing persons and allowing them slowly to build confidence in you, especially when they are in conditions of crisis and extreme distress. The behaviour in such circumstances of people who are basically sane and normal is most interesting, and it is rewarding that so much can be done to help such patients. You aim so to say to reanimate them psychologically and for them to resume their life and work again. I worked at one time with people who were mad, and this was in no way as satisfying, because truthfully only drugs can help such people and control them. Sadly they are not reachable at all by psychotherapy, and I do not like this. It is necessary for any doctor, not only in the Soviet Union but anywhere in the world, to feel that he has some power to help and to heal. If all he can do is offer control, well I cannot think any proper doctor would gain satisfaction from that.

The patients we have here in our Suicidological Centre could in most cases be described as persons who are healthy but in need of help, and have recognised this. We also give temporary treatment to a few so-called borderline cases between those who have mental health and those with mental illness, and also to a few more who are actually mentally ill. The thing in common they all have, the reason for their being brought here, is that they have already tried to kill themselves, or it is considered there is immediate very grave risk they will do so. Before we can perform what may be called intervention into their crisis situation, we have first to try to discover if they are in the normal or the abnormal mental-health group, and then give treatment accordingly. For those in the first group we have individual and group therapy, and at the present time we are experimenting also, with some few cases, with the technique of hypnosis. For those in the second, well as I have said to you there is not much we can do. We use all the same modern drugs which are used in such cases in the West, but not of course under their brand names. But we do not use treatments which I have heard are still in use in other countries, such as brain surgery for mental illness. This is now illegal in the Soviet Union. Electroconvulsion therapy and deep-sleep treatment are examples of other methods which are now not much used, because they are considered to be old-fashioned.

We will perhaps have here thirty patients at a time staying in the clinic, and they have come to us either through referral by ordinary physicians at the polyclinics, or perhaps at their own initiative. A number have come too as a result of them being in contact with something called 'The Telephone of Trust'. You have heard of it? Good, then I do not need to waste our time describing it for you. It has been in existence for many years now, and I think it is something which we can feel does very good work.

Last year your great Englishman Chad Varah visited us at our invitation, because we had heard he was responsible for bringing into being something similar that you have, which is called I believe 'The Samaritans'. He was most interested in our work and the method in which it is run, and we equally were interested in your organisation, which he gave some lectures and speeches about. We all learned many interesting things from each other, some of which will be adopted in our respective countries I am sure.

The similarities between us and your Samaritans we discovered were many; but the great difference of course was that all our workers and consultants are trained medical doctors, psychiatrists and therapists. We do not use voluntary workers at all. I am sure they do good work but my own feeling is that it is better to do it in the way that we do, although Chad Varah's voluntary workers are given some kind of basic training I know. I have the impression it is not possible really to tell if one system is absolutely better than the other or not. The greatest benefit from his visit, I think, was our two organisations met and recognised each other, and we hope it will be beneficial to both sides.

Excuse me for one moment please as I answer my telephone. Hello? Nella, I asked you please if you would not allow me to be interrupted while – what? Yes yes I know all about it, it is tomorrow afternoon. What? It is not tomorrow, it is this afternoon now? But why did you not remind me? You did remind me? Oh yes Nella I remember now, you did: I am getting very old. Thank you Nella, yes I will come to the taxi in a few moments tell him, thank you.

You must forgive me, I am so sorry, I am a forgetful old woman, I have an appointment to lecture at the university in one half-hour exactly, so I must hurry to get there. I am so sorry, now we must conclude our talk which has been of great interest for me. I must take my papers for my lecture and put on my coat. If you should speak in London before long to your great Chad Varah, give him please my regards. And my coat, where – oh it is here, it has fallen to the floor behind my filing cabinet. You like my other photograph also? Ernest Hemingway yes, only this one is not inscribed for me as I never met him. I regret that I never did, it would have been without doubt the greatest moment of my life. Of all the writers in the world there have ever been, he is the most favourite one to me. I have read all of his books, though in Russian only, I cannot read English. *To Have And To Have Not, Across the River and Into the Trees, Death in the Afternoon, The Old Man and the Sea* – some of them I have read three or even four times and know long passages from them by heart. My favourite one of all? Oh there is no question of it, it is *For Whom the Bell Tolls*, and I can even say the epigraph on the title page of it for you – and in English too. Let me see, it is from the writings of your English poet John Donne is it not? And it says 'If you hear the bell that is tolling, do not ask anyone for whom the bell is tolling because it is tolling for you.'

He also killed himself, Ernest Hemingway, is that not so? How interesting it would be for me to stay and talk with you a great deal more about him. But alas I cannot, I am so sorry. Excuse me, I think I will take with me an apple from my filing cabinet to eat in my taxi on the way. You would like one also?

Fyodor Petyavin,
Red Cross & Red Crescent*

A middle-aged man with his black hair cropped close to his head and wearing an immaculately cut dark blue suit and red tie, he fastidiously arranged and rearranged his notes on the desk in front of him, from time to time clearing his throat nervously while he read his prepared answers from them. He gave them doggedly and in order, whether a question relating to them had been asked beforehand or not.

– We do not have many visitors here at our headquarters who have not come so to say on official business, and it is my pleasure to welcome you and give you all information you require of any kind. I will tell you something first of the history of our society, and then of its work in the present day.

The international organisation for the relief of suffering which is known as the Red Cross came into being as a result of the efforts of a Swiss banker whose name was Jean-Henri Dunant. He was moved by the sufferings of wounded soldiers he had seen at the battle of Solferino, a village in Lombardy where the French and the Pied-montese defeated the Austrians on 24th of June 1859, and three years later in 1862 he wrote and published a book which said there should be an international body to give help to the wounded in all battles, and its neutrality of purpose should be recognised at all times by the combatants. As a result of this an international congress of sixteen countries was held in Geneva, and in the following year the first Geneva convention, which agreed to this, was signed. As the emblem of the organisation's neutrality, it adopted a red cross on a white ground, which are the colours of the Swiss flag reversed.

It was four years after that date that the Russian Red Cross Society was formed and affiliated to the principal organisation. The original convention has been revised three times: in 1906, in 1929 and in 1949. There are now 140 countries who are signatories to it. Because in the Soviet Union there are four republics which are in their population almost entirely Muslim, their emblem, the Red Crescent, has also been approved and recognised by the main body since 1923.

One of the most conspicuously remarkable episodes in our history occurred between the years 1941 and 1945, at the time of the Great Patriotic War. The Red Cross and the Red Crescent were entrusted with the task of training all those who volunteered to care for our wounded soldiers in military hospitals and camps, and at the height of our efforts we had over one-quarter of one million nurses and other helpers, who worked by the side of our Army doctors or in such things as medical evacuation units. During the time of the war five and one-half million Russian people donated their blood to Red Cross & Red Crescent units, to help save the lives not only of their own husbands and brothers and sons, but also those other nations including those who were fighting against us.

The wartime years were sad and terrible, and everyone hopes with all his heart that such times will never come again. But there will always be need for our society: it now works very extensively in charitable ways to assist those in need. The Soviet Red Cross & Red Crescent has a voluntary membership of more than one hundred million people of all ages. Our main purpose is to train nurses and others, and to be an educational organisation in schools and factories, as well as of course to collect funds. Some money is given to us by the State, but mainly we finance ourselves through charitable gifts and donations. In recent years after much discussion we have reallocated our resources and priorities, and we recognise now four main areas of our work. One is educational, to encourage in people the spirit of humanitarianism and charity; the second is to develop our health-instruction and preventative work; and the third is in extending our services of emergency aid and relief to people afflicted by disasters, such as the earthquake in Armenia. The fourth and no less important theme to our work is in the area of medical and social assistance which we give to families of people who for reasons of health have low incomes.

The first subject I mentioned, our educational work and the necessity for it, is one that concerns us greatly. I will say frankly that in my opinion at least, there is a shortage of merciful and charitable attitudes. It is not that our people are by nature cruel or indifferent or lacking in warmth of heart. But it has been part of our culture for many years now that every citizen's needs will be provided by the State, and it is enshrined in our constitution that this should be so. It is, if I may say it like this, an attitude of mind, and one which many people cannot think beyond. If a person needs assistance he has only to turn to the State, and the State will provide. No one of course will suggest that this principle is wrong; but it unfortunately does not allow an attitude to grow which arouses in people an awareness of the need for them also to give charity.

Our second activity, that of educational work, is now very extensive. At present we pay from our budget the salaries of 14,500 fully trained medical nurses, whose job it is to assist with the care of the elderly, the disabled, the war veterans, and those who are confined by long-lasting illness to their homes. These nurses, who work alongside State nurses and in exactly the same way, are fully trained: they give injections, in certain cases prescribe and administer drugs, and help people who are not so sick that they need to be admitted to hospital entirely. And for those nurses we provide voluntary helpers, whose training of course is not so complete, to act as their helpers. There are three hundred such nurses who are as I have described, who have been trained by us, and they can call on the services of approximately two hundred voluntary helpers who give them some of their time. It is a small number, you may think, in a city as large as Moscow; but as I have explained, the idea of doing voluntary work is one which is only very slowly beginning to grow.

I will also say that another of our activities, that of raising money for the provision of medical equipment, is one that gives us many problems and causes much discussion. Our State-provided health care is in most instances adequate, and in some cases very good. But there is no doubt that on what may be called the material side of medical services, in general our standard is very low and by no means equal to that of western European countries. For example, the industry which provides artificial limbs is run of course by the

State: but it is inefficient as well as providing things of poor quality. We can give financial contributions to help those in need to obtain better things from abroad, but then there is the dilemma of whether we should use our money for such things rather than for the educational programmes I spoke of earlier. In Moscow just now we are providing some funds for the setting-up of a special factory, run as a co-operative, to produce artificial limbs for such people as men who lost limbs serving in Afghanistan, because we feel they deserve better-quality ones than those the State provides them with.

Another project we greatly need money for is a centre we have set up in Armenia for the treatment, help and rehabilitation of the many thousands of people who sustained injuries during the earthquake there. It was as you know a most terrible disaster: it will be many years, perhaps even a decade, before the effects of it on many people have been overcome or even significantly lessened. This centre is being financed entirely by the Red Cross & Red Crescent; and it makes me happy to say to you that the money comes not just from us, but from our International Society of organisations. It was a most moving experience for us that so many countries all over the world sent money to Armenia at the time of the earthquake, in her hour of need. Seventy-six different countries gave aid through the Red Cross and we received money to a total of seventy million Swiss francs, which all will be used for the construction of such centres as I have described, as well as rehousing programmes. It was a wonderful example of international friendship, and we in the Red Cross & Red Crescent can never express our thanks adequately.

Perhaps I may add as a personal observation that at the time the earthquake occurred, many of us here were deeply impressed by the speed with which medical relief teams were assembled and sent to Armenia by several western European countries. In particular Britain, France and Germany were able to have such teams arrive within less than twenty-four hours. Such a thing was beyond possibility for us ourselves: this was because of our terrible bureaucratic methods. We have studied how it was done by you, and we have learned much from that. To us it was quite remarkable.

In these last few years, I am glad to say, relationships between our organisation and other Red Cross societies in capitalist countries have vastly improved. Last year we sent a delegation to the United

States, and this was the first time such a visit has occurred in the
past seventeen years. What hope can there ever be, some of us were
beginning to wonder, for such things as world peace and co-
operation if even the different countries' branches of the Red Cross
cannot visit and talk with each other? But I say with all my heart
that that has all now passed for ever, I hope. We now at last are able,
for the first time, to work together to formulate programmes for
joint action all over the world. Nothing but good can come of this.

I thank you that you should have taken the trouble to come and
visit us and learn something of our work, and I send fraternal
greetings to all who are members of the Red Cross in your country.

5 *Faith*

Vassily and Lora Kashirin, teachers

Father Valery, White monk

Father Boris, Black monk

Natasha Nadirova, historian

Vassily and Lora Kashirin,
teachers

Their apartment was the ground floor of an old three-storeyed house, which stood incongruously on the boundary of an estate of modern tower blocks in the southern outskirts of Moscow. Both were in their early thirties: she was small, delicate-featured and brown-haired with large brown eyes, and wore a faded blue T-shirt and jeans. He was thin, tall, fair-haired and bearded. Both laughed frequently at and with each other as they struggled to find English words.

Lora: It was decided by us after very long arguments –
Vassily: No it was not for us arguments, that is quarrels.
Lora: It was decided for us after long quarrels? Vassya, we did not quarrel.
Vassily: No no I mean the first word that you used, you said long arguments and arguments is the same as quarrels, and that is what I say, that we did not quarrel.
Lora: So what is the word then I should use?
Vassily: I think 'talks': we had long talks, and then we decided.
Lora: Very good, I will say we had long talks and then we decided –
Vassily: Discussions, I have remembered the word now. We should say we had long discussions.
Lora: Very well, we had long discussions and then we decided we would ask you not to bring interpreter and then we can talk more freely.
Vassily: Interpreter you see, well sometimes it is difficult because you do not know the person, so we try to talk to you with our poor

English, but if you are not happy with it then we can meet again at another time with interpreter.

Lora: We have friend, she is teacher at the English department of the Pedagological Institute and she has said she would be interpreter for us, but at the moment she is vacationing after next week.

Vassily: We should say it is until after next week: it is until after next week that she has vacation. No, I think it is holidays in English, vacations is what American people say.

Lora: So if you can understand us, then first we will try to talk with you together on our own. And in our – not arguments Vassya?

Vassily: No, discussions.

Lora: Yes I am sorry, in our discussions we agreed also we would try to tell you of our religious belief, by Vassily and then by me, and then you should ask us questions and together we will do our best for you.

Vassily: Or we shall talk and discuss with you so to say not in a formal way, but as friends. It is better now in our country, it is possible to speak more openly and not have fear. But always like all other people we are thinking will this situation continue, or will it soon again be that everyone must be careful what he says, you know?

Lora: You see for us, well it is something that is not too difficult that we have religious belief. But we have our daughter Tamara, and she is young to understand and so it is difficult for her. Now she goes to a different school which we have founded – found, that is near to this house. There there are twenty other children whose parents think of these things in the same way as we do. It is a private school, we pay for it ourselves, the salaries for both of the teachers, the paper and pencils, everything; but you understand it costs much money and we do not know how long it will be able to last.

Vassily: We shall tell you why it is so that we send her to this school, but I think it better that you should hear it from Lora, because she was the one who was more involved to it all, the setting-up of the school and so on.

Lora: Well it happened like this. Always we have been feeling that because of our belief, Tamara should follow us in it and therefore in our house it has been where we have spoken freely of what it means to us to have religious faith and what we believe. When she was five

years of age, which is three years ago now, she went to attend the
school of the State which is situationed on this housing estate. I was
not happy because I am teacher myself, but for music only and so it
is not a thing which affects me: but I know such matters as what
others teach, the patriotric songs all children learn to sing, later the
joining of the Young Communist League and all the rest. And I do
not like this. But I was willing at first for Tamara to go to this
school until she was a little older, and then we could see. But in
only few weeks, I think it was perhaps she has repeated there
something she has heard at home, but one night before Vassily is
coming home, the bell on the door is pressed; and when I go to
open it, standing there there are three men from the militia. They
have in their hand a paper, which is an official authority to come
into our home to look for things. So they come in and they stand
here in this room, just here. One of the militiamen shows – showed
– me the paper, and then he said to me 'Put on to the table there if
you please any guns that you have, any narcotics, and any books for
children of a religious nature.' Tamara she is in bed and she does not
hear this. So from the cupboard there I took some of the books we
have for her, picture books, and put them here. And the militia,
they took them away. They did not search any more, they took
only the books I had put out on the table. And I think this action by
them was in the form a warning, you see. It was so unbelievable.
But you know, it frightened me, I felt it had been something very
horrible that had happened here.

Vassily: And it was immediately as a result of it that we decided we
must take Tamara from that school. With our friends we decided
there must be some other form of schooling, so this is how we came
to set up this school of our own. We have heard nothing from the
authorities, they have not been to the house of the person where it
is, and none of us have had enquiries made why our children are not
attending to the official State school any more.

Lora: We do not know why it is so. Perhaps it is that the authorities
know and they have decided to let us continue with it so long as we
are not too openly speaking about it. Or it could be so – it is just as
possible – that somehow it has become overlooked that Tamara and
the other children are not seen at the official school.

Vassily: It is many times like this in our country – you do not know if something is now being tolerated, or whether it is because of bureaucracy and inefficiency that some matter has not yet been discovered.

Lora: Or even if the authorities are too lazy to do anything about it. Anything is possible. So we continue with what we do, and do not talk loudly about it.

Vassily: But as you can see, so perhaps it is not necessary for us to say this to you, the fact we are breaking the law in this situation – well it is not a source of fear for us, and we do not hide our faces all the time. The Church, religion, such things are part of life for us and give us happiness. Myself, I am engineer at a factory which produces material for computers to work on – its name in English I think is software – and at my work I do not hide from my colleagues such things as that I go every Sunday to church for example. Many of them are men of my own age; some have belief and some do not, but it is more and more so that we exchange our ideas with one another and have tolerance for the different points of view.

Lora: It is not quite so at the school where I teach. I think this is because you see it is a school of the State, and tolerance of the ideas of religion is not so ready to find. In particular some of the older teachers, all their lives they have been taught to think of religion as something to be frowned upon. Religion is not in favour. In fact I can say this was the case with my own parents, when I was a girl. Sometimes even I would hear on the radio beautiful music and singing, and if it was of a religious nature the radio was at once switched off. But it is true is it not, sometimes such attitudes by parents do not produce the results they intend? What happened to me was that one day when I was seventeen and a schoolgirl still, I was walking and I passed by a church. From inside it there was coming such very beautiful music of the kind I had never been allowed to listen to in my home. It was of course a Sunday morning, and it will seem strange to you that I say it but it is true, I had never put together in my mind this music I liked and a building such as a church. So I went inside to this church, and there was going on what I think is called a service. There were many people there, and all of them surrounded by this singing. And I looked, and I saw that all the people in the middle of the church, they were being led in their prayers by a priest; and then at this side there was an old woman who had become dead and she was lying in her coffin. Standing all around her were the members of her family, and they were crying, and a priest was giving prayers for her. And at the other side over here was yet another priest with a young couple who had brought their baby to be christened. My feeling, it was something I cannot explain, something that came at once to my heart. Here was death, there was birth, and it was the whole circle of life in front of me. From that moment onwards belief in God came into me, and it has been the same always for me ever since that time.

Vassily: For me it was not so simple a happening. In my family, such belief had always been present. My parents were Roman Catholic, and it was the great wish of my mother for me to become a priest. But before I became engineer student at the university, I began to think carefully about this. It seemed to me I could not believe women should be nuns and men should be priests, and they could shut themselves behind walls and cut themselves away from life. So I turned against the idea. And then it was later when I was student that I met Lora, and my love for her was confirmation that it was possible to love God and to love a person, and they are both warming to the heart. I think both of them are the same thing, our love for God and our love for each other.

Lora: The time when we feel this the most strongly is when we go together to the church, perhaps with Tamara also. It is best when it is not a great holy day, but one of no importance especially, and the church is perhaps nearly empty, with not more than fifteen or twenty people. We feel then at home in faith, because always all the saints and angels are there so you are not alone. Faith is not just for the brain but for the heart and the soul. Religion is you could say something like a communication with God. We pray, and God is here on earth in the church.

Vassily: This to us is the Holy Spirit, and it is everywhere.

Lora: Yes everywhere all around us, it is completely the – well I do not know the word. What is it, how do you say it Vassya? If you have religious faith, then it is your . . . you used this word the other day, what is it?

Vassily: Environment?

Lora: Yes exactly, that is the word. If you have religious faith, then God is your environment. This is the way we feel.

Father Valery,
White monk*

An affable, heavily bearded, shaggy-haired man in a sports jacket, gesticulating and smiling all the time he talked, he seemed to fill the tiny room in his apartment he used as a study. Its shelves were filled with papers and books and rows of neatly bound typescripts.

– In my case it was a little different from what is usually heard of other people about why they came to religion. For many of them it was due to sadness, some kind of tragedy, perhaps the death of someone close to them who they loved greatly. Or sometimes for others it was the fear of death, an awareness that this is not the only life, there must be something afterwards which will be better. Sadness or the fear of something, and when all else is failure they turn to God. But with me it was nothing to do with any of those things, instead religious belief came absolutely and only from joy of life: for me it was a great and wonderful experience that led to my conversion.

It was at the age of seventeen when I was a student. I was due to go to college where I was to study biology. And then suddenly there came this day, I went to the library to read something for one of my exams, and I saw sitting in front of me an angel. Of course she was not a real angel, she was a student also like myself. But I was heavily struck with her beauty, with her loveliness, with the strange aura which was all round her, and I fell deeply and instantly in love with her though I had never even seen her before. I asked her if we could meet the next day and she said Yes; and the next day I asked her if we could meet the day after, and the day after, and the day after that. I was helplessly in love, and it gave me such a feeling as I had never had before, that the world was a place of beauty and happiness, and I wanted to share this joy with everyone. After some days I could keep it secret inside me no longer, and so with great enthusiasm I began to tell people about it.

It had made me realise, I told everyone, that the only explanation for such a beautiful thing to happen, the only way it was possible for it to happen, was that someone must have made it happen – it could not be just a coincidence. And for someone to make it happen, this meant therefore there had to be such a person who could make that it happened. It could only be God, I said, which therefore showed me he must exist.

My mother was very angry indeed when she heard me speak in that fashion, and she told me so. She was not herself a member of the Party, but my father, her husband, had been before they were divorced; and many of her friends were Party members, so she was very embarrassed, because it would show she had not brought me up properly in the way of the State, which of course was atheism. She said I would bring disgrace on her, and she threatened she would inform on me to the militia – and there would be trouble made at my school about it because they had not taught me properly. She did not mean such things I know, she would never have informed on her own son, but all the same this gives an idea of how distressed about it she was.

I told her if she could only meet this most beautiful girl she would understand my feelings. She said absolutely she would not meet her, she had no wish at all to come into contact with a person who had filled my head with such ridiculous ideas. I said to her what was true, that it was not at all from the girl I had got my ideas, but my mother would not listen. When I told her it was now my one and only desire to give thanks to God and to go to church and be christened, my mother wept.

And I went to the girl, and I told her of my feeling also. I said I had fallen deeply in love with her, and the experience was one of such enlightenment and discovery to me that it had opened my eyes to what I had never known before, the knowledge of the existence of God. I told her I was going to go to a church and talk with a priest and ask him if he would prepare me to be baptised into the Christian faith. I hoped, but naturally I was too shy to say it to her, I hoped that perhaps she would say too, that she was in love with me in the same way, and also would feel it was due to God and she would like to be christened as well. But I am afraid instead her response was like my mother's, what you would call very negative. She said to me how could I believe such foolishness, that God existed, when everyone knew there was no such person. And she said if I ever mentioned it again to her, she would have no more to do with me. This was what could be described as an ironic situation was it not?

But it did not change my belief. And so it was that I lost my girlfriend, and deeply upset and angered my mother as well. But I carried out my wish, and in a short time afterwards I was christened and admitted to the Russian Orthodox Church. This was something that I prepared myself carefully for. When it finally happened by then I was already a student of biology at a college. For three years after that I studied very hard, and in time I went on to further study at an institute of genetics. When I had finished my studies there I was then at the age of twenty-five, so I did not have to go to the Army.

I liked work at the institute very much, and I did some good research in the field of genetics. If I may say it, I was a good geneticist and there would have been a career in that field for me. But the older I became the stronger grew my religious belief that the foundation of every society is what it always must be – the quality of its religious and spiritual life. So finally when I was at the age of thirty, I felt I must make a decision as to the way my life should go – whether it should be further into science, or if I should change completely and devote myself to religion and the Church. Very strongly I was feeling I wanted to try to do my best to serve God. At that time also already I had met my wife: we were married and had two little girls, and they were tiny babies so it was a big decision for us. I should add by the way that they were what are called twin babies: my wife says this happened because I was a geneticist. So it was that I chose to give up my research work and became instead a student for the priesthood at the Moscow Seminary. The transition from the scientific world to that of religion is an unusual one and people sometimes comment with surprise at it: but of course for me it is all part of God's intention.

The period of seminary study for the priesthood is eight years, and part of it is to serve as assistant in a parish. It was here at this church that I did this, and for part of the time I broke off from my studies and worked here for payment. This was necessary because we had so little money and we had our children to support. In fact it came that what I had hoped would be eight years of study in the final total became almost fifteen, because I could only continue my studies by correspondence while I worked. Last year I took my final qualification examination, but I am glad I am still able to be attached to this church as the assistant priest. I do not regret in looking back that I decided to become a priest though we still have little money, and I am sure if I were to return to the beginning of my life I would follow the same path. But of course to be married also. In our church we have two kinds of priests or monks – those that are called in popular terms the White monks, married and with families; and the Black monks who have taken a vow of celibacy.

Because I am as we say a White monk, so I do not have the religious contemplative life, but am involved with many things which are part of the parish life outside the church. I help with the services but am also involved with parishioners in religious discussion-groups, study of the sacred books and other such things. Our church is open every day from eight o'clock in the morning until one o'clock, and on Sunday it is open all day. There has always been a church here for perhaps three or four hundred years; in the past even, ours was always allowed to remain open although many others were closed. Now times have become easier, and for example a new cathedral is to be built soon in Moscow to mark the Orthodox Church's millennium.

I would say we have perhaps three hundred people or more who come to our services here, but I am a little sad also to say that although there has been an increase in the number of attenders, I am not sure it is the same as an increased number of believers. I think it is not more than a vague feeling for most people, perhaps just if they have a baby it would be nice for them to have a christening ceremony; or before a burial, to bring the deceased person for prayers. Perhaps it will take as many years for religious belief to grow once more to its full strength as the number of years it has taken that the Church has had to suffer persecution. For many years many of our books have not been allowed to be printed: I do not mean only the sacred texts but also the works of commentary and promulgation, and so for a long time there has been almost no literature of religion in our country.

The only way, in fact, that many of them have been preserved is in this fashion you see here all around you on my shelves. These manuscripts, some of them typed and some of them copied laboriously by hand – well these are what are known as our 'samizdat' publications. It is not so necessary to do it so much now, for many of them can be openly printed and published – but it was always part of my work, as it was of every priest, to make copies of these works and circulate them. It was hard long work, day after day and week after week, to continue with the copying of them; and until only a few years ago, in every church and religious academy, you would find it being carried on all the time. Sometimes the KGB would come, and if they had such instructions as to do so, they would be looking for works by named authors and if they found them, then they took them away. Of course there would always be other copies somewhere, and you would get one and begin to make more copies again, and so it went on. There was an occasion when they came here once to my home and took away over seventy different titles – but those times, now all of us have the hope, those times are gone for good.

But you know it is my opinion that the persecution of the Church is not in fact the most important thing facing us. That is as you may say an outward problem, and not an unknown one in the past. At many times in history, and in many countries, the Church has been oppressed. But it has always survived, and there is no doubt it always will, because there is no way the truth can be prevented from existing, however much is put on it. So that is not so much a problem for the Church: it is almost a tradition of Byzantine history that the Church shall suffer and be oppressed.

The problem is more difficult than that, because as I have said, there could not be any such thing as that the Church became completely wiped out. But what did happen was that during the years of the Soviets since the Revolution, the State was most careful in the selection of which heads of the Church it allowed. Those only who could be relied upon absolutely to conform – they were the only ones the State would tolerate. There was, and there is still you see, the system of dual control. On the one hand is the Council for Religious Matters, and this is so to say the officially recognised control. And with this goes the invisible control exercised by the State and watched over most carefully, undoubtedly, by the KGB. They monitor anyone who is candidate for high office in the Church, and if they are not acceptable, they are not accepted. Anyone who has been accepted and then begins in any way to make trouble or even perhaps seem as though they might be going to be troublesome – well, they are removed from office and sent somewhere far away. The Church has sustained itself only by agreeing to this subservience to the State. Now this so dominates the hierarchy of the Church that I think it will take many years for it to pass. This is the problem of our church today: it compromises still.

I have enjoyed our conversation, and I am sorry that it concludes on this note of pessimism. But it is my honest belief.

Father Boris,
Black monk*

The journey from the front entrance of the monastery to his office was a long one: up and down staircases, along corridors, across reception offices, in at one door of an empty meeting chamber and out through the other one at the far end. He walked briskly ahead, his long black robe flowing, his black shoulder-length hair unkempt and flying. There were frequent halts for greeting colleagues as he passed, with a ritual of hand-shaking, embracing, kissing on left and right cheeks. Finally, at the end of a fifth-floor landing he unlocked a door into a cell-sized room, moved files and folders and papers off chairs with voluble apologies and perched himself on the edge of his desk, smiling, with his legs drawn up under his gown.

– Our monastery as you see, it caters for the soul but it also takes care of the body in providing regular physical exercise. During the day, if you wish to see someone and ask his advice, or discuss some point with him, you pick up this telephone and enquire where he is. Always – you can rely on it – you will be told he can be found at the furthest point away from you in the complex of the building, so you spend much time going to seek people. But advantages also: if you feel anytime you would benefit from walking after sitting perhaps for several hours, then you may take yourself in any direction and go for a half-hour, even for an hour – and no matter how the weather is outside, rain or snow, you will always be warm and under cover. Through the windows you can see all its beautiful exterior architecture from constantly changing angles, so it is an interesting walk.

It is fortunate our monastery still remains as it is. In 1928 the State decided it would do away with all monasteries, and many were destroyed or altered inside so that they could become factories. This one, can you imagine what they did with this? They did not change it but they used it as a prison.

It was ideal as you can see, with its high walls all around it, and many hundreds of rooms in it just like this one: so it was preserved. But then during the war when Stalin discovered he could not stamp out religion however hard he tried, and that people had more and more need of the Church for the spiritual comfort it provided them in their time of suffering, he allowed it to be put back in use as a monastery again, and so it has remained ever since. Our great good fortune; of course also for myself, who wanted always to be able to come here, ever since I can remember as a small boy. If it is not being unhumble to say so, in our church this is a place of great prestige, and anyone who is appointed to the staff as I am, well it is an honour you know, to be at Danilov Monastery.

To speak more of myself, I am a monk who is a researcher: I am a contemplative, a student rather than a constant priest, but I do some priestly work for some part of my time. I take services at a church which is not far from here, but irregularly, mostly on Sundays or holidays. My research work involves me in much travelling, so I therefore cannot commit myself to a regular timetable of church services. I should say that I prefer this situation, I prefer the intellectual activity of study to the daily activities of parish and ceremony. This is something you cannot foresee when you first enter the priesthood of course, and it was something in myself which I had no idea of at the beginning of my career. But if you are a child and you think what you will be in manhood, you see yourself as a figure: for me the figure I saw for myself was that of the priest taking services in a church, not someone sitting all day long at a desk, reading and writing, that would be something I did not imagine.

I had no other idea ever than to be a priest: I cannot recall a different one at any age. It is a vocation of course, as is said a 'calling'. It is what I always had. It is common among the clergy of our church that there are many who did not receive any kind of religious upbringing, because religion was frowned upon by the State. It was never actively suppressed because it was realised by the State that this would only create martyrs. My father had died when

I was too young to remember him, and I received from my mother a constancy in religious belief. She took me regularly to church; she said to me more often than one occasion that she would be happy and proud if I were to enter the priesthood. This naturally was the first and greatest formative influence on me.

When I came to leave school at eighteen it was accepted without question by her and myself that I would enter an ecclesiastical academy. But here a difficulty arose that we had not foreseen. It was at the time of Brezhnev and because of the official attitude to try to hamper and discourage the Church, there were severe limits to the number of students such academies were allowed to accept. They took therefore only the most brilliant or most promising of applicants; and I was not one of those. If you were the kind of person I was, I would say perhaps of average ability, then the only other way to be accepted to an academy was to have connections – even perhaps through someone who was a member of the Party. But again, I was not such a person and nor was my mother.

Always though as I have told you, I was determined to enter the priesthood; so I worked at different occupations but always in my mind on a temporary basis. I was a postman, lorry driver, cleaner in a factory, manual worker, many things. But most importantly I made regular attendance at the church in the area of Moscow where we lived and became friendly with a priest there. He knew of my ambition and he encouraged it: he recommended to me books and theological papers I should read, he allowed me even to take some small part sometimes in services in the church. That was how it remained with me from the time I was eighteen until I was twenty-five. But always I was making applications for acceptance to be a theological student, and at last and to my great joy a place was offered to me at the Ecclesiastical Academy of Leningrad. It would mean that I would have to go away from home and leave my mother, but as it had always been her desire for me to be a priest she at once encouraged me to go.

I must say it was a late age at which to achieve what I wished. But I had been patient and persistent because as I have told you, never in my life had I wished for any other occupation. At the academy I worked and studied hard, and there after six years I was offered by the Principal to consider taking the vow of celibacy and to become a monk. As you can imagine, little consideration was needed. I agreed immediately: to be a Black monk is very special, and there are many fewer of us than the so-called White monks who marry and have families. This was now seven years ago, and ever since I took the vow it has been by far the happiest period of my life. So I may say without hesitation that here and now, at the age as I am of thirty-eight, this to me is the time of culmination of my greatest desire.

The major work with which I involve myself is that I am part of the team which is preparing background material for the translators of the new Russian Bible which is in preparation. It will be a scientific and critical edition of the Slavonic Bible, of which the one presently in use is now more than seventy years old. There is a new Hebrew Bible, a new Greek Bible, a Roman Catholic one, and many other different editions and adaptations. So our task is to produce a similar such edition of a Russian Bible which will stand by the side of these. It has of course also the extra importance that it will be a new formulation of the base of the language of the whole of Russian literature. It is an exciting prospect and it gives me great pride and great pleasure to be involved in it. I think it by far is the greatest way in which I can serve God. Others find their satisfaction as I have mentioned in church and parish work with their congregations, but for me research and writing is of greater enjoyment and importance.

Well, it is so because it is so, I do not think I can express it in any clearer way than that. The church that I go to when I take services is small, perhaps a congregation of only little more than two hundred persons: and I do not get great satisfaction there, apart of course from the liturgical singing which is always of great beauty. I do not of course want to lose contact entirely with the ordinary people; but I will admit to you that sometimes when I have returned from long travelling only the previous night, or have been working late into the night here at my desk, I think it would be nicer for me to have a long sleep in the morning rather than have to start early on Sunday to take services and confessions. It is of course my duty to do so, and I would not do other: but I regard it perhaps as some kind of additional voluntary work that I have to do, as what I may call a due that has to be paid for the privilege and enjoyment of my other work.

Also, to me, there are too many people who give me their confessions who I do not think at all understand what may be described as the basic beliefs of our religion and the fundamental aspects of Christian morality. Many many people do not at all understand that the life they are leading is one which is sinful in every respect, and I do not refer only to sexual and physical over-indulgence, but also in the way they place material values regarding possessions and standards of living above spiritual values. I try to impress upon them that they should change their way of life completely, and not be as they are, entirely concerned with comfort and enjoyment. But this is not an easy task, especially when people cannot see, or will not see, that the fundamental base for all life and the way it is lived, is the belief in God. This is the stone on which the Church itself is founded and nothing will shake it or remove it.

I regret it very much when it is said, as some people do say, that the Church has a history of compromise with the State. They do not properly understand that, at all times in history, the Church's first priority has always been to survive. If compromise is necessary for that, then it will compromise – but this in no way has ever altered its fundamental beliefs. The hierarchy of the Church has always had a different time-scale in which to work: it is eternal, and it must always struggle to maintain itself as a fundamental source of comfort.

My greatest regret is that we cannot return in history to the time of perhaps eighty years ago. I would describe myself not as a conservative but as a traditionalist. I mean this in this sense, that conservatives try to maintain what exists, and traditionalists try to restore faith in an ideal – the ideal that the Church should embody the foundation of society. I have always belonged to that part of the Orthodox Church which believes in this tradition. But I am realistic, and believe that it is impossible for the Church ever to set itself too strongly in opposition to the State, or identify itself too closely with those who insist on rebellion. After all, the Church has no material power: its power is only a spiritual one, and it is one which will always triumph in the end. I repeat very firmly my belief in the Church's primary duty, which is to protect itself and to survive.

I do not find the present times in which we live, as some people do, as exciting ones in which there can be great hope for change. I see this as a period for concern and caution – and caution in particular against the seductions of promises of new freedoms and false ideas which are now being promulgated in many places. It is the duty of the Church to resist these and to continue to call for a return to traditional values. This is my belief.

Natasha Nadirova,
historian

A slender dark-haired woman, with an oval face and high cheek-bones, she wore a smart navy blouse and light blue trousers. Her voice was soft but firm, and she chose her words thoughtfully and precisely.

– I think now I am not a Quaker lady, not yet – as you would say in English, nearly but not quite. I am fifty-two, and there is time yet for me to decide: I still have much to do, to study and to write, and it will influence me of course – not to change my religious faith, but to decide the final direction it will take.

To tell you how this came to be, it is necessary for me to go back to the early part of my life and to speak with you a little about my childhood. I may do so? I have then to say the first thing – and it is that I owe my life to Stalin, and without him I would not exist. He would be surprised to hear, I think, that it is due to him completely that there is this nearly-Quaker lady today.

This is the way that it came about. My father lived in Leningrad: he had his family there, his wife and two children, and his work was that he was an architect for bridges. But when the terrible repressions of Stalin began in the 1930s, it was reported that he had said something against Stalin, and so he was arrested and told he would be put into a labour camp. This happened to many people and the result of it was great loss of good workers. The people my father worked for, it was at the Building Ministry, they did not want to lose him so they proposed to him he should go to the north, to the Novosibirsk region, where there was being constructed a canal. It was agreed if he should do that, he would not be put into a labour camp. So he said to them Yes, and he went to that place.

His wife and children, they did not go with him and they rejected him. In those times it was safer to do that or else they would have lost everything, their home and his wife's work and everything else. My father worked for five years in the north, and it happened that after a time while he was there he met my mother. She was younger than he was and very beautiful, I have photographs of her. They lived I think together for a while and then they were married when he became divorced from his wife. I should say that this is my own reconstruction of the situation, because my mother has always been very unwilling to talk to me about it. She did not want to have children; I do not properly know the reason, but she told me that whenever she became pregnant she always had an abortion.

Then there came the time that Stalin was told the population of our country was declining very severely. He himself had been responsible for this situation because he had caused the deaths of so many people, and also because he had put so much fear into peoples' lives that they did not want to have children. But to try to bring to an end the decline of population, then he issued a decree that it was no longer legal to make abortions. And it was just in that time that she became pregnant with me. So that is how I came to be born, by a decree of Stalin.

Through all my childhood, everyone lived in fear and no one knew what their own life would be. It is one of the first things I remember, that in our apartment we kept a bag packed with clothing for me in it, and I was told by my mother that if it ever came to happen that she and my father had been taken away by the KGB I was to go with that bag to her sister's, my aunt, and she would look after me. All the rest of my life, I have never been able to remove this fear from myself that one day something might happen like that: I still have something of it in me now.

Then there came the war. My father was an ill person, and he was sent to work at a factory in the Urals. My mother came with me to Moscow to live with my aunt; and one day she heard that my father was dying and went to him, and when she got there and found he had died she came back to Moscow again. Then at the end of the war she too died: I was then eight years old and I was very sad because I loved her dearly. So it was my aunt who took responsibility for me and looked after me in my childhood and adolescence.

I was very young when I met and married my husband, who was fourteen years older than myself. Soon we had our son Nicholas who is now aged eighteen; and it was when he was twelve that my husband came to me and informed me he had fallen in love with someone else and was having a romance with her. I answered him that if he wished it he should go, which he did at once that same evening.

Life was very hard with me, and I went with my baby son to live again with my aunt. She was also an ill person, but we made the arrangement that she should look after my son while I went to work to try to earn some money for us to live on. It was on my shoulders, but I was prepared to do anything – be a secretary, give lessons to people for English which I had studied myself at school and after it, to translate articles, and every kind of thing. I began also to write short articles for magazines on a number of subjects: one of these was on different periods of English history which had especially interested me and which I had read about. One day an editor of a magazine who had published some of my articles, he said I should go to a publisher and propose to him a book, because they had already indicated to him they wished to publish a work about Oliver Cromwell. I had written articles about the English Civil War and I knew a little of Cromwell already, and that he was of interest to colleges and schools. I went to see these publishers, I proposed to them the book and they accepted I should do it.

This was a time which was very unhappy personally for me, because it coincided with the time of a most painful arranging of divorce with my husband. But I did much research for my book, I met many people, I submerged myself in my work, and more and more I came to find that I enjoyed writing. Finally I came to the Historical Institute, and they proposed to me that I should go there to a part-time job with them, to finish my book and also to teach for them. This I did, and when my book was finished three years ago they offered me to stay with them, and this is where I am still and I like it very much. When my book came eventually to be published, well there are already many books in Russia about Cromwell, so it was not a great success: it sold I think only perhaps a hundred thousand copies. But I have a job and I do research, and I also earn some money again by writing articles. This has now been my position for several years, and I can say with truth I am very happy.

I will make for us some tea so that I may rest my voice for a little while, and also gather my thoughts in preparation for how I shall continue.

– Now I will try to tell for you the rest of my story. Always from my childhood I have had religious belief, and I was brought up in our Orthodox Church. There are many ways it has supported and consoled me, and one of my most vivid memories from a child was how at every Easter, my aunt would take me to the church which was near where we lived. Not to go inside it, because at that time it was always so overcrowded, but we would go to stand outside it in the square. Just as it was coming to midnight, the square would be packed with people who stood all of them absolutely silent. Then, in the minute before it came to twelve, everyone would light a candle: in every hand there was a candle, and the whole of the square was filled with thousands of candles glimmering. Exactly at midnight the doors of the church were flung open and a priest came out to the top of the steps of the entrance. He told to the crowd 'Christ is risen!' and everybody answered him 'Christ is risen indeed!' And after this we went home with these candles through the streets, everyone carrying them. So you see, that is a precious memory of my childhood, and it still means much to me. It satisfied me, and I shall remember it always as a wonderful experience of childhood.

But yet somehow today our Orthodox Church does not quite satisfy me any more. When I go to visit it, I can say only that I feel lonely there. I see in front of me wonderful performances by the priests – they perform their ceremonies, they read something, they tell something and so on. Sometimes I understand the language and sometimes I do not, and always the choir is singing most beautifully. But I have now this feeling all the time that it is a performance by the Church, and the people are not part of it, they do not seem to have a relationship with the beautiful performance. It is performed for them, but it is not admitted for them to have a part in it. You must forgive me that I do not explain it well in English, but of course it is something I am trying to speak of which is deep inside me here. I still visit the Orthodox Church now and again, it is necessary for me sometimes that I should, but it is not too often now.

I know also that I am not alone in another feeling which I have, because I have spoken of it among my friends. It is that somehow our church has not quite given the people of our country all that it should. It has been I would say a church of consolation, but not a church of reform. This is true of other churches in Christianity also, and perhaps other people may feel it the same with their churches – that it asks for belief and obedience, and if you give that and will follow, then it can offer no more. But if you want to have discussion, if you want to have opening of the mind – then no, it does not care for that.

And so it came, you see, that I was affected by my study of your English Puritans. Because when I was making my studies of Oliver Cromwell and the background to his times, naturally then I came to learn about George Fox and the Quakers, and from then onwards I came to discover others of the different reforming of beliefs. It was perhaps coincidence that it was at the very time when I was beginning to question the forms and ceremonies of our Orthodox Church; but however it was, I became drawn more strongly and more strongly towards the Quaker way – that there is something of God in everyone, and everyone has something of God in them. There is growing now in our country everywhere a feeling of cynicality about everything – about Communism, about the State and about the Church – and I find it is for me too in my religious belief, that I do not want the outward shows, and like better the more simple things.

6 Crime

Joseph Chernov, militia patrolman
Vladimir Milovich, Ministry of the Interior
Yevgeni Piratin, prison governor
Mikhail Dolmano, long-sentence prisoner

Joseph Chernov,
militia patrolman*

On the front row of the empty and echoing meeting hall of Militia Station 37, Slavinsky Prospect 13, he sat stiff and upright in his metal-blue serge uniform, his cap carefully placed on the tip-up seat next to him. At first his hands tightly gripped his knees, and he looked ahead as he spoke, frowning in concentration and stumbling to order his words carefully.

– My name is Joseph Chernov, I am Militia Patrolman Number 917 at Station 37 in Moscow Central District. I am twenty-five years of age. I am unmarried, and I live with my parents. I have been in the militia for four years and seven months. I like being in the militia, it is a good occupation. Well I do not know your country but I think what you say is correct, from what I have seen on television and read in the newspapers what we call the militia you call the police yes. We are the official arm of the civil authority, and it is our duty to fight crime and to maintain law and order.

I am a graduate of secondary school. After it I did my military service in the Army for two years, and after that straight away when I came home from the Army I joined the militia. It had always been my ambition as long as I can remember: at school and in the Army I became friends with people who were in the militia, and I never wanted to do anything else. Also I have an uncle, one of the brothers of my father, he was also in the militia. Sometimes he would talk with me about it, and tell me it was a good and worthwhile occupation, because an officer of the law is someone who upholds justice. What seems attractive to me about it is that I am doing something creditable in society, something which is really for the good of my country, and so I think I can respect myself because basically it is doing something which is good.

It is an occupation that I would say yes, anyone who does this most definitely has to have a vocation for. It is not a job someone would do for money, because the average pay of the ordinary militiaman is small, only a little over two hundred roubles[1] a month. This is, as I think most people would agree today, a rather insufficient wage, and it is one reason why many people who do not have a vocation for it do not stay in the job. I am sure in these modern times it will eventually soon be seen that a militiaman's pay is quite inadequate for the sort of work he does. So if someone is uncertain of their vocation for the work, soon they become unhappy and try to find another job which is better paid.

Speaking for myself I must say honestly I have never had such feeling. But I have many colleagues who have, and so now they no longer serve in the militia. The work is complicated and indeed at times it is a fact that it is dangerous. In this respect I am fortunate that I am not so far married, because if I were I would have to think about the poor pay and the dangers involved, and whether it was justified from the point of view of my wife and family if I had one, for me to do such work. But as I have said, I think that before long the pay will improve. There is a phrase, and it goes like this: 'One of the most expensive things the State can have is a cheap militia.' I think this sums it up exactly, I think this will soon be seen by everyone.

There are several things about the job which I like and am happy about, and there are also things which I do not like and am unhappy about. Yes, if you will permit me to do so I will tell you a little about both these things. I will begin with what I am happy about. In the course of my work I arrest a number of criminals: I would say that on average it is perhaps eight or nine persons a year who are guilty of serious crime, and many more than that who might be described as petty offenders, such as people who are drunk, or hooligans, or have no proper papers, persons of that kind. It gives me satisfaction when someone who has committed serious crime is

[1] About £200.

detained by me or one of my colleagues and then punished appro-
priately in court. That is the triumph of justice, and as such it gives
you good feelings. You have to be careful at all times to be just, but
it has to be said there are also bad people who escape punishment,
and this is a matter for sadness. Also there are times when a criminal
is in your opinion not punished severely enough, but this is
something you learn to accept as part of the job, however much it
angers and disappoints you.

As to the things I am unhappy about, well the most important I
think is the very vague legal status of law-enforcement officers in
the Soviet Union. The exact thing I am referring to is the insufficient
level of legal protection which is extended to a law officer, which
definitely in my opinion is not enough. Certainly I will be more
specific with an example for you, yes: I will do so by referring to
the story of an incident that was described in the newspapers and
also on television. It occurred only just a few days ago, and it
illustrates how imperfect the regulations are, and how little protection the law offers to us.

We have a regulation which I can quote, and it goes like this.
'Regulation 407. A member of the militia may fire his pistol only if
his life is directly threatened.' In practice that means that I am only
correct to fire my pistol five seconds after I have become a corpse.
But a continuation of this same regulation permits me to protect an
ordinary citizen in a somewhat better way. It goes on to state I may
fire my pistol to protect citizens from a direct threat to their life, or
– and this is the important addition – 'in case of danger to their
health'. So you see that as far as the militiaman is concerned, there
is no mention that he may fire his pistol to protect his health or save
himself from injury. I have the privilege to make the decision about
possible danger to the citizen's health, but not to my own.

This means for example if there should be an incident let us say of
riotous behaviour by what we may call a bunch of roughs, perhaps
eight or ten of them together – well, they are not armed but they
are running wild, and a militiaman who attempts to control them,
he cannot do so even by firing a warning shot into the air if they
come towards him. But if they set upon some poor harmless old
man they see, well then he can. This is very unsatisfactory, I am
sure you will agree.

To return to the incident I was going to describe to you, I will now speak directly of it. It occurred in the 17th District last Wednesday, in Barbinsky Street, in one of the blocks of residential apartments there. Three criminals entered the building and broke into an apartment where was living a twenty-seven-year-old woman, and they murdered her by stabbing her to death with knives. Then they collected many valuable things from her apartment – the total value I believe has been assessed already at forty thousand roubles – and they took them downstairs to the street, where a motor car was waiting for them to make their escape. Well it just happened that a militia patrol car was passing, and seeing the criminals loading boxes of goods into the car, it pulled up to a halt. One of the two militiamen in the car got out and went to the criminals to ask them what they were doing. Quite justifiably he thought they looked as though they were thieves, but at that stage he had no idea they were dangerous murderers also. As he approached, one of them pulled out a knife and said to him he should come no closer to them, otherwise he would be dead. At this point the militiaman turned his head in the direction of the patrol car to call for help – whereupon the criminal with the knife produced a pistol and pointed it at the patrolman's chest and pressed the trigger.

It is at this point that I think you as a writer will be very interested by hearing now what happened next. If you were to write it in a book, no one would believe you because they would say you had made it up. For what happened was this, that the criminal's gun did not fire: it just made such a noise as like this, 'Click!' Yet later when it came to be tested, it fired a bullet correctly every time. It is a situation I am sure an author would find it very difficult to invent such a thing.

Then the criminal leapt into the car with his accomplices and they drove off at high speed. The militiaman drew his own pistol and fired after them, and the bullet from it entered the car at the rear and hit the criminal who was driving in the neck, and so the car came to a halt. By this time the militiamen in the patrol car had called for help on their radio, and within a very short time other patrol cars arrived to assist them: all four of the bunch of criminals were detained, except one who managed to escape by running away. He was the one who had been injured in the neck incidentally; but he did not remain free for long because he was bleeding badly and went to a hospital for treatment, and the medical staff of course reported immediately that they had someone with a gunshot wound.

So the point of this story, as you will see, is that it illustrates what a difficult and dangerous job we have to be a militiaman, and the risks that have to be taken. If the militiaman had been able to approach the criminals with his pistol in his hand, as for example I have seen them do in American films that we see sometimes on television, then he would not have been in any such danger in that situation, as he was from the criminal who drew his gun and attempted to shoot him. People do not understand this very largely at all, and the newspapers and the television often say things that are unfavourable about us. No no, I have never myself been in such a situation yet where it has been necessary for me to draw my pistol – but those colleagues I was telling you the story about, well they were only a few kilometres away from our district, so one never knows at any time where and when something like that could happen.

Well finally my ambition of course is to go higher in my profession: for this reason I am attending law studies on two nights a week, and in two years' time I hope I may graduate and could then perhaps progress to the rank of junior sergeant, then after that be a senior sergeant by the time I am thirty. We shall see, but promotion is slow: it is based on your age and the length of service you have performed, rather than on your ability.

And finally there is one thing I would like to say, and it is this. I would like to give you my very best wishes, and through you to send greetings to the people of your country.

Vladimir Milovich,
Ministry of the Interior*

The hospitality-room of the Ministry was on the sixteenth floor of a towering rectangular modern building near the city centre. It had green-upholstered small settees and armchairs arranged round glass-topped coffee tables, floor-to-ceiling curtaining of light blue, and reproductions of Impressionist paintings on some of the beige-distempered walls. Two young women in stylishly cut white blouses and black skirts brought coffee and biscuits.

The Ministry's spokesman was dark-suited, politely friendly, at ease and urbane. He was in his early forties.

– You have as much of my time as you wish. I apologise that I do not speak English. And allow me also please to apologise that you have had to wait over one month for an appointment with me, and that it has been necessary for your assistant to make a total of eighteen telephone calls to achieve final confirmation of this date and time today. I will not try to take refuge in the excuse that we are very busy. Of course we are very busy, as I am sure all ministries in your country are always very busy too. But frankly our fault is not so much in that, as in our celebrated bureaucracy: for some reason it seems always necessary for every letter or memo to be examined first by three people before it can be passed to a fourth person for further examination. We are trying to improve, and I am sure if you were to return to visit us in ten years' time, you would find us still saying we are trying to improve. It is like this in your country also, it is as bad or is it worse? About the same? Well I am sure it is so everywhere.

But you have had some members of the militia provided to you to talk to and choose which you wished to interview? And that has been satisfactory? Good, and I can tell you also today that your request to visit one of our prisons, and to talk to the governor and to a long-sentence prisoner on your own – these matters have now been attended to and all has been arranged for you. Next Tuesday you have permission to go to Labour Colony Number 7, in the Belivsky region outside Moscow. The KGB, well we do not have good contact between us, so I am afraid we have had no success with them for you.

Now to your questions for today. Do not hesitate to ask me anything whatever that you wish, in relation to the crime situation in Moscow. This morning's newspaper? Yes I have seen the headlines on its front page: I have it with me here, in case you had not yet seen it. 'Rape and Murder Increasing in Moscow', 'Crime Figures Rising', 'Interior Ministry's Alarm'. Well I suppose such headlines would be typical in a newspaper anywhere. As you know, it was not the policy of our government until recently to issue figures about crime or release any information: in fact it might almost have been assumed that we had no crime. Citizens could learn nothing about it at all. Now the policy has changed: this year is only the second one in which figures are issued. And I greatly wish they were reported in a different way. But some newspapers seek for what I believe are called 'angles', and the more sensational they are the better.

It is true to say there is an increase in the number of cases recorded in certain categories of offence. But from my own reading of the translations of foreign newspapers which we receive, I get the impression, you know, that there is a similar situation in both London and New York. Increasing crime – if you want to find evidence of it you can, and always in the published figures. In this newspaper it makes me smile to read such words as 'Interior Ministry's Alarm'. 'Alarm' I think is really not quite the correct word: 'worry' perhaps, or excuse me if there is no such translatable word, 'perturbation'. Who anywhere, either in the Ministry or even an ordinary citizen on the Metro, would not feel when reading the figures of crime, worry or perturbation? But it is not quite the same thing as alarm I think.

We suffer our figures, as you do in your country I am sure. I mean by that that figures are never an exact guide: they cannot be regarded as strictly reliable in ways some people presume. To give an example, our figures I have here for burglaries in the last three-month period show an increase upon those for the previous period. Does this mean there have been more burglaries? Well the answer I think is No: it means more burglaries have been reported and recorded, but that is not the same thing. People hear our police, or militia as they are known, have better methods now of catching burglars; so they will report a burglary of their home. Before, if only a small amount of property was taken, they did not bother to report the matter because they did not think the police would catch those responsible.

There is also the problem concerning how law-enforcement agencies register crimes. They do not like to show a picture which reveals that a large number of crimes are unsolved, so they may sometimes adopt one of two methods to obscure it. They may catch a criminal and ask him to confess to some unsolved act of burglary, to make their figures look better. Or they may, as we say, put the figures under the table – not bother to record some of them, that is. I do not know if it is true or not, but I have read that in some Western countries, the police will sometimes do the opposite and record more crimes than have occurred. They do this to show how busy and underpaid they are, to support their claim for higher pay; and it could be that this happens here also. It is only my personal view, but I think here in the Soviet Union, the militia are very poorly paid. In the West, so I have read, they are highly paid; and I think this should be so. The result for us of poor pay is that we have problems of recruitment all the time.

To consider now the general picture of crime in our country, my knowledge of other countries is based only on my reading. But I would say that in most ways the types of crime we have in Moscow are similar to those seen in big cities everywhere. One type of crime which we do not have compared with London, however, is one which I believe takes up much time of your law-enforcement officers. That is the type which covers motoring offences of all kinds. We have only a very small number in Moscow. This is not because Moscow motorists are better behaved of course: it is only because we have so many fewer cars. For instance with a motor vehicle there is no problem ever that you cannot find somewhere to park it: you will be able to do so usually in the same street wherever you are going, or within easy reach of it. Our streets are wide and cars owned by private citizens are few, so the result is a free flow of traffic. We have cases of course where someone drives dangerously, too fast, perhaps under the influence of alcohol, and these are regarded very seriously. They carry heavy penalties if it has involved the killing or injury of another person. But motoring offences of all kinds do not figure highly in our criminal statistics, as I believe they do in yours.

For the rest, as I have said, crime in Moscow is much the same as anywhere else. The most common offence is theft. A worrying recent tendency has been the increase in the number of armed burglaries into people's homes. A reason is possibly that as more people are now engaged in business ventures on their own, in such forms as co-operatives for example, it is known or suspected they keep money and valuables in their homes. This attracts the activities of gangs who use violence, both to break in and then to force the occupants to hand over their possessions. And it is not only gangs who use this sort of violence: only yesterday for example we caught a girl of sixteen who had broken into an old lady's apartment, terrorised her with a knife, and forced her to hand over money and jewellery.

Much crime in our country is alcohol-related: much crime and of many different kinds. It is shown in violence, within a domestic context, by a husband against his wife and children. And it features in sexual offences also: in rape very often. I am sorry to say too alcohol leads sometimes to offences against children by people who are mentally ill or disturbed. We have a benevolent attitude towards children in Soviet society: offences against them are looked upon very seriously, and those who commit them are severely punished. But I do not want to suggest we regard punishment of itself as the answer to what is fundamentally either a mental or social problem. It is commonly accepted that in many cases of delinquency of all kinds, attempts merely to punish bad behaviour out of offenders have been singularly unsuccessful. When they were not accompanied by other forms of treatment, and some attempt at understanding, they usually failed.

We do not know, and I'm sure no one anywhere else does if we are honest about it, how to get rid of crime. If you look at any of our old Party programmes, it is usually said in them that one of the aims of the State is to eliminate crime completely. It gives the opinion, or perhaps a better word is 'dogma', that crime has its roots in the structure of society, and that once society is completely changed it follows naturally there will be no more crime. As there is only common property and common ownership, therefore there is no need for criminal activity, since people should not want to steal what they already own. Well, I think that was a Utopian vision. We no longer regard the problem of crime as being so simple in its origins, or a solution to it being so simple to find either.

Nowadays we believe that perhaps our best aim, our most realistic one, is to try to hold back crime. We are improving law-enforcement methods, and trying to maintain law and order in an acceptable way. If one may use such a phrase, I would say we hope at best to stabilise the crime rate. Perhaps we shall eventually find a way to decrease crime; but if we do, it will be very slowly, only after much study and thought, and not by blindly chasing any simple single idea such as punishment or reprisal.

If I may do so myself, now I would like to ask you two questions. The first is whether you felt in your approach to our Ministry, tedious and with all its long-drawn-out delays though it was, that a co-operative attitude was extended to you in giving you the facilities you asked? And secondly whether you can suggest ways in which we can improve assistance to those like yourself who come to us from other countries with questions? We have not yet been for long an approachable Ministry, and we do not have much experience of it. We wish it to be known that it is not necessary, as one might say, to batter down our door: just to turn the handle we hope will show it is not locked. If we learn how things are done in other countries, by your own Home Office for example, this would provide helpful guidance to us.

Yevgeni Piratin

*prison governor**

Standing at the edge of a housing estate in a suburban town, the prison compound was surrounded by a thick wall and a thirty-foot-high wire fence. Inside, the main prison building was of red brick, old and three-storeyed. Around it were about a dozen smaller buildings: dormitories, workshops, a hospital and a short terrace of four small houses. The prisoners wore brown jackets and trousers of a coarse material, and had their hair cropped.

The Governor, a large heavily built man, wore the uniform and peaked cap of an Army officer. He walked unhurriedly and unescorted along the concrete paths between the buildings, giving an occasional nod to an inmate as he talked about his work.

– This prison is called Colony of Corrections Labour Camp Number 7, and it is forty kilometres from the centre of Moscow. I came here when it was built twenty years ago. Hard to believe, is it not, that in those days it was in the middle of a forest in the heart of the countryside? It was very remote and isolated: the idea was ordinary decent people would be protected by being far away from the dangerous criminals it contained. Now look what has happened since then: a whole new town has grown up next to it. The people who live in those blocks of apartments there, if they want to on a Sunday afternoon they can sit on their balconies and see over the wall to watch the animals in the zoo. So much for the idea of protecting them: now they have criminals all around them almost. They do not mind: if they do, they will live somewhere else.

Would you wish me to give you a guided tour with an official speech of commentary? Or would you prefer to walk round as we do now and give me questions I will do my best to answer? Very good yes, I also would prefer the second course. Let that be the way we proceed then. Our autumn weather is pleasant, yes?

Our prisons are known as 'penal colonies': this one is of the type called a 'general standard' institution. It holds 514 men who have a wide range of sentence for many sorts of offence. The average sentence length is perhaps between three and five years; but we have men doing a longer time than that, in one particular instance a man who is serving fourteen years. Most of those confined here have not been considered by the courts to be the very severest type of criminal: such offenders are usually sentenced to a regime of hard labour, which is stricter and less relaxed. It is for only the most dangerous or persistent criminals. Of those here, it is felt there is still some hope for them, even if only a little: they may still be able to benefit from what is offered by way of rehabilitation, or have some possibility of changing their ways. But of course we have many failures, because many of them are incapable of changing their ways.

It is possible for a man who is here to earn a reduction in his sentence: it depends on his behaviour. His remission could be as much as one-third of the original sentence; even in some few cases a very well-behaved man might leave on licence after he has done only half his sentence, if we consider he would benefit from leniency. But you will understand that like any other prison, this is a place where people who have broken the law and are offenders in society's eyes are sent to as a punishment. So the regime they have is strict; some perhaps would say it is too strict. I would not make a claim that we want a man to be happy while he is here, that would be ridiculous; but I would hope that if he feels he has been treated severely, he will feel also he has been treated fairly.

For all prisoners the daily routine begins at six o'clock in the morning when they get up. There is then exercise and physical training, followed by breakfast in the dining halls. You may ask of any prisoner you care to what the food here is like. If you find one who has any praise at all for it, please let me know because it will be a miracle. At seven-fifteen or seven-thirty there is counting of the prisoners to make sure everyone is present, and all then go to work. There is a choice of enterprises they can work in: we have a light-engineering factory which makes tools, a large garage workshop which is engaged on contracts for the repair and servicing of vehicles for different ministries; and there are simpler forms of labour for those less capable of work, which include the making and painting of road signs, street signs and so on.

The working day consists of eight hours: there is a time in the middle of it for lunch, and at 4.30 p.m. work finishes for the day. All the men are counted once more, and on a random basis some of them are searched to ensure they have not concealed about them tools, for example, from the workshops. From 5.30 p.m. onwards some go to school classes at their own request, where they can learn basic educational subjects like reading, writing and mathematics, which a number are deficient in. Or they may go to vocational training to learn some kind of skill which they would like to have proficiency in for when they leave prison. For the rest, if they do not wish to do either of those things they may spend their time at leisure in association with the other prisoners, playing games outdoors if the weather is not too unpleasant, or watching television. We prefer them to be active, but the choice of course is theirs. At eight o'clock in the evening they have dinner, then there is a further short period of free time until ten o'clock when they go to bed.

They sleep in dormitories, normally eight to ten men in a room, usually in two-tier bunks. The accommodation is bare and simple, but each man is allotted a small area of his own for a few personal possessions such as books and photographs which he is allowed. Each dormitory has its own sanitary arrangements: toilets, washbasins, baths and showers and so on, the necessities of life but no more. The standard of tidiness and cleanliness has to be maintained at a level similar to that which is required in the Army.

For the work which he does in the prison workshops, each man is paid the equivalent sum to what he would earn if he were working in such a job outside in freedom. But the difference here in prison is that part of such money, perhaps fifty per cent of it, is taken from him to pay for his food and accommodation. Further sums also may be deducted: the court which sentenced him may have ordered that in addition to being imprisoned, he should also pay in instalments a fine, or compensation to someone if he has robbed or injured them.

I would estimate the earnings of a prisoner would be about the equivalent of fifty pounds a week in your money. Half of it is as I say taken from him in deductions, so this leaves him with a total of twenty-five pounds a week. From this sum he is permitted if he wishes to send money to his wife and family; he does not have to, and of necessity if he does it cannot be very much. But at least then he may feel he is contributing something towards their welfare. Finally, from what he has remaining, he may buy himself small luxuries such as tea, soap and tobacco from the prison shop. Prisoners barter such things among themselves: luxuries are far more important than money in prison. The biggest luxury with the highest value is tea: one might almost say it was prison currency.

We think it is very important for a man, even if he is in prison, to maintain contact with his family if he has one. For this reason a prisoner is allowed to write and receive as many letters as he wishes, and also if it is necessary at a time of family crisis such as illness, to make telephone calls. But the most important contact is the visits he receives: each prisoner is allowed a total of four short visits from relatives a year. These last up to four hours at a time, so he has sixteen hours of visiting in a year. We accept this is not very much. Also if he is a married man, a prisoner may have two visits per year of three days at a time from his wife. You perhaps noticed when we passed them a small terrace of houses: they are for these conjugal visits. The houses are simply furnished but they have the necessities for cooking and so on, and the wife brings food in with her when she comes. For the whole of the three-day period they are independent and are left completely alone. It is far from normal life, but perhaps during that time they are able to pretend the man is not in prison and unable to be close with her.

As for discipline, for prisoners who are very badly behaved, for instance by showing violence to other prisoners or the staff, I have a range of available punishments to use. First I give reprimands and warn as to future behaviour; then I may fine, or refuse permission for a man to buy in the prison shop for a period, or most severely of all restrict or refuse to permit a certain number of visits. If none of these methods alters a prisoner's behaviour, I have finally the method of taking him away from the other prisoners and confining him in a punishment cell. These are very spartan: they contain only a bed, a table, a chair, and a washbasin and toilet. I can order a man to be placed in this sort of confinement for up to fifteen days. It is of course a very severe punishment, and one which I use rarely. We do not have any solitary confinement: if a man is put into a punishment cell, he will have at least one other prisoner there too, as we do not think it humane for any reason to keep a man entirely alone.

That, I think, is a brief description for you of our penal system. You will of course be able to compare it with that of any prisoner you may wish to talk with alone.

I am sure no one would claim our system is other than far from ideal. We have two main tasks, I think: the first is to contain the offender for a period of time, as the punishment society demands should be inflicted on him. And secondly, while we are doing it, we should try to help him prepare himself for a more satisfactory sort of life when he is released. I often feel we have fallen short of our objectives in this; the only comfort I have is that penal regimes in most other countries in the world are similarly ineffective.

There is not much of interest about myself. I have been here for twenty years, as I told you, from when the prison was opened. As you see I am an Army officer and I have specialised, perhaps I may say, in penal matters for the whole of my Army career. All the staff of this prison are soldiers: it is customary that a man may be ordered to do prison-warder duty as part of his period of conscription. We think this is preferable to having staff who spend their whole lifetime as warders: it is felt they could become as institutionalised as the prisoners.

So I hope you have found your visit of interest. A last question, certainly yes please go ahead. Why do all the prisoners have their hair cropped close to their heads? Well, it is so they could be quickly identified as prison inmates should they escape. How many escapes have we had? With respect, you said one last question and now you have asked two. However I will answer the second one also. We have never had any prisoners escape.

Mikhail Dolmano,
long-sentence prisoner*

He was sitting waiting in a bare-walled room at the end of a corridor in the administration block: it had nothing in it apart from four wooden chairs round a small table, and its barred window was too high up the wall to see out of. Sallow-complexioned and short, he wore a battledress type of uniform of thin brown material and a collarless striped shirt. His fair hair was not cropped.

– Yes I have been told I do not have to talk to you if I do not wish to. But I am willing to do it, to be frank, because life in prison is very boring and anything is welcome that is a change. I have also been told that nothing I say will be repeated to the authorities here or in the ministry, and so I may speak frankly and say whatever I wish. Yes I believe that to be true: in my opinion the Governor is always a straightforward man and speaks honestly.

My name is Mikhail Dolmano, I am twenty-nine years of age, and I am serving a prison sentence of fourteen years. This was for driving a motor car when I was drunk: it was involved in a serious crash with another car, and the four people in it were killed. I think by law what I received is the maximum sentence for this offence that could be passed. The sentence was for each case, you understand, so I was given it four times. But the sentences will be running together all at the same time, not one after another. I have spent three and a half years of my sentence in prison so far, and I have been told no consideration will be given to the idea of my release until I have served at least half the time. So it is possible in theory after seven years that I might be considered for release on parole licence.

I say in theory because I understand only that it could be possible.

I have to say that I think it would be very unlikely. I would realistically expect no hope of consideration for release until after perhaps nine or ten years at the soonest, because of the seriousness of the offence and the number of people who were killed. I have set my mind to expect that as the amount of time I shall be imprisoned, but if it happens it is less, naturally I shall be very glad. I say truthfully though that I do not think it will happen: it is a hope, perhaps I may say a wild dream, that is all. We shall see. Two things might have some influence on it: one would be how I behave here in prison, and so far I have been careful not to make trouble of any kind. The other possibility to influence it would be what sort of an occupation I could have on release. The place where I worked, the bosses there have said when the time comes they will offer to give me back my own job. They said this at the court, when I was sentenced; but they may not be the same bosses there in ten years' time, so I don't rely too much on it.

My job was that I was a mechanic in a garage, making repairs to motor cars and small trucks. Here in the prison I am employed in the motor repair workshop; it is the same kind of thing, but on a much bigger scale, since we repair very large trucks belonging to government departments. Many of them are of considerable size, so I am getting experience of a much better kind. While I am working I am also preparing examinations on the subject. When I pass those, which I hope to do in two years, I shall have proper qualification certificates as a motor engineer. That may be one benefit of imprisonment for me and help me in getting a better job when I am released. But a disadvantage is that as well as being given a sentence, I am prohibited from driving ever again in my life. This will mean I shall never be permitted to collect or deliver vehicles as part of my work. But you will understand, all these such things which I think about are far ahead in the future. I try not to lose hope for myself entirely, but I know what worries me most: it is the thought of having to start life all over again, at the age of perhaps nearly forty. This will be a huge task.

I have a wife and one child, my son who is now aged four. A dream I sometimes have is that when I am finally released from prison, he will still be of an age young enough for me to take him to school. In my dream I walk holding his hand with him to his school, and then I stand and wave goodbye to him while he goes off for his lessons. My wife is a very good woman: we had been married only for one year when I committed this offence and was put into prison. We had one small piece of good fortune afterwards: she had an aunt who lived in this town near here, so she was able to come to live with her. This means a great saving for her in time and money when she comes to visit me. She and our son have one room of their own in her aunt's apartment, and when she comes on her three-day visits she is able to leave him there and her aunt looks after him. She has found herself a clerical job also, at a factory in the town: it does not earn her very much money, and she has to do without all luxuries of any kind. I am only able to send her from the wages I earn a small sum, the equivalent of perhaps about one hundred pounds in a month. It means she and my son can survive, but not much more.

It would be nice if she could bring my son with her on one of our family visits, we would all enjoy it; but it is not permitted. So I can only see him when she brings him on one of our short visits. There is entitlement to four of these a year, lasting up to four hours in length on each occasion; but so far since I have been here, I have had only three of these visits a year lasting two hours each. I do not know why this is: it is certainly not because I have done anything wrong. All I have been told is there is a shortage of time available for using staff when visitors come.

The family visits are satisfactory, but the short visits are not. They take place in very uncivilised conditions. There is a large room like this, or a series of cubicles rather, smaller and with bare walls. But conversation in them is not allowed to take place as we are talking now, face to face across a table. We are separated by very thick glass, so no contact of any kind is possible. We speak with each other by means of a telephone on each of our respective sides. As you can imagine it is very unsatisfactory. I do not understand why on such occasions I am only allowed to communicate with my wife like that, while on the family visit we live together on our own for three days at a time. If you enquire, you always receive the same answer: 'It is the regulations.'

The regime of the prison is quite hard. We go to work early in the morning, and we are not allowed much time for recreation and hobbies. When the weather permits, there is some sport such as football outside, and I do gymnastics and weight-lifting in the gymnasium which I enjoy. The food, well I would say it is sufficient, but of little variety and not palatable. You are given the same thing for your main meal almost every day: meat of poor quality, potatoes and perhaps cabbage, and this you will have sometimes for four or even five days in succession. The uniform we wear as you can see is poorly fitting and thin, and not warm enough in winter.

I look slightly different from most of the other prisoners, yes, because I do not have my hair cut short as they do. This is not a special privilege extended to me because I am a long-term prisoner, the reason for it is medical. I have a scalp condition, and the prison doctor has recommended I do not have my hair cut short.

What else may I tell you about? Please ask me anything else you would like to know. I am not a very well educated person so it is easier for me if you ask me things: I cannot think myself of what might be of interest for you.

The prison shop? Well it cannot really be described as much of a shop at all. I will show it to you later, as I have been told I may take you and show you a dormitory and anything else I wish. When we go to the shop, you will see it is a small room no bigger than this, with not enough space for more than six people at a time, so there is always a queue. There are very few goods for sale in it: some tins of small fishes, bars of chocolate, cigarettes and tobacco, and little brown-paper packets of tea. Smoking is not restricted so you may buy as much tobacco as you wish or can afford, but the thing everyone wants is tea. No one can get much of it, but there are some who manage to get it in quantities large enough for them to resell it at inflated prices. It is not a nice thing that those who are in difficult circumstances such as losing their freedom should take advantage of others who are in the same situation. But it is human nature. There are some very unscrupulous persons in prison – almost perhaps as many as there are outside, this is a common joke that is heard.

There are also some decent men. This is one thing I have learned from being in prison. It is not always necessarily the case that a man who has committed a very bad offence is one of the worst persons. You can for instance meet a murderer who has killed his wife or lover in a very savage and horrible way, but when you talk with him and get to know him you discover he is almost in every way a nice person. But you will meet some other man and you do not like him at all: he is a bully and a boaster, and an objectionable character completely. And you then discover his offence was of a trivial nature, he is perhaps a thief of only a small amount of money, and not in any way to be regarded as serious a criminal as the man who is a murderer. It is strange to realise this, it shows you that previous opinions you had of many things like crime and criminals were not correct.

The most unpopular type of prisoner to others? Well without doubt this is the person who has committed offences of a sexual nature against children. Such men are completely despised by all other prisoners: many feel as I do myself, as the father of a small child, that such creatures should not be permitted to go on living either in prison or anywhere else, but should be immediately put to death. They are animals, and they should not be allowed to live. I am one among many here who would kill them with our bare hands if we could capture them. But they are kept for their own safety in a separate part of the prison, which is heavily guarded at all times, and so it is not possible to get access to them. I think it is wrong that they should be protected like this: they should be left to survive if they can in with all other prisoners, who would know what they had done. On the ladder of social position in prison, these people are at the very lowest point; in fact it can be said with truth they are not regarded even as being on the ladder at all.

Thank you for having this conversation with me. It is the first event of interest to me that has occurred since I came into prison. Please now accompany me back to the main building.

7 *School 257*

Alina Pashkova, headmistress

Grigori Valentov, teacher

Class 8: Leonti, Sasha, Lisa, Ida

Class 11: Andrei, Sergei, Nika, Galya

Alina Pashkova,
headmistress*

A slightly built woman with short fair hair, wearing a brightly coloured summer dress, she sat behind an old-fashioned desk in her large bare-walled office. She spoke with quiet self-assurance.

– We have here at School 257 Moscow Central District 780 pupils, approximately half of them boys and half of them girls. They range in age from six to about fifteen or some few of them sixteen. We particularly remember of those who are among our youngest children today, that they will be attaining school-leaving age in the year 2000: so it is an interesting thought, both for them and for us, that they will be the first adults of a new millennium. Therefore we think of them as very special, because they will be the carriers of education into a new age. And of course we greatly welcome the challenge to us of preparing them for this.

The school itself, well I have to say that I hope we shall not still be carrying this building also with us into the next century. It was built I think in 1936, and as you will have seen when you were shown round it by the two older pupils, much of it is shabby and old-fashioned. But our hope is that its age is the only thing which is old, and what it contains in learning and the passing-on of ideas is more up to date. Our task is to make sure that between the time when they first come to us, aged six or seven, and when they leave aged fifteen onwards to go into senior education or technical school, every pupil by then will have received a thorough grounding in basic matters such as reading and writing and mathematics, and also a good knowledge and appreciation of the world's great literature, paintings and music. We feel education should consist not only of facts, but should include also an appreciation of all things including the eternal values in life.

Myself, I am forty and I have been working here in this school now for almost twenty years. In fact I was a pupil here. I worked for a short time at another school as a teacher of physics, but then returned to a post here when there came a vacancy. I became Headmistress eighteen months ago when the previous Head retired, and this was as a result not of my application and appointment, but by an election. We have this system in many of our schools: when there is a vacancy for the position such as Head, all the teachers vote to say which person among them they would like to have. In my case I was fortunate and honoured to be voted for by thirty-six out of the total of thirty-eight members of staff. I did not vote for myself of course, and the only teacher who voted against me told me afterwards that he had not done so on personal grounds, but because he believed in principle that it was better for someone from outside to be appointed. This is an alternative the staff can vote for too if they wish, but apart from that one person no one did so here.

It is a system which I feel is good. I say this not because it resulted in my own election, but because I do sincerely believe that the loyalty and friendship of those who work for him or her are by far the greatest working aids any Head can have. Also I should mention our school's particular tradition, which is that it has been common now for many years for a high number of its teachers having been pupils here themselves, as I was, and this gives us all a feeling of belonging here. We have already now in our senior classes six or seven boys and girls who have stated that when they leave, after attending teacher-training college their first preference will then be to work here if vacancies occur. It can even happen – we have an instance of it now as we speak – that a teacher herself, when she was an older pupil, knew some of those she now teaches when they were pupils. I think this is helpful to all those concerned. In total more than a quarter of our teaching staff were pupils here themselves: so they regard themselves as carrying on the tradition I spoke of earlier, of coming back to work at the school where they had their own education.

Perhaps now you would like to hear a little about our daily routine? It is typical I think of most Russian schools; although I have not visited your country and do not know from practical experience, I think you may also find in many ways it is very similar to your own system. Our first lesson begins at eight-thirty in the morning, and on average the pupils have six lessons each day, lasting for forty minutes. There are two principal breaks – one at ten o'clock when all the pupils have breakfast together, and another break soon after midday when they have their lunch. School finishes at two-thirty in the afternoon, but at midday on Saturdays. The general curriculum, for all pupils at levels graded according to their age, covers a variety of scientific and technical subjects. It also puts equal emphasis on what are called general humanities such as history, the social sciences, and literature. As far as language-teaching is concerned, besides Russian pupils can study one other: the choice is between English or German, with by far the biggest majority – more than two-thirds – taking English. This is both by their own wish, and that of their parents. This is because English is throughout the world the language of information. Wherever you go or whatever you do in life, it will be of great advantage to you to have a knowledge of it. An engineer, an airline pilot, a historian, a medical technician – whatever you can think of as an occupation, anyone with a knowledge of English will be able to communicate with many others in it whatever their nationality. They can also read articles in journals and newspapers which will keep them up to date in their field. I regret very much that I did not study it at school myself, but twenty years ago I am afraid it was not encouraged.

Other languages can be studied also of course: we make arrangements for lessons in them to be given as extra teaching after school hours, in for example evening classes. Such lessons are free of charge, but are not included in the general curriculum because small numbers of pupils for them do not justify a full-time teacher on the staff. Of all other languages, demand for the teaching of Japanese is most definitely showing signs of increase. The reasons are that Japanese people, particularly those engaged in commerce and large-scale construction projects such as the building of hotels and trade centres, are engaged in growing numbers in the USSR, and so obviously there is a demand for knowledge of that language.

Discipline? Well it is not a matter which causes us very many problems or much concerns us in our thinking. I do not know if

Russian children are basically all well-behaved, or what the reason for it is. But I can truly say we have few instances of bad behaviour by school pupils. We think it is perhaps because nearly all Russian children like school and have good relationships with their teachers. The responsibility for the exercise of discipline is emphasised as being that of the class teacher; but the highest punishment of all that can be used is being sent to me here in my office for reprimand. It is something which happens rarely: I do not remember how long ago such a thing last happened, but I think it was about six months ago, so that will give you an idea of its infrequency. No, of course I do not use corporal punishment, what an absurd idea! Even if it were permitted, which it is not, can you imagine someone my size attempting to administer it to a big strong young boy? I would think both he and I would collapse with laughing at the idea of it!

If a pupil behaves badly in any way, including such instances as in regard to other pupils, or does not attempt to do his or her schoolwork properly, it is usually sufficient to correct it by the teacher speaking after class with the pupil concerned. If that fails to put the matter right, then the teacher may threaten to bring the subject up for discussion by the whole class, and of course to carry out this threat if there is still then no improvement. The pupil has to be given the opportunity to speak and explain why the behaviour is taking place, and if it is felt that the pupil's complaint or grievance has substance, there is discussion about what should be done.

If bad behaviour or work still persists, then the pupil may be sent to me. And it is possible, I suppose, that in a very extreme case a pupil who refused to behave in a proper fashion could be expelled. I have heard of it occurring in other schools; but in my time here both as pupil and teacher, I have never known it happen at this school. My own opinion – I'm sure it's that of all the staff – is that if children are not happy at school, do not behave well there, do not work and most importantly do not enjoy working, then there has to be some cause in the child's out-of-school life for this. Therefore instead of punishing the child, we should try to establish the reason for the behaviour, and see what can be done to ease the problem for the child. I believe all children have a natural tendency towards wanting to acquire knowledge, and they enjoy doing it. Anyone who does not have that belief, I think perhaps they should not be a teacher.

I think that the happiest time in a child or young person's life is when they are at school. It is where friendships start, not just with one person but with several: you feel yourself part of a group who are all having the same experiences. You are preparing for life, or you are being helped to prepare for it, and this should be a happy and pleasant experience for you. A way to judge this is I think to consider the way so many school pupils spend their summer holiday, in the period between the end of July and when school begins again early in September. Many activities are arranged for them by the school, or through it: they include summer holiday camps in the countryside, in the mountains or by the sea, and trips to foreign countries. For many years of course these have been to what were known as Eastern bloc countries, but now in these changed times more and more holiday visits are being experienced in countries such as England, France, Italy and Spain. The demands for them and the numbers who wish to go on them are all increasing, and I am sure these visits will greatly help us to understand the way of life and the peoples of western Europe, and their understanding of us. But the point that I make is that so many activities by schoolchildren in the holidays are really, one could say, almost an extension of school. I think if you were to ask schoolchildren if they liked this, or if they would prefer to go away and have nothing to do with school for a while – then most of them would say they had no wish to go away from contact with their school. We would regard our whole school system as a failure if our children were not to have this attitude that they wanted to keep in touch with this school.

What I have been able to say to you in such a short talk as we have had, well of course it has had necessarily to have been sketchy and superficial. I will gladly make arrangements for you to speak with one of our other teachers, who may give you views different from mine. And also of course if you would like it, I would be happy for you to talk without teachers present with one or two different groups of our pupils.

Grigori Valentov,
teacher*

A quiet-voiced man of forty-two with long dark hair, at first while
he talked he kept his eyes fixed on his clasped hands on the table in
front of him; but as he gradually relaxed, he looked up from time to
time with an occasional smile.

– I do not think I shall have much to say that will be of interest to
you, because I am just a person who has an ordinary career and there
have been no great events in my life. I have been a teacher at School
257 ever since I became a teacher, the subject that I teach is history,
and it is to pupils between the ages of eleven and eighteen. I have
been doing this for five years now, from when I began teaching.

I had been before that a clerical worker in the militia section of the
Ministry of the Interior. I was so to say a policeman or detective,
but working in an office, not out in the streets face to face with
people. What I did was to read through material which had been
collected about a case, and put the facts together for the prosecution
to present to the court. I would index the information so that
reference could be made to it in the future, if the same person or
persons involved were again to be charged at another time with a
further offence. It was I would say very boring, a routine sort of
job; if I had had higher qualifications I could perhaps have progressed
further, but I think it was not of sufficient interest for me to want to
make further studies.

The Ministry has its own training schools for such people among
those it employs who wish to make studies, and at the age of thirty
I applied to go to their college where they were offering a course in
early Russian history from the twelfth century. At first I was not
accepted, I could not attain the required standard in the selective

examinations; but after a year I applied again once more and was admitted as a part-time student. This I think was mainly to the credit of my father: he himself had a great interest in that period of history, and he passed on his enthusiasm to me and lent me many of his books to read, and would talk to me at length about it. He has died since seven years ago, but I think had he lived he would now be quite pleased to see what has resulted in me from his interest.

I had been intending also to study law at the Ministry's college, my intention being to make that a principal subject in which to get at least a diploma of higher education, with the historical study as what might be called a specialised area of interest within that. But often we never know what is in store to us, how things will turn out so to say: and it so happened that after I had been studying there for a time, I became friendly with other students who were like me, by which I mean of an age older than the majority of other students. Many of them were training to be schoolteachers, and gradually it seemed to me it would be much more interesting to do that than to confine my vision to working only in an office. Also by that time I had two growing children myself, a boy of ten and a girl of eight, and I liked them very much, and found it always enjoyable to be with them. So that is how my interest began to change towards the idea of trying one day to become a schoolteacher.

It was not easy because I had my regular day-to-day job at the Ministry, and most of my studying therefore had to be done in my spare time in the evenings and at weekends. It took me six years almost to gain the necessary certificates of qualification to teach in a secondary school such as this, whereas if I had been a younger person and done my study full-time at a university, it would have taken me not more than at the most two years I think.

So that was how it happened that I became a teacher, and so far I have not regretted it at all that I made such a change in the middle of my life. I like very much to work with young people of all ages, and at present besides teaching general history from early times to the present, I am also spending in my curriculum a few hours a week with some of the older pupils teaching them elocution. This is because some of them want to become teachers themselves, and wish to learn how to speak clearly and confidently in front of a large group of people; and also because some of them feel that later in life, whatever occupation they have it will always be a useful skill for them to have. Undoubtedly they are correct in this, it does build up an individual's confidence. Perhaps if I had learned it myself at a younger age, I would not have spent such a long time sitting at a desk in the Ministry of the Interior talking only to pieces of paper.

I do not have my own son or my daughter as pupils here at this school, because I do not agree with such situations. It would be very convenient for them to be here because it takes only five minutes to walk from where we live. But I feel that the dangers which would be involved would be too great. Well, by that I mean it would be possible for me to give them greater marks than they should have, because they are my own children – and even if I were not to do that, their classmates may feel that I had done it. Or on the other hand, for the reason that they were my children and I did not want it to appear in anyone's eyes that I was favouring them, it is possible equally that I may give them lower marks than they should have. So it is my decision it is better from every point of view their school attendance should be elsewhere.

I will add that I would be happy for them to be at a school of this standard, and with a good atmosphere such as this one has. I think most of the children who attend are happy here, and tribute should be paid to our Headmistress Alina Moreovich Pashkova for achieving this. However, lest you should think I am perhaps hoping what I have said to you may be repeated to her to my own advantage, let me also add that I do not agree with the system we have in which the Head of a school is chosen by the vote of the staff. I do not think this is a good idea, and I myself was not one who voted for her at the last election. My opinion is that the Head should be appointed by the Ministry of State Education from outside the school, because otherwise inevitably there is a situation where certain groups are friends of the headmaster or headmistress, and favouritism in return occurs. Alina Moreovich has so far avoided this, but I think it will eventually happen here as elsewhere.

What are the principles on which the teaching of history is based in Russian schools today? Well of course this is truly very interesting at this time. There are many changes, and there is much – well I do not think it is too strong a word to use – there is much turmoil in our country. There are so many changes that one simply cannot keep pace with them. I wonder often to myself how I would have fared under the old regime, when the history that was taught was not – well, when it was concerned with modern times at least – it was not history at all: the only word which could be used for it was 'propaganda'. My father used to say to me 'If you are going to talk about history, then you must not deal in lies. If you are instructed to say something which you know is untrue, then you must not say it: you must remain silent about it, never must you tell something which you know to be untrue.' It will not surprise you I'm sure when I tell you my father was on several occasions called in front of the authorities to explain something he had said, or something it had been reported he had said. And he was warned many times that if he continued to say such things, he would be punished for it. He was not a teacher himself: he was a poorly educated man, a peasant farmer only, but he was never afraid to speak his mind at the meetings of his local management committee.

And now, you see, we have the situation since the last four years that we may say openly what we know to be true – that for instance Stalin did many good things for his country, but he was also a tyrant. He was a dictator who caused millions of his own people to die, such as the farmers of the Ukraine by starvation, or by sending anyone who opposed him to prisons and labour camps, and by perpetrating executions and murder. We may also say, it is no longer forbidden to say, that we have many problems in our country: economic problems, crime problems, problems with national republics which no longer want to be part of the USSR. These are now things we can tell, and encourage discussion of the situation, whereas before we were not even allowed to admit they existed. History teachers had to teach – but fortunately not myself because I was not yet a teacher at that time – that everything in the Soviet Union was perfect and every person was happy; the problems that there were in the decadent capitalist countries of the West were of their own making, and demonstrated the corruption of their systems.

The situation today is that in many instances we are still using for example in our classes textbooks which contain these untruths. So we say to our pupils 'These words that are printed here are lies. It is part of our history that untruths were printed in school history-books as though they were the truth, and no one was allowed to say otherwise.' It must give strange feelings I think to older teachers than myself, those who have been willing to perpetuate falsehoods, and now have to stand in front of their classes and tell them that they did so.

I think the children must find it very confusing for themselves too. You cannot teach mathematical lies or chemistry lies or Russian grammar lies – but history yes, you can teach lies about everything that is contained in it, and so it is now the most interesting almost of all subjects to have the responsibility of teaching. That is why, I think, that Alina Moreovich invited me as one of her staff to talk with you, because she perceived it would be an area of interest to discuss, and because she knows my feelings about the subject.

And I would like to say that I think it is of the utmost importance that we teach our children correctly and truthfully now. I remember many years ago when I was a young man I had to do my military service in the Army like every other young man. One of the things I was taught was how to clean and look after and fire a rifle. Well, you know, I have long ago forgotten how to do those things. We do not need them any more, it is no way to solve anything at all by military force. Today, it is our children who must be our rifles.

Thank you, I have enjoyed our conversation very much. I was a little nervous at first because I have never been interviewed in this manner before in all my life. I hope I spoke satisfactorily for you.

Class 8:

Leonti, Sasha, Lisa, Ida*

They sat on chairs in a small wood-panelled group-teaching room at two-thirty in the afternoon; from outside, the noise of traffic came up from the street below through the wide-open windows. The girls wore blue skirts and white blouses, with Young Pioneers' red scarves neatly knotted at their throats; the boys wore black shorts and open-necked short-sleeved shirts.

– *Lisa:* I am Lisa, I am thirteen years of age and I am here today to meet you with some of my friends who, like me, are pupils at School 257 in Moscow Central District.
Ida: I am Ida, I am twelve years old and I am in the same class with the others.
Sasha: My name is Sasha and I am twelve too. If you do not know it already, I should say my correct name is Alexander, but that Sasha is the shortened form of this name in our country.
Leonti: I am Leonti and I am also twelve and in the same class as the others.
Ida: How it happened that the four of us are here is that our teacher asked our class, who all of us have begun to take English lessons, if those who would like to meet a person from England would put up their hands. There are twenty-three pupils in the class, and that was the number of hands that were put up – twenty-three. Our teacher then explained to us that you had said you would like to talk with just a small number, perhaps two girls and two boys. She thought the fairest way to decide who it would be was for us to write our names on pieces of paper and mix them all up together, boys in one group and girls in another, then she would draw out two names from each. That is what we did, and we four are the lucky ones.

Lisa: I would like to welcome you to our country on behalf of the rest of the pupils of our school, and to say we hope very much you will enjoy your visit to Moscow, and meet many interesting people during your stay in our country.

Leonti: This is for all of us our first year of studying English, so at present we have only two English-language lessons a week. Our teacher told us it would be good practice for us if when we met you we tried to speak some English with you, but we have talked about this among ourselves and we feel that as we know so very few words of English yet, it would make us shy to try: so with your permission we will speak our own language.

Ida: Also trying to speak in English might stop us from saying properly what we want to, in answer to your questions.

Sasha: But it is helpful to us to listen to you saying things in English to your interpreter, and then to hear her repeating in Russian what you have said. We do not know what English sounds like when an English person speaks it. Our teacher is Russian, and although I think she speaks a good English, already we have noticed how different many English words sound in the way you say them.

Lisa: I think we should tell you also you are the first real live English person we have ever met.

Ida: You do not look anything at all like what we expected. Perhaps when you came in you will have heard some of us seemed to be a little rude, because we giggled. This was for the reason that it was a surprise to us to see you looked just like an ordinary Russian man, and in no way any different from one.

Leonti: Well since you ask us, I will be the one brave enough to tell you more about what we mean. I hope you will not think it is very rude of me. There is an English writer we read, called Charles Dickens, and in one of his books he writes about a man called Mr Pickwick. There is a picture of him in the book. He wears a coat with a big collar like this, and a scarf and a high hat; and that is how we thought you would look, like him.

Sasha: But we have also seen modern English people on television, on the news and sometimes there is a modern English play, such as one last year which was called *The Forsyte Saga*. We know it is true that people today in England do not dress like Mr Pickwick: really we all know he is what I think is called a caricature, but we still think sometimes that English people look like him.

Ida: But also I think you are different in the way you behave. English people in the play *The Forsyte Saga* and on the TV news and so on, I have always had the impression they are all very tall and have thin faces, and do not talk much. You do not seem to be like that.

Lisa: I have always thought English people were all very serious in their ways, and did not laugh or smile very much.

Leonti: Your country itself and what it looks like, well also it is true that the picture we have of it comes just from what little we have seen about it on television. It is a small country, I think, and you do not have great forests and deserts and plains.

Sasha: My impression is that many people live there in cities that are close together. Once I read in a geography book that you can travel almost the whole length of the country, from one end to the other, in perhaps only a little more than a day's journey on the train.

Ida: I know it is a warm country because of something called the Gulf Stream, which is an ocean current which keeps most of western Europe warm because it comes from near the equator. I think this means also that it rains a great deal in England.

Leonti: And there is always fog, at all times. In all the pictures I have seen on television of London, there is always fog.

Lisa: It is a country that I would like to go and see. Particularly London, because I think there are many interesting things there. There is a bridge that opens in the middle and folds upward like this, I believe it is called Tower Bridge.

Sasha: Yes and it is near somewhere called the Tower of London, which is a very old historical place where they keep prisoners before they are executed.

Lisa: I think they do not keep prisoners there nowadays: today it is just somewhere for people to go and look at.

Ida: Does your Queen live there? I do not know very much about her.

Leonti: I only know that she does not have very much power and is what is called I think a figurehead. And she has some little dogs which I have seen with her in pictures. I do not understand how it is that she can be a queen but not rule the country.

Sasha: My father has been there, he works for a newspaper, and he has told me your country is ruled by a president whose name is Mrs Thatcher. She travels about to different countries and has been here to the Soviet Union.

Ida: Yes, I have seen her on television: she wears smart clothes and looks as though she is a nice person. I understand she will rule your country until she dies, and then you will have to have an election and choose someone else to rule you in her place.

Lisa: I think that is about all we know about England. So now, as you ask, we will take it in turns to say what we like and what we do not like about our school. I am the first who will say. I have tried hard to think what I do not like about our school, but there is nothing much about it that I can think of that I don't like. The building is big and old, and old-fashioned, and I wish it looked nicer; but inside, it is a very friendly place and I think nearly all the children here are happy. Most of all I like the fact that a big number of our teachers were pupils at this same school themselves when they were younger. This gives it a nice kind of atmosphere, with older people and younger people all mixed together in it. I feel it is very important that you like school because that helps you to learn there.

Ida: That is something which I too like very much about the school. Some of the teachers are really very young; not so long ago when some of them were here as pupils, they were happy and so they want to keep that same atmosphere. Another thing I like is there is no fighting in the playground, or perhaps I should say not fighting but rough play. I think this is because most of the boys are too sensible to behave like that.

Sasha: Well, not just the boys but the girls as well.

Ida: Girls don't fight.

Sasha: Oh yes they do, I have seen them.

Ida: Girls fighting – in our playground?

Sasha: No not here at this school, at another one. I saw girls fighting there one day.

Lisa: But you do not come to school to fight, you come to school to learn. You would get into trouble for it here: the teacher would put your name in a book and you would have to go and see Alina Moreovich Pashkova, and she would speak very severely to you.

Leonti: Like the others, I cannot describe anything very much that I don't like about school. But it is easy for me to say what I like: it is all the things that are arranged for you in the holidays if you want to do them. I am soon going to summer camp in the mountains, where there will be a lot of skiing with good instructors. My brother went to such a camp last year, and he says he enjoyed it so much he wishes he was still a pupil at school and could come again this year.

Sasha: Perhaps the thing we should say that we most do not like about school – I think this is true, that most of us do not like it – is that we have to wear school uniform. It makes you feel you have to try and look like everyone else, and think like everyone else, and in every way be like everybody else. I think most of us, if we were given the choice, would prefer to wear our own clothes rather than uniform.

Lisa: But why should we not wear uniform? What is wrong with that? It shows which school we belong to, and that we like it and feel it is a place where we are proud to be pupils.

Sasha: Well I am saying we should have a choice whether we wear school uniform or not, that is all I am saying. I can still feel the things about it that you have described, and I do; but it isn't necessary for me to wear a uniform to do so.

Ida: I agree with Sasha. I like my school very much, but the only thing I do not like about it is having to wear uniform all day. As soon as I get home in the afternoon I put on casual clothes and then I feel more at ease.

Leonti: I asked one of the teachers about this one day, and he said he thought that in only a few years' time, schoolchildren would no longer have to wear uniform if they did not want to.

Lisa: It has been a very enjoyable experience for us to talk to you, and it has been our pleasure to stay after school to talk with you. We thank you for visiting us, and please convey our good wishes to all schoolchildren in England when you return there.

Class 11:

Andrei, Sergei, Nika, Galya*

Perhaps because they were seniors, they seemed more anxious to appear mature and responsible in the way they talked, and this made them less relaxed than the younger pupils. None of them wore anything resembling school uniform: one girl had a blue skirt and white blouse, the other a track suit, and the two boys wore T-shirts and casual-wear trousers.

– *Galya:* We are four pupils from Class 11, which is one of the older pupils' classes, and is mainly for those who will be leaving school next year. Three of us are fifteen years of age, and Sergei is sixteen. We will tell you first who we are and what each of us hopes to do after leaving school. Then after that we will give you our thoughts about some of the subjects you gave us the list of last week, and asked us to tell you our ideas about them. Sergei should speak first because he is the eldest.

Nika: And also because he is a man, and in Russian society it is customary for men to speak and give their opinions and females to hold their tongues.

Sergei: Well very well Nika, I am sure I do not mind at all if you want to speak first yourself. We must not let our visitor think we are as old-fashioned and out-of-date a country as you suggest. So yes please, you speak first.

Nika: Very well then, I will. I am Nika, my favourite subject here at school is biology, and so when I leave I would like to go first to a college of technical education and study it further, for perhaps two or three years in such a college, and then continue with my studies in the same subject at university. I do not know yet which branch of biology I would like to specialise in, but I think in fact possibly it might be plant-biology research.

Andrei: I am Andrei, I am fifteen, and when I leave this school I would like to go to a pedagological institute and be a teacher-training student. I have talked about it with some of the teachers here, and all of them said the same thing, that it is good to be a teacher and they themselves enjoy it. I would not necessarily want to come back and be a teacher at this school: it is something I have not yet made a decision about. That I would like to be a teacher is as far as I have got up to now in thinking about it.

Galya: I would like very much to study law when I leave this school, but I do not yet know if it will be possible because there are certain preliminary examinations to pass first, and I may not do well at them. But that is what I would like to do if I could; and also of course I would like to get married and have a home and one child at least.

Sergei: And now I will be the last one to speak, to show you that it is not true that it is men who always speak first. My own favourite subjects here are economics and international affairs and history. I would like to stay as long as I can as a student, and go to university. But for all young men of my age there is the problem of having conscription in our country and going to the Army: you do not know whether you should get your two years' service over as soon as you can, and then go on with your education, whether you should interrupt your education for two years in the middle of it, or whether you should try to postpone going to the Army until the end of your studies. As I have said, it is a problem for everyone of my age.

Nika: Perhaps before long there will not be conscription any more, and the law will be altered so that those who do not want to go to the Army are free to choose. It is ridiculous that we have such a large army anyway. I think we do not need it at all, or at least not in such a great size as we have.

Galya: I think this subject of conscription was not something you put on the list of things you would like us to talk about, and of course it concerns Sergei and Andrei but not Nika and me. The subjects on the list which do concern us all are, in the first instance, where you have asked us to say what we think will be the most important problems facing our country during our own future lifetimes. Each of us has something to say about it.

Sergei: To me the biggest problem we have to face is the desire which is growing all the time in nearly every individual state in the USSR, for them to break away from the Soviet Union. Many of them are demanding independence immediately, and this is going to be a most difficult problem both for them and for the country as a whole. You cannot just say to the Baltic states such as Latvia, Lithuania and Estonia 'Here is your independence, take it and enjoy it.' All their economy depends upon their trade within the Soviet Union: they depend on it to provide them with essentials such as fuel, power and raw materials – and they depend on it to buy the goods that they themselves produce.

Nika: Before long the whole country will be having a big economic crisis because of this, and so I agree this is probably the most important problem that is likely to face us. Not just the Baltic states but nearly all of the others too in the Union, they have been under the power of the central government to such an extent they have never developed their own realistic economy. I wish some way could be found so that they would have their own government and the freedoms they want without suffering economically. But I think there are many hot-headed people both there in the different states, and here in central government, who are going to make it difficult for it to happen.

Galya: There is a possibility that violence and even civil war could occur because of it. It is important that those in power on both sides should take a wide view and try to reach compromises rather than defeat one another. And another important part of this matter is that because in all their lifetime the peoples of these states have never had freedom and independence, when they get it they will not know how to deal with it properly. Independence means not just freedom for you, but you giving freedom to other people to do what they like too, so I hope people will be tolerant with each other.

Sergei: It is very interesting for me, and I think for many other people too, to see what is happening at exactly the same time in both eastern Europe and in western Europe. It is two absolutely opposite things. In the East many of the republics of the USSR – and as well what were called the Eastern bloc countries – they are all determined to become independent. And just at the same time in the West, all those different countries are trying to come together into one great united European country. Perhaps both sides will learn from each other the difficulties and problems of trying to go in these opposite directions.

Andrei: There is also another problem which I think will grow in size during our lifetimes, as well as this one which we have just been talking of. It is that of the increasing damage which is being done all over the world to the environment. I think people are becoming aware more and more that it is happening, and that we should try to stop it. But matters that we hear constantly about on television, or read about in magazines – such as the destruction of rain forests, the ozone layer, the number of now-endangered species of animals and plants, the pollution by chemicals of seas and rivers and lakes, acid rain and many other things – these are all doing great harm to our environment. We are only just beginning to learn how, and to what degree; and I think there are many cases where we have not even yet woken up to what we are doing. Also our governments will not give us full information about their activities. They are keeping many secrets from us about the way they themselves are causing damage, so it is difficult for steps to be taken to stop them doing these things. I read not long ago about an organisation called 'Greenpeace'. It tries to take action against such things as polluting the oceans with waste matter from nuclear power, or stopping the killing of whales on a huge scale for commercial purposes, and making many other protests of this sort. But it is only a tiny organisation and its opponents such as governments and industrialists have enormous financial resources. So it does not have much power to bring about change. I think these ecological problems are the ones which are going to be the most difficult for us in the future.

Nika: My choice of subject as the most important one we shall have to deal with in our own future lives is – or I hope it will be – the question of how we are going to handle the question of the place of women in society. In USSR we are very backward about this indeed in our attitudes, and we must try to do something about it. Even in the West, according to magazine articles I have read, there is still much progress which needs making. A lot of women are looked upon as no more than slaves and servants, whose only purpose is to marry, raise a family, look after their husband and home, and be content with that for the rest of their lives.

Sergei: That is what a lot of women want to do with their lives, they are very happy and contented that their life should be like that and they do not want anything more.

Nika: Yes of course: it is women themselves who contribute to the problem by thinking like that.

Sergei: But if they are happy to do it, why should someone come along and tell them they shouldn't be happy, they should be unhappy about it?

Galya: Well, I would be happy to do that myself so long as I had a husband who loved me and I loved him. But I would not want to do only that, I would like to do my own work and have my own job as well. I think a problem connected with this is that many men and women get married when they are much too young, perhaps only nineteen or twenty, and then after a few years they find they do not love each other any more, and we have many divorces.

Andrei: But there is a problem too that if two people love each other and want to be together all the time, they cannot find somewhere to live unless they are married. So this means they have to get married to find out if they are suitable for each other. I have read that in the West it is not uncommon for young men and women to live in the same apartment together without being married. But if you would want to do that here, you would not get an apartment allocated to you.

Nika: In most cases a girl's parents would not allow her to live with her boyfriend, who she wasn't married to, in their apartment. So this is another reason why I say the question of women's position is such an important one: a young woman should have the right to choose whether she gets married to the man she likes, or not.

Galya: And finally all of us together think that a very important problem which faces us now in our everyday lives will have passed in a few years' time, by the time we are adults. We hope that it will have been solved, but we are also all agreed that it may not have been. This is the problem of the great shortages of food and other things in our shops. It would be very depressing for us to feel that such a problem was still going to be with us when we are adult.

Sergei: We will try to be optimistic. But I think in our hearts we are not, we are pessimistic.

8 *Are you now, or have you ever been?*

Alosia Buninova, textile factory worker

Klara Paramova, lecturer

Vadim Koronov, art critic

Anatoli Teresov, Party official

Philip Andreyev, professor of English

Alosia Buninova,
textile factory worker*

A well-built woman with her sleeves rolled up, a strong voice and a ready smile, she sat at a table in a small office at the end of one of the vast weaving sheds. She wore white overalls and a white headscarf fastened tightly round her hair.

– I hope you enjoyed looking round our factory and I am sorry it was so noisy that we could not talk together so I could explain everything to you in better detail. But here with the door shut it is much quieter, and now I will be happy to answer any questions you may wish to ask. I have finished my shift for today and I am at your disposal for as long as you wish.

I am fifty-two years of age, and I am the head weaver. We have in this shed a total of 250 looms, and sixty-eight women work here. Some women look after three or five looms, some as many as ten; I look after eighteen because I am the senior and most experienced worker. I love the work, and I do not notice the noise because it is the music of my life. This is why I am going on working still, although I am past the official retiring age of fifty. I have devoted all my life to it, for thirty-seven years ever since I was a girl of fifteen. I hate leaving it, I do not like it when I have to take my holiday, and even going home at night I am only looking forward to coming back again the next morning. What do I like so much? Well, it is just everything, it is good to work here, it is interesting and it is exciting.

In the whole of our factory together there are three thousand workers, and we produce all kinds of cotton fabrics for dresses or for shirts. There are three what we call shops: one for weaving, one for spinning, and one for colouring and decorating. The goods that we produce go to all parts of the Soviet Union, to many parts of eastern Europe such as Hungary, Bulgaria and Czechoslovakia, and we also send goods to countries in Africa, to Pakistan, to China – everywhere you can think of. This is why I say the work is exciting, because we can think every day of all such countries where people are wearing the things we have made.

How I came here first is that I was allocated a job as a textile weaver when I was at school, and then I was placed here. I was happy at once, and I have never wanted to go to some other factory because this one is the best in the Soviet Union. All its workers are happy: you could go to any of our women who we have out there, and I am quite sure you would not find one to tell you she did not like being here. There is great competition to work here, and if there is someone who leaves, at once there will be as many as twenty or thirty who come to enquire if they can have her place. This is because we are well looked after and the conditions are good. It has always been so, and this is widely known in Moscow, that if you are a worker at Factory 33, you will have a good life because there is always thought about improvements.

I married when I was twenty, and when I had my first child there was a nursery nearby and I would put her there while I worked. When my second child was born, by that time there was a nursery within the building; now for new mothers in present times, we have a big kindergarten which provides very good child care. If she wishes, a mother now can leave her child there for the whole of the time from Monday until Friday and only take it home at the weekend. This is of help in cases where there are domestic problems, or if the mother has a long way to travel to come to work, or if she is a mother on her own. Whatever difficulties she may have in any way, she needs only to ask for assistance and it will be given to her.

Now that my children are grown-up, it is possible for me when I go on my holidays to go for some of the group tours that are arranged for us. I have been three times in Hungary, twice in Bulgaria, once in Finland and once in Romania; and also for one visit to France, which is so far the only country of western Europe I have seen. It would not of course have been possible for me to make such visits, because of their cost, unless I did it in this way, with a group from the factory. It was four years ago that we went to

France, and I am sorry to say I have forgotten the name of the town. My impression of it was that it was a very beautiful town, with many things available to buy in the shops but very expensive. People were very hospitable to us and made us welcome, so in every way it was a good visit. But I must also say there were times when I felt strange and uneasy – for example to see so many things in the shops and the rich people buying them, but also to see poor people who wore rags and slept at night in the streets. I would have liked the opportunity to talk with such people and learn how it came about for them to be in that condition. I do not think I could be happy to live in a country where such a thing is possible. But it was interesting for us to see, and important, because it makes us aware of the many good things we have in our own lives.

It is all due, without question in my mind, to the Party; for me there has been no question ever that I should not belong to it, because it has always been the greatest thing in my life. My mother and father before me were Party members, and I have always wanted to belong to it since I first joined the Young Pioneers, and it was my dream to become a member of the Young Communist League as soon as I could. I worked hard, behaved well, and always did as I was told, and at the age of fifteen achieved my ambition. That is why then at that age I was very happy to come here as I did. It gave the opportunity to me to show that I was a good worker and was willing to do my tasks in the shop, and after work to take part in meetings in which production problems were discussed. If your achievement is good and you take responsibilities, then there is a chance you will be offered Party membership.

This was what happened to me, when I was eighteen. I was proud and honoured of course that I should be asked to apply. But I did not, because I examined myself and I did not feel honestly that I was yet ready: I felt that I should spend some more years continuing to prove to myself that I was a worthy enough person. To me Communism is when people are very conscience-minded and always ready to follow a right way of life. It is not something that you will say 'Oh yes, I will join the Party because it will be good for me.' It is much more that you should ask yourself in what way you can contribute good for the Party. It is to live not for yourself only, but for other people, and you must be sure in your mind that this is what you will always do. I think there have been some bad Communists who have not done good for the name of the Party. I think that they joined not for its benefit, but instead only for their own.

I did not become properly a Party member until the age of twenty-seven. All the time I was thinking of it and thinking of it, and I am being frank to say that until then I was uncertain in my heart – not that I wanted to be, but that I may not be good enough to be, and may not be able without hesitation to dedicate the whole of the rest of my life to it. With this result: that when I did make my application, I was completely certain of my feelings. And it is not, you see, simple that you make application and are then accepted. Instead, if you are considered suitable possibly to be accepted, you are then given a period of probation. It lasts for one year. Your duties and your obligations are explained to you; and so you then once more have the opportunity to make final reflections about it. At this same time of probation also, the Party Membership Committee carefully considers you and decides whether to accept you. Everything will be looked at, your work record, all you have done in your life so far, if you have played your part as a good and honest citizen in every way, and if you have devoted voluntary time to Party activities. In this way all information about you that is known is gathered together, as well as opinions sought from others who know you.

The day that I was told the probation was over and I was to be accepted into the Party was one of the days of the greatest joy and pride for me that I had ever had. I had at last the feeling inside myself that I was a fully grown-up person, there is no way better I can explain it than to say that. You have proved something to yourself, and from then onwards you are aware that people are going to look to you for example in every way – in your work, in your home, in what your activities are, and in how you conduct your whole life. So it is natural that from such a time forward you will always keep this in the front of your mind, that people are judging from you the whole of the Party.

In your community where you work and your community where you live, you must be prepared to be a leader; and one who is such not by appointment but by example. At all times you must behave well and considerately, and do only that which is fair and just. Then perhaps you can consider you are fulfilling your obligations. But it is important to say you are doing so only up to a point. You have further responsibilities on top of those of your personal behaviour, by which I mean also to attend meetings of committees, discuss matters of importance, and arrange affairs generally. To give you one example: I spoke earlier about the matter of the visits we had made from this factory to other countries. Well, they do not happen without much preparation; and as a member of the Party you must not see how much work of the arranging you can leave to others, but how much of it you can take upon yourself.

It is not right to boast of such things, because one gladly accepts responsibility and obligations. But I would like to mention this also, that the highest body of the Communist Party of the Soviet Union in Moscow is what is known as the Central Committee. It consists of delegates from all fifteen republics of the Union, plus other members from other sectors of the community including twelve different representatives of industry such as construction workers, machinery-plant workers, light engineering and so on. It is my honour to be the representative of the textile workers: it is something I am very proud to be, and I hope you will not think it wrong of me to have mentioned it. There are in total only 565 members of the Central Committee, so to belong to it is achievement for me that gives me a feeling here in my heart which really it is not possible to describe.

For an ending I would like to say that most of all what we want is for all people to live in peace and friendship together. There should be many more people from the West who come like you to talk with us, because it is always best that people meet each other and talk and decide not again ever to have war. I am sure such meetings will grow in number, because it must happen for the sake of the whole world. I send fraternal greetings from myself and my fellow workers here to the whole of the people of your country.

Klara Paramova,

lecturer

She kicked off her slippers and pulled her feet up underneath her on the sofa and lit a cigarette. Laughing often, lively, animated and articulate, she wore a plain green T-shirt and blue trousers.

– OK, you want to know about being a good Party member, well I will tell you. I'm not a good Party member, but I know many people who are, so I will tell you about good ones and this one particular not so good one. Let me work it out: I'm thirty-nine and I joined the Party at twenty-four so that means fifteen years as a member in what is the phrase, good standing – paying my dues, sometimes going to a meeting to elect a delegate to this conference or a representative for that occasion, but not much else. I'm not an active member, I don't take my share of responsibilities. Why? Well because I am not a good Party member, as I told you. And I'm not a good Party member because I don't believe in Communism, it is as simple as that. Nor do a lot of Party members, does that surprise you? It should not. Shall I give you the picture for myself and see if it helps you understand what I mean?

From since when I was twelve or perhaps thirteen, the thing I wanted most in life to be was a teacher. I don't know why, my family were not in any way academic: my father drove a train on the Metro, my mother worked in a factory that made fittings for machinery which was used in heavy engineering. But for me only teaching was what I was going to do, I was determined about that. And to be not just a teacher of any kind of subject, but only one, which was English. I liked doing English at school, it came to me easily, and in all my spare time whenever I could get them I read English books. Everything, anything: the classics, old-fashioned writers, modern ones – Shakespeare of course naturally, Dickens, Walter Scott, H. G. Wells, Bernard Shaw, Agatha Christie, it didn't matter what.

From school I went on to higher education, university, and then a language institute – the same one in fact where I'm now a lecturer. I was a good student, a very good student, always high marks and having commendations, being praised as the best pupil in the class and such things. You know sometimes I felt almost a cheat, because I was doing so well, but not because I was making huge effort. It was only because it came so easily to me, almost I didn't have to try. English was truly like my mother tongue by the time I was twenty.

Then there was the matter of the Party, and being a member of it: that too was a great help in moving me upwards in my career. Like every person, at school I was a Young Communist, a member of the Komsomol. You didn't think about it, you just were: you didn't want to be any different from anyone else in your class or your age group, there was no question of being so. It's taken for granted at school: you're a member of the Young Communists because every-one else is. It's not something at that age you even think about.

What was the important question was whether or not after that you went on and joined the Party, or whether you didn't bother. Most people in fact, they don't bother. In the Soviet Union I think it's only one person in ten who's a Party member, that's all. And the proportion's all the time now becoming less and less. They never used to publish figures of course, but now under the new regime they do. There's a radical weekly called *Moscow News* which regularly publishes information of this kind; a few years ago it would not have been allowed. It's printed in I think nine different languages, and when I can get one I get the English edition. That had the latest figures last month and it was commenting that recruitment was now declining very sharply. I particularly liked their headline to the article: it was headed 'The rising fall in Party membership' which I thought was nice, though I don't expect they intended it to sound so funny. I wanted to write and say to them something like 'Never mind the rising fall, what about the falling rise?'

Anyhow to come back to the membership subject. What I've just been saying, well I think now I wouldn't bother to join. But in those days fifteen years ago, there was no doubt that if you wanted to get on it would be a great advantage to you to be a Party member. In certain spheres, if there was a vacancy and two people applied for it and one was in the Party and the other wasn't, it would be always the Party member who got it. In fact it was more than that: if there were nine people applied and only one was in the Party, there was no point in the other eight bothering. In the world I was in, what you might call the academic world in which the number of teaching posts was limited, it was very much like that. I am speaking of higher education: which had been the position I wanted, not that of a schoolteacher.

Yes, I am saying that precisely – joining the Party was for me entirely a calculated way of furthering my career. It had nothing at all to do with ideals. But of course you can't just open the door and walk in: when you apply, there is first a period of a year when you are what might be called a conditional member. You have to prove yourself in that year, not just by giving correct answers to questions about the Party's principles and beliefs, but also by attending a certain number of meetings, volunteering to go on certain committees, and give up a lot of your spare time to Party work. It might be more difficult for a manual worker, I don't know; my parents by the way, neither of them was a Party member – but in the academic world it wasn't difficult to give the impression that you did more than you actually did. You contributed ideas to debates and discussions, you nodded your head seriously when things were said, you tried your hardest to look as though you were very involved in everything.

I was accepted into full membership after the year: I was then aged twenty-four. And I would think it was at the most three years afterwards, or more maybe like two, that I became a complete dissident. I've stayed one ever since. Principally it was because once I was in the Party, I could see it in a clearer light and understand it better. So for me then there came the belief both that Communism was wrong, and also that Communism didn't work and would never work. Originally Communism was based on the ideology of Karl Marx, on ideals of equality for all. From this he tried to ensure a system of daily life which followed these ideas. But those who came after him, when they came to power, where real life wouldn't fit in with the system, instead of changing the system and adapting it to circumstances, they tried to change people so they would fit the system. First it was by persuasion and then, horribly as everybody now knows, by Stalin with persecution and oppression, killing and lying and deceiving and every other wicked measure there was. The astonishing thing I think though is that people allowed it to happen. As to why they did, I suppose that has to do with our history. We were a people who were slaves and serfs, without rights and without any concept that we should have rights. I think deep down inside of us, most of us still have this idea: we're not a governing people, we're a people who accept that by some kind of natural law, it's we who should be governed. I don't think we have much pride in ourselves as people: we don't have much sense of ourselves as individuals. My parents were like that. It disturbs me a lot, and quite often too, that I can still feel it remaining in myself.

But well, I am still a member of the Party and I shall remain one. At its simplest it is because if I was to do something that would draw attention to me, like not continuing my membership and stepping down from it – well then I think almost certainly, I would lose my present job as senior lecturer. I got it because of those who were in contention for the vacancy, I was the only one who was in the Party – and from this it is correct to deduce yes, the members of the appointments committee were nearly all themselves members of the Party.

I feel a little freer now in the last few years to say things and do things that are critical, even things that are against the government. A thing I feel strongly about for instance is the lack of information there has been about the after-effects of the disaster at the nuclear power station at Chernobyl. Information about it is released only a little bit at the time, piece by piece you could say, and more or less only when it has to be. But many things are still covered up, on the grounds that such information is they say 'not in the public interest to be divulged'. Most people still do not know the true facts because they haven't been given out – exactly how many people have died from radiation sickness, how many malformed babies there have been born, exactly how many surrounding villages and towns have been not just evacuated but actually rased to the ground. It's an almost endless list, all these things we haven't been given the true facts about, or in some cases not yet even any facts at all.

What I am saying is this: or rather two things. One is that I am no longer afraid of speaking out on the subject to my students. I do not think any of them would now be inclined to inform on me for it to the authorities. And the second thing is that because I am still a Party member, I have more freedom to speak as I do than somebody who is not. It is in some ways a very ironical position I think. I regard myself as a soldier of the cause: but only a foot soldier, perhaps almost no more than a mercenary. Some I suppose might describe it as a form of cowardice, but I don't see it as so myself. Perhaps it is cynical, perhaps it is sceptical; I think it doesn't greatly matter, because to me most of all it is realistic.

I am not a Communist, and don't believe in Communism, for the simple reason that I think it takes too rosy a view of human beings and it doesn't work. You could say I am not a Christian either, for almost the same reasons. I know there are good Communists and bad Communists, and not all the bad things done in the name of Communism are the fault of the system of itself. But I think it lacks things, and some of the things it lacks are serious. First I would put self-respect or a feeling of the value of people as individuals. I have never been to the West, but of course at the place where I work I have met a lot of people from the West – and there is something about their manner, their self-assurance, which is unlike that of Russian people. I think this can only be the fault of Communism: it may have done, it has done, many good things, but it has never somehow built up dignity in people. There are many catch-phrases, 'the dignity of labour' and such sayings; but there isn't one for the dignity of a person as a person, it's an idea which doesn't even exist.

I think I will not change in my views very much now, not at the age of forty: I think I will remain as I am, a Party member but not a good one because I don't share its beliefs.

Vadim Koronov,
art critic

A tall, broad-shouldered man, with a mass of unruly fair hair and a gingery beard, he wore an open-necked check shirt, black corduroy trousers and sandals. He sat drinking mineral water at a table outside a pavement café on a mild autumn evening.

– I am art critic and writer and my English is not good, if you will forgive me: I read many books when I was younger man, but it was not until ten years ago I travelled outside USSR, to England and USA, and heard there people saying English. Before that only on the radio. You think it is good, well thank you; I think like all Englishmen you are polite and would not say it was not good even if you thought so yes?

Well now, to talk to you about the Party and what I think, I will do my best. The background of my family I should tell you first of all, and perhaps it will surprise you. You look at me, you see me like this, and this is how I am always: a mess, that is what my wife says to me, that is what she tells me how I look. And she is so beautiful herself you know, smart, neat, always tidy: she despairs that I will change. But I may not have been like this, I could not have been like this, it is very possible if I had followed the career my parents wanted for me. Then I think you would have seen me look completely different. Because you see I would have been a soldier: in uniform, very smart, sit up like this, you know what I mean?

I am only child, both my parents are dead now, and all his life my father was an officer of the Soviet Army, a high-up officer so to say, of considerable rank and good position. We lived many years in Moscow because this is where he worked, he was to do with the ministry that supplied Army vehicles. He was at one of the central depots and was in charge of it. So we had a good apartment with three bedrooms, which was because of his position both in the Army and also in the Communist Party, he was a high-up person in that too.

Until fourteen years of age I went to a special school for those who were children of Army officers and the sons of Party members. A place of education for the children of privileged people; but that does not mean it was an easy place to be, or you did not have to work hard. You had to work very hard, harder than at ordinary school I would say, because it was to prepare people for careers that their parents wanted for them. For me it was intended that I should follow my father into the Army.

Well, I did not like this very much. The school studies were quite difficult for me, many things to do with mathematics and scientifical subjects and they did not interest me, I preferred artistic things such as music and painting and literature, things of that sort. And I did not like the training camps we went to all the time, where they teach you to be tough, to do running and sports and boxing, the physical things you will need to learn to be the good Army officer. Not for me all that side of it, thank you.

But of course it made for great difficulties. From when I was eleven I think, I became aware that to follow the example of my father – well really it was outside any possibility for me to achieve it. I remember an occasion when I had failed some very necessary examination to pass upwards to the next grade. 'Please Vadim,' my mother said, 'please Vadim try harder, your father is so disappointed you do not do better at school, he wants so much for you to succeed.'

I knew it but I did not know what to do. He was a kind man, always very kind, and he would never have said such a thing to me as my mother did. That was not his way. He hoped I would do better but he hid his disappointment in me, you understand? It was never his way to give me punishment or reprimands even, if I did not do well. Instead he would try to find things he could give me praise for and encouragement. My father was always a kind and good person, always so to say a man of ideals, which was why he was always a Communist. The second thing in his life, it was always the Party: the first was the Army, and then the Party. He was very enthusiastic for it and for all its ideals: when I was still only a little boy as big as this, he would tell me stories about the Revolution and its heroes. It was from him I heard for the first time the saying of Karl Marx that each person should give according to his abilities, and should be given according to his needs. My father would say it often, it was his guiding principle.

Every person should live and work for the benefit of others, my father believed that with all his heart. I also remember another thing he said: the Great Patriotic War had shown to the world what a fine society we had in USSR. It was proved: so many millions of people had been ready to fight to their death to defend it. The end of it, the final victory, was the year of my birth; and his view was that I had been born into the perfect society and would be brought up to be a good citizen of it. I have spoken with friends often of this: it is difficult for those of us who are too young to have memory of those times to know what it meant to people then. They saw it as such wonderful achievement never to have surrendered to an enemy which had conquered almost every other country in Europe. It is true, it was; but you can never feel it so deeply as those do who were there and took part.

And then we come to Stalin, and how it came that he could do such cruelties to his own people at the time before the war and then to continue in the time after it. I think it should perhaps be said like this: there were those, the greatest number, who did not know of the things that happened, there were those who did not want to know, and there were a few who did know but remained silent. I think my father was in the middle category. One or two times as I was growing up, no longer a child but not fully an adult, he would say to me 'Vadim, there have been mistakes and wrong things have been done in the Party,' and he would look very sadly and shake his head. It was no longer possible you see for those who did not want to know what a monster Stalin had been, for them not to know. At the time after his death what Khrushchev had said became knowledge generally, and I think my father would have been among those who learned early. I remember that he talked with me once and he did not say to me what he knew, but he spoke of something he called 'protecting the Revolution' and striving always to carry out Lenin's ideals. It was never my father's way to lie, but it was not his way either to throw away the whole philosophy of his life because of Stalin. The Revolution had survived the war, and it would survive Stalin's atrocities too, I think that was his aspect towards things.

If I talk again now of personal things, when I came to be eighteen and to leave school, I knew definitely in my mind I was not suitable to have an Army career, and my father knew it also. But it was then the time for my conscription, and my father talked with me frankly about it. He said he knew I did not like the Army and would not want to have my future in it, and he said that he would like me to tell him which of two possibilities I would like to do. He was very honest, he always was, very frank about it. There was the possibility that because of his position he could make it sure that in my period of service I would not have to go very far away from Moscow, as is the rule in most cases. He would do it he said if I told him it was what I wanted. But he said he would like me to know also he did not think it right influence should be used in this way, and in his opinion I should do my service like every other young man.

Of course when he said this I agreed immediately: all my life he had influenced me towards a way of thinking that what should be done was what was right, not what was the most comfortable and convenient. I could see from his face that when I said this he was immediately pleased. And so I went away from home, in fact to the Odessa region which was perhaps two thousand kilometres to the south. I had an easy time, but this was not because of who I was the son of: it was just that you are allocated to jobs and positions by what you might say was a lottery system. For me it came that most of my time was spent in clerical administration, because of my knowledge of Army methods and procedures which I had learned at school.

The Commanding Officer of the camp I was in had been in previous years in a similar position in Moscow, and he was a friend of my father. He did no favours for me because of it, but sometimes he would sit and talk with me and tell me stories of the times they had had together, what good friends they had been, what a good man he was. They of course were true. Soon I felt I could confide in him, he was a fatherly person to me: so I told him one day that I knew how much I had disappointed my father by not going forward into a career as a professional soldier. He nodded his head that he understood it; but he was like my father also, because he did not reprove me about it. Instead after some days when we were talking one evening again, he said he knew of something I could do which would please my father as much, or perhaps even more, than if I joined the Army as a professional soldier – which would be if I joined the Party. I was astonished, the idea had not occurred to me; but he said that if I wished, he could arrange for me to meet certain people who could help me achieve it.

About that, I was not unenthusiastic: I had absorbed all these ideals and ideas from my father already, and I saw them not only as dogmas or creeds but as standards to live by. So in the two years I was away from home that is exactly what I did. Like all other pupils I had been in the Young Communist League, the Komsomol, at school, and so I went on from that point. Let me tell you, I was good Party candidate: I did all the things it is necessary you should do, attend meetings, volunteer for work in your spare time, everything. Let me say as well because it's true, that I enjoyed it. The Commanding Officer must to a certain extent have used influence to bring me to the notice of important Party people; I am sure of that, but I am also sure that I was not an unwilling candidate for membership. I was doing it entirely because I wanted my father to see, when I returned from my conscription service, that I had at least one achievement.

I had told him nothing about it in letters written home; so that when I got back, I was able to surprise him and say what was true by then, I had become a member of the Party. It was like coming home and laying it as a present at his feet. I did not know it, but he was ill at that time, and it was only in a few months afterwards that he died. So I was very glad at what I'd been able to do.

I am still a member. You might almost say it is in memory of him, I am carrying on the family membership. My mother also is dead now, but I continue to belong to the Party. I am not enthusiastic, I am not unenthusiastic; but I am sure I shall stay always a member. In my daily life, in my occupation, I would say almost it is irrelevant, if I am talking about if it advances my career because it does not. My membership is valuable to me only for personal reasons, that is all.

Anatoli Teresov,
Party official*

A small plump bald man, while he talked he kept his hands clasped lightly in front of him on his large desk, which had nothing on it except a blotter, a notepad and a telephone. Behind him on the wall above his head was a large framed drawing of Lenin.

– I am Deputy Chairman of the International Section of the Workers' Union for Peace and Friendship, and I came to this position three years ago. Before that, from a young man of twenty-two, I had different responsibilities to do with such things as financial affairs, economical developments, conference organisations, the forming of delegations to conferences world-wide, and the accommodation and host arrangements for delegations which came to us from other countries. I travelled a great deal to do with my work: to Eastern European countries, but also to Greece, Italy, Spain, Israel, Iran – there are too many to name all of them, but I will mention also Japan and USA. It has not been my fortune yet to visit your country, but I hope I shall have opportunity to do so next year.

Our union began its existence at the end of the Great Patriotic War, when it had the name of Workers Against Fascism. It had the chief function then of affiliating with similar bodies both within the Soviet Union and outside, for mutual help and assistance and the making of contacts: so to say, the building of bridges between workers in the same industry in different countries. Miners, steel workers, railway workers – our purpose was to make it possible for such groups of people to visit one another and talk together of mutual problems. At the end of the war, it extended its efforts with the purpose of including those who had been engaged in such occupations but perhaps in the war on opposing sides, so that they could come together in peace and friendship. This is why the name of the organisation was then changed: it called itself no longer against something, but instead for something.

We now today have friendly contacts with 350 different organisations in 120 countries, which you will agree I am sure means a very broad activity. Our committee is everywhere the official representative of the Party, and is very glad always to have the opportunity of making welcome guests from any country anywhere and to extend the hand of friendship to them. Within the agenda of the visit, in all cases we try to do two things. One is that groups of people who have shared work-interest, they can discuss such matters freely in what are so-called open forums. They share their problems and working difficulties, listen to each others' methods of overcoming such problems, exchange knowledge about methods, and very many other things which will be of use, or if not of use then of interest, to their own worker-colleagues when they return to their own countries and tell them about them. But as well as activity of this kind, what is just as important to us is that they should get to know Soviet people as individuals. This is the second thing we do. For this purpose there is time for them on a visit to have the open forums and to go sightseeing in Moscow – but also it is arranged that they should meet people privately in their homes, see how they live, and talk to them person to person on such a level as you and I are doing now.

Often it is said afterwards to us by our visitors, that of every part of the programme agenda, it was that one which they found to be the most interesting and of the greatest value. And I think this is so, it is truly of the greatest importance. When people have opportunity to know each other in this way, much progress is made in the way affairs are conducted from one nation to another. You see someone's difficulties, you speak with them and hear about them from that person, and so you understand of the many different viewpoints which there are.

I would like now to tell you a little of our financial situation. Principally our funds come from the Party's own funds, but there is also something we have which is called the Workers' Annual Peace Day. Its purpose is to allow people to each make an individual contribution to peace, and in a practical way. On this day, all workers are invited to give that day's work to the Peace Fund: whatever they would be paid on that day, they nominate to give it to the Fund. It includes every person to have the opportunity, even those such as myself who are responsible to administer for it. For that day's work, which is concerned only with work for raising financial support and nothing else, we do it ourselves entirely for nothing. It is our duty, so to speak, to give the example for others to follow; and of course to do it willingly and proudly.

Yes you are correct, that is the way always with the Party. It is called the path of example, and it is to return thanks to the Party for what it has done for us. Well I would say in answer to your question that it has improved the quality of our lives – not just the lives of the people who are its members, but of all people of the Soviet Union.

That it brings privileges to be a member? This is a difficult subject to speak of, and one which there has been a great deal of wrong information about. It has been said in the past, there has been talk of it, that some Party members in high positions used that fact to obtain for themselves such things as better accommodation, food of better quality, more easily obtaining permission to travel abroad – talk even of such things as large motor cars, big dachas in the country with swimming pools – many many things have been said. So well I will tell you: there are instances of such things occurring, yes it is true. But two things must be said also on the matter. One is that I do not think you would go to any country at all in the world and find it different: those who are in the higher positions, they do have certain things of a higher standard, yes. It is not the doctrine of Marxist Leninism, which is that all men should be equal: it contradicts that entirely, but I will say again yes, it is sometimes that it is so. Undoubtedly.

And the second thing to be said is of equal importance or more. It is that there have also been cases where, when such discoveries have been brought into the open, those who have taken advantage of their position to obtain privileges to which they were not entitled – well then, they have been punished and they have been removed from their positions. There have been in fact some celebrated cases by people who, shall we say, were brought to justice when they did not expect it, because they thought that their position, or the fact that they were related to someone who was very high up, would protect them. Well, it did not.

Allow me to speak more to you of the subject of my own privileges. I think it is better to answer your question in this way, to talk of myself instead of other individuals. I will then be speaking exactly what I know, not repeating statements about other people which I may or may not know the truth of. My own privileges are these. First, I do not have a splendid apartment; my apartment has two bedrooms, one used by my wife and myself, and the other by our son who is sixteen. It has also a kitchen, a bathroom and a toilet – and one very great luxury, which is what you would call a dining-room which in size is less than half the area of this room we are in now. No, much less even, perhaps even only one-quarter of the size. You may if you wish come to see it. I think already during the time you have been here you will have been in larger apartments, and most of them owned I think by people who are not Party members.

Secondly, the subject of my son's education. He goes to an ordinary school in the centre of Moscow, where there are six hundred pupils. He has never had special education because my wife and I have never sought it for him, we think his schooling should be of the same standard as any other child's. And now, a dacha in the country: let me talk of that. Yes I have a dacha in the country, as do many thousands of other citizens of Moscow. It does not have a swimming pool, indeed it does not have a bath or a water-flushing toilet, since there is no plumbing for it. It does not have central heating, it does not have a carpet on the floor, it has an old table and chairs, and two old beds. What it is I will tell you simply, it is what may be described as being like a small or medium-sized shed. For many people, of whom I am one, a dacha in the country is a place where you go at the end of the week for two days to lead the simple country life and to rid your lungs of the petrol fumes of the city. There is no electricity there of course, and no road near it, only a long path in the woods. It is not near a town or a village, so therefore always you take your own food. And last I should say of it that it was not purchased for me through Party funds, it was something I bought for myself and my family ten years ago from the uncle of my wife, because he was becoming old and found it was no longer habitable. It is still not greatly habitable, but one of the things in my spare time I like to do is to make repairs for it, to paint it and to do things to it with my hands.

Now my car. Yes I have a car, a small car which I drive myself. This perhaps I think might be under the heading of a privilege, since it is provided for me by the Party. I have much travelling to do in my work around Moscow and so it is used for this. You will see every day that thousands of other people in Moscow also have similar cars, not just members of the Party. If I use it for my own purpose, such as going with my family to our dacha, I pay for the petrol I use myself.

And what else for my privileges? We do not shop at the special shops that are available to some individuals who are in higher positions, and it is for two reasons: one is that I do not agree there should be such places, and the other is it is anyway very expensive because most of the contents are what would be described as luxury items – drink, clothing, perfumery and such things. If you came to my home, it is true you would see a small number of such items – good coffee, Indian tea, a little French wine – and these things I obtain from the one privilege which I do have in being a Party member of some position, which is that for many years now it has been easier to travel to other countries than it has been for most other people.

This is the privilege that I do have as a Party member, and if it is something some people would say is wrong, then I cannot agree. As I have told you, it has been part of my work always to travel, for the arrangements I was speaking of earlier. I may say incidentally that sometimes, quite often, I did not enjoy the fact that I had the privilege of travel. I would go let us say to Helsinki for two weeks; and on my return would be told that in two days' time I was to be in Cairo because there had been some mix-up of something which was necessary urgently to be put right. So travel was not always a privilege but a duty.

I answer always that I do not think it is wrong that for their work Party officials should travel; and perhaps if they like some country and make some friends there, another time to take their wife with them for a short holiday. Why not? There is nothing wrong with that. What is wrong is not that we can travel: it is that other people cannot travel, and this is wrong, yes.

There are as you say many questions to discuss and it is true we have spoken of only a few of them. It has been interesting for me, because not many persons come to speak of them in this fashion, it seems often they would prefer only to set down their opinions which are to be put forward as facts.

Philip Andreyev,
professor of English

The walls of his study at the university were lined almost from floor to ceiling with shelves crammed with books. The room was small and so was his desk: he put his swivel chair in front of it, swinging himself slightly from side to side as he talked. He wore a shabby green corduroy jacket and an open-necked shirt; he was bearded and in his mid-forties.

– First let me say when you telephoned and asked if you could come and see me, and indicated something of what it was you would like us to have a talk about ¬ well perhaps it may surprise you when I say I had not ever given a great deal of thought to the subject of why I was a Communist and why I was a member of the Party. Why, what else would I be? I thought; and then after that, Why should I not be? The subject, the question, the thought – it surprised me a little that it should ever occur. Living in an ivory tower, perhaps that is what I am, like many other academics do you think? Not here only in this country, but everywhere: I suppose we all do this, take ourselves and our beliefs for granted.

Stalin, you know, was extremely determined in his policy of fostering xenophobia, the dislike and suspicion of all foreigners, and his influence remained strong in this respect at least for many years after his death. Through almost all of the Brezhnev era and right up until a few years ago in fact: it can still be detected in a considerable number of the older generation of people. They were taught to see enemies everywhere, to be suspicious, on their guard – and who more easy to direct this at than foreigners? So although now they are told all the time foreigners are not all bad, some of them are good and we need their friendship, they still have the unease and the fear they were born with, which was ingrained in them when they were young.

The other people who kept much of this attitude, they were the members of the Party, the 'old guard' Communists as they are known. One of my earliest memories of the first school I went to is of several of the teachers there who were always propounding this idea, in the most crude basic ways. In geography, here is our glorious USSR and then here is the rest of the world, full of countries which are small and unimportant, or else they are big and corrupt and no one who lives in them is happy, because they would all like better to be living here. In history, on such a date we beat such and such a nation in battle, then on another date we beat so and so: no one ever beat us, unless it was that we were betrayed or our generals were aristocrats and fools. In literature, our great Russian writers of whom we have so many that we are the envy of the whole world, in music the same, and in painting too of course. Even in science; this invention was originally made by our scientists, this discovery in medicine was ours. On and on, and nothing else.

But what happened with me was something quite different, I suppose because of my ancestry. My father and mother, both were Russian and so also were my grandparents; but on my mother's side, not her grandfather but her great-grandfather, he had been Dutch. It's from him that I have my name, I think he was perhaps a sailor who had come here and met and fallen in love with a girl, and married and stayed. So I never, if I may put it this way, I never had the feeling there was anything to be feared from people of other nationalities. I didn't protest at what the teachers were saying, I don't recall I felt awkward about it even: I just had the conviction it was not correct. I was impervious to their influence, I will put it like that. It brought disappointment to me later in my life, because the first time I visited Holland ten years ago, to stay for a term as a visiting Fellow at one of their universities, I was expecting I would feel much at home, as though I was returning to my native land. Unfortunately I felt nothing of this kind. I did not find Dutch people to be friendly as I had expected, I did not understand them in any way, and my predominant feeling was one of homesickness.

It surprised me too that I found so many of them to be aggressive towards me: to have, I can almost say, the same kind of negative feeling about all foreigners – certainly in my case Russian foreigners – in reverse to the one which was then common in USSR. A man at the university, a professor in fact, said angrily to me one day when we were having – well it was not even an argument, only a mild difference of opinions on some small matter – he said 'You Commies are all the same.' I was completely astonished, because I had never at any time so far as I could recall entered into political discussion with anyone, and certainly not with him. It astonished me also that he should take it for granted I was a Communist. He was an educated well-read man, but he was making – though on no grounds at all – the assumption that all Russians were Communist Party members. Of course only a minority of them were, even at that time.

Where his assumption was doubly incorrect was in the saying that all of us Communists are 'the same'. We are very far indeed from that, very far. I think I could summarise my meaning by saying that as it is possible to be a Communist without being a member of the Party, so it is possible – and it happens in many cases – to be a member of the Party without being a Communist. The second category, you may say, are members because it is expedient, not out of fundamental belief.

It is very complex, all of it. You will find the man who has been a Party official all his life, and who you may say has always dedicated himself to the function of saying whatever is the Party line on everything. He repeats words and phrases: he does not always understand them even, but he will go on repeating them like a parrot until he is told to say something else. I have known it literally happen that within perhaps one week only, a person will say two things which are completely contradictory. One clear example was at the time of the war in Afghanistan: I have heard with my own ears one Party official who was defending the need for our troops to be there on one day, and then only within a few days was saying with equal force that it had been a bad mistake, an unjustified incursion of Soviet armed force, and was to be brought to an end as soon as possible. It happened that I met him only a few days after this; and I spoke to him directly about it. I quoted to him his words on the two occasions, I asked him how he could say those two completely different things. He answered me calmly; it didn't seem to me he was aware even there was anything wrong with his answer. Which was: 'It was what I was told to say.' He was not angry at the matter, it was just as a soldier says 'I was obeying orders'. That is sufficient, that is the justification and no more is needed than that, 'It was what I was told to say.'

Party members of that sort – well let us say frankly, there are many of them, and it is almost a time now when one begins to feel sorry for them. A lady last week approached me, she said she had been asked for guidance by one of her students; it was on this very point in fact of whether he should, or he should not, make application to become a Party member to improve his chance to further his career. She went to see the Principal of her department, who himself is a lifelong Party member, to ask him what advice she should give her student in reply, and was told 'Say to him whatever you like.' This lady, she was struck dumb, she was dumbstruck, yes? She came to me and she said 'I am forty-five, for the first time I have been told I may say whatever I like – and I don't know what to say!' She was truly distressed, truly, in completely a dilemma.

So that is one kind of Party member, so to say the loyal one who is happy to follow instructions, but is lost absolutely when they are not given. Then there is another kind, which is the one who is always arguing and discussing, to the end of every small detail. It surprises me sometimes – no, I would say more that it surprises me quite frequently – how critical members can be of the Party and themselves, and I do not mean in an abject way but in a way that seems to have only the wish to behave honestly. You have heard it said perhaps that the Communist Party is a party of puritans, and I think it is true. It is strongly opposed to such things as prostitution, drugs, sexual immorality, pornography, to any kind of fraud or corruption or stealing, genuinely on the grounds that it believes such things are wicked and sinful. It is strange to have words with religious connections like 'wickedness' and 'sin' in a State where religion is not at all encouraged, but that really is the strength of their feeling. These people too you see, they also are now in a dilemma: so much every day is being heard of people in the Party discovered giving and taking bribes, abusing their positions of power, of being some way or another by whatever definition you choose, corrupt – so for them it is as though they were seeing a dream of what shall we say, the natural goodness of man, crumbling to a dust in front of their eyes. The sadness it causes them is very great. Some, many, have gone on trying to close their eyes to the existence of so much corruption. Now it is no longer possible for them to do so, and it is very painful.

So as to what is my position, how do I stand on this subject – well as I have told you I have been asking myself, in preparation for our talk. Very well: the first thing to say is that I am a born Communist, in the same way that in other countries other people are born Roman Catholics, born Quakers, born aristocrats, born paupers or whatever label they may wish to use. I am not a passionate Communist advocate: I take it for granted as the natural and correct way of life. And because of that I am a Party member, just as because of it my parents too were Party members. It would be to say in the same way to a religious person, you cannot really call yourself a true religious person if you do not go to church. So, you cannot call yourself in the same way a true Communist if you do not belong to the Party.

If the Party shows itself to have been corrupt and to have been misused by many individuals only for their own advantage, does this mean I will turn my back on it? No it does not. It means I will remain a member of it and try to ensure that the Party will get rid of those individuals and become upright again. This is an unlikely event that all corruption will be ended for ever, perhaps it is not within human nature to achieve it. But I will hope that it could happen, and I will stay in the Party and try hard to bring it about.

If certain people in the Party show themselves to be unthinking, if they say this one thing yesterday and another different one today – does that mean I will think the Party is only for fools and people who don't have principles and say only that they obey orders, and turn my back on it for that reason? Again no, because I know very many people in the Party who are not like that, who are people of ideas and principles completely.

I accept that the Party has failings: it has always had, sometimes very great and terrible ones as in the time of Stalin. I do not know what it is, your own personal belief, but I hope in saying this I am not offending it: so has the Roman Catholic church, in the days of the Spanish Inquisition – but so far as I am aware, that has not stopped people in any great number from following the Catholic faith. I shall not, I am sure, change: I shall defend the Party from criticism when there is need to, but I will never say, I hope, that it should not be criticised.

9 Visitors

Katerina Rovno, schoolgirl

Marina Belskaya, Academician

Larissa Bishop, library assistant

Dmitri Nemirovsky, tourist

Katerina Rovno,
schoolgirl*

Only five feet tall, she wore her hair tightly drawn back from her pale and delicate-featured face, and fastened in a braid on top of her head with a black velvet bow. She played with a small silver locket in her long-fingered hands while she talked.

– It is with pleasure that I welcome you to the home of my father and mother and myself here in Moscow. I am seventeen years of age, my name is Katerina, and I am in the highest grade at my school. Just last week only, I returned to Moscow from a visit to England, where I had been on a visit for two and a half weeks with a party of twenty-three of my fellow school-pupils, both boys and girls. It has been agreed that the same number of English boys and girls will come here on a reciprocal visit later on in the year; and like we did, they will stay in the homes of families of other school-children, and perhaps spend also some time in lessons at our school.

We went to stay for the whole of our visit in the big city of Manchester, which is an important city in the north-west of England. The only other country I ever visited before, outside Russia, is Cuba. My father when I was ten years of age worked there for four years as an engineer, and my mother and I lived with him there. So for that reason I had the idea in my head before I went to England that Manchester would be like Cuba, with sandy beaches and blue skies and palm trees waving in the wind. But when I got there I found that it was not so: Manchester is not in any way at all like Cuba, it is different in every way. And I liked Manchester very much better than I liked Cuba. One thing for me that was important is that Manchester is not as hot as Cuba: Cuba was all the time hot, even hotter than we have it in summer in Moscow, and I do not like this. Although the people of Cuba were very friendly towards us, I think the English are much more friendly still than they are. I love all English people: they are like us in their looks and their ways. I was so happy there.

I stayed with a family called Mr and Mrs Wilkins. They owned a small shop on a street corner in the Longsight area. People were all the time coming into it to buy such things as newspapers, tobacco, pieces of butter and other small groceries, as well as ice-creams and sweets for children, and many other things. You could even get pens and pencils and such items as sausages in packets there, all in this same one shop. We do not have shops like this in Moscow.

Every person who came to the shop was always friendly and cheerful and ready to speak with me, even though I know only three or four words of English well enough to say them. I understand better to hear than to say. At first I am feeling awkward and shy, but everyone was so friendly with me that such shyness lasted perhaps two days only, that is all. Mr and Mrs Wilkins allowed me to stand with them behind the counter, and to everyone who came to the shop they were introducing me as 'our family daughter from Russia'. Everybody shook my hand and said they were very pleased to meet me. I think it was the case that Mr and Mrs Wilkins had told many people beforehand that I was coming, and the people came to the shop not to buy something but to see me. Many of them said they had not had the pleasure to meet a young Russian girl before.

At the beginning of my visit, it was still a holiday period for the English schools, so I went to lessons only for three days of the final week. We did not go on visits to many other places, because Mr and Mrs Wilkins asked me where I would like to go and what I would like to do. When they did I said always what was true, that the thing I liked best was to stay with them in their shop and meet all the time all the friendly people who were coming. It gave me also good opportunity to practise my English which is very poor. In all the time I was in Manchester I did not meet one English person who spoke Russian, so this was very good for me because I had to try to understand and to make myself understood.

The only trips we went on were to the centre of Manchester city, to look at the big stores which are there. I think people in England have much more money than we have, there are many many more things to choose from in the stores. I did not have so much money with me, we had been allowed to bring with us each pupil only the equal of fifty pounds in roubles. One day in a store I made myself brave enough to speak some English, to ask the lady how much were a pair of jeans. When she told me, I could not afford them. I said to this lady that I am from Russia, and she took me to show me on the other side of the road where there was a street market. She said to me I would get a nice pair of jeans there but much cheaper than in the store. So that is what I did, and I thought it was very kind of this lady to make such a suggestion to me. This was something that made me happy all the time in England, that whenever I entered a shop I was greeted always by people who smiled and asked me how was my health that day. When they talked with me and discovered that I was from Russia, they said such things as 'It has been nice to meet you, goodbye and good luck for you.' This is not something which happens very often here in the Soviet Union.

Mrs Wilkins or her son Christopher who is fifteen, they came with me to the centre of Manchester if I wanted to go there, or sometimes I went on my own to look at the big shops. In the evenings Christopher took me to many discos and places like that where young people meet, and always people would buy for me cups of coffee and fizzy drinks. All of Christopher's friends were nice to me: this was because always he was careful to choose only good places to take me to, which were full with friendly people. I did not see any of the rough type of person you can see sometimes in Moscow discothèques. Another thing I liked very much was that after we had been dancing, we would go then to look for a special shop which sold chips. We also of course have such places in Moscow, but English chips I think are much better. Then we would go home, and we would sit and talk with Christopher and his parents until a late hour about our two different countries, how we would always want them to be friends with one another.

It is difficult for me to say something I liked best of all in England, because I liked everything there was, there was nothing at all I did not like. The people, the homes, the way they lived, everything I ate or drank, I liked it all very very much. The only thing there was which took me a little time to be accustomed to, was that English people drink their tea with milk in it, which we do not. This was their custom, and so I all the time drank my tea with milk in it as they did. Then very quickly I came to like the English way better than we have it, and since I have returned I continue to drink my tea in this way. My mother and father tease me and say I am pretending to be an English lady, but it is true that I do like it better now like this.

When I first came to their home, Mr and Mrs Wilkins said they would treat me as if I was their own daughter. And they hoped I would look on them as my English father and mother, and that I was a member of their family. That is exactly how it was: I really did feel a member of their family in every way, and I was very happy that it was like that. Mrs Wilkins told to me one day she had always wanted to have a daughter herself but she was not able to do so. And she said if she had had such a daughter, she would have wanted her to be exactly like me. She was a very warm person, not at all as I had thought an English person would be like; when it came time for me to leave, she kissed me and cried, and I cried because of my feeling for her too.

Of all the people from England that I miss most of all, Mrs Wilkins is the second. The first one of course is Christopher, because he and I came very soon to fall in love with each other. He was very kind and considerate to me, and I know he feels for me what I feel for him. This feeling is a very great experience, it is something which I have never felt in my life before. Sometimes at night before I went to bed he would kiss me good-night, and sometimes even in the morning when I came to breakfast he would kiss me also, in front of his parents. So I know he is serious in his feelings for me, and it makes me very happy.

Before I came back to Russia, he offered for me to marry him when we are both a little older. I think this is something which will happen definitely, because of what we feel for each other. We discussed it when we went for a walk together along a path through a small wood near his home. He told me what he wants to do when he leaves his school next year is to go to London and be an actor. If he is successful in doing that, he would send some money for me to come to England and marry him. I would like it, and so would my parents, if he could first come to Moscow to meet them. There is the possibility for this to occur later this year if his school will accept for him to join the party that comes to us on a reciprocal visit. However he may not be able to do this, because before he met me he had not entered his name on the list of those who wished to come to Moscow, so perhaps he will have to find another way to come.

I have written to Christopher a letter each day now since I have come home, but it takes a long time for letters between Russia and England – four weeks, or sometimes as many as six. I have also written him some poems in which I have tried to express my love for him, but this is difficult for me to do. It is hard to express correctly intimate and sincere feelings in a language that is not someone's own, especially when as in my case I do not know what are the proper English words. I hope when he receives the poems he will understand what I am trying to express to him, even though they are in bad English. He says I must teach him Russian words of love also, so that in the same way he can write poems to me.

When we went out for our last walk together and he proposed me to marry him, I of course agreed. He then gave me the next day this silver locket. Sometimes I wear it on this chain it has, round my neck here, but I prefer to carry it. It opens like this, and inside as you will see there is his photograph: here opposite to it he has written 'With all my love' and signed his name. I could not give him such a picture of myself in return, because I had not taken any to England: I did not expect any such thing to happen to me as to fall in love. But I made him the promise I would send one to him on the first day I was back at my home, and this I did.

My father and mother and I would now be honoured if you would take some tea or coffee with us in our kitchen, and I have made for you a pie.

(The pie was a sponge cake.)

Marina Belskaya,
Academician

Small, dark-haired and lively, she sat cross-legged and barefoot in the middle of the white-coverleted divan in her living-room. She wore a scarlet cotton blouse, a long loop of small black beads and trim black jeans. She kept a packet of cigarettes and an ashtray next to her; smoking, sometimes she'd put her head back and blow a thoughtful jet of smoke up in the air before going on talking.

– So, I am forty, I am member of the Soviet Academy of Sciences, and I am research sociologist studying the interaction of state and government in Great Britain. My interest in particular is in the British Civil Service, the administrative arm of central government. The subject fascinates me because in Soviet Union we have division between workers and intellectuals, although the words do not have the same connotation as they do in Britain. Here it means what I think you call blue-collar and white-collar workers, but we designate all of the latter as intellectuals. Anyone who works with his or her head rather than hands is called an intellectual. I am an intellectual, a brain worker, myself; but this does not mean I am mentally superior to someone else: it describes only the type of work I do. In fact for many years in our country it has meant more lower status than higher one, since the blue-collar people, called 'proletariat', controlled the State. But I think in England, people who have controlled the state have been always white-collar workers, in particular civil servants. So this is my study, my area of interest, and my fascination. I am sorry I do not explain myself very well: my English is OK for talking and reading, but not so good when it comes to trying to explain an abstract concept such as this.

Why the subject has been of such very great interest to me since I was, well a schoolgirl of fourteen, I don't know. I think what happened, you know, is something ridiculous but very common. At school you are shown a list of subjects and they ask you to say if any are of special interest. You say that one and that one, and they say OK, that is what you shall study. What's ridiculous is it is when you are fourteen: you are expected to make an informed choice. But so, that was one of my choices, the influence of intellectuals or some such vague title. That was what led on to studying English society, because it is something more visible there than in USSR.

Also it fitted well with my other choice of subject to specialise in, which was English language. Why I chose that is simple to explain: it was no more than that I liked it, and soon was transferred to a special school for it. We had very good teachers: most of them Russian, but a good number English and American. They taught us not just construction and use of the English language, but English literature and culture also. We were taught not only how to read and speak English, but also the everyday way of communicating in it, by reading newspapers, listening to broadcasts from England on the radio, watching films, everything. Also of course there was in the school the very strict rule not one word was spoken all day that was not English.

But most of all, you know, for a young person like myself, the one dominating influence in my life was the Beatles. In those times their music and songs they were heard everywhere. They had special meaning and importance for everyone. Maybe now I am older their words seem in some cases a little too much sentimental, but earlier I used to think they were perfect. So did nearly everyone of us in my generation. 'Strawberry Fields', 'Eleanor Rigby', 'Michelle', 'Yesterday', 'Yellow Submarine' – I could go on and on. I know every word of twenty at least of their songs: they are still in my head after all these years. They were good you see because they were not just songs only about personal problems of young people, but about problems and concerns in the lives of everyone.

I find it funny you know, that they were English, the Beatles. It is considered in this country, and I am sure in other countries in the world too, that English people have as their main characteristic reserve in their dealings with others. they do not show their feelings, they have what I think you call 'stiff upper lip' yes? But the Beatles were English, and they sang all these universal things which found response in millions of hearts. It was my knowledge of them which made me confident, when the chance for me to go to England came, that underneath this English exterior there would be warmth of feeling. For many years it had been very difficult for Soviet people to go as visitors to abroad, except to eastern European countries. Then suddenly the chance came, for me to go to help my studies and also for partly holiday.

I went to London with my husband for one month just two months now ago. My first visit to England – of course it was like a dream for me to be there, I was at last in this country which had occupied so much of my life in my head for more than twenty years. And immediately I felt totally at ease with English people: they were not like foreigners at all. I hope at least, they did not find me too much foreigner either. Reserve was there, but I discovered soon what I knew: that more than anything it was politeness only, and under the surface there was quickly warmth and kindness in absolutely everybody. Even though it was winter as it is here now – such warmth!

For four weeks we were in London; it was so exciting for me, and I liked everything very much. We did all the things that tourists are to do, saw all famous sights like the Tower of London and Buckingham Palace and many more. But what I enjoyed the most was just to be there, to walk, to look at the faces of the people and their expressions. In Moscow you know, everyone looks always to be so serious; but in London no, it seems always they want to smile. English people have very much the thing which we do not: it is self-assurance in everything, their manner, the way they walk and talk. They are people I think who have much self-respect, they are proud of themselves, sure of themselves, but in no way to make it offensive. And to me it seemed they extended this respect always towards everyone else. People everywhere were friendly to us, this I noticed many many times, and on every occasion but once they were helpful and so polite. Of course I am fortunate that for me there is no language barrier at all, so it was always easy to have conversation with everyone: strangers in street, children, shopkeepers, when a friend of a friend was met. It was excellent for me that I could do that.

I cannot pick out one memory above others, because truly there were so many of them. Perhaps one that was very special indeed for me was that we had an invitation from a friend who is professor at Cambridge University. He invited that we should stay for two nights with him and his wife. Cambridge, it is so beautiful and the weather was sunshine always, again it was all for me like a dream. He took us to the library of, well I think it was King's College. This was a place like I have never seen before in my life: so big, so huge, such atmosphere of calm and quiet. It was like you were standing in the heart of human civilisation, you know?

Well to sum it up for you, I would say I had most of all the feeling that England was a country where I felt at ease completely, and at home. I had thought that perhaps it was possible I could after all find the reserve English people have their reputation for, that it might be something I could not penetrate. But it was not so at all. And what was especially interesting for me too was how it compared for me when I went six months ago for the first time in my life to Italy. I know I am a person who is unreserved and shows her feelings; so I thought in Italy I should feel at home. From everything I read and heard about the Italian people, they had the same temperament as me and so I should feel at home there. But you know, when it happened that I went there, to my surprise I found I was not happy at all. I found the Italians too much expressive, too emotional and volatile: they had much more than I wanted. They seemed to me like our Soviet Georgians perhaps, expressing too much emotion and passion in both happiness and sadness. I was not comfortable there. But in England, well I think the phrase is that for me, I thought the English had it exactly right. My husband commented on this also: he told me he had thought I would feel that I fit in Italy but not in England, but it was the opposite.

Did I say that phrase 'On every occasion but once' in England people were helpful but polite? Well no, it was nothing, it was a trivial occasion. I think it was because it was so unusual behaviour that it remains in my mind, that is all. It was a day when we wanted to visit to the House of Commons, there was a queue for those who wished to go in that we joined. We did not mind this: who from Moscow could mind that for something there was a queue? It was a day that was very hot, I think almost a record for London summer ever, over ninety degrees Fahrenheit. So after half an hour it was making me that I felt ill. My husband could see this, so he suggested to me I went to sit under some trees a little way away, no further perhaps than across this room. I did this, and he remained in the queue until it began to move as people started to go into the building.

So I stood up and went back to the queue to stand again with him. At this time a young policewoman came to me and said 'You cannot join the queue like that, you must go to the end of it.' I explained to her, and my husband he explained to her also, that I had been with him in the queue but had sat a few moments under the trees because of the heat. And he said to the policewoman 'I think you saw her go from the queue, because you have been standing here all the time.' And the policewoman she said 'I did not see her here, she must go back to the end of the queue.' So then my husband said to the people in the queue in front of him, and those in the queue behind him also, that some of them must have seen me standing with him. And he said to them politely 'Please tell this lady policeman that it was so.' But you know, this was what shocked both of us very much, there was not one person before or behind in the queue who would speak to help us, everyone looked away in silence. The policewoman then said to us very roughly that we should both of us now go to the end of the queue, and that was what we had to do.

But so, it is such a small and silly thing to speak of, in all of the four weeks that were the happiest times ever in my life. The behaviour of the young policewoman, well perhaps she herself was hot and tired from standing in the sun also; you can find everywhere in the world, I am sure, people in little official positions who will be rough and rude. I think it was that no one would speak up for us against her that was the thing most surprising to us. When we told it later to one of our English friends, he said it was an illustration of typical English behaviour, that people do not like to become involved in such instances, and will say instead they did not see what happened. But his wife said no, it was perhaps the truth that all the other people in the queue were foreign visitors as well, and they were afraid that if they spoke, the policewoman would order them to the back of the queue also.

But really you know it was nothing, nothing at all. You can receive such treatment ten times a day in Moscow. My husband says it was good, because it showed me all English people they are not angels.

Larissa Bishop,
library assistant

Sitting at a table just inside the door of a small restaurant, she sipped at a glass of lemon tea and talked in a quiet voice, sometimes stumbling over her pronunciation. She wore a plain white dress and her long fair hair flowed loosely down on to her shoulders.

– I am in age twenty-one years, and two weeks ago I return from England, where I have been for my first time, on holiday with my husband Jim. He is Englishman, and we have been married one year. He is student of illustration for children's books, and he came to research at the Moscow Children's Library where I am working, and that is how we are first meeting.

We went to England for him to take me to see his parents who live in a small village in Devonshire. It is called I think Dartley, it is near the town called Newton Abbot. It had been my dream to go to England more than any place in the world, a long time even before I met my husband. I had studied English at school and a little while at institute. One day it is my hope I will speak it much more better than I do now. Jim has learned to speak Russian: in two years he has been student here he speaks my language in a much better way than I am speaking his.

First we flew by aeroplane from Moscow to London, then at once we caught train to Devonshire and we spent ten days there in the home of his parents. They have small house but very nice, in small village which I liked very much indeed: there only perhaps two hundred people in total live. It was fifteen kilometres from the coast in one direction and only ten kilometres in another; also not far away you could go to a place called Dartmoor which is very barren country but beautiful. Jim's father is what I think is called retired; he has motor car and he and Jim's mother took us to many different places to show them to me. We went to seaside, three times to countryside, and once to the big city called Exeter which has beautiful cathedral. Jim's father and mother were very kind to me: Jim's father is what I think is the right word, jolly. He was always laughing and making jokes for me, and I was happy about this because of course always I had been wondering in my mind whether they would like it that their son had married Russian woman, and perhaps they would think I am not right person for him. But I think when we meet they did not think this after all, and we became good friends.

Every evening of our stay, Jim and I we walked to the village. It had what is called an English pub, and I learned to drink there English beer which is much stronger than we have in Moscow. All people who came to the pub were very friendly. The manager of it told everyone I was Russian girl, and always they came to the corner where we were sitting and shook hands, and many people bought for me drink of beer. In USSR I am in what is called Army Reserve for special emergencies, I am nurse, and I showed a photograph of myself in my uniform. The manager of the pub, he liked this picture very much and told everyone of it and asked me to show it to them. One man when I showed it, he went out of the pub to go back to his home: in perhaps five minutes only, he came back again and in his hand he had his sailor's cap from when he had been in war, and he insisted I should keep it as present. He put it on my head and stood like this with his arm round my shoulder, and several people came with their cameras and took a picture of me with him. It was very nice that everyone was so friendly, and I was not any more frightened that English people would not like me.

The part of England is very pretty there in Devonshire. There are beaches with sand at seaside and pretty places everywhere, even in winter. But I think I would not like to live there myself: for a young person it would be very quiet and with not much to do. Jim has said to me that one day if we go to England to live there which we might do, we will go to his parents for our holidays. That will be very nice, but not to be there for all time.

After we had had our stay with Jim's parents, we then went to London for one week to stay with some of his friends. It was house

of rooms for students in a part of London called Camden Town;
one student had gone away for one week to another part of England,
so we could have her room for ourselves. It was very nice, and a
cheap place for us to stay.

It was also very interesting to me to stay there you see, because
the friends of Jim who owned this house, they lived there themselves
and were what in Moscow we call 'blue', which your English word
for I think is 'gay'. They were two men, each of them about thirty
years of age, and very kind and friendly to us. What was such a
surprise to me you see was these men were entirely open with the
fact they were homosexuals who lived together. It would not be
possible for men to do this in Moscow, they would not allow it and
they would be punished by law. But in this house where we were in
London, everybody took it for granted that they were homosexual
and lived together as they wanted to. In Moscow people would have
been very unkind and cruel to them for that.

One was called Malcolm and the other's name I think was Pete.
They looked after the house and kept it neat and clean everywhere,
including the kitchen which everybody used together, and it was
altogether a new experience for me, and I liked to stay there very
much.

Jim took me sightseeing and we went to one place where I have
forgotten what it was called; but there were many statues of famous
people which were made from wax. We went also to Westminster
Abbey and Tower of London, and I walked in all the famous streets
such as Piccadilly, Trafalgar Square, Oxford Street, Regent Street,
Strand, and many others. Also to a street market called Portobello
where there were many good but cheap clothings for sale.

It was exciting of course for me to be in London, but I was
shocked at how dirty and untidy it had been. I am sorry to say this,
but my impression was that people who lived there, I think they
could not have very much pride to allow it to be like that. I saw
everywhere black plastic bags of rubbish that had burst open, and
everything inside had spilled out on to the pavement. People just
walked by and did nothing; I think in Moscow if such a thing
occurred people would stop and help one another to tidy it up.

Of course London was not like Devonshire at all, with everybody
rushing all the time and very much traffic in the streets. Sometimes

there was so much noise and rush that I had headache: I think this was because air in London was not good to breathe, also somehow it did not seem to me to be clean. I think it would be hard to live in London because of this. And all food and clothing was very expensive there also.

What I liked most of being in London was to go into the pubs in the evening with Jim: we went each night into a different one. None of them was like the one in the village in Devonshire, but every one was interesting for me. One was for young people only, where there was all the time loud music and dancing; another was for people of all ages. They sat together talking quietly and sometimes they were singing songs together, when a lady played for them a piano which was there. One night Jim's friends from the house took us to a pub which was for gay people, both men and women who were homosexual. It had a nice atmosphere, and many people bought drinks for us when they were told I was from Russia.

Another evening we went to a pub in the City of London, which is the business quarter. All the people who were there were young and rich: Jim told me the name for them was I think 'yuppies', but I do not know what it means. They were only people I met all the time I was in England that I did not like. They were not at all friendly, and many of them had their nose turned up at the end like this in the way they look at people. They were all shouting and each one trying to show he could spend more money than the next person to him. They were not like all other people who said they were interested to meet someone from Russia: when we were introduced they just said things like 'Oh you come from Russia, how interesting,' and then they did not ask me any questions but went instead to talk and shout again with their friends.

But that was on one night only that I met such people. At all other times people were not like that, and I enjoyed myself very much. What I liked most about English people of my age was something it is difficult for me to explain in English, but I will try. It is something that is different from what young people have here in Moscow: it could be called great confidence in themselves. They are friendly, they walk in the streets with their heads held up like this, and they do not look so worried as people here seem to do all the time. Perhaps it is because they do not have so much to worry about, there are not the shortages of things in shops. I do not know what it is with young English women, but it seems they are as if they like themselves. I explain this very badly so I will try again. It is not that they like themselves in the way that makes them what is the word, conceited. What I mean is they are happy to be themselves, and they are happy that in return you should be yourself. But I want to say this is not because they have a lot of money. Many of the students who were in the house where we were, they did not have money, but they had this atmosphere about themselves that I have been speaking of.

I noticed this very much with girls of my own age, that they wear whatever clothes they like, and no one thinks what they are wearing or what you are wearing, they do not pay attention. I saw girls with trousers, girls with long skirts down to their ankles, girls with jeans and girls with very very short skirts, which in some cases came for example down almost only just to the top of their legs. I have myself a leather skirt which I like, and it comes to my legs but here. Jim had told me it was not especially short compared to what I would see in London, and he was right. But once when I wore it on the street in Moscow, well it is more than once, it has happened two or three times, older women have come up to me and said I should be ashamed to dress in that way. One woman who was a stranger to me completely, she even pulled at it and said it should be very much lower down on my legs.

I could not imagine this would happen anywhere to a girl in the street in London. What is there is freedom to be as you like, and it is very good. If you know that you have that, this gives you the confidence to find your life more enjoyable, and I would like it if it were so in Moscow also.

Dmitri Nemirovsky,
tourist

An elderly man with white hair and blue eyes and a white beard, he wore a light grey suit, a white shirt with a button-down collar, and a dark blue tie. His voice was strong and deep, his manner ebullient and lively.

– Well, to talk about America, what can I talk about America? Four months ago I have been there three weeks only, in one small section of it: what is called I think the East Coast. Does this qualify me to talk about America? I think not, I was just a tourist. What I have to say, they are impressions only: snapshots with a camera, you know? Well OK I try for you, I try. Then if you do not like it and it is no use for you, you can throw it away, put it in the trash can or the garbage can, whatever it is they call it. So there you are, that is my first impression of America for you – in all the time I was there, I was never able to discover what the difference was between the trash can and the garbage can. If a man cannot do that, I think what else he says is not reliable and has to be treated with care, do you not agree?

How it came about that I went there was like this. Until I retired last year I was teacher at our English Institute in Leningrad, and I met there a young American man and his wife who were on a visit. He was professional photographer, he worked for himself as free-lance, but he had high reputation because he was coming to Leningrad on what Americans call an assignment, to do pictures for a magazine article. His special interest was in people, not in beautiful or historic buildings. Ordinary everyday people that you see in Leningrad, with the buildings only as background. That is unusual:

visitors to Leningrad see it usually the other way round, they look at the buildings and do not see the people.

He came to me to ask advice; someone in America had mentioned my name because they had read some article somewhere I had written. He was younger than me but immediately, you know, we were empathetic, we had the same view of things in many cases. He asked me to bring my wife to his hotel, and his wife and my wife they liked each other very much also, so it was immediately a good rapport that we had. They came also to our apartment some evenings to eat with us. He was in Leningrad I think for three weeks, and before they departed he and his wife said 'Please, you must come to visit us in America for a holiday, we shall invite you as guests to our home.' Well this was very nice you know; but I think people often say such things, but they do not mean them.

I will tell you frankly, we were a little surprised when only perhaps one month later we had from them this very positive invitation to go to visit them. So suddenly we decided yes we would go, it would be a holiday to celebrate that I was retiring. We applied for all the necessary papers, our exit visa, our entry visa, all the things you have to have: and then one day it was all concluded – and there we were, we were going to USA. We had been not outside the USSR at all ever before, so it was a very exciting feeling for us. We thought also we were very brave, to go so far away and to such a place as America. To do that, oh yes, we thought we must be, you know, rather exceptional people. Then not long after I heard one day on Moscow radio in the previous year more than thirty thousand Soviet citizens had travelled on holiday to America at the invitation of friends. So I knew we were not so exceptional people after all.

We made a long flight from Moscow to Boston, and there when we arrived our friends were waiting to greet us with their big motor car, to drive us in great comfort to their home in New Haven Connecticut. This was an important thing I learned in America: when you give the name of a place, you also give the name of the state where it is located. Boston Massachusetts, New Haven Connecticut, like that. I do not know why, I think because they have perhaps twenty different places called Boston, twenty different places called New Haven and so on. The second thing I learned, immediately when we arrived, was how true it was the amazing hospitality American people give to their guests. They arrange everything to make it sure you are comfortable; it is in one word overwhelming you know, their kindness. There is their phrase 'Nothing is too much trouble', and it was so that they were demonstrating it to us all the time.

The house of our friends was by our Russian standards magnificent in size, standing near a lake with beautiful countryside everywhere all around. I think it is not unusual in America, but I think it would be for people in any other country. It had in it five or perhaps six bedrooms, each one equipped with own private bathroom, a huge kitchen so beautiful it made my wife's eyes pop out of her head, big big sitting-rooms, a garden, a tennis court, everything. I think in Moscow it would accommodate perhaps twenty-five to thirty people you know? And always they were saying to us when we expressed ourselves about it 'No no, it is not anything special, many of our friends have houses like this, you will see.' And it was true, they took us to meet their friends and they did have such houses also, in some cases even bigger.

I think this was a very strong impression I had from many American people I met, you know, that they knew their standard of living was high. And they were half-proud about it, but also somehow they wanted to show you that it was not so important to them. They wanted to be how does one say, casual about it and not boasting. So their way to do this was to share it all the time, with as many other people as possible. I think this may sound like not a kind thing for me to say, but in a way it is like when a child has a toy, it wants to show it to others. What is the point of having it if other people do not see it and enjoy it with you, you know? You enjoy that they should enjoy it, that is how I would say.

I think perhaps in many ways they feel this about their whole country too. They know it is very rich and beautiful country, and they want everyone else to come and see it and enjoy it with them. So our hosts had prepared very carefully an itinerary for us, so that we could see their part of America. For one week therefore they took us on a tour by car: to New York for two nights, to Washington for two nights, and also for two nights to Norfolk Virginia. In each place we spent one night in a very first-class hotel, then the other night in a motel: some small place like that, away from the city and perhaps by a lake if there was one. This was a very interesting experience, because it meant in each area we would spend one night with luxury, and the other with what they would call an ordinary standard of accommodation, where we could meet and talk with ordinary American people. It had been worked out with great care.

The countryside everywhere was very beautiful and the weather good, it was like we have for our autumn here. Often in many places it was too late for what they call 'fall' when all the trees have beautiful colours, but all the same for us it was an experience we shall remember always, to see such good countryside.

Then there was New York. What shall I say about New York? What shall I say after two days, only two days, in New York? A very big city, a very noisy city, a very ugly city, a city with great beauty and grandeur – all of such descriptions are true. And some very poor areas we went to also, with black and Hispanic people living in places you could not imagine it would be allowed. In USSR no one has big houses like those of our friends, but no one either has such places to live as the poverty quarters of New York. It was very confusing to us that these two standards of living could be not only in the same country but in the same city. But when you ask, people shrug their shoulders like this and they say 'There is nothing to be done, it is a problem is too big for anyone to solve.'

This was another impression I had of America also, you know, that people are very honest. I do not mean in not stealing things or your money being safe or anything like that: I am saying it about the way not only our friends but many others too would talk to us, to tell us what was wrong with America and ask did we feel it was also. They would tell us what was wrong with their government, how it spent too much money on armaments and things for war, and not enough on helping people who were sick or poor. More than that, they were always insisting what a material society theirs was, how people were thinking only money money money all the time. You did not have to go round with a notebook to write in it faults of America: American people were anxious always for you to make sure you had noticed these things, and they were all the time telling you of them.

We met one night when we were at home in our friends' house in New Haven two professors from Yale University with their wives. We had long discussion with them, and they said so many things critical of America and the American way of life that my wife commented on it to them. She asked them to tell us some good things about America. They thought about it for some time, and then one of them said 'Well, that we can talk about it like this I suppose. But that is no great deal, only to talk.'

We had heard many times before we went there, you know, that American people were all of them very proud and patriotic about their country. I do not mean to say they were not patriotic, they were I am sure. But there was no impression to us at all that Americans thought their country was perfect and did not have failings. This was a refreshing feeling for us to have, it made us think many of our ideas we had had about America were wrong. Perhaps this happens always when you go to a country and meet its people: you find they are not as you had thought. I should say also that there was one particular thing. Small, but I think it is an important one, and it shows how mistaken ideas can be if they are not founded on knowledge. It is simple: we thought Americans talked always with loud voices. But they do not. The Americans we met, they were thoughtful and spoke quietly and calmly. Not at all in the way that for example I do myself, you know? A small thing: but a good impression, one that made me think.

Those are my impressions for you of America. Could I live there? Oh no, never, it would be absolutely impossible. Yes of course I will tell you why. They do not know at all how to make tea, they make it with powder.

10 Women 2

Polina Medesova, parapsychologist

Irena Valkeva, hotel cashier

Lily Golden, Institute of African Studies

Roza Lemskaya, toy maker

Ella Kirova, office receptionist

Olga Nadimova, writer

Polina Medesova
*parapsychologist**

She lived in an eighteenth-floor apartment high up in a modern tower block. Its walls were covered with astrological charts and graphs, posters advertising ESP conferences in India and Australia, and a map of the world with envelopes pinned on it with pencilled arrows marking the places they were from. A chubby elderly woman with short-cropped grey hair, she wore a floral robe and chattered animatedly, sitting at her writing desk.

– There have been here in the last two years people who have come to visit me from all over the world as my reputation spreads. It is something that means much to me because I am an old lady and I know that before long I shall have gone on to another life somewhere else. I would like to say at once also that I think your interpreter is a very beautiful young woman, and it gives me additional pleasure that while I am talking with you I can look at her. Do not be embarrassed my dear when I say such a thing. It is true: you are a very beautiful young woman, and I like to have beautiful young women near to me all the time. See, she moves her chair so she will be sitting further away from me. But I will not hurt you my dear beautiful young woman, there is nothing you should fear except those who do not speak to you the truth.

So sir: you have come to Moscow from England, and you like to meet with the famous parapsychologist and healer Polina Medesova and talk with her, and now here you are. You do not need to tell me of course how you found me, because this I already know. The knowledge of my work and powers spreads so rapidly now that everyone knows of me, everyone has heard of me. Sometimes it seems almost every day there is an article about me in a newspaper

– not so much here of course in the Soviet Union but in other countries all over the world – and then come the letters and telephone calls from that place, and so it goes on and on. If you had been here in the morning yesterday at this time, you would have heard the telephone ring there on that shelf, and it was a gentleman from Jakarta the capital of Indonesia, calling me to ask me to help him. The day before that someone from Paris. All the time it goes on. But I can tell you it was two years ago only that I was poor and had no money. I could find no work to do and was all the time afraid I may be taken to prison. As you can see, now it is a very different situation for me. This was due to our kind dear Mikhail Sergevitch Gorbachev, who at last permitted that I and other people like me who have extra-sensory perception, we no longer have to hide and be afraid. It is still forbidden by our laws to study parapsychology and practise healing, but it is so that this law is no longer applied. A great wrong had been done to persecute and outlaw such people as myself, but perhaps before too long now the law itself will be abolished.

For twenty-six years from when I was a student and left school and after that left the institute, I worked at the Ministry of Foreign Affairs as an interpreter and translator. I could speak Portuguese, Spanish, German, French, Italian, together with some Finnish, Swedish, and a little Dutch and English. It has never been a problem to me to learn to speak almost any language, because of my earlier experiences. In a very few weeks or at most between two and three months I become fluent in any language by studying textbooks and attending at classes for a short time. At the Ministry I put this facility to good use for example at technical conferences: if I was given some notification that gave me sufficient time to do so in advance, I would study the languages of the countries of many of the participants, and immediately when the delegates from that country arrived, I would go to them at their hotel and ask them to allow me to practise speaking their language with them before the conference began.

Then it came the day that someone informed on me. This was at the time of the middle of the Brezhnev era. I do not know who told to the authorities about me, and many of my colleagues at the Ministry were very sorry about it, but they told me I was no longer permitted to work for them. The reason you will guess: it was not that I indulged in activities against the State or anything of that kind, but that I had as a friend someone who was older than myself who was also a parapsychologist and faith healer. I had been seen going to meetings at her apartment of small groups of others who were interested in the subject. Books about extra-sensory perception which were banned at all times in the Soviet Union were found in my desk at the Ministry, and I had on one occasion lent one of these books to someone where I worked who enquired about the subject. Also, I had written an article under my own name for a magazine of parapsychology which was circulated illegally in Moscow. Such activities had been unwise for me to do, there is no question of that; had I done any of them as an ordinary person I do not think anything very terrible would have happened to me, perhaps no more than a fine. But for someone who worked for the Foreign Affairs Ministry to do this, well it could not be permitted for a moment and so I had to be dismissed when it was discovered. After I had worked there twenty-six years!

My parents were long since dead, I was not married, I had an apartment but it was smaller even than this one, and I did not have savings of any large amount. Because I had worked for them for so long, and I was already then becoming near to the age when I should retire, the government gave me a small pension to live on. As you can imagine, there was only one employer for interpreters of the kind which I was, and that was the State: so there was no further prospect of employment for me. And that was how my situation continued, one of complete unemployment for a period of thirteen years. The only thing there was in my life was my interest in my subject of parapsychology, and so I studied it even more deeply because there was more time I could devote to it. I knew a small group of other people with the same interest, including my friend I have already told you of, and that was how I spent my time, in clandestine meetings and discussions with them.

It was at one such meeting which I think was seven years ago now, that I met a lady who had come there and she was from India. She talked with me of yoga and meditation, and the practice of spiritual healing. She told me she was able to know instantly of a person whether they had the gift to do this or not; and she said I was such a person, and having been given this gift it was my responsibility to use it. You can learn how you can use it, there are ways in which you can direct your mind so that it operates, and all that is required is that you should practise how to channel your thoughts in this way. Different people have different methods which suit them best for the exercise of their powers: for some it is necessary that they should have physical contact and actually touch a person with their hands, but for me it is not so. My healing power is so great, and I have worked so hard at making it so, I can now operate telephone healing to a person anywhere in the world. It is only necessary they should make a telephone call to me, that they should then answer some questions for me, just a few, and then I can heal them over the telephone. The knowledge of this ability which I have is spreading very rapidly now throughout the world. I am very happy to do this, and I do not charge a fee for it: I leave it to those I have helped to send me whatever payment they think I should have, that will sufficiently express their thanks. It is interesting for me, it is exciting for me, and it makes me very happy that I can now do this openly and without fear.

There is one thing only which gives me some sadness: it is that now it has come at a time when I do not yet have much money and so cannot travel, and also that I am not twenty years younger and with more energy and strength in me to do such travelling. It is still in our country that you need invitations and permissions. There are so many regulations which first have to be satisfied wherever you wish to go, that it is all so difficult now for me in every way.

And there is one country above all where I would like to go if it were possible, and that is to Brazil. It is a country which is very close to my heart, and the reason for it is that in one of my previous incarnations I was Brazilian. As you know, we all have had many different earlier lives, and it is that one which I have the most feelings and recollections about, and for which I have the clearest memories. I do not know why it should be that one earlier life is more vivid than any other, I know only that it is so. I cannot say exactly when it was precisely, but I do know that my name was Luís Escardos, that I was a peasant with very little education, and that at birth I was a bastard, having no father for my name. Of course you will know this is so with most peasant people in Brazil.

I think, though I am not sure, sometimes I have this feeling strongly and at other times not, but it is my impression that this person who I was, was what is called a mulatto, that is a person with some blood of descent from a white person. This young man that I was, he worked in the woods, he did heavy labour for which he was poorly paid. Also he was a very lonely person, with no knowledge of his family and not many friends, and so he was unhappy. That part of his nature has remained in me and brings me very close to his feelings, because I too in my life have been often lonely and unhappy too. He was a modest and simple person, nothing of great adventure or drama happened to him ever in his life, and he lived in a shack on the edge of the town of Pernambuco, from where he walked every day to his work. When he was twenty-five years of age he was killed by a tree that fell upon him while he was working: it had been cut in the wrong way by mistake by some other person, and so that was the end of his life.

This as I say is the clearest of my recollections of earlier existences, and from time to time additional small revelations of other details concerning it come into my mind. Some of them I think must be inaccurate because they do not fit in with the rest of the picture, and those I reject when I have thought sufficiently about them. But what has joined my life most clearly from Luís Escardos is the speaking of Portuguese, because of course that was his language. I remember when I first came to learn it, I could not understand why it was so easy for me, and I had the feeling that in some way I had been speaking it all my life. At that time of course I was a student and I knew nothing of such things; it was only when I began to learn of them that I realised the fact that indeed yes, I had been speaking Portuguese all my life – only not in this existence, in another earlier one.

The only other existence I have recollection of it is one which I do not see so clearly yet or feel many details of. But I know I was also a French Army officer at the time of the Franco-Prussian war in 1871. I have the feeling that that life too came to an end at an early age, and that it was as a serving officer. But it was neither in battle nor as a result of illness or accident. I think it is possible that it could perhaps have been as the result of a duel, but this is not something I have a strong feeling about. If there is more to be learned it will be revealed to me if I am patient, I am sure. It was something of him for example that makes me respond as I do to your beautiful young lady interpreter you have brought with you. He had what is known as an eye for the ladies, and so therefore dear young madam I do also. But please, there is nothing for you to fear.

Irena Valkeva,
hotel cashier

She sat near the window which led to the apartment's balcony, looking out at the heavy rain falling in the afternoon's fading light. A round-faced fair-haired woman in a short-sleeved grey dress, talking quietly and thoughtfully, and gently twisting her wedding ring round and round on her finger.

– I like this time of the day, it is the best time, for me the summer days are always too hot. Moscow is a big city, all through the summer it is noisy and dirty and dusty, it is uncomfortable to live here. I would like to live in a forest somewhere. My uncle who is dead now, sometimes he would invite my mother and me to his dacha. It was small, no bigger really than this room with another room there as a bedroom. No water, no sanitation, we had to take all our food with us and it was a journey of four hours on the train. But once we were there it was like to live in paradise, or so it seemed to me as a girl: the air so pure and so many scents in it of the woodland. My daughter is fourteen now; she has never experienced anything like it yet, she has lived in the city all her life, but I hope she will do so one day. Perhaps she will find a boyfriend for herself who will take her at weekends to the countryside. She misses much because of our life at present and how it is, but she is a good girl and does not complain. There are many things though I'm sure she would like it to be that they were different.

The rain is good, I like to sit and watch it like this, it cleans our city and I am thankful to it. If my daughter is out with her friends as she is now, I sit here alone and thinking. I hope it does not sound to you I am unhappy person. I am not unhappy, I am not unhappy at all: the word for what I am is contented.

I am forty years of age, I am a cashier in the accounts department of a hotel in the city, and I have lived here in this one-roomed apartment with my daughter since my husband left me twelve years ago. At that same time my mother died also, so it was difficult for us. My husband, well he agreed that he would send me money for her upbringing, but twelve years have gone by and I wait still for the first payment. I considered at first I should leave Moscow and go to Kiev where my sister lives. But I knew no one there, and besides I have to say honestly my sister and I, well, we are not the closest of friends. So instead I stayed here, and I think now it was the right decision.

For my life, well at that time I was twenty-eight years of age, and I was optimistic I might meet another man and marry again, but I did not. There was once a man for a short time, he would leave his wife he said and marry me. But you know how it is with men, or perhaps you do not; in any case, it came that he did not leave his wife and it is perhaps for the best. Why do I say that? I do not know: one has to persuade oneself these things are so. And you know I was happy with my daughter, to feel I was working for her. I had a job then also as a cashier, in the accounting department at a clothing factory, and they had a crèche there where mothers could leave their babies to be looked after for them in the daytime, so it was a good arrangement. My daughter of course she was only very young, and I was happy I could have her near to me at work. I was happy at the end of the day too when I could bring her home with me without difficulty. The time that I told you of when there was the man, it was one of a little awkwardness of course; but as I have said, it did not last for very long.

A thing that also I was able to do was to continue my studies of English. It had been my favourite language at school, and I had the opportunity that I could do much reading and studying just for my own enjoyment. I had much free time in which I could do it, without worrying if I passed good examinations or things like that. Many people in Russia speak English to some extent, I do not know if you have come across this? It is our second language of course in schools.

The time that I was speaking of, it was not too bad a time. Only rarely could I go to concerts or to see friends, so mostly I had to entertain people here in my home. I like to cook, to give a little dinner party for two or three of my friends. Most of them were like myself divorced women: there are many of us in Moscow. So we would come and we would eat and we would talk about things between ourselves, about such matters as the selfishness and cruelty of men, and such things as that that women talk of when they are together.

But, you know, time brings changes. Some of them have married again, gone to other places to live. But I remain here, and I do not have too many worries. At the present time Anita my daughter is now grown-up enough for us to be friends, and I like it very much that we can talk about things together. I think though it will not last for more than one more year or two in this way, then naturally as she grows to be a young woman we shall become apart. But good friends still I hope.

It is beginning to be hard for her though you see, to bring her friends here in the evening: the apartment is so small. As she grows up I think it will become more difficult still, especially when she has perhaps a boyfriend. She will not always want to be at discos or cinemas with him, sometimes she will want to be with him on her own. This is only natural, it is the same for all boys and girls, they want sometimes just to be together without anyone else. And as you see, our accommodation here is not enough. We have two beds in the bedroom there, and it will be awkward for them if I go in there to sit on my own, or into the kitchen, it is all very near together. I cannot always in the evening though go out myself to friends, in winter especially. 'May I come to see you this evening, Anita wants to spend the evening with her boyfriend in our home' – I cannot be saying this all the time to my friends. But it is not a problem that is uncommon anywhere is it, so I think something will be arranged so that we do not quarrel about it.

Or also of course it could be that I have my own woman's summer, and then the problem will be reversed. I have no plans, there is no man at present in my life, but it could happen in a year or two that it is me who wants it that Anita goes out for the evening and leaves me with my boyfriend. 'A woman's summer', you do not have this phrase? Well for us, if there is coming a time in the autumn when for a few days the sun is shining and it is warm, we say that we are having a woman's summer. It means that in life for a woman perhaps when she is my age or a little older, she has a last late blooming, and that is how it is with the weather. You say 'an Indian summer'? Why do you call it that? It has something to do with the country of India where the British used to have their empire? Well if an Englishman himself does not know, who else should I ask?

But to speak of problems again, well perhaps everything will be OK you know with my daughter. I am like all mothers, I worry of course that she might one day become pregnant. I talk to her about such things already but who can tell, I think perhaps there should be more information for young people about such matters, they should have teaching at school or there should be books that can be borrowed from the library. I must say to you, you know, that I think you would be surprised at how little I myself know about the subject for example of birth control; I think you would think it was very surprising that a woman of mature years could still know so little. My mother taught me nothing about sexual things and at school it was not even mentioned ever at all. Sometimes I think this is one of the things that caused it to happen that my marriage lasted a short time only. It was shocking to me what happened between a man and a woman when they were married: to speak frankly to you I found it was distasteful. I understand from some of my friends that it should not have to be so, and for some of them it is not always so. They say there are books you can find which come mostly from the West, which will teach you about such things. But it is not a good situation here, when a woman of my age is still so very ignorant that she does not know how to teach her own daughter how she should be better informed. There are women who write sometimes informative articles in magazines, but only rarely; I had wondered if I should perhaps write to one of them to ask for advice.

The way our society is constructed, you know, I think sometimes it has all been created by men and for men. There is much talk about the equal place of women in society, and recently they broadcast on television the discussions of the Supreme Soviet when it was in session. There were many hours of talking of new laws and criticisms of old ones and how they could become better. Even such matters as how the position of women could be improved, because everyone knows it is much in need of improvement. But you know, all those people who were talking of such matters, almost every one of them was a man. Men discussing how to improve the lot of Soviet women, and scarcely a woman's voice or opinion to be heard, what do you think of that? No one pointed out that it was so, that it was wrong not to hear very heavily and clearly many women's points of view. There is very little awareness among men in Russia that women's views need even to be heard. For a man from the West it must seem we are a very backward society still I think. Equality for women is much spoken about and there are laws designed to ensure it; but what it means I think is that so far as doing for example heavy manual labour or things of that kind, well yes the opportunity is there for women on equal terms with men. But in all very top influential positions in government and in business, you will find there are few women anywhere. The idea that there should be such a person as Prime Minister of our country who is a woman, as you have with your Mrs Thatcher – well I think it must be many years before a thing like that could happen here.

Usually, as I have said to you, I sit alone and think about such things, so it is interesting for me to talk of them instead: thank you.

Lily Golden,
Institute of African Studies

She sat on a saggy leather-upholstered settee in her apartment, a large handsome black woman of fifty-five in a brightly multi-coloured long dress. She had a bad cold and had to keep blowing her nose on a small handkerchief tucked up her sleeve at the wrist.

– Oh dear I am so sorry all the time to be doing this, please forgive me. Yeah, like I was saying, many folk are surprised to hear that, they did not know it. But Pushkin was a black man, that's for sure: he was the son of an aristocrat, but his grandfather came to live in Russia from Ethiopia. So there's no way could Russian people ever be colour-prejudiced, not when their greatest poet comes from a background such as that. In the southern republics like for instance Uzbekistan where I was born, there are thousands and thousands of people who have darker skins even than mine. And any number of Tartars and Georgians, Tadjikistanis and Armenians too – many of them are dark-skinned. The Soviet Union has over one hundred different races, so here it's of no consequence at all whether you're black, brown, yellow, white or any other colour. I've never experienced anything in the nature of colour prejudice, I don't think it exists.

I am of American origin in the sense my father came to live here from the United States. He was the son of someone who had been a slave, in Kentucky I think, and he then became a student at the famous university for black people, the University of Tuskegee, which was founded by Booker T. Washington. Then he came from there to be a student of agriculture at Moscow University, and after that he went back to America and gathered a group of black agriculturists to return with him to Uzbekistan and form a farming collective. Altogether I think there were about thirty people he brought back with him to start the project, and he married a Russian woman. My father was a man that all my life I've wished I had known better; but he died when I was six years old only, my memories of him are very few. You often hear stories of Russian people emigrating to other countries after the Revolution, but less about those who came to live here from other countries: there were many of them.

Until the beginning of the war in 1941, my mother stayed on at the farming collective, but when I became eighteen she moved to Moscow so I could be a student at the university. When I did, the subject I chose to specialise in was African studies. Well, the reason for it was I'd become interested in the history of black people from when I was very young, and I used to talk with the people of the collective who'd come to this country with my pa. I discovered they knew just nothing at all about their own history. Like him they were the children of slaves, who'd been taken to the United States from the Caribbean or Africa, or their parents had – and they didn't even know which country they'd come from. They'd been regarded by their masters as so insignificant they'd come to look on themselves in that same way – completely unimportant, with no thought of their origins whatsoever.

And you know it's still today common to find this among black people in America. A few years ago I went there on a short lecture tour, speaking mostly to black students at a number of universities. To take one example only, on my visit to Mississippi I found I was talking to well-educated and well-read young people who'd never even heard of Booker T. Washington. You know here in Moscow you can read about him in almost every school textbook there is, and you think everyone in the world must know of him. So it's very strange when you discover in America itself, even many black people know nothing about him. I've often tried to explain this to myself, as to why it should be that in USSR we know of his work and achievements in America – but among black people in America, nothing is known. It's as if they feel that in so many parts of America they're looked down upon simply because they're black, so they feel in other countries with populations which are predominantly not black, they'll be looked down on in the same way. They find it hard to believe that in the Soviet Union at least this is not so. Oh dear I'm sorry, excuse me.

I've been at the Institute of African Studies ever since it came into existence, which was now almost thirty years ago. It was during the time of Khrushchev, and how it came into existence was because the great singer Paul Robeson came here on a visit to the USSR with his wife and his family. I don't know how it was, but he'd known my father from back in the United States and he wanted to meet up with him again, I guess to hear about the communal farm project. Of course my father by then had been dead many years, so Paul Robeson instead wanted to meet my mother and me, and talk with us about him. He was in Moscow a while, but he wanted also to travel to other parts of the USSR: so he invited me and my husband and my mother to accompany him and his family as he travelled. We did this for two months with him, and I've looked back on it always as one of the very great experiences of my life. Paul Robeson was in every way a very great man – a great singer of course, but also a very civilised person with a wide outlook, and a great interest in everything he came across and every person he met. He could be described with truth as a truly internationalist person. He spoke English, French, German, Chinese and Russian, all of them fluently.

He had much trouble in his life in the United States of course, because he was accused of being a Communist. In fact he was not, or at least he was never a member of the Party. But he loved the Soviet Union, he thought there were many good things here, and he was always ready to say so. But to me you know, knowing him as well as I did, I think it was never sufficiently appreciated how much he owed his wife. She also was a marvellous person – very good-looking, well-educated, and looked after him and watched over his interests in every way. Of course like many women married to great men who are famous and popular, she had difficulties with him, but I think mostly they were happy enough together. I liked her so much.

But let me tell you now about the setting-up of the Institute. It followed that tour we made together, during which time Paul Robeson became very interested in the subject I was speaking of earlier, how black people knew nothing of their own origins. When we returned to Moscow he spoke about it to Khrushchev, saying he thought there should be a special separate Institute for African studies. It tells you what kind of a man Paul Robeson was, and how strong the impression he made on people, that Khrushchev agreed immediately. There was an Institute for African Studies established within three days. I joined it at once and I've been there always since that time: it's been the work of my life, it's brought me great satisfaction and I may also say pride in its success.

The Institute's always been there for me, and it's been both a joy and a comfort in my personal life. I can tell you that's not been too smooth. I've been married three times: my first husband was a young Russian man who was a musician, a pianist, but we'd been married only three months and then he was killed in an automobile accident. For a while I kind of felt almost I didn't want to go on living. Then I fortunately met at the Institute an African man from Zanzibar, which first gained its own independence in the 1960s, and was united with Tanzania when that became independent also. Those were at first very unstable times, and he felt he should return to his country to try and help with the situation. And a short time after his arrival there, he was killed.

It's by him I have my only child, my daughter who's now thirty-five and is a well-known journalist and broadcaster on television here. She works mostly for the radical newspaper *Moscow News*, and she was the first ever Soviet journalist to go to the United States and work on an American newspaper in an exchange programme. We're good friends with each other I'm glad to say, which is nice when your child becomes adult. Finally some years ago I married for a third time, to a Russian writer. So as you can see, my own life in personal respects has not been an easy one. But two things have always brought me happiness – my work at the Institute and my friendship with my daughter, who's both a clever young woman and a kind one.

At the Institute there's always so much to do which interests me, you know? At the moment there in particular, with my colleagues I'm trying to bring into being not just a place for students to study, but also provide something of a social centre for them as well, and even in some cases for their families. This is something which at present is our main project, to develop this. And we want to show African films and present theatre productions, to put on musical concerts, establish a restaurant and other things like that. We also want to offer counselling services and social help. Unfortunately it happens quite a number of African students while they're here, they marry Russian girls and then at the end of their studies return to their own countries without them. They leave them sometimes with babies, and there are great problems then for young mothers who have to bring them up on their own. We're not yet ready to offer much practical assistance, but perhaps within a short time now we'll be able to offer more support and facilities, such as for them to have their babies cared for during the daytime while they work and earn money.

So you see how it is, my life's full and interesting, and I've never once at any time regretted my father came to Russia, and I was born a Russian citizen. What I am to myself? Oh yeah that's easy for me to answer. I am a Russian, absolutely a Russian. Despite the origins of my parents or my father at least, despite the colour of my skin, despite the concentration of my mind always being on African affairs – fundamentally I'm a Russian. More than that, I'm a through-and-through Muscovite. Wherever else I go, always after only a few days I miss my Moscow. I've lived here so many years now. Russian is my main language: my English I learned of course as a child from speaking with my father, but inside my head I think in Russian and I speak to myself in Russian. As I speak with you this afternoon, I talk in Russian then translate it in my mind into English before saying it.

Well, to say what it means to feel this way, to feel Russian, I guess that's something pretty hard to put into words. I'm not a member of the Party though: when I was younger sometimes I thought I'd like to be, but when I enquired I was told it wasn't possible because my husband was not a Russian. This was at the time of my second marriage, so I lost interest. Since then working at the Institute has brought me so often into conflict with the Party bureaucracy that my feeling now is positively against it. You know, I think I must be an anarchist, and I'm too old now to change my ways, that's for sure.

Well, I've talked so much my head is full and my nose will never let me breathe again. How long does a cold last in England? Uh huh, it's about the same then as here. Oh excuse *me*.

Roza Lemskaya,

toy maker

We met by arrangement at an apartment belonging to one of her friends. Tall and green-eyed, her untied dark hair flowing down to her waist, she walked barefoot for a while on the parquet flooring of the sparsely furnished sitting-room, before flopping into an old wooden rocking chair with her billowing patchwork skirt wrapped around her legs. She was thirty-one.

– Here it would not be nice to live, in this horrible what you call it, tower block? When I see what it is like, all buildings everywhere, I could not ever live here in such a place. I like to think there is no one else in the world but me. I love my children, I love my parents, I love them very much – but they tie me to the earth, I cannot fly away up among the clouds, I cannot walk in this direction or in that, because I must think always I have to come back again.

What is the word, *gitana*, you have it in English yes? It is what I am, someone like me who wants to be a free spirit and she never stops for long in one place: *gitana*, gypsy I think in Spain. There is another word also: I am heapy, what I am is a heapy you would say, is that right? Good, it is good for me to talk with an English person, I practise my English upon you. All I have is what I remember from school, and a man that I knew a few years ago, he also spoke English a little and we would talk it sometimes together.

The first thing to say to you is that I live my life in freedom, always as much as I can. I do not mean with this the phrases politicians use, free speech and democracy and such things like that. I mean freedom to live outside everyone else's society, to live exactly as I wish. With my friends I put away all the values that other people have: money, possessions and such things as that. We have a camp where we live in the summer out of doors in the woods, and in the winter we go further out from the city to where there are empty buildings in which we shelter. I am sorry I cannot take you there to show you, but of course we do not do that, we do not let anyone know exactly where it is that we live, then no one can come to find us. We do no harm you understand, we do not rob or steal or have drugs. It is just we want to be separate, to live in peace among ourselves, to have no laws, no obediences we must make to authorities. Many people you know, they do not like that, they feel you should not be against the conventions, and they try to force you that you belong. I think they want all life to be the same for everyone.

I have two children. My daughter is twelve and her name is Darya and my son is seven and the name he has is Denya. All of us as heapy persons we bring up our children together in community, one big family, and try that we should all live together in peace and love. Oh yes and I have a third member to my family, our little dog to whom we give the name Mathilda. For us this is a joke: in Russia if you hear that someone is called Mathilda you expect she will be like this, very big and fat, someone who is like an elephant. But our Mathilda, she is only as big as this, and so everyone laughs when they hear her name.

How I became like this, heapy, well I will tell you. My mother and my father, he is from Ukraine and she is from Georgia, and they have son who is older, and then me. My father is Party member and he works in the heavy-engineering factory which makes loco-motives, and my mother she is the daughter of a peasant farmer who likes to cook and to sew, and all things to do with the family. She is a good woman and a kind woman, and my father all his life he has worked hard to provide the money for his family. My brother, when he is born they have very high ideals for him, he is going to be hard-working at school and he is going to be in every way a good boy. And it is true, that is what he is. He is clever student, particularly with engineering and physics. He goes to school and then he goes for his conscription into the Army for two years, then after that he comes home and he goes to study at the university. In every way he does everything that is right for him, and he makes his parents so that they are very proud.

But with me it is quite different, I am how do you say exact opposite? I am not clever at school, I will not work at my studies, in the evenings I go out with my friends, I am rude to my parents and I do not obey them. Do you understand how it is in this country for members of the Party, that they must always give good example of how to live and behave for others? So you can imagine how it was for my father, that he has a daughter who is such bad example of how a schoolgirl should be. What is the word you would use that he would be? Embarrassed, yes, thank you I remember the word now – I am embarrassed for him.

When I am child, my father he is not cruel to me you understand, he does not beat me or things like that. But I run away from home, I stay with a group of other young people like myself, and nothing he can do will make me change my ways. It was something you see that was inside me, I became that I could not exist in such surroundings of my family. My father tried many times to talk with me, and he could never understand. And of course he could not, because I could not understand either myself why my feelings were as they were. All I could tell him was that I did not want to live in that sort of existence. It was an unhappy situation.

You will guess what it was that happened before long, which was that I lived with a man and married him and had his baby. This was my daughter. He was you know a nice man, kind and gentle, and he was like me that he did not like our modern society in this world. He made his living from painting. No, I think instead I should say he did not make his living from painting, you understand? He was good artist but not a genius. He sold his paintings to anyone who would buy them in the streets, or he made portraits of people in the streets, things like that. To help to make extra money for us I also did painting, but this was designs of decoration for matryoshka dolls. They go one inside the other, perhaps four five six, or even with the big ones as many as twelve or sixteen. Each one is the same as the one on the outside, the same face and figure with perhaps only a little variation of the dress as they go smaller and smaller inside. Anyone can do this if they have just a little ability to copy, that is all. In the small villages all around Moscow there are men who make the dolls in plain wood, and you go to them and buy a supply, and you paint them and then you take them and sell them in the street. It is very boring to do believe me, one day after another the same face and the same design. And there are so many people who can do them, you cannot get much money for them. A souvenir for the tourists, that is all; and a demand for them all the time, everyone who comes to visit our country, he has to take one back to his own country to show he has been to Russia.

Well my husband he was an artist person, and I was a painter of matryoshka dolls, and that was our existence with our daughter and of course our marriage came to an end. I think now he lives with someone else and sometimes I see him; he is nice person, I like him and I think he likes me, but we no longer love each other. It is often like that between people.

Sometimes now today still I paint the matryoshka dolls to make some money. But I like much more instead to paint the little toys I sold to you in the street: the bears with strings, the wooden snakes and cockerels and clowns on their ladders. They are nicer than the stupid dolls I think yes?

What to do now, would I like? With my life? It is strange you ask me that question you know: it is something I have been thinking about in my mind very much at the present time. Most of all, you see, I have to think I am no longer young woman, and I have to think of the future for my children. I cannot just live my life for myself, and hope that always it will suit them for the future. I did not want my parents' way of life, and therefore perhaps my children will not want for themselves the same as me.

So I think if it was possible, what I would like most to do is go to America. I have friend who has gone there with her husband: he is musician and he plays in an orchestra, and she writes to me about life in America and it sounds that it would be good to live there. They are in the state called Utah. At the present time it would be very hard for me to get permission to leave this country because of our laws. But there is much talk now that it may be made easier before long, and so if it is I think that I shall apply to go. Then there will come the big problem if I would be accepted to live there by the United States: I do not feel they would always be demanding for people who can paint matryoshka dolls and make wooden toys. My friend, she has written to me that she with her husband would support me and my children for some length of time, but before long it would come that I could not just go on in that way, I would have to make the way which was my own.

The reason for me to want to go to live in America, well I would say it is the very opposite one to that you will hear from many people who also tell you that is what they would themselves like to do. I have talked with many who have said it, and they say it is because in USA there is higher way of living, bigger standards, all the people there have motor cars and refrigerators and nice clothes and things like that. That is not the reason for me: because of my belief in the heapy way of life where nobody owns anything and everyone shares everything, such things are not important at all. Instead what is important is the freedom that there is there: and I will say again to make it clear to you, I do not mean the freedom of speech and all these things.

What I mean is the freedom that there is in such another country as USA to go right away from cities and towns, far out into the country or the desert if you wish, and do not have anyone come after you and tell you that you cannot do that. Always here you see you have to have papers and documents, such a thing if you can imagine it as an internal passport to travel to some other place in your own country. Laws, rules, regulations, everywhere, all the time – that is what we have here. No you cannot reside here because your registration is for you to reside there. That it should be like that in your own country, well it is hard to imagine, but it is so. In USA if you want to go from one state into another you do not first have to go to ask permission; but here, yes. In USA if you want to move your homes to live from one state to another, there is no one you should ask, you just do it. But here, no. I have read these things and I have talked with people about them, and so I know. If you are in New York and you want to go to San Francisco, you go just like that. Here no it is not possible: it is not possible even to imagine that you could do it.

I am not political person, I know there would be very many things in America I would not like. But I think that there I could turn away from them and go to live somewhere in another part of the country. I would have the freedom to choose what I did and how I lived, and so would my children also when they are older. It is this feeling that you have the freedom to choose how to make your own life that I want for them to have; not as it is now, that if you want truly to be free then you have to go and hide.

Ella Kirova,

office receptionist*

Smartly dressed in a dark green skirt and jacket over a dark blue blouse, her straight brown hair was cut in a fringe. She sat in her typing chair at her desk in the outer office of her employer, a lawyer; in front of her were a typewriter and a manual telephone switchboard. She talked in a soft voice, from time to time lifting her hand and running her fingers gently through her hair.

– My boss is away this week in Leningrad on business. Now it is my lunchtime hour, but because he is away I do not have very many things to do, so we may talk as long as you wish. I came to work here only one month ago, but I think my boss must be pleased with my work when he is ready so soon to leave me to look after everything for him while he is away.

My name is Ella, I am forty-five years of age, I have a son of seven years of age and his name is Leonid, and I am not married. I have never been married. The father of my son is a married man, and many Russian women when they found themselves in my position, they had become pregnant and they were not married, it could be said the usual thing for them to do was to have an abortion. Abortion is common, or perhaps it would be better to say instead it is not by any means uncommon. Often there are, as in nearly all other countries I think, love affairs between men and women who are not married to each other but who are married to other people, or as in my case who are not married to anyone. As a matter of fact, I will tell you this married man who is the father of my child, he was the first man that I ever had made love with in that way. It was because I loved him, and I have never loved any other man. But do not think I am a person of tragedy: I am not, one has to be philosophical about such things. He did not love me in the way that would make him want to divorce his wife and give me his love instead, but I do not now make myself unhappy for it. I am quite happy in my life now, with my son who of course I love very much and he loves me in return.

Why I did not have an abortion when I became pregnant as most women would have done, well we will speak more of it later. Permit me first to tell you something of my background before it happened, and in this way I think you will better understand why I did not do it. When I was at school, the thing that I liked to do most of all was to learn the French language, and the teacher who taught it to me, she advised me that I had a good feeling and understanding for the language, and also a good pronunciation. She herself was from French parents, and she said she did not advise all her pupils to do this, but for me she advised that when I left school I should go to a language institute to take qualifications to become myself a teacher of French.

This is what I did: I took my diploma at an institute and then became a schoolteacher of French. From the age of twenty-one until the age of thirty-four I was a schoolteacher, and I was very happy to do that because I enjoyed it very much. I would have liked it if I had been able to go to France and stay for some months there, so that I could hear how ordinary French people spoke their language; but this was not permitted in those days, although I went to Morocco for two years as a teacher, and French is widely spoken there. But France itself no, I could not obtain permission to go there.

I had the misfortune in Morocco to contract an illness of the throat. At first it was only that I had many bad colds and sore throats, but then it became worse and worse, and there were many times I could not speak at all. I was like this you know, I would open my mouth and speak and no sound came out. It was finally necessary that I should give up my job and come back home to receive better medical treatment, and I did this. But after many tests I was told by doctors that nothing further could be done, and I would never be completely cured. So it was not possible that I should continue as a teacher, because a teacher who on many days could not talk – well that is of no use at all.

I was unhappy about this, I may say I felt almost it was completely the end of my life, because I was so happy to be a teacher. But the fact had to be accepted: that is how it was, and I resigned my position. I went again to an institute to learn some secretarial skills instead, and then I worked in the clerical department of a factory, and this was for eleven years. I was happy with my colleagues, I lived at home with my mother and father in their apartment, but it seemed to me when I had come to the age of thirty-seven that really life had passed me by. I had not married, I had not met any man whom I had loved or had loved me, and I had lost my career. Oh and also at that time my father had died perhaps one year before, so altogether – well it was for me as though life had no meaning so to say.

Then as I have said, my path crossed with this man, and what happened – well I will say what is true, that it was such a feeling and such an experience as I had never had before. For a short time we were lovers and I found then I had become pregnant. I told my mother about it and she knew that such things happened and did not blame me in any way; but of course she expected that I would do what other women in such a position always did, which was to have an abortion. The man who was my lover and the father of the baby, he was also of course of the same expectation.

But then I began to think seriously to myself of my situation. I was thirty-seven years of age, nearly thirty-eight; I was not married and I had loved only one man in my life, but he was himself married and had children, and was not going to marry me as I had always understood. So it was unlikely for me that I would ever meet and marry some other man; almost certainly if I did, at the age I was then it was unlikely there would be another chance to have a child. So it was that I made the decision that I would not have an abortion, I would remain pregnant and when the time came I would have my baby. I told this to my mother, and I told it also to the father.

He, well perhaps the simplest way to describe his reaction is to say that he was very angry. He said it was my fault that I had allowed myself to become pregnant because I had taken no precautions, and it was my responsibility to terminate the pregnancy. He said if I did not, he would not admit that the child was his, and that in fact he would have no more to do with me. You must understand that I do not in any way blame him for this: I am quite sure any other man would have said the same thing, it is normal for a man to react in that way. So it was the end completely then of our relationship.

For my mother, it was much more difficult. In our country it is frowned upon that a woman who is not married should have a baby. Why should anyone do such an extraordinary thing, when it is so simple to have an abortion and no one thinks less of you that you should do so? But to be so obstinate and stubborn that you go ahead and have a baby, especially when you are not married – well, this is a very bad thing to do, it is against convention, and you are behaving in such a way it is almost as if you are trying to be insulting to everyone. This is almost entirely the attitude of all people of the older generation like my mother; people of my own age are becoming I think you would call it slightly more modern in their outlook. In the office of the factory where I worked, the women of my own age when I told them of my intention, without exception they were understanding and did not withdraw their friendship. But with some of those who were older, it was not so.

For my mother, I am sorry to say that the situation has not changed even now. I live with her still, and she looks after Leni while I work to earn money for the three of us. She is very kind to him, she takes him to school and fetches him home again, and all things of that nature. There could be nothing I could say, of any kind that would be true, to suggest she does not treat him all the time and in every way with affection.

But between us, between myself and her, I am sorry to say there is always unease and strain in our situation. He is now seven, and in that time she has come to love him greatly; but in that same time, her attitude to me has not altered from when I first said I was pregnant. I may say in fact it has become worse, and we have many quarrels and disagreements. I think that she misses very much my father, and would like to be able to talk to him about what attitude she has, and if he could advise her as to what she should do. But she has what I may call an unchanged non-acceptance towards me, because what I have done is unusual. She said to me once that she thought I had done it in a deliberate way to try to hurt her, and I had not taken into account her feelings, what people would think of her that she should have brought up her daughter to allow her to do such a thing. She tells me many times that a woman with a child should be married and part of a proper family unit, which is something which consists of one man, one woman and one child or perhaps two. She tells me also that a child, especially one who is a boy, he needs the presence and influence of a man for his upbringing.

It may be so, it may be that in that last way she is correct. But it is not something which in any way I can do something to bring about. When I worked at the factory I worked long hours so that we should have enough money for three people to live. Now that I work here the pay that I get is better, it is interesting work and I enjoy it in such quiet surroundings. But the responsibility is more, and the hours are even longer still. So how should I have even the opportunity to meet a man who would marry me? I am a little old I think to go out dancing on my own, or to restaurants or such places where a meeting might occur. And anyway I would not like to do it: at the end of the day and at weekends I am tired. I like only to go home and spend time with my son, I am not interested to find a man for a husband. I do not think such a thing anyway could now occur. It was my decision when I was pregnant to allow things to take their course and for me to have a child, because I thought it would bring what I may call some fulfilment to my life. And it is so, it is true, that is what has happened: my life does have meaning for me now, because of my little boy. And it is my responsibility to work hard for him, to earn money to feed him and to clothe him, and to see he has a good home and education, and put as much of my spare time as I can to be with him. I am happy with this situation that it should be so, it is what I myself chose how it should be.

But you know, shall I tell you what it is sometimes I amuse myself to think? Yes? Well there are pages in some magazines that you see, where people write to say they would like to meet another person of the opposite sex: perhaps for friendship, perhaps for marriage, or perhaps even for something else. I would put such an advertisement myself in such a magazine, that is what I amuse myself to think. I would say that I was like all those lonely people must be, with a need for a husband to look after me and my child. He should work all day to earn money for us and for my mother also, it would make a funny joke would it not? Yes, I looked at such a magazine once I think, but I did not think I fitted to what any man described as a partner he was looking for. This is something I tell you to make you laugh, please understand: it is not such a thing I would ever do in reality of course.

Olga Nadimova,
writer

Her apartment was on the ground floor of a large old house in a tree-lined square, in a residential district near the city centre. The sitting-room was large and high-ceilinged, with rows of books on the shelves and modern abstract paintings on the walls. Short and plump with a shock of short frizzy brown hair, dark green trousers and a thick pullover with a patchwork design of bright colours, she walked about while she talked, drank coffee, munched biscuits, and smoked long thin cheroots.

– I shall become too fat if I continue to eat eat eat, that is what my husband used to say. Well, he is gone, we are divorced since one year; I do not have him, but I still have my biscuits. He has his new woman and one day she will become fat too. Next year I am fifty and one day she will also be fifty. I have my man-friend and life goes on. These paintings are all done by my daughter: she is only amateur, and she likes very much everything with bright colour. This pullover was made by her for me, it is her design and then I knitted it myself. You would have liked to meet her you know, she is a very interesting person. What can I tell you that you want to know?

I have always been writing always, ever since I was little girl. That is always what I wanted to do: poems, stories, anything made from words. My husband was a sculptor, he worked for the State, and he made all the time sculptures or how do you call them, monuments. Of Lenin, all the time of Lenin, and so he was never without work: a commission for a new monument to Lenin to be placed outside this building in this city, then another one for that city, on and on all the time like that. Making statues of Lenin, you could work for ever all the rest of your life. He was respected, he was well-paid, and so he was a good person for me to marry, my father said. Well, he was right: I was a good wife for twenty-five years.

He was a good husband also, we are still friendly. He gave me a comfortable home, but most of all he gave me time to write. I did not have to go to look for work, I could stay at home and write and that was all I wanted to do. He did not beat me, he did not have liaisons with other women; well after all, how could he, he was too busy making his sculptures of Lenin. 'Are you happy Olga?' he would say to me. 'Yes Leonid' I would say to him, 'I am happy.' 'Then why do you always write unhappy poems and unhappy stories?' he would ask. It made him sad you see: when he read something I wrote and it was sad, he thought it meant I was sad myself. 'Leonid' I would say to him, 'I do not write about myself, I write about other people. Tolstoy did not write about Anna Karenina because *he* was sad, he wrote about her because *she* was sad.'

It is true I suppose, it is sad people who are more interesting to write about than happy people, especially if they are women. But then I think all women are mostly unhappy, so that is why they are interesting to write about more than men. But men, I do not know: are all men unhappy too? Why are all women unhappy, do I think? Shall I say because of men? No. No, I will think about it and we will talk more of it later.

Yes I am a member of the Writers' Union, but only since three or four years. It was the system until then that you could not be a member until you had had I think it was two books published; and you could not get your books published unless you were a member of the Writers' Union, so it was a circle like this all the time. I wrote articles and I wrote short stories, but I could not get them published in Russia. They were translated into English and were published in America, and into French and were published in France. But not here, no one would publish them here. I think there were two reasons for this: the stories were about women and they were about women's subservient role in Soviet society. The men who made up the committees of the State publishing houses, they did not like this: they said it gave a picture of Russian women that was not true, women did not feel like that. You understand? These bastards are telling me, a Soviet woman, what were the true feelings of Soviet women?

But there has been change now. I have had one book that is published in the United States and another in France, so for the committees I am now someone whose work they wish to publish, because it shows to everyone what freedom we have. OK but I am cynical, I am afraid: I think just as easily it could happen that if there is again a different political leadership, they could throw me away. I do not trust very much these people: they are not writers themselves but they have the power to say who shall be given the designation 'writer'.

It is the same both with the committees of the publishing houses and with the Union of Writers. Some of them, they themselves they write a book; and it is worthless. But because of their position they can approve that it can be printed, in an edition of several million copies. We do not have the royalty system that you have in the West, that you earn royalties on how many copies of your book are sold. Here you are paid for how many are printed. So you see if you are in a position of power, you can order yourself a fortune and one for your friend. Then you will see the situation that the book appears in large numbers of copies in the bookshops, and it sits and sits on the shelves because no one wishes to buy it. So finally it is recalled, and it is pulped. Then what can happen is hard to believe: but it is true, a new edition of the book appears, reprinted on its own recycled paper. This a good system yes? I think you would call it in your country 'Alice in Wonderland'.

Certain of these producers of what we can call such 'authorised' books, something is happening now that they cannot understand. They begin to travel much more abroad and see how things are in other countries; and so to show what a reputation they have here in Russia, they take with them copies of their own books. They show them to publishers in the West, and they say 'Look I am famous author of the Soviet Union, this book I have written had printed there five million copies. I am sure you will want to publish it here, and also in USA, Germany, United Kingdom or Australia or wherever it is.' The publisher takes it to read: but it is not good book, so he says No thank you, he will not publish it. The writer of the book cannot understand this: he thinks the publisher can be given the order to publish it. So he thinks there is conspiracy or something, and he has enemies working against him. Well, these things will change but it will be slow; here the State controls if the book shall be printed, how many copies it will have, whether it should have allocation of paper, the means of distributing it, and the bookshops it is sold in: everything. Can you imagine how many years it will be to change this?

So I am not very optimistic you know for the future here for a writer such as myself. Perhaps you wonder why if I feel in this way, I then belong to the Union of Writers even, why do I have association with it? Well I will tell you. It is something you may think is cynical. Yes it is cynical: I join it for the advantages. Not to have my work published, because I do not need to worry now about that. But the Union of Writers is a trades union, which gives benefit to its members. They have the description of themselves as 'writer', officially; and this means that when they are old and do not wish to write any more, they will have pension. If they are ill, they will have financial support. If they have nowhere to live, they can go to the Writers' Union and ask for help. If they wish a holiday, there are holiday houses where they can go. So there are many benefits, and it is for these that I am a member. Only for these: nothing else. They do not tell me what to write and what not to write: this now they dare not do.

Let us return now to your interesting question at the beginning, when you asked why do I think all women are unhappy? Well it is true you know that in our society, in this Russian society, there is no question that women feel their chief purpose is for the benefit of men. If there are problems which are of concern for them only, men will pay no attention and regard it as something for women to solve. I will give you an example. It concerns the ordinary everyday matter, the provision of sanitary towels. Always, but always, there is shortage of them. A shortage of what is for every woman a basic necessity of life. A man will complain if his wife has not got a good reserve supply in their home of tea or soap. But of sanitary towels? Well that is her problem. You would not believe how many Soviet women, since their age made it necessary, have become completely accustomed to using for themselves such things as cotton wool or cloths, because they cannot get sanitary towels. They regard it as perfectly normal. But you will never see this problem brought to public attention in newspapers or magazines: there is never discussion about how to avoid such shortage and what should be done about it. Yet it affects perhaps one out of every two of all our citizens. If it were men who had such a thing as menstruation, something immediately would be done.

Another thing that is regarded as normal is for women to have abortions. Several abortions in her lifetime, most women will have had: six or seven has been said to be the average. And it is not for fear of illegitimate births: abortions are mostly by women who are married and do not want another child. And you know, this is because the pregnancy is regarded as the woman's problem. And you see it is regarded in that way not just by men, but by women themselves also. They have been brought up all their lives to feel like that: if they become pregnant, it is not the man's fault, it is theirs. They have been in some way negligent, or lazy: she has not counted the days of her month properly and said No, or she has just not bothered. Methods of birth control such as the pill or the coil, they are available to some degree but they have a bad reputation. There is no tradition for a woman to try to avoid pregnancy, I will put it like that. If pregnancy comes, then abortion: that is the tradition.

Shall I tell you something? I think of myself as modern woman: in many ways, influenced by my reading of writers in English, I have become Westernised to a great degree. I know about this, I know about that, there is nothing new I can hear of that would surprise me or shock me. Modern in ideas, up to date, sophisticated. But you know, at times when I became pregnant, although in my head I knew it was not correct, here and here in my heart there was always the feeling very strongly still, driving out all others, that it was my own fault. In this, and in many other things, it is same. The woman is pregnant, it is the woman's fault. Men look for others to blame, anyone except themselves; but for women it is the opposite. They are the first person they blame. They have low self-esteem. Always when something goes wrong, the fault must be theirs because somehow they are not worthy. So I will revise it, what I said: it is not sad that women always feel, they feel uncertain, doubtful of their worth. It is interesting for a woman to think of, on a day when it rains.

11 *Men 2*

Dr Oleg Alyakrinsky, Institute of American Studies

Arkady Forminsky, car driver

Georgi Robinson, retired translator

Pavel Rudov, private detective

Alexander Ilyinarko, entrepreneur

Dr Oleg Alyakrinsky,
Institute of American Studies

An energetic and quick-talking man in his mid-thirties, he wore a tan-coloured linen suit and black boots with Cuban heels. Assured and self-confident, he spoke fluently and with a slight American accent. We talked in his modernly furnished office.

I'll tell you my favourite modern American poem. It's by William Carlos Williams. Some people say these are the sixteen most famous words in the American language. It's called 'The Red Wheelbarrow'; it goes in short lines like this:

> So much depends
> Upon a red wheel
> Barrow
> Glazed with rain
> Water
> Beside the white
> Chickens

I could quote you reams of his other poems too, but that one's always stuck in my mind from the first day I read it. Why did I choose the works of William Carlos Williams for my doctoral thesis? Well obviously because I liked his work very much: of all the modern American poets I liked him and e e cummings the best. Also I guess I wanted to choose a poet who'd not been studied very much before in USSR, not someone widely known like Whitman or Robert Frost. Someone else I considered too for studying for my doctorate was Ezra Pound: but you know, he's so erudite and obscure I think you'd have to be at least fifty yourself before you could learn enough to understand what he's referring to in some of the things he writes. Cummings I find very attractive, particularly in what you might call his 'eye poetry': you know, the typographical arrangements of words and letters on the page to convey effect. One of his I especially like is – well I should really write it down, but I'll trace it in the air with my finger to show you the way it appears. It's a single vertical line of letters put one underneath the other on the page:

A
l
e
a
f
f
a
l
l
s
l
o
n
e
l
i
n
e
s
s

I think it's wonderful. But you know I'd be happy to sit here and quote my favourite poems all day long, so unless that's what you want I guess you'd better ask me more questions instead.

OK right, I'll try and summarise things. Where we are is the Institute of American Studies, which is one part, only one small part, of the USSR Academy of Sciences. It was set up around twenty years ago now; I was still a schoolboy of course then. It's the centre of research in our country for the study of the USA, and there are similar centres for the study of Europe, Latin America, Africa and all the other continents.

We concentrate on learning about, and studying, current affairs in the USA. Every different aspect of contemporary American life – literature, painting, social life, the country's economics, politics, thinking, military planning – everything that happens there is studied by our researchers. We each have particular areas, like mine which is modern literature. We gather all information we can find, on every aspect of our subject, and then analyse it, summarise it, and prepare memos on it for the Foreign Ministry, the Central Committee of Government, the Supreme Soviet, individual ministers at all levels – anyone, in fact, who wants knowledge and information in order to formulate policy or decide exactly how to respond to American actions of any kind, whether they're economic, military or to do with any other matter. They can negotiate, or talk formally or informally at any level with an American person better, if they know as much as there is to know about his background, culture, history, psychology and everything.

We prepare feasibility studies, options of responses that our government could make and then forecasts of what the likely responses would be to our government's responses, and so on. But our work though is confined only to providing information for others to make informed judgements and take decisions on. It's not our function to do such things ourselves, or recommend one course of action in preference to another. Obviously there are similar studies being made of the USSR in the USA: I think I've seen somewhere a reference in the press describing such people there as 'Kremlin watchers', so we might therefore be described in a similar way as 'White House watchers' or 'Washington watchers'. Know your enemy? Well, no, not really, no.

I haven't any what you might call first-hand knowledge of the US to any extent; I went there for a very brief visit once, but that was some years back. I came to the Institute five years ago from Moscow University; there were several American professors there under whom I'd studied – and always of course all the time was speaking nothing but English with them. And when I came, I was hoping at first to confine my work to studying modern American writing. At that time I was reading and writing papers about the work of those who were known as the 'Beat' writers – Kerouac, Ginsberg, Ferlinghetti and the rest. I very soon began to feel a spiritual closeness to such writers: they were alienated from the accepted values of society – not just American society, but our own also. I don't think many people are aware of the similarities: on both sides they prefer to concentrate on the differences between us, which of course are all the time stressed by propagandists in a constant exchange of denigration.

You can't consider a country's literature in a vacuum, or its writers as detached persons not connected with everything around them. Whether they're praising their own society's virtues, and being propagandists for it, or rejecting it and turning their backs on it, you have to know and understand that society, and its values and its powersprings, so that you know exactly what it is the individual contemporary writers are accepting or rejecting. Gradually since coming here I've tried to extend my knowledge of such areas as the more general ideological aspects of Russian and American societies: I wanted to see where they coincided and where they were irreconcilably opposed. I studied as many aspects as I could of American ideology, because it's important to understand the basis on which American policy decisions are made. And so I read not just learned books but popular novels, magazine articles – everything I can find. I suppose now I've produced altogether about thirty or more papers, many of them of considerable length, on ideological aspects of the USA.

I'm not alone here doing this work: as well as writing, I have meetings and discussions with others, so we can exchange information and views. You may be interested by the way to know that now almost without exception, all of us here feel it's useless to continue trying to maintain barriers between our two societies on purely ideological grounds, whether this is done by the USA or by the USSR. And we've had some achievements. For a considerable number of years our government jammed the radio broadcasts to this country of something called *The Voice of America*. We were all very much opposed to this: it seemed foolish to try to stop people hearing what the Americans had to say. Unless people knew what it was, how could they come to any informed decision about their own attitudes? You see *The Voice of America*, which can now freely be heard, might be described as being how America advertises itself and its values. It's of course propaganda, and propaganda's very often self-defeating. If they say things which are not true, and which people know are not true, then they've reduced their future credibility. And *The Voice of America* calls itself that, but it's not really the voice of America at all. It's only one of many voices, some of them diametrically opposed to everything it stands for; it's only the way chosen by a few people to present themselves and their ideas. So people come to understand that, and compare what it says with the views of American visitors they meet – and this doesn't reflect well on *The Voice of America*.

Another aspect many of us here feel strongly about too in this area, is that neither of our two countries, Russia or America, should presume our own particular ideology is suitable to be a universal model for the whole of the rest of the world. Many countries will accept for example economic aid from the USSR, but they don't want the Communism that goes with it; and in exactly the same way, countries that take American aid don't want at the same time to have to embrace the American way of life. I don't think either country should make it a policy aim to spread their own ideology, in an almost Messianic way, wherever they go.

An example of how mistaken such a policy can be, can be easily quoted one from each side. Take the Americans: they believe in the cult of the individual, and in the virtues of self-sufficiency and personal advancement. But this is an idea which is not even faintly grasped by Russians – they've no historical background of the pioneers or anything like that. So the Americans can't export that idea as a whole parcel of virtues. It doesn't take into account the Russian people's history, culture, philosophy or ethical values. So it's a mistake for them just to reject the whole of the Russian way of life and try to substitute theirs, on a presumption the Russians would like it better.

And from the other side, the Russian side, it's equally as big a mistake to presume the only valid social system is the Marxist-Leninist one. It has its ideals, but people can't and shouldn't be expected to live on ideals alone. In fact they won't, however much you wish they would or think they ought to. And to try and impose it on people by force, well I think this can never work; and also once again, it's counter-productive.

Such ideas are spreading a little now in our country, and I like to think we've had some influence at least through our work here in bringing it about. But you know, what I was saying to you a few minutes ago about *The Voice of America* not being the only voice of America – well this would also be true here. I don't know whether people fully understand this in other countries, that just in the same way, not all Communists have the same stance. I'm not myself a member of the Party, but know sufficient people who are to be able to say that it, the Party, seems more and more every day to be dividing into two completely different and opposing camps. There are the old-fashioned Stalinists who call themselves the 'traditional-ists'; and as well there are those you might describe as 'liberals'. And they even further subdivide into ones who want reform but slower, and those who want it to push forward much more quickly. You can even find some of the traditional ideas and some of the liberal ideas not only within the same party but sometimes within the same individual: a person will want both to reform, and to preserve some of the old ways as well.

Particularly you'll find this in areas of argument such as military spending and the maintenance of a large Soviet army. I think almost without exception everyone here is opposed to military thinking, to so-called military 'solutions' to problems. We don't think the Soviet Army should be the size that it is, and not long ago we produced a brochure arguing there should be a cut of at least fifty per cent in military forces. This made us very unpopular with the military establishment of course. And there was also another problem connected with it: one I mentioned earlier, tradition. Compulsory service in the Army, conscription, it's part of the basis of our society. The USSR idea is that you have a truly people's army, one that everyone belongs to. You don't have a sort of élite of pro-fessional soldiers. So if you did away with the Army, you'd be standing tradition on its head. Some people do already think that conscription's a bad thing and suggest young men should start refusing to do military service. But this will take years to happen; not least because universal military service is enshrined in our constitution, there's a law saying we should have it. Any attempt to break the law or refuse to obey it – well this also isn't a tradition in this country, people can't conceive of the idea of saying No to the authority of the government.

It's an interesting time to be alive in our country and see what's happening; and I think I'm young enough to aspire to being alive long enough to see quite a few changes. I like that idea, it gives me a good feeling. And I should say in the finish I think they'll be for the good. I'm optimistic.

Arkady Forminsky,

car driver*

He was sitting at midday in his car where it was parked in the shelter of the buildings along one side of the courtyard. He dozed, his elbow resting on the ledge of the open driver's-side window; his eyes were closed and his head was supported on his hand. A big and amiable man with curly ginger hair, a moustache and a thick beard. He woke up with a start.

– Ah my friend how are you? Where do you wish to go today then? Nowhere until this afternoon? Good, very well, I will still be here waiting for you, do not worry. But yes of course you may sit in the car next to me and our friend in the back and talk, get in. It is warmer in here than out in the snow. You smoke? You are good; I smoke smoke smoke all the time, and it will kill me in the end. What? Well I am astonished: you would like to talk to me about *me*? Truly that is astonishing – but certainly yes, if you wish.

My age? Ah my age – well I can say to you that I am forty-nine, and that is true. I may be forty-nine and one-quarter, I may be forty-nine and one-half, I may perhaps be forty-nine and even three-quarters; but whatever it is, I am forty-nine and I am not fifty. Life is like a swamp, is it not? You go on and on slowly, it becomes harder and harder as you walk, and in the end you disappear with the mud up over the top of your head. But others follow. I have three children – my son who is twenty-three years, my second son who is twenty and has gone to the Army for two years, and my daughter who is thirteen. And I will tell you something that is very strange: they all stand higher than their parents, even already the girl. Perhaps it is good: they will last longer above the swamp than we did I think. My wife says she does not mind at all that our daughter is taller than she is, but she hopes she does not become wider this way, because my wife you see she is let us say just a little plump, you know what I mean?

I have two brothers and two sisters, and all of us live in Moscow except my senior brother. He used to live in Moscow with his wife, but then he became acquainted with another woman and moved with her to Kharkov. Such things happen, it is life. Then I have a second senior brother who lives in the district where I live, and a senior sister who lives in that part also. I left out something I should tell you: it is that my second senior brother works in Moscow and he drives a taxi. I was myself a taxi driver and he liked the idea and became one too.

But then three years ago I left that occupation and came instead to work for this car-hire company which supplies cars and drivers to such organisations as this, the Union of Soviet Writers, and to other organisations too. I like the days when I am designated to work for the Union of Writers, because there are interesting people from all over the world who they ask you to take for them to different places. I have driven only one English writer before: he was a writer I think of detective stories or criminal stories. His name was John Mortimer: is he a well-known writer in your country? Oh he is a very well-known writer? Well I have driven him in Moscow and he was sitting in this same seat you are sitting in now.

I have been doing this work almost for thirty years: a taxi driver first and then I came to this company. I would not say I like it very much: there must be other things to life than sitting behind the driving wheel of a motor car in such terrible traffic as there is here in Moscow. But if there are such things, it has not been my good fortune to find them.

My philosophy of driving, well it is easy to say. In one word I would describe myself as a driver who is calm. I never go at high speeds, and even if somebody comes suddenly in front of me so that I have to put on the brakes sharply to avoid collision, I do not bang on the horn like some drivers do, and shake my fist and shout. This is the most important impression I like to give to my passengers and to other drivers, that I know what I am doing and nothing will disturb or upset me. Sometimes a man I have come to fetch, perhaps he is an important person and he comes running to where I am waiting, and he says 'Quickly, quickly, I am an important man and I am late and I need urgently to get to the Ministry!' Well you know it always seems to me they can continue to wait for him for some more minutes at the Ministry, but I am not going to take risks in my car for myself or other people because he is late. If that was the case he should have come to me sooner. There are some drivers they have to make such speed they drive first in this lane, then in that one, then back to the other again; and when you come to the traffic lights at an intersection, there they are sitting waiting impatiently, and you have caught up with them doing your own steady speed. All they have achieved is to have given some other people nearly a heart attack; and one day perhaps they will give themselves a heart attack too.

The thing I like least of all, well it is when the motor car I am driving breaks down and stands at the side of the road and will not go. To be a driver you have also to know how to get it to go again and mend it with your hands: it is very hard in Moscow to get even the smallest spare part of any kind for a motor car, so you must know how to make repairs, even to tie things together with string so you can go along. And the most important thing of all is you must be a student of psychology. Not of people, but of motor cars. Each one is different, so you must find how to handle it correctly when it breaks down. One will respond only if you speak with it gently and give it sympathy and encouragement; another, you must become angry and shout, and even perhaps strike it with your fist or give it a very hard kick, because that is the only language it understands. Each one is different, it is like a horse you see; and if its days are over you must accept that, that all life comes to an end, it is not the motor car's fault or yours, it is life.

So that is the formulation of some of my ideas. As I have said, the main one is to be calm. But sometimes, you know, it is a great strain to remain calm. Perhaps there is a very bad day with the traffic, and a very difficult passenger as well, who says he wants to go first to this place, and then changes his mind and says he wants to go somewhere else, then changes it again and demands you take him once more back in the opposite direction. All this and all the other drivers in the traffic trying to kill you – well believe me, to stay calm as I do, it lasts only until I get to my home in the evening, and then sometimes I may explode. With anger, or with tears, or with both. My wife has some tablets she gives me, and they are good: in one hour, or two, I feel better again and ready for driving once more the next day. But it is not good for health to take tablets.

It is better to do what I do if I can, which is to save up all my feelings until the end of the week, and then take one day completely away from all such things, and relax. The greatest relaxation of all for me is to go fishing, either to the Moscow River or to a lake in the countryside. It is a very healthy thing to do, and for the four years now that I have been doing fishing, I have not had a single day from work with illness. Winter or summer it does not matter, I fish whatever is the weather or the season. In summer I sit on the grass by the lake under the trees, and in winter I take my little tent and little stool and I sit on the ice in the middle of the river. It is safe to do this but you must wait until the ice is ten centimetres thick at least: then you can sit on it and make a hole in it and put in your line. But you have to take great care that the ice is sufficiently thick for a person to sit on, very great care indeed. Every winter in Moscow there are children who go to fish without an adult with them, and they are impatient and will not wait another day for the ice to thicken. So they go through it and they are carried away by the water beneath; no one can rescue them, and they drown. That is how children are sometimes and it is sad; but of course, well, it is life.

It came to happen four years ago that I began to fish for this reason I will tell you: I used to spend very much too much of my time in beer parlours. You have not been in one? Well I will not offer to take you because I go into them no more, but I will tell you what they are like. They are just a small room with ledges round pillars and on the walls; and in one corner there is a dispensing machine with paper cups. You put in your kopeks, I think it is forty now, and hold the cup under the spout, and it fills with beer. The beer is put into tanker lorries to come to the parlours, and I may tell you that there is water also put into the tankers, so the beer is very weak. And water is again put into the dispensing machines in the beer parlours as well, so you can imagine how many hours it is necessary to remain there drinking this liquid to gain any effect that is different from drinking water. You can sit there a whole day almost. Then the drinker goes home in the evening and shouts at his wife, and she shouts at him, and so it goes on. And well, you understand, I was such a man: that was the main way I got my relaxation after driving.

But one day it happened to me that I saw another driver at work, and he was putting a fishing rod and other equipment in his car, and I asked him what he was doing. It was a summer evening, and he told me he was going to the Moscow River to fish, and he invited me to go with him. This was what I did, and I liked it so much I went with him the next evening and the next evening as well. I was, I may say, exactly like a fish on a hook: I was caught. He lent me some copies of the magazine *Fisherman*, and I spent every moment reading them while I was waiting for people. It gave advice to beginners on everything: what bait to buy for different fish, how to tie it if it was necessary, which were good fishing rods and lines – everything.

It seemed to me this was a much better hobby to have than going home every evening to shout at my wife, and so I do not do this any more, nor does she any more shout at me. Also, she likes very much to eat fresh fish, and so she is every time very happy when I take home something I have caught. I have invited her to come with me to watch this fishing, but so far she has not done so: she says it is the woman's place to stay in the kitchen and prepare the pans and dishes and plates, and lay the table to be ready for my return. This has made our life together very much happier now, I assure you. And my daughter – well I have invited her also to come sometimes with me; but she is a young person and would sooner do other things such as dancing to pop music with her friends. That is how life is when you have a child, the child will not always be interested in the same things as you. It would be a great advantage for me though if she or her mother would come: fish are not fools you know, and I suspect sometimes they can scent the nicotine from my fingers on the bait, and will not take it because they know I am waiting for them. But if it were tied by a woman's hands, they would not be able so easily to tell. They trust women more I think.

The thing that gives me the greatest joy? I will tell you. I have always been something of a scientist, with an interest in inventing things. Last year I constructed for my fishing a small tube like this to carry a certain bait on a hook below it. The tube contains a little flag, and when the fish takes the hook, it slides out of the tube and sticks up like this in the water. I tell you, when I see the little flag go up and can say to myself that such an invention was my own idea, it is a moment of pure happiness for me.

Georgi Robinson,
retired translator

A well-built white-haired man, dressed in a dark suit and collar and tie, he sat in a high-backed dining chair at his kitchen table, his pale eyes looking out of the window of his high-up apartment. His voice at first was tight and tense, and until he was more at ease he talked stumblingly.

– It's difficult to suggest what description you should give of me. In my life I've done many things and I've been many things. You could say I was a retired translator, a retired private schoolteacher, a retired artist, or even a retired draughtsman. They'd all be true, I've done all those things. You could even say I was a retired prisoner from a prison camp, that'd be true as well. The operative word is 'retired': I retire from people, I don't tell them much. I'm keeping it all for a book I'm going to write, or that's what I tell myself. Whether I'll ever do it of course is another matter.

One of the things about my life which makes it difficult to talk about is that I don't know much about it. I mean in the sense that I've arrived at the age of sixty-seven without really knowing who I am. Perhaps it could be better put by saying that I thought I knew who I was until about ten years ago, and then discovered that I wasn't at all who I thought I was, I was someone completely different who I knew nothing about. It's very confusing.

Let's start by saying I'm English. Or I think I am, I'm fairly convinced I am now, but for most of my life I'd thought I was Russian. My mother was Russian and my father was Russian – until, that is, I discovered my father was really someone else, and in fact he was English. I officially retired from work when I was sixty, and I've spent the last six or seven years since then trying to unravel it all, and to help it along I've given myself this sort of half-and-half name. It's not my name but it'll do to be going along with kind of thing. If it sounds very confusing and incomprehensible, that's because it is. As I expect you can tell, I get very nervous talking. It'd help me if I smoked a cigarette, so if you don't mind. Right, well now perhaps I'd better try and start again.

With your childhood you remember little bits here and there, then as you go through life you pick up more little bits. You learn things about yourself and your past: you didn't know them, but other people tell you. 'You used to live in such-and-such a place' they say, and you think Oh did I, well fancy that, I remember the sunshine and the house, so that was Cape Town was it, well I never knew that. That's how it was with me. I was there in Cape Town as a very small boy, and I think I was born there too most likely. My mother was an Englishwoman but I've no recollection of my father, I don't know who he was or at least at that time I didn't.

Because what then happened was what you might call in the nature of a sudden change, and the next thing I recall is I was here in Moscow, living with my mother and the Russian I call my father. I haven't the faintest idea how it came about. My mother never talked about it; but she did talk to me in English, which is how I come to speak English naturally, almost as what you might call my first language. So far as I recall she never told me anything about South Africa, or what she'd been doing there, she never mentioned it. Or how she came to be living in Moscow married to a Russian who was my father, so I was always led to understand both by her and by him. With them I talked Russian also as my first language. She and he talked mostly Russian together and I don't think he talked any English at all. She never gave me any reason to think she wasn't Russian, or that I wasn't either. When you're a small child you just accept things as they are and you don't question how they came about, or at least I didn't.

So anyway that was the situation. I'd been born in the 1920s, probably in Cape Town, and then something happened, and my mother and father split up. That's if they were married in the first place of course. Then somehow or other she met a Russian man and came to Moscow with him and me. She let me grow up thinking he was my father and he went along with it. The only curious thing, though I didn't think it was curious at the time, was that for a short period, when I was still very young, I'd say under ten certainly, she sent me to a private Anglo-Russian school here. Therefore I received what you could call an English primary school education. Then after that I was put in a Russian school and continued my education there. I don't know why, probably the money ran out or something. Or – but I don't really know this, it's only conjecture and it's only occurred to me recently – perhaps the man who was really my father had been sending her money for me, and then for some reason or another he stopped. I'm only guessing though.

After that I continued to grow up as a Russian boy, and then my mother died. I don't know what from, I don't know what the illness was that she had, but she must have been fairly young, perhaps in her forties or somewhere around there. I'd be about twelve or thirteen then, and though of course I didn't know it at the time, that was the end of any chance of me ever being able to ask her questions about the circumstances of my origin. This wasn't apparent to me, and my Russian father as I'll call him, he continued to bring me up just as if I was his own son. He didn't marry again and I know we didn't have a lot of money because he wasn't particularly highly qualified at anything; but I never went short of food or clothing, and of course all Russians have this extended-family idea, so there were plenty of aunts and uncles and grandmothers to look after me and see I was all right.

Then the war came. It started in 1941 when I was eighteen. In one of the very first air raids on Moscow that there was, my father was killed. He was in some office building or other, and a bomb fell on it and that was that. One morning he went off to work as usual, he didn't come home to our apartment at the end of the day, and one of my aunts I think it was came round in the evening with the news, and said she was going to take me there and then to live with her and her husband. Naturally I was very upset about his death, I seem to recollect I was much more upset about it than I was when my mother died. As I say, I didn't at that time know he wasn't my father; but even if I had known it wouldn't have made any difference, because he'd been in every way like a father to me.

Not long after that I was due to go in the Army like everybody else, but I didn't pass the medical examination because I had poor eyesight. It must have been very poor indeed, because they were taking everyone. Instead I was drafted into a job with the Moscow radio station, translating news bulletins from English into Russian, and sometimes reading a few pieces of news which I'd translated from Russian into English. There was bombing and shelling and food shortages and heaven knows what else, and it was a pretty tough time. But I had the great consolation that at the radio station I met and fell in love with a young Russian girl, and we got married. We found a tiny one-room apartment of our own, and we were more happy under those circumstances than hundreds of thousands of other people were in those times. We're still married to this day: a little while ago we celebrated our forty-fifth wedding anniversary, and we've two daughters grown-up and married, and we've four grandchildren.

Then round about 1948 or '49 came the Cold War, and the Stalin reign of terror. What he'd done before the war had been fairly dreadful, but it was nothing to what he started to do afterwards. I was one among tens of thousands of people arrested: the KGB came for me one day at work saying I was arrested for spying, and they took me off to the Lubianka gaol. They weren't too bothered about producing any evidence, they just said in my work at the radio station I'd been in contact with British and American visitors, and some of them were spies and they'd taken back information I'd given them to their own countries. I was kept in the Lubianka for six months, and while I was there like everyone else I got regular beatings. Their idea was to break you down and get you eventually to confess to whatever it was they said you were guilty of, then take you to court for trial and sentencing based on your confession. In my case I hadn't done anything so there was nothing I could confess to: so finally they didn't bother taking me to court, just came into my cell one day and gave me a piece of paper, which they read out to me. It said I'd been found guilty of being an enemy of the State and indulging in anti-Soviet propaganda, and the court had sentenced me to ten years' imprisonment in a labour camp. So I was taken off to Archangel and I worked digging ditches with hundreds of other men who'd been punished in that way for crimes the State said they'd committed.

Everyone was in the same boat, there was nothing you could do about it, and nobody was going to come and help you. I didn't know where my wife and children were or what was happening to them. I did know that so long as she herself wasn't arrested on some trumped-up charge, other members of her family would look after her. And what I didn't know at the time either, and it would have made me worry very greatly about her if I had, was that she was keeping up a continuous one-woman campaign for my release. She kept writing letters to government departments, going to government offices and demanding to see people, and all the rest of it. If I'd known about it, I would literally have begged her to desist, because she was putting herself in such terrible danger.

However, I was one of the fortunate ones. After 1953 when Stalin died, under his successors Malenkov and Khrushchev there was a period of a few years of what became known as 'the thaw'. Amongst other things in it, they started releasing people who'd been given long sentences even though they weren't guilty of anything. They must have had thousands and thousands of cases to look at, but mine was one which they saw and rescinded, so I was only in the labour camp five years and then they let me out. I came back to Moscow, and tried to resume normal life again. I say 'tried' deliberately, because you'd be surprised how difficult it is. You all the time lived under the feeling that you were being watched and under suspicion: you couldn't rid yourself of the fear that if you did or said the slightest thing just a little bit wrong, you'd be arrested and imprisoned again. Everybody else had the same fear; but they hadn't done anything, whereas you were 'a known criminal' as it were, so you felt you had to be doubly careful.

And you know, it lasted for years, that feeling. I remember once, it must have been five years after I'd come home at least, and one night my wife and I'd gone to a hotel to meet some friends and have a meal with them. While we were waiting for them to arrive, a man and a woman came in, and I recognised him as an English person I'd known from when I was working at the radio station, ten years or more before. I went over to him and he recognised me and we exchanged just a few words; then the friends we were waiting for arrived, so my wife and I went off into the restaurant with them. We'd been in there only about ten minutes, and then suddenly I burst into a cold sweat, sweating violently, my hands started trembling, everything. It was fear, pure fear at what I'd done in going over and speaking to the Englishman I'd known before. I started thinking I shouldn't have done that, I shouldn't have done that. He was one of the people I was arrested for consorting with, what if I've been seen talking to him again? It was no good, I was in such a state about it I had to apologise to our friends and say I was ill, and my wife had to take me home.

It's still present in me, to some extent, even now: once in a while, just for a few moments this fear comes back that I'm being watched. It's quite irrational, but I'm not by any means the only person who's got it. It's all part of the KGB's psychological success: for years, until quite recently really, they liked to give the impression they were everywhere. They wanted everyone to believe everyone was watched, everyone's telephone was bugged; and they liked tourists and visitors to the country to think it too. Your hotel room was bugged, you were being watched wherever you went by unobtrusive men in mackintoshes and fur hats, all that sort of nonsense. I mean if you only just pause to think about it, it has to be nonsense. If it was true, it'd mean the KGB'd got a staff of millions listening in on telephones, opening letters, keeping watch on everyone. It's just not a feasible idea at all. But what is feasible is what I've said – and a jolly good job they've made of it too: the KGB's done nothing to contradict the idea they're all-seeing and all-knowing. It's in their interest, or it was until quite recently, for people to think that.

Anyhow: to get back to the time when I came home from the labour camp. Somehow my wife had managed to keep her job, but they wouldn't take me back into broadcasting because of my foreign background and being in prison. And that's more or less how it's gone for the rest of our life: my wife's been the main bread-winner with the steady job, and I've taken what I could get when I could get it. A bit of coaching of children privately in English, a spell as a mechanical draftsman for an engineering factory: I do technical drawing quite well, but I'm self-taught and haven't any proper qualifications. Now and again I do some translating for foreign digest publications. We get by: my wife's a small pension, I've an even smaller basic State one, and that's it.

As for the other matter, well the reason I'm still not very far on, is that I've not got enough money to go to England and really start making a search. The story of my conception and all that South African business – well all this was told to me by one of my aunts some good few years ago now, who said she'd been told it by my mother. My mother had told her she was going to tell me 'when I was old enough' was the phrase, but of course she didn't survive that long. I suppose my Russian father had the same idea, that he'd tell me when I was grown-up, or at some such suitable time, but he didn't get the chance to either. I call myself 'Robinson' because that's a good old English name, but I don't know what it is really. I suppose the sensible thing would be to forget it altogether. Only somehow I can't, it keeps nagging away at the back of my head: more so in recent years, I don't know why. Perhaps because I'm not working and have got more time to think. Or perhaps it's because I'm getting old, and just feel I'd like to know a bit more about myself before time runs out. But I think I will definitely try to put it into a book.

Pavel Rudov,
private detective*

A thin man of forty, short and smart in a dark suit and open-necked shirt, with a moustache and deep-set brown eyes, he appeared suddenly by the table in the corner of the crowded cafeteria, standing formally to attention. A quick handshake, then he put on the table for inspection his identity document with its colour photograph of himself, and a printed business card.

– May I sit? Thank you. Allow me to present myself: Rudov, Pavel, of the Alexander Detective Agency. We have as you see two branches, one here with our Moscow address, and the other with the address on this side is our office in Leningrad. I am the head of our Moscow branch, and the senior partner. Thank you yes, I will have some mineral water.

Shall I now continue? I am in charge of our Moscow operations, my partner Mikhail Gregorovich with whom I founded our enterprise takes care of things in our Leningrad office, and I go there twice in each month to ensure everything is functioning smoothly. We have no problems between us and a good working relationship; I started the business now just one year ago, and my partner joined me shortly afterwards. It is the very first of its kind in the USSR. Why it is called the Alexander Detective Agency? It is because Alexander is a Greek name meaning 'defender of men', so I chose it for that reason: we see ourselves as offering security as well as detection. Protection, security, surveillance, industrial counter-espionage – it is not possible always to define where they overlap each other, and so this is a comprehensive name for all we do. It is the first such organisation of its kind in the USSR, but I think before long others will follow our example. We have shown there is a need, and a growing one, for such a thing in our country now businesses of the private-enterprise type are being allowed, and they begin to flourish. Companies from other countries in the world are now beginning joint ventures with Russian businesses here, so we offer our services to them also.

The idea for this type of private agency, it must be said that it was entirely mine. I was working in the Interior Ministry, in the State police system, the militia, for almost twenty years, and I was a plain-clothes detective in the department concerned with economic crime, such as fraud on a large scale. I was specifically concerned for six years with that particular aspect of law-breaking, and as a result gained a wide spectrum of experience. By this I mean not just of the detection of criminal fraud, but where opportunities for it would occur. I was aware of the possibilities of it happening before it actually did so: the weaknesses in various businesses that could be exploited, so to say. Naturally I cannot speak too specifically of these things and describe individual cases; but in time I had more knowledge of the subject than almost any one other single individual who exists.

You see the State cannot, as you will understand, act to prevent crime of such kind: it can take action only after it has been committed and detected, then it can prosecute. But what I can offer, what my agency can offer, is advice to private companies in advance: warning them of flaws and weaknesses in their accounting and financial systems, studying business dealings they are proposing to engage in and pointing out to them how they might be taken advantage of by opportunities for fraud against them. All such things as that: we demonstrate to them how the spending of a little money in advance to us for advice can prevent the possible loss to them in the future of huge sums. It is not giving away secret information, I am sure, to say that in a huge bureaucratic system such as we unfortunately have, there are many opportunities for corruption and malpractice. I may quote, it is well known now from newspapers, that there are many instances of such things as goods not reaching their destination, or being detained and sold where they should not be. So you will be able to see why, as the extent and number of private business ventures here increase, as they are now doing so rapidly, there is considerable opportunity for us.

We also offer other services to business companies, such as the guarding of premises against robbery. We provide patrol guards, with or without dogs as requested, and night-security guards for offices. We can also provide personal bodyguards for businessmen who for example may be carrying large amounts of valuable jewellery or gold and silver with them when they are travelling about the country, or visiting to it from countries abroad. Our operators who perform this kind of work are all highly skilled athletes who are trained in unarmed combat. They give what we name 'visible protection' to an individual who wants it to be obvious to potential assailants that he is guarded, or invisible protection to him if he prefers it to be like that. Some of our men work for all the time in this way, others we call upon just for periods when they are needed. We train them in knowledge of the law, to know what steps they would be permitted to take and what they would not be permitted to. Up to now at least, we have had no problems in this area. None of them is licensed to carry firearms.

Forgive me, yes your interpreter did exactly translate to me your question, and your repeating of it, as to whether they carry firearms. He will also translate to you exactly again my answer: none of them is licensed to carry firearms.

As for other aspects of our work, I will tell you some of the other things which we do. An important one is the tracing of missing persons. This may be a simple matter, a wife perhaps wishing to find the whereabouts of her former husband, who is avoiding paying her money which he has been ordered to do by a court for the maintenance of their child. But it also covers such situations as an employee missing from his firm with possession of money, or merely information perhaps, which his firm wishes to recover from him but does not have sufficient evidence to take to the police. Always of course if there is such firm evidence, we advise the client that that is what he should do at once, to put the matter in the hands of the proper authorities.

We do also such things as offer assistance to large companies who are engaged in manufacturing of a technical or scientific nature, and discover that information about their processes or methods is being given by someone within their company to let us say one of their competitors. You will again understand I am sure that I am not willing to give you too specific a picture of our activities, except to say that we are in a position to offer several methods, all of them effective, in discovering who the culprit or culprits are. It is then up to those who have employed us to take what measures they wish against those concerned. As you can imagine, industrial espionage is extremely difficult and the most sophisticated of methods must be used for it.

I am sorry, I think your interpreter and I are having confusion here in understanding one another. Permit us to speak together for one moment please. Ah yes I now understand, the words are somewhat different in meaning: the service we provide is that of counter-espionage, we do not offer industrial espionage, that would be illegal.

One further and perhaps final aspect of our work which might interest you, and for which we are now receiving an increasing number of requests, is that of the surveillance of children and young persons. It is like this: parents for example are worried that their daughter or their son is getting into bad company, perhaps associating with young drug takers or drinkers, or even young persons of a criminal nature. So they come to us and ask us to keep watch on them for a period of say one week or two, and then give them a report on what places the child goes to, who his or her friends and associates are, whether they are of good character or not, and their backgrounds and whatever information we can obtain about them. We then prepare a complete report to the parents on their child's behaviour and it is of course confidential to them. No, I do not have any idea why the parents should come to us rather than talk themselves to their child, but it is a fact that they do. It demonstrates the amount of worry that children cause their parents these days: as I have said, work of this kind now makes up a considerable proportion of our activity.

Forgive me I am sorry, I do not understand your remark which has just been translated to me, may I consult again for a moment with your interpreter?

Ah yes, I think it is that I have given a wrong impression to you by using a word which your interpreter translated as 'surveillance' in the case of young people. We have of course available to us many highly trained operatives who are very skilled in working with teenagers, talking to them and gaining their confidence and so on. In every case we prefer it if parents will give us permission to try to reach a situation where we ourselves can talk to the children about the worries they are causing their parents, try to discover the reasons for their behaviour, and point out to them the risks they are running if it seems for example they are taking drugs. We ask them to consider where their conduct is leading them, the dangers that may soon confront them, and things of that kind. In every case we try hard to get them to see where they are behaving wrongly, and how the situation with their parents may be improved. We hope they will see their parents' point of view and, if their activities are wrong, will take steps to correct them such as for example becoming a member of an appropriate youth organisation.

So I think now you will understand what a great variety of things we do and how many different services we offer, in areas where the law and order forces of the State are not able to operate. I would say that without doubt within the next few years there will be an outbreak of demand for what we can provide in other parts of the Soviet Union. It is my ambition that we should before long have branches of our agency in at least thirty cities. Now that the climate of opinion is changing and private business is being allowed to develop, I think the future for us looks to be very good.

Two things only are hampering us. One is the shortage of modern technology equipment in our country. Such things are either not manufactured or they are of poor quality. We would like to have for instance radio monitoring devices, and also in particular car telephones, so that our operatives could keep in touch with each other and with their headquarters. Unfortunately they are scarcely yet in existence here: a few taxis in Moscow have radio-telephone communication with their central office, but beside that there is nothing. And the other thing which restricts us of course is money: we cannot buy such equipment from abroad because we do not have the hard currency to do so, and we have no individual sponsor or sponsors. All the money of myself and my partner is invested in our enterprise: we do not owe anything to anyone else, and we have not taken out large loans. But – I am hopeful for the future. It is interesting and necessary work that we do, and after all we are now only at the beginning of our project.

Alexander Ilyinarko,

*entrepreneur**

Slightly built, thin-faced and fair-haired, he wore a beige corduroy jacket, light brown trousers and trainers. His handshake was firm. While he talked, occasionally a look of cautiousness came into his eyes: he seemed uncertain whether what he was saying would be regarded as heretical.

– My age is thirty-two, and I have been resident in Moscow now for four years. I originate from a small town in the north Caucasus region, but there would be little purpose in me giving you its name, because it's very unlikely you would have heard of it. I live here in Moscow with a friend: she and her husband have an apartment on the western side of the city, and through their kindness I'm able to have one room of this, for which I pay a proportion of their rent. Let me assure you I have the necessary permits to reside in Moscow should you wish to see them; I carry them with me always, because as a businessman it is necessary for me that everything I do is proper and correct. In a bureaucratic system such as ours, if I may say so, it's always easy to get into trouble if some person thinks your papers aren't correct. You never want that to happen: it risks giving a customer with whom you may be trying to negotiate a large contract, the impression the person he's dealing with is not all he appears to be. This has not happened to me, but I have heard of it; so it's better never to take the risk that it might. Coming to meet you and talk with you this evening, for example, you could be suspicious of things I said, if you'd reason to suppose I was not a thoroughly respectable person.

Since the arrangement for us to meet each other was made, I have thought over carefully what I should say to you and what I should tell you. I have decided that the best thing would be to tell you openly and without hesitation everything you wish to know. It seems to me if we meet as two honest persons, with an arrangement to talk for a while, that is the best. This is exactly how I always like things to be, and I am therefore most happy to meet with you like this. We may call it an arrangement for friendship, if there could be such an expression.

I moved to Moscow from the small town in the northern Caucasus where I was born and grew up because I had a great desire to develop myself, I wanted to attain a higher standard of living. I have an ex-wife and two children there, and I return to see my children perhaps twice a year; in the meantime I send their mother regular payments towards their upbringing. My ex-wife enquired of me the last time I was there, which was just before Christmas, if there was any chance that in the future I might return – to the place of course, it was not a personal enquiry with reference to her, since she now has another husband. I told her what I will tell you now, that I could never again live in a place like that, because it contained nothing progressive or imaginative that anyone could find to do. The only place I could live now is Moscow. It would be wrong to give the idea that I came to Moscow only to seek success. Here I feel the possibility of that exists, and in my work I think I shall attain it. But there were also personal reasons.

They were to do with a woman naturally. I do not know if you have yet met many women in Moscow, but if you have you will understand what I mean when I say they are different from other women anywhere else in our country. It is to do with their eyes of course. Well, that is an expression which we have. It is because of the great shortage of accommodation in Moscow and other such cities that there is very restricted opportunity for men and women to speak to each other about intimate things without being over-heard. So therefore all such conversations are conducted through the eyes only; and Moscow women are particularly noted for their ability to convey to you most frankly what they are thinking and feeling, simply by looking at you directly with their eyes.

But before I tell you of that circumstance, first I will continue my account of what activities I had been engaged in in my town of origin. I went to do my service in the Army, and I was there in a communications unit. I found it fairly interesting, but it did not provide me with any knowledge or experience I could put to use after my service ended. At that point in my life, I then decided to try and form some kind of business of my own. This as you know is very difficult in the Soviet Union, because almost everything is concentrated in the hands of the State. I tried to form a small business to do with the transportation of farm produce; but there were difficulties for that in every way, because the State had the monopoly not only of transport but also of the produce of the farms. Then I attempted to run a taxi business, but again I was thwarted by the need for filling in endless forms and obtaining necessary permits. I tried, also unsuccessfully, to bring into existence what you may call a kind of accountancy business and advisory centre, but this failed also. Under Soviet conditions, it is never easy to thrive if you are trying to do something which is outside the main roads, if you understand me. I am sorry to say that the person who least of all understood my desire to work for myself and my family, and take something other than an ordinary occupation which involved only routine activity, was my wife. She was discouraging towards anything that required enterprise, and was always trying to persuade me to be no different from others, and questioning why I felt such need to act on my own. This misunderstanding between us gradually widened until it became a deep rift, and it's what finally made it necessary for us to part.

For perhaps one and one-half years before this came about, I had made a number of trips to Moscow, five or six in that period, for the purpose of visiting a friend I had been at school with. He had married a young woman who was a ballet dancer, and she was a Muscovite and he had come to live here with her. We were close friends and he had much more understanding of my nature than my wife had. It was he who first told me many of the ideas and desires I was expressing were known in the West, where they were described as 'private enterprise'. He introduced me to a friend of his who had the same outlook and was of the same age: she was working for one of the first Russian-American joint business ventures to be established, in a large office. There she was gaining a great deal of experience of such matters as the importing and exporting of machinery, and general methods of private trading and business.

There are no such things in the Soviet Union as schools where you can go to learn business matters, since all such activity has always been in the hands of the State. This put this young lady in a very advantageous position; she was aware of it, and she was taking full advantage of it and all the time learning and learning. I found this a very attractive quality in her: it seemed to me she was a person of great character and enterprise, who knew what she wanted from life and applied herself to gaining knowledge which would help her acquire it. It was just beginning at that time, four years ago, that our State system was starting to allow private farmers to come into Moscow and sell their produce; and she saw in such things the possibilities there were. In our understanding of such things we were the same; and there was also developing between us, through the eyes if I may express it like that, another kind of attraction also.

Then an extraordinary event occurred: some people might call it that, though I do not myself. Many hundreds of thousands of people in the USSR take seriously the matter of reading their horoscopes which are printed in the newspapers and magazines. They do not blindly commit their actions and reactions to whatever they read there, but take into account what is forecast for them each week, before they decide whether to follow a certain course or not. One of the most popular, because he is one of the most accurate and sensible of these astrologers, is from Nepal; his predictions and comments are very widely known in our country. It will give you some idea of his popularity and of his reputation, when I tell you he is quoted regularly on State TV at weekends in the late-night news.

What I am telling you of what occurred is this. I had been several days in Moscow, and during that time had begun to discuss with my young lady the idea that we might go together into partnership in some kind of business venture. Then on my return home at the end of the week, I was reading in the newspaper the horoscope for my birth sign by the Nepalese astrologer. In it was a suggestion, very strongly made: that if I was considering some new venture in my life, what the stars foretell for me was I should immediately take any necessary steps. If I delayed, the astrologer said, a good opportunity would not present itself again for a long time.

I therefore returned at once to Moscow. I went to see this young lady and asked her what I did not know: it was what the date of her birth was. When she told me, I realised it was not the same as mine and we had a different sign of the zodiac. I told her what the astrologer had said in my case, and together we looked for what he was advising for her; and we agreed before we did, that if it was in any way contrary to mine, we would abide by what he said for her. So, I will tell you that the prediction for her was not the same as the one for me. No: it was even more emphatic, saying something of the nature of 'You will be presented with a new and completely unexpected opening in life, and you should take it without hesitation.' As you can imagine, it was a most exciting moment for us, to find this prediction in each of our cases, which so accurately referred to a matter we had been talking about only some days before.

And that is how I came to set up a business partnership with her, and soon afterwards came to live in Moscow. I have spoken already this evening of the difficulties and frustrations that attend almost every step you try to take in a bureaucratic state. It is only correct therefore that I should say now that on both the matters of getting a permit to reside here, and in setting up and registering our private import-export agency, everything went swiftly and smoothly: either bureaucracy was nodding asleep and could not be bothered to put difficulties in my way, or else the complete nature of the Soviet State has changed overnight. My own tendency is to think the former is the case.

We progressed slowly, we are still progressing slowly. We did not require a large sum of capital to equip ourselves: we are after all, shall we say, middle people, as it were between those with demands and those with supplies, putting one in touch with the other and taking our commission on the deal. We are also all the time on the look-out for new opportunities to expand in any direction, and we are building up what may be called a consultancy. People come to us asking 'Where can I get this?' or they approach us from other countries abroad and say to us 'I have this, who could I sell it to in your country?' With the relaxations which have occurred in the past few years things, though they are not always easy, have become easier. When we can, as we now quite often do, act as agents in business matters which bring us the so-called hard currency, naturally a number of doors are opened for us.

As everybody knows, since the Revolution very many Russian people fled their country and emigrated to others. Some of them were successful settlers and founded businesses, and their children after them developed these, sometimes into large companies. We have approached by now quite a number of them, offering to find them equipment or machinery, and also to become their agents in this country for their products. I will give you an example: we are at present supplying to a Canadian farming consortium small helicopters, Soviet-made, which are much cheaper than those they can purchase elsewhere, but of equivalent or in some instances better quality. This is a large contract, and for regular supply.

So perhaps I may say to you it is not only the stars' predictions which suggest good omens for this business being profitable. To hear such a phrase as that – 'profitable business' – spoken by a Soviet citizen, well I think it is something you may not have heard said very often, is that correct?

12 Big names

Stanislav Sorokin, GUM Department Store Manager

Vitali Rossolov, Bolshoi Theatre stagehand

Ludmilla Orlova, Intourist guide

Marc Winer, Director, McDonald's Hamburgers

Stanislav Sorokin,
GUM Department Store Manager*

Smartly suited, polite, confident, quietly spoken and in his early fifties, he sat at the glossily polished conference table in his office on the third floor of the huge old-fashioned building overlooking Red Square.

– Oh yes, many hundreds of years ago there has always been market-trading here in the square, long before GUM Store was built in 1893. In one of his novels, I think it is *Fathers and Sons*, Turgenev describes some of the stalls that were here displaying goods, and the people all round them doing their shopping. As you have seen, basically it has kept to its tradition: GUM Store is like a big covered market hall. It has three landings, with individual shops or stalls arranged all the way round each one, and the open space in the centre goes from the ground-floor level right up to the glass roof. Under a decree which Lenin signed in 1922, it became the first of the State Trading Shops; he laid great emphasis on the importance of trade to the economy and I think his ideas about it were far-seeing.

GUM Store is the largest department store in the world. Its area of floor space is fifty thousand square metres; other such places elsewhere in perhaps USA or some other countries may be bigger in size, but in number of customers and purchases I think nowhere approximates to it. It has been estimated for us that each day almost one-half of a million people come in through our doors. Some enter only to look, but the average daily number of purchases is at least half that number, 250,000 or more. The visitors come from all the republics of the Soviet Union: in some instances they have made journeys of many thousands of miles. Some of them, perhaps they will make only one journey to Moscow in the whole of their life; and as they always do, they make a pilgrimage to Red Square to visit the tomb of Vladimir Ilyich Lenin. And most of them rarely fail to come here then into our store too. We have the saying that every day it would be possible for you to see here not just someone from every one of the republics, but as well someone from every single town and city of the USSR. The annual turnover in trade, well I do not know its exact figure: but again, it has been calculated that it approaches perhaps the equivalent of eight to nine million pounds in sterling or twelve million US dollars. These are astronomical figures are they not? They must I am sure be perhaps more guesses than as you would say precise calculations.

The building of it was what would now be called a joint venture: that is, it was done in co-operation by engineering and construction firms from several different countries. Most were Russian of course, but there were many parts such as drainage, foundations, scaffolding and so on that were made by French, German and British companies, and you can still see their names on certain parts of the installations. And the structure itself, well of course by now it has to be said that it is of historical interest; with all that that means in a place which is trying to become a modern centre for trade. Those who built it one hundred years ago did not have good machinery and all the advantages in electronic technology that we have nowadays, so it took them three years to complete it. It is fifteen years since we ourselves began reconstructing it, and we have not finished it yet nor in any way approached the amount that they did, so you see what truly marvellous progress we have made in our ways.

When I first came to my position here, I may tell you I was very surprised to find how little the day-to-day functioning of the store had been interrupted by the extensive building working which was going on. It had all been very carefully planned in advance and with much thought: you will find many people I am sure who are still not aware of what is being done. Then one day suddenly inside, the whole complete transformation will be revealed. I have been here for four years now and there are many things I am still finding, that are happening to make improvements. I have passed often within a few metres of them, but not known such things in my own store: even though I am the head person, I in no way know everything that is happening. It makes it interesting for me too; when I was first appointed to my position, I may say that although I readily accepted it because I regarded it as my duty, I was not as one might say very full of excitement at the prospect of coming here. I thought it would be an administrative post of great responsibility, and of course it is this; but I confess I also thought it would be somewhat dull, and not what I had had in mind for myself as a career.

When I was young, my early career as a young man was in the Army: my occupation there was being a pilot. I enjoyed it, it had excitement and of course to some extent an amount of prestige. But then in the era of Khrushchev at the time of the 1950s there were many military cuts, and I decided to leave the Army as I could not foresee a great future in it. I was an enthusiastic member of the Komsomol League, the branch of the Party which is for young Communists; and I progressed from there to the Ministry of Trade, where I was Secretary of the Party organisation. By that time I had grown older and become shall we say less romantically minded: I no longer wanted to pilot aeroplanes and possibly fight in wars because I had a wife and family. But the work I was doing at the ministry was varied and active, and to study trading methods abroad I was sent on several trips to different countries in Europe, and all this was of great interest for me. Then alas there was a scandal involving some people in high positions here at GUM Store; it received publicity all over the world I think, because very well-known names were involved. The outcome of it was that I was offered if I would take the post of Manager and try to recover the situation, which as you can imagine had become embarrassing for our government.

Now I have come here, as I say I have found it to my liking much more than I expected I would. I have begun to make trips abroad again to see other big department stores and to become acquainted with their methods; so far these have taken me not only to eastern European countries, but also to such cities as Vienna and Munich. I have not yet been to America or England; but I have an invitation to visit your country in what I hope to be the near future. The owner of one of your big department stores in London has said to me last month that as soon as I inform him I am ready, he will immediately send his private jet for me. Well of course that is very kind, but we are not yet at the stage in the Soviet Union, I am afraid, when one can have the use of a private aeroplane to come and go as one wishes. Perhaps one day such a thing will be possible, who knows: we shall wait and see. It will certainly be very interesting for me to go to United Kingdom, because I think you have good tradesmen in your country. There are people from whom it will be possible to learn much, and I am anxious to set up links and good relations between us.

It will also be important for me to buy in world markets. The prospects for this are extending, and as soon as it can GUM Store must improve the range and quality of the goods it offers. We are beginning already to take part in joint trading ventures, but of course we have the problem to obtain the currency we need in order to buy in other countries. We have at present a monthly trade turnover outside the Soviet Union to the value of about three million pounds; but it is my ambition, and I think there is a good possibility of it, to raise this to ten million pounds. Like all other problems we have, everything is connected with the economy of the State in a wide sense: if there are reductions for instance in the expenditure on military spending, and if further development of co-operatives is allowed, then this would help us greatly, I believe. Nothing will change all at once, but there will be steady improvement I hope.

And there is one particular aspect of going to western European large stores and seeing how they do things which will interest me: it is how they deal with the problem of what is called 'wastage', losing goods to people who take them without paying for them: in a word yes, stealing. From what knowledge I have, there are very sophisticated surveillance systems in your big stores. We have nothing of that kind here. I believe they cost a great deal of money to install, and if we change our policy of display, which we are considering to do, then we shall need to give great consideration to this subject. We do not have many goods at all which are openly displayed. Our system is that articles are shown under the glass of a counter, the customer points to which one he wants, and the assistant then takes it from the storage bins and gives it to the customer. Your system, or so I believe, is that goods in quantity are on open display within easy reach of the customer so they can examine them before buying; and that many sales are made on the principle of impulse, when the customer picks up something that has caught their eye. As we get more goods on offer for sale, we shall I am sure have to adopt these new methods of display, and in turn that will bring these problems of theft.

Perhaps something else which I will be able to study too is one of the most important things which is lacking in our retailing here, which may be called the complete absence in our shops of such a thing as a culture of service. Since there has always been a shortage of goods in USSR, it has never been necessary for our assistants, in GUM Store or anywhere else, to make effort to sell things. Whatever they have to put on display, the customers will – literally sometimes – fight to buy it. The assistant never has to try to persuade, or do anything more than give an indication when the next delivery of something may be expected. If he is asked does he have something by a customer who requires it, his answer needs to be no more than No. He can be as rude and as arrogant as he likes, and it is indifferent to him whether the customer comes back again to GUM Store or not.

If the day comes when there is no longer such a shortage of goods in the Soviet Union, I think this is one of the biggest problems those in retail trading will have to face. Almost the whole of the workforce engaged in it will have to be retrained and instructed in the importance of good relations with customers. It will be a major task. Already I have been most interested to notice the contrast between the manner of assistants in Moscow shops, and that of those in the newly opened venture not far from here, the 'Golden Arches' of the American hamburger purveyor, McDonald's. Polite and welcoming assistants who are eager to serve you: in that respect alone, Moscow has seen nothing like it ever before. Well, we learn, I hope.

Vitali Rossolov,
Bolshoi Theatre stagehand*

The proscenium curtains were drawn back and the empty auditorium seats were in darkness, but the stage itself was lit. It was as crowded as a railway-station concourse: overalled workers were putting up backcloths and scenery for the coming evening's performance, electricians raised and lowered and experimented with floodlights on gantries, carpenters hammered and banged at scaffolding, performers in rehearsal-clothing consulted with musicians and choreographers, secretaries made notes on their clipboards, and an advance party from a German opera company to be performing the following week were trying to find where microphones and other sound equipment would be placed.

A muscular young man in jeans and a T-shirt with 'Sadlers Wells Ballet' in neat lettering on it, he sat on the floor at the front of the right-hand side of the stage, dangling his legs down into the orchestra pit. He was twenty-nine.

– There is nowhere very quiet today, but if we sit here we shall be in no one's way, so I hope we will not be disturbed. I am afraid it is the same every day almost: this has to be changed, that needs to be altered, nothing is quite good enough so that everyone is completely satisfied. Ah well, the Bolshoi is one of the world's greatest theatres, so its reputation has to be upheld; it is because it is like it is, with everyone trying to make it the best, that it has become famous. Does its age and the old-fashioned nature of so much of its equipment surprise you? Many people comment on it and wonder how the standard of its productions can remain so high.

The official designation of my job is that I am what is called senior stage operator: in England I think I would be called stagehand. My work is to put up the scenery for the productions with my colleagues, and move or change it when necessary during the performances. Together there are thirty of us: ten work at this side, ten at that side, and ten at the back. Out of sight always of course. If someone is seen it is a terrible mistake, that the audience should catch sight of a hand or a foot. It is not very often; but it can happen, and when it does there are always huge arguments and quarrels about it afterwards. It should never happen, it is not professional that it should.

I have been working here for five years now, almost six. Already when I was fourteen or fifteen, as a schoolboy I had no other ambition than to do some kind of work in the theatre. I do not know why it was; but I would read all books and magazines that I could find which had anything at all in them to do with theatre. But I was a shy boy, and I never wanted to be an actor or appear in public: I knew I would always be too frightened to act in front of an audience. That I realised it was good I think: there are so many who want to be actors, and they try and try and hope one day they will be stars but they never succeed. I was not like that, all I wanted was just to work as some kind of an assistant in the theatre.

There are special schools for stage people, and I attended one of those for four years. It is not easy to be accepted into one as a student: first you have to pass examinations in such subjects as Russian and European literature, and history and mathematics. Then if you are accepted, at first it is like a continuation of your ordinary school: you study the subjects I have mentioned, together with physics and chemistry, for one year. The following year you then begin to take special subjects such as history of art and history of theatre. After that, the next year you progress to mechanics and engineering, and begin to learn about stage design and equipment. There is one special department where you study stage lighting, and another the handling of stage equipment; I chose the second as the one I wished to specialise in.

During part of my course I came here and worked at the Bolshoi for one and a half years to have practical experience. I also spent one year working in the same way at the Stanislavsky Theatre. Then for me like for everyone else, there was the interruption of two years' conscription for the Army. When that was over and I came home again, I was lucky immediately to be offered temporary work at the Bolshoi. Well you know since I had first come here in my training, there was nowhere else I wanted to work. So you can imagine my great happiness first to have that opportunity, and then after that to be offered a permanent position.

I am young now, but I hope I shall still be here for the rest of my working life. It is something which is really fantastic for me: to be so fortunate as to work here is like a dream, but a dream more amazing than I could ever dream, to work for one of the world's big names!

There is also still a little part of it for me that is in some way frightening. To work with so many of the famous names in opera and ballet, to be an essential part of this company – it is always exciting, but at every performance, there is still that moment to come which you look forward to with apprehension. Will the audience have liked it? It has been done for them, but has it been done well enough so that they will rise from their seats and applaud, and go on applauding perhaps for twenty minutes or more even than that? And will their applause be because they have been inspired by what they have seen, or will it be something that is formal and polite because they know it is expected of them? It is most strange, you know, how when you stand at the side of the stage and listen to it, you can sense whether the applause is absolutely happy and with genuine excitement, or whether it is not. Everyone in the company can sense this difference, every single person knows which it is.

To me the show that we have in our repertoire which I like the best, well it is unquestionably *Spartacus*. The old favourites, well they are very good of course, and sometimes everything comes together so perfectly with the dancers and the music and the scenery you feel it is perfection. But they are not, if I may express it in this way, they are not quite so challenging any more after you have done them hundreds of times. You know you can do them, and do them well, but with little need to think of them; but with such a ballet as *Spartacus* which is still in so many ways fresh and new and exciting, it has in it many problems to be overcome in the staging, and so you cannot be entirely sure you have got it right in every detail. I have worked on the performance of it one hundred and twenty times. Every time it has been with special pleasure and I am never bored or too familiar with it once, not at any moment. The music, the choreography, the costumes, the dancing, the scenery, the lighting – everything about it is exciting to me. But it is exhausting too: it is necessary for me to be at the side or the back of the stage for every second of it, for the whole of the three acts.

So that is my favourite, and nothing else can compare with it. I do not have one which is my least favourite. Naturally I like those where I have the most to do. But another one, it could be the favourite of a dancer or the people who operate the lighting, so I will not hurt anyone's feelings if I do not mention one by name. A ballerina, she will have her favourite, which will be the one which gives her the most opportunity and scope to display her skills; and so it is with us all, and that is why my own favourite is *Spartacus* as I have said.

The dancers, well perhaps it will surprise you to hear me say this, but it is true: I have found that all the great stars, they are very easy to work with. It is because they are professionals absolutely in every way, to the tips of their fingers: they work and work and work at their performances, they always give of their best, and they are very appreciative of the efforts of those like myself and others who do not receive the audience's attention. If you are a worker and good at your job, which is to make it possible for them to be the stars, they do not overlook this. They know how important to them you are, and they will always give you their thanks and praise. This of course makes you enjoy your work and be satisfied with it.

The difficult ones, shall I tell you who they are? They are those who have not yet made their names, who are insecure in themselves, and seek to blame others for what they think is the fact that they have not yet achieved all the recognition they deserve. Just last week only, there was a young lady who is not yet at the very top, though I am sure she will be – and she was dancing her solo in her performance when she made a slight error, and for a moment her feet became in a tangle. When the curtain came down at the end of the act, she came furiously on to the stage and began to search and search on the floor where the incident had occurred. And finally she found near there a tiny scrap of paper no bigger than this, the size of a postage stamp. She took it in great anger to the company manager, and she shouted at him 'Look, look, how can someone be expected to perform properly when the stage is covered with rubbish like this!' Well she is very young still of course. But you never have behaviour of that kind from a big star: if she makes a mistake the only person she curses is herself.

A part of my work I greatly enjoy is the opportunities we have for travel. We have several different touring companies, and sometimes you are here in Moscow or sometimes you are away with one of them. For instance tomorrow we go on another European tour: today I am sitting here talking with you, on Thursday I shall be starting my work on the stage of La Scala Milan. I have been during the last year on a tour of America, in New York, Washington, San Francisco and Los Angeles; the audiences were very warm towards us and appreciative of our performances, and we hope next year to go again.

Also we went to Great Britain this year: I think this was the most exhausting trip we have ever had. We went for a few nights to Switzerland and Dublin, and then to London, Birmingham and Edinburgh. In fifty-seven days we did fifty-five performances, so you can imagine how tired afterwards we were. My wife, we have our son who is one year old, and she says she hopes I am not away so much I miss all his childhood. But it is not so bad as that, I am sure.

This shirt was a present to me from an English stagehand, and in return I gave him one from the Bolshoi. Incidentally, and I do not say this because you are English yourself, but because I mean it: I found it very enjoyable to work in your theatres with English stagehands. We took only a part of our stage team, and so we were dependent to a great degree on them. Russians, you know, well we are very excitable if something looks as if it could be going to go wrong. But the Englishman, no matter what happens he stays calm: he does not shout, he thinks quickly in his head how something can be put right, and he does not wait for you to tell him how to do it, he does it immediately himself. Then afterwards when you thank him, he tells you it was nothing: I think the word he uses is 'It was nothing mate.'

One other thing in England I enjoyed was to look in the big music-record shops in Oxford Street of London. I love music, and I bought many, though there were still some unfortunately I could not find. Well, if you mean it and will as you say be coming again back to Moscow, of course I would be most delighted if you could find them for me, yes. The ones that I most want are *The Other Side of the Moon* by Pink Floyd, *Wish You Were Here* also by Pink Floyd, and *Presence* by Led Zeppelin. And anything of the group called 'Cream'. Oh that would be truly wonderful if you could, I would be most grateful.

Ludmilla Orlova,

Intourist guide

A tall woman with fair curly hair, she wore a bright two-piece red suit, toning dark red shoes, and a high-necked white blouse trimmed down the front with lace. Relaxed, she sat on the edge of her desk, swinging her legs a little and smiling. She spoke almost faultless English.

– Well what would you like me to tell you? I am forty-five, my husband is in charge of the design department for a factory which makes tractors, I have a son of eighteen who is a student, and I have been an Intourist guide for twenty-one years. I am happy with my home and my husband, and I am happy with my job, I would not like to have any other occupation in the whole world. So there you have the story of my life, and anything else you wish to know please ask me questions about. No it is my pleasure, I am at your disposal for as long as you wish, I am not at all busy today. It is my day off, I came especially for talk with you.

I began to work with Intourist immediately I graduated from Moscow University where I had studied English. Our system in this country is that straight away when you are leaving school or university, you will be placed in a job. If you do not like it you do not have to stay, you can find something else for yourself; but many graduates from Moscow University who study languages go to Intourist. For example if they speak German or Japanese or Italian or whatever it may be, then they go there if they wish, automatically. Then after a little while if everything is OK, Intourist ask you if you want to stay with them. If you tell them yes you do, then they send you on courses to learn about the countries people come from who you are going to be a guide and interpreter for.

I did such special courses for six months. I studied the history and customs and way of life of English people; and I also studied what you might call – well, to say it was psychology would be to give it perhaps too scientific a name. But learning the way of thinking of English people, what they like to find when they come to our country, what they do not like to find, and matters such as that. For an example well I must think for a moment. Yes now I have thought of one. We were taught most English people are very relaxed and easygoing, they do not get excited or angry quickly if something goes wrong. So when you are their guide, you must behave in the same manner yourself: you must put right what is wrong for them, but in such a way as they would do it themselves. But with other countries, I will not specify them obviously, people who come from them, if there is some hold-up or frustration they shout and scream and wave their arms. So with them you must do the same as that, otherwise they think you are not as sufficiently concerned about it as they are.

I have never been to England, not yet, no; but of course I would like very much to make a visit there because I feel I know so much about it. The only place I have ever been to in England is Sunderland: this was just for a few hours, perhaps twelve years ago now. I was one of the guides for a party of Russian passengers on a cruise ship: I think perhaps there were about three hundred or more. The cruise began at Leningrad, then the ship went to Stockholm, Copenhagen, Hamburg and Sunderland, and then it came back to Leningrad again. The passengers went ashore just for a few hours at each of these places, that is all. I remember at Sunderland one of the party, he was very enthusiastic for me to get him the famous English dish he said he had over and over again heard about. He must have this dish he said, he could not come to England and not have it; and it was called fish and chips. There was a shop not far from where the ship was docked, so I was able to get it for him. I have often wondered what they must have thought in Sunderland, of the day a woman came from the big Soviet cruise-liner to ask to buy fish and chips.

There is one very enjoyable part also of the job as Intourist guide, and that is you learn a great deal about your own country. Let us say a troop of English visitors come – oh forgive me I am so sorry, that is the wrong word – I mean a group of English visitors come and they are visiting not just Moscow but also Leningrad, and then to the Ukraine to Kiev, and even sometimes as well to Odessa on the Black Sea, or far north to Murmansk or to the furthest east even, to Vladivostok. And so you visit them all. There are many places that at the beginning, although they were in my own country, I had never hoped to visit them. Of course your guests ask you questions about the history and architecture of all these places, so at first you have to study very much to become familiar with them. I have many times been sitting late into the night in my bedroom in the hotel, reading the guidebook about the place we are, because I've never myself been there before. I know the next day I shall be expected to know the answers to all questions. Well, I can say I know where to get fish and chips in Sunderland, can I not?

That there are also things I do not like about my job, oh yes of course. Mostly all our visitors who come to our country, they like the Soviet Union and are friendly; they are curious about everything, interested in all that you can show them. An ordinary guide like myself, I meet perhaps one thousand English tourists in a year – and there is no doubt, for most of them to come to the USSR is an experience they enjoy and find very exciting. But from that number, there will be a few, but only a very small number – well, when they get here for them it is a big disappointment. They have saved up their money for a good holiday, and then they do not like it. So you can understand that they are unhappy. They do not like the hotel, it is not a good one and it is not up to English standard – and this is often true, everyone knows it. And the food they do not like either – it is so different from what they are used to. The meat is of poor quality, the vegetables poorly prepared and so on. And again it is true: we are a long way behind your standards, there is no question of it. Or a plane is late for departure, or a coach does not come and everyone is standing for an hour waiting in the cold, all these things. We are trying to improve, but it is taking a long time for us. But the guests of course they have no idea what I am doing to try to have everything sorted out. When there is a complaint about something that is wrong in the hotel for example, I am going to have big argument with the hotel manager that he should allow our guests to be treated like this, or with the restaurant manager that his food is being so badly cooked, or I am telephoning and telephoning to the Intourist ticket department – all these things, it is my job to have them put right. But sometimes the guests do not know I am doing this, they complain I am doing nothing or they cannot find me. To them I am Intourist, I am she who is responsible and that is all they see.

I must not exaggerate to you: it is not very often such things happen of course. But when it is the end of a hard day and everything has gone wrong that day, everything, then I say to myself you know, Why am I ever an Intourist guide? But as I have told you, most English people, they are not like that: they come and they do not expect it to be just like their home for them. They see new things and have new experiences, they are happy and so friendly all of them. So it is good for me, and I try to make it good for them. Do you know what it is my name means, 'Ludmilla'? 'Ludmilla' means 'good for people'; that is a good name for an Intourist guide yes?

There are funny things too, oh yes. The one that is the most often, I think it is when you give the commentary on the coach when there is the sightseeing tour, you know? You tell about the architecture and the statues and the buildings and the history; and then when it is finished, someone of the group comes to you and they say 'Thank you so much, that was very enjoyable, I never knew Moscow was such an interesting city, it is so beautiful.' Well I have still not found a way to say in reply yet, without it sounds you are making fun: 'I am glad you liked it, but I am sorry, it is not Moscow it is Leningrad.' It amuses me also of course but I must not show it, when someone says to me of my suit for example like this one, they say 'What a smart suit you are wearing.' And I say 'Thank you' and then I wait for the question to follow: sometimes it does not, but there are many times it does. It is 'Did you buy it here?' You think you would like to respond, very politely of course: 'What did you think we all are, peasants in bears' skins?'

The best thing? Oh it is now. That you can talk freely and naturally, that is the best thing there has ever been. Part of your training to be an Intourist guide, it used to be you were told exactly what you had to say in answer to questions. Not to lie, you understand: but how to divert a question, or not answer it but instead to give the answer to a different one. You became expert at it. And now that is all gone, you can answer how you wish, you can have discussions, anything you like. Someone asks me something and very often you know it seems they are taking it for granted because I am an Intourist guide, so I must be a member of the Communist Party. Now I say immediately what is true: 'Perhaps you think I am a member of the Communist Party? I am not and I have never been, in all my life.' Before, you were not allowed to say that: you could not say you were a Party member if you were not, but you were instructed you must not deny it if it was thought that you were.

And you can make little jokes also. The other day an English visitor said to me 'How does it feel for you now to have so much freedom?' And I said to him 'Well for myself I am very happy. But it is hard for me to get used to, because you see I came out of prison only last Tuesday.'

All this now makes me enjoy my job even more every day. I have a very understanding husband who does not mind that it takes me away from our home so often: he has always said if I was doing a job that I liked, that was the most important thing. And just recently my son said to me when he has finished his studies, he thinks he might like to be an Intourist guide too. So his life cannot have been too bad for him so far can it, even if I am going away so much? It pleased me very greatly that he said that.

Marc Winer,

Director, McDonald's Hamburgers

His private office was one of a suite of comfortably furnished rooms on the eighth floor of a hotel in the city centre. It was small, neat and uncluttered, with a desk, two swivel chairs, a telephone, an intercom and a fridge. A dark-haired man in his early forties, he wore a short-sleeved open-necked shirt and lightweight trousers, and a gold wristwatch.

– Hi, good to meet you Tony, come in, make yourself at home, siddown. We have nineteen minutes OK then I have to leave for the airport? Hope that doesn't make me sound like someone out of *Dallas* or something, it's just I'm going on vacation with my family and they'll be there already waiting for me. OK so switch on your tape recorder and fire away. Say that's a neat little machine you got there, where'd you get that? Do you mind me asking you how much it cost? Wow that's pretty good. All set then, right, let's go.

How's it going? Well you're looking at a happy man Tony: I'll tell you in one word how it's going, it's fantastic. Today when we talk now, we're just two weeks after the opening of the first McDonald's Hamburger Bar in the USSR. The results so far, they've been tremendous, wonderful, great, far better than our hopes and dreams and expectations. And it's just so exciting for everyone connected with it, because there's been so much hard work in the last two years to bring it about since the final contracts were signed. But now here we are, open at last, on Pushkin Square right in the centre of Moscow, and we're serving more than thirty thousand people a day. Isn't that something?

We open ten in the morning until ten o'clock at night every day in the week, and from hours before we start up and open the doors there's a constant line right around the square and back again. Even on a below-freezing day like this, it stays there all day whether it's snowing or raining or whatever, people queuing to get in. And you know what's to us the most important thing? Not only that there's so many wanting to be customers, but that when they come out they go away happy, really happy with what they've eaten and how they've been treated, and they're telling themselves they're going to be coming back.

That's what matters to us most of all, it really does. I guess anything that's new and different is always interesting to anyone – but this, well it's so new and different to Russian people they're just absolutely knocked out by it. It's clean, bright, sparkling, up on the second floor of the building so's everyone from outside can see it, the boys and girls who do the serving are in smart uniforms and always smiling and friendly and cheerful, the service is quick, the food's hot and it's good, and Moscow's never ever seen anything like it. We've a problem which we knew we would have, which is that the customers once they're inside, they just don't want to go. We discourage them from stopping too long by first we don't have smoking: a Russian can't exist if he can't smoke immediately right after he's finished eating or often while he's doing it, so that moves a lot. If that doesn't work, then we have our floor managers who firmly but in the nicest possible way ask them would they mind moving along so's some of those who've been waiting outside so long can have their turn. We've had no trouble on that so far, which makes me think maybe we've got our method right.

But I think the place's greatest attraction, you know, has to be that plaque right by the entrance there which says payment's only in roubles. It's not and it never is going to be a hard-currency restaurant for the privileged and the élite. It's for the Russians themselves, where they can spend their own money in it, and we've adhered to that as a principle ever since the idea came into being fourteen years ago. Yeah, that's what it took, fourteen years: that's how long ago it was when the McDonald's people first began negotiating for a mutually acceptable agreement between them and the Russians. And I guess it's no secret there was more than once when it looked like the thing'd never even get off the ground.

But somehow it did; right across the street there is what came out of it, the biggest McDonald's in the whole world. It seats seven hundred people, it has twenty-seven cash registers, and there's a crew of eight hundred staff, maybe one twenty-five full-time and the rest doing three to four hours a day on a rota. And you know what Tony? When we first started recruiting, if we'd known then what we know now about how it was going to go, we'd have taken on twice maybe three times the number of people we did. Everyone we have is Russian except for maybe two dozen from Germany and I believe two from Hungary. Below myself there are four managers who we trained for eight months in Toronto, and they run the restaurant along with three experienced managers we've brought over from the States and Canada. We pride ourselves on our service and quality, it's as fast and efficient as it is in every other McDonald's everywhere in the world – and it's our policy gradually for the Westerners on the staff to make themselves obsolete. First they'll work towards being just a shadow presence, then gradually we'll develop self-sufficiency among our young Russian staff and promote people from the floor to right up as high as they want to go. It's no secret too that we've hopes and plans now for opening several more branches right across the USSR. We've so far had letters from thirty-one other different cities here asking us to go there and open one of our restaurants. The Soviet government has been profoundly welcoming, and if we can develop the necessary infrastructure to support the branches, in theory there's no limit for many years yet to what we might do.

Each place we go, we obtain equipment and furniture and lighting to the standard we require, and make sure it's replaceable when replacements are needed. We have to find the right locations, get all the necessary permissions, and check we can find enough of the right kind of young people to train as our staff. Then as for the most important thing, the food supplies – well naturally we take the most enormous care about that. We're happy the way things have worked out here in this first venture, and if we can operate the same way in other places then everything'll be just fine. For the whole of two years before our restaurant opened its doors on the first day, we had our agricultural and food-production experts working in and around Moscow doing all the necessary enquiring and checking on what we were going to need in the way of produce. We grow our own beef, we process the meat into frozen hamburger patties, we take local potatoes for French fries, and the milk we use for ice-cream and milk shakes comes from locally too. Our explorations have had to be very thorough and they've been checked and counter-checked. Naturally enough, when it was finally known for sure that we were coming, dozens and dozens of suppliers approached us wanting us to sign up a contract with them and do a quick deal at maybe a cut price. Well, we don't do things like that. If someone for example tells us he can supply us with a certain quantity of potatoes on a regular basis, we have to make absolutely sure that those potatoes are of the type and size and quality that he says they will be – and also just as importantly, that he can keep them coming to us in a regular flow without hiatuses of any kind. If he can't do that, then he doesn't get his contract; and if he does, before he and we sign it, we make sure he fully understands the very stringent conditions there are attached to it. Suppliers have to realise we don't accept being let down.

Then there's the other just as important matter of quality control, which takes place at every single point of the whole supply process. Not one single item of food escapes checking: before delivery, during delivery, on reception, and repeatedly as it passes through storage, the kitchens, over the counter and on to the customer's plate. There's uninterrupted and minute checking of freshness of food and cleanliness of the equipment it comes into contact with, the trucks that bring it, and the people both outside and inside who handle it. And on top of that, finally senior personnel go constantly into the restaurant among the customers to check on the quality of the finished product, almost up to the moment it goes into the customer's mouth. McDonald's has been in business thirty-five years now, and it's been successful because every individual knows what's expected from him, whether he's a supplier to us or someone who works for us: it has to be right, it has to be the best, it has to be exactly when required – and if it isn't, as far as he's concerned that's it, he's gone.

As a job, I guess the word I'd use for it is exacting. You get a pride, you know, in working for a big company like this; and we try to instil that feeling into everyone we have on our payroll. You can't do that unless you have it yourself: I certainly do, and to be put in charge of a unique operation such as this, and one with such high standards, well what else is there I should feel but pride? It's been the greatest experience of my life so far, that's for sure. The Russians are a really good and nice people to work with and to live among, that's something that I can truly say. Before I was appointed to this position I'd already worked several years here in the USSR for the Coca-Cola company, so therefore I already had good experience of business here. I speak Russian, naturally, a little French and some fairly good German, oh and some Hebrew too. And fluent English of course, though maybe you'd not say so yourself; but I was born and raised in New Hampshire which we consider to be one of the most anglicised parts of the United States, so that's why I speak the way I do.

No, I don't miss living in the US, not in any way. I don't mean I don't love my country, but my family and I consider ourselves fairly Europeanised. My wife and I have two children, a son of eighteen and our daughter who's twelve. Our son was at high school in the States and then went to college for a semester; but then he asked could he come here and be with us because the whole idea of living in the USSR fascinated him. He did that last year, and already he's picking up the language pretty fast, and I don't think it'll be long before he's pretty fluent in it. What he'll do then I don't think he's decided yet. Our daughter's in seventh grade at the Anglo-American school here: she says she's happy there, and until she says different that's where she'll stay. As for my wife, and this of course is the Number One important thing, she's all in favour of us being here. If you knew her, you'd know that if she wasn't she wouldn't be here and neither would the kids – nor me either, so it's as simple as that. She and the kids, they've been supportive to me every step of the way: we like to think we're a family who all talk things over together and know how the others are thinking and feeling, and I guess so far we're pulling together. I think they think of themselves as being Europeanised too, which makes things a lot easier. We all had a few years together in Germany when I was with Coca-Cola, and that was another thing which gave us a pretty open outlook, I guess. In any country wherever you are, so long as you accept the way of life there is neither worse nor better than yours, but just different, I think you'll get along OK.

Eighteen minutes? That's the kind of time-keeping I like Tony; it's been a pleasure visiting with you.

13 Couples

Igor and Leonora Vitaliev
Rudi and Kira Falin
Slava and Julia Vadimsky

Igor and Leonora Vitaliev*

Stocky, clean-shaven and fine-featured, with curly fair hair, he wore a smart suit and an open-necked white shirt. She was shy and quiet in manner in an off-white dress with a small pattern of sprigs and leaves and flowers on it, and had her fair hair in a pony tail. They sat side by side on the settee in the apartment's living-room. At first he did most of the talking, and she constantly looked at him to confirm what she said.

Igor: We are living here temporarily: this is the apartment of Leonora's grandparents. They have said we may stay here until we have a place of our own, which we hope will be in about three months' time, when our names come to the top of the housing waiting list for newly-weds on this estate. Now we have just one room of our own here, and share the bathroom and toilet and the kitchen.

Leonora: It is very kind of my grandparents to do this.

Igor: Her mother and father are divorced and each of them lives with a new husband and wife, so we could not live with them.

Leonora: They have children and no room for us.

Igor: And my parents do not live in Moscow, my mother is in Kiev and I think my father is dead, I have not been in contact with him now for seven years. But I think it will not be for too long that we are here, perhaps only three months.

Leonora: Or four, but no more than that we hope.

Igor: It is a start anyway. We can manage, most young couples do the same, the important thing for us is we are together.

Leonora: So far it has been OK.

Igor: Yes, so far it has been OK. If the rest of our marriage goes no worse, then we shall have no complaints. After all, we are now already an old married couple: our wedding was the day before yesterday, so that is three whole days it has survived for us so far.

Leonora: I hope you will understand that Igor likes to make jokes: he is doing it all the time, but people do not always understand that.

Igor: Sometimes even Leonora does not understand, and then we have a quarrel.

Leonora: No please do not say that Igor, it gives the impression we are not all the time happy together.

Igor: Very well, I will say we are always very happy together, because it is true. And also I will say we never have a quarrel: that is also true, but not as true as the first thing. However, we should now give some description of ourselves. First Leonora will tell you about herself and then I will speak after her.

Leonora: No Igor please I am too nervous, I would prefer if you spoke for both of us.

Igor: Well then to begin with I will say that I am twenty-three, and Leonora is nineteen. I work at a farm factory as a driver of a truck which delivers vegetables in the Moscow area, and Leonora is a teacher at a nursery school.

Leonora: Well I am not quite a teacher, because I do not have any certificates. But I look after the children and play learning games with them. They are very young children, very small, from two to four years old.

Igor: Later on you hope you will go to college and study to become a nursery teacher with qualifications.

Leonora: Well yes perhaps. We shall see what happens, but I would not like to go very far from the nursery where I am working, because it is on this housing estate. It is very convenient for me, both where we are living now and where we hope to get our own apartment.

Igor: Unfortunately it is not very convenient for me though to live here. This is on the south-west limit of Moscow, and where I work is almost at the north-east limit; so every day I have a long way to travel in the morning, then a long way back again in the evening. I have a motor car but it is a very old one and almost broken down, and to drive it so far each day through the traffic of the centre of Moscow, well I do not like this and neither does my motor car. I think one day before long it will expire, or perhaps it will be me who expires first, I do not know. I shall be glad to get rid of it, it is all the time breaking down and brings nothing but worry for me.

Leonora: You would not have met me, Igor, if you had not had your motor car.

Igor: Yes that is true you see: as I told you it has brought me nothing but worry.

Leonora: Igor!

Igor: I was driving home one evening from my work, and near Kalinin Street I saw a friend of mine standing talking with two very nice-looking young girls. So I pulled up my car and went back to talk with him. One of them was his girlfriend, and the other one was her sister who was Leonora. I thought she was the prettiest girl I had ever seen, and she thought I was the most handsome man she had ever seen, and so that was it, our fate was sealed.

Leonora: I did not think you were so handsome, because you are not. You asked me to give you my telephone number which I thought was very bold of you. I was very uncertain whether to give it to you.

Igor: You must have hesitated for five seconds at least, I am sure. However so that was how it was, and then it took a very long time for us to get to know each other before I could decide whether to offer her to be my wife.

Leonora: Three days.

Igor: Was it only as long as that? I am sure it was four.

Leonora: I remember I wondered why it was taking you so long to ask. If you had asked me on the second day I would immediately have said Yes.

Igor: Well I am very shy you see. So well, this was now three months ago from today. Immediately Leonora agreed that we should marry, we went the very next day to register our intention. When you do that, then they offer you two or perhaps three different times and dates when they can marry you. It is usually as it has been in our case, about three months ahead.

Leonora: Sometimes it can be much longer, so we were fortunate they offered us a date so soon. Then at once there were many plans to be made and all so quickly. To try to find somewhere to live, which of our friends and members of our family we would ask to the celebration party afterwards, to find a hotel restaurant where we could have the wedding meal, and many many other things.

Igor: You have forgotten the most important thing of all, your wedding dress.

Leonora: Oh yes that is true, yes of course. It was made for me by one of my aunts, and it was very beautiful with a long white veil. Then I had all my other wedding things to buy also. We have a tradition that when you marry, everything that you wear must be brand-new, from your head right down to your toes. It symbolises that you are beginning a completely new start for your life, and bringing nothing with you to your marriage that you have had before.

Igor: We went to the Marriage Office at one o'clock on our wedding day, and of course because there are always so many other couples to be married, we had to wait a little time before it was our turn. We had two friends who came with us as our witnesses, and Leonora's little brother who was there because he wanted for the first time to see a marriage performed. Leonora and I exchanged our agreements that we should be married, and gave each other these rings which we are now wearing, which are identical. Then our friends came with their cars, and they took us on a drive round the Moscow streets. After that we went out to the Lenin Hills which overlook the city, where the view is very beautiful.

Leonora: It is the custom for most newly married couples to go there. We took with us some bottles of champagne and drank toasts there, and our friends took photographs. Then we went in the cars again, to go to the Church of the Epiphany which is near here where we live. We went inside and stood quietly together with our friends for a little while. There was no church ceremony; but a lot of people like to do this nowadays. When we were there there were two or three other newly married couples with their friends doing the same. It gives a nice feeling if you have just got married.

Igor: We stayed for half an hour; then I lit a candle for my name saint, and Leonora put one for the Sacred Mother. After that we went to Leonora's aunt's apartment for a little while, then for a dinner in the afternoon at the restaurant of a hotel, then returned to the apartment again for a big party which we had arranged for about forty of our friends. Everybody was very happy, and we ate and drank until two o'clock in the morning. The next day Leonora had to go back to work and I had to go back to work, and both of us felt we did not want to, but that is life.

Leonora: It was the start of a new life, which we now look forward to. We shall both continue with our jobs as we are doing at present, but we hope for two things that might bring changes. One is to have our own apartment, and the other is for us to have a baby, which we would like very much.

Igor: But we are agreed that first we must work as hard as we can, so that we have enough money to buy certain things which we shall need when we get our apartment. So far we have nothing, no furniture of any kind, not even what might be described as basic kitchen equipment for Leonora. We do not have plates or knives or forks or anything.

Leonora: We shall collect them gradually, and people will give us things of theirs which they can spare from what they have. Igor is good in handling and saving money, and I am learning how to be the same. Most of all I would like to have, after we have sufficient of the everyday things, a washing machine for our clothes: we have put down our names on a waiting list for one and it will be about a year before we get it, by which time we hope to have saved up the money for it.

Igor: Then next after that we shall buy a television set. First a washing machine for you, then a television set for me.

Leonora: No Igor, it will be a washing machine for you and a television set for me.

Igor: You see, now she also starts to make jokes.

Rudi and Kira Falin

A tall man with a mild voice, he had shoulder-length fair hair which fell like a curtain round his face whenever he tilted his head slightly forward. He wore a check shirt and old corduroy trousers and sandals. She was small and dark and vivacious, and wore a green T-shirt and jeans. He was twenty-four, she was eighteen.

Rudi: I will be interpreter. This is a one-room apartment and this is all the furniture we have – the bed there and this kitchening table and these three chairs.

Kira: It is enough. Many people like us do not have place at all to live because the authorities will not let them.

Rudi: Well they will not let us either. They do not know we are here and we should not be here because, well for many reasons.

Kira: This is true. The reasons are I am not resident of Moscow and I do not have permission. And Rudi he is unemployed, he has no work and he does not try to get work, and he should have been to the Army and he has not been, so altogether he is a very bad person you see, are you not? Edik says we can tell you these things.

Rudi: Yes a very bad person, we both are. We do not do as we are told, we do not confirm.

Kira: Conform.

Rudi: Conform, yes. Officially this apartment is registered as the apartment of someone else. He lets us stay here because he does not need it, he lives in another place with someone else.

Kira: It is like this all the time in Moscow everywhere, many people do not live where they say they live.

Rudi: And many people live where they say they do not live.

Kira: In Russia if you are against convention it is better if you make all things as much as possible to confuse everyone. The bureaucracy also itself makes everything confusing; it does not mean to do this but it makes the situation that will help you too because it is like that. We enjoy it, to live like this is something that makes us laugh.

Rudi: One day we shall be caught perhaps. Edik says you will not have us caught.

Kira: No I am sure you will not. I know you are peace person also. But now we will talk something serious for a while. First I will tell you about myself. I come from a small town, it is about two hundred kilometres from Moscow, and when I was at school I did not like my lessons very much because all I wanted to do was to draw and to paint. But they said I could not do only this, so I told my sister who lived in Moscow if she would enquire for me if I could come to stay with her and her husband and try to go to an art school. She said I could come for a little while, and that is how I came to Moscow. It was not easy to find an artists' college, but I was lucky that there was one which would give me a place.

Rudi: What Kira is not telling you is that she is good artist, very good artist so much so that college was very pleased to take her because they could see she had very good talent.

Kira: Well perhaps. But they did not know I had talent not just for to paint and to draw, but for other things too. There was a well-known painter here in Moscow and he became in trouble with the authorities because he was given the opportunity for an exhibition of his work, and he made it entirely of anti-war paintings he had done. They were not pleased and so they closed the exhibition. At the college we made a petition which most of the students and teachers signed, to protest about this and sent it to ask that the exhibition be opened again. This was done, an official protest from our college, and I was the one to take it and present it. I added to it a peace mark, I think you have this symbol in United Kingdom and other countries of the West, it is called I think CND. And so the college were very angry that I had done this, because it made it seem they officially supported CND which they do not. And so they would not let me have my place there any more.

Rudi: They proposed to Kira that she should write a letter of apology but she would not do this. She is very obstinate person.

Kira: No, only of some things. If they are to do with peace. With other things I am not like that. You also are the same.

Rudi: Oh yes, and that is why we are suitable for each other.

Kira: Tell something now about you.

Rudi: It is like Kira says, I am obstinate person also for peaceful things. At school I was good student for mathematical subjects and so after it I went to an institute for electronics for two years. We have this system in Russia that a job, a position, will be found for you by your school or institute when you finish your training, and I was told one was to be given to me in a State factory.

Kira: He was a clever student and it was a high position.

Rudi: I will say as you say: well perhaps. But I found it was to do with the production of fighting aeroplanes and I said I would not do this work of this kind because I did not agree with it. I was told if I did not take the position then I would have to leave the institute and go to the Army. But I would not do that either because I am pacifist, so after much argument there was no choice for me, I had to go away altogether. My parents, they live in Moscow and they were anxious for me. But I also was anxious, for them. I told them to say I had gone to the Ukraine which they did, but it meant I could no longer live with them. Fortunately at that time I met Kira one day at a peace demonstration, and so we have each other all the time now.

Kira: How we live is that Rudi knows much about all things to do with television and radio, so people ask him to do work for them: for example in their apartments, to repair such things as TV or fridges or to do wiring repairs. And I also, I make things, I sew and knit and decorate dresses. So we make a living.

Rudi: It is interesting that all the time so many people are asking us to do so many things, and they are willing that it is all without official documents or permissions for us to work or to do it.

Kira: It is quicker for them to get things done that they need, and so they do not ask many questions of us.

Rudi: Sometimes there are arguments. If someone asks me my opinion of something to do with the government, I say that I am opposed to it but I say also that I am opposed to all governments everywhere, if they make war. And sometimes there will be a person who will tell you they think it is unpatriotic not to fight for your country, or not to be willing to defend it with fighting if it is attacked. They will ask how can there be a belief in pacifism completely, when such countries as America talk openly of attacking us and threaten us with rockets and missiles. They say we have to tell the Americans if they did such a thing, we would fight back. When I say no I would not fight back, they say then I am a traitor.

Kira: But they do not say this until after you have mended their television set for them yes?

Rudi: Yes and they ask do I have a religious belief that makes me think like this. It would be easier for them to understand me if I had, but then when I say that I am on the whole a Christian, but mainly my belief is you cannot just kill people never mind for what reason, well that makes it even more difficult for them to understand.

Kira: You see this idea, well mainly in Soviet Russian society the idea, or the ideal, it is that everyone is together for the same thing, and that no one rebels against the establishment. If they did, they don't know what else to do.

Rudi: I think it is part of our history that we have always been like that.

Kira: Everything is planned out for you. You are born, you are looked after when you are a baby, you go to school, at school it is arranged for you to have work when you leave, you are married, you are given somewhere to live and that is how it is all through your life. So it is difficult to break away from this pattern.

Rudi: If people see someone who is different, they do not like that at all, and they will all join together to be against such a person. Communism you see, it means a system for living for everyone, and there are good things to it; but it cannot work properly if everyone wants to go his own way. I do not respect my government for this: I would like to respect my government, but there are many cruel things in Communism. I think it would be good if more Soviet people could speak with people from America and England and everywhere else in the world, and exchange their ideas.

Kira: For us in the Soviet Union it is very difficult to travel, there are so many forms to fill and everything, and it is very expensive too. But I wish many more people would come to see us from other countries, and to meet us and to talk with ordinary people like we are. This would be very good. They could see what is human in Soviet society and tell us what is human in theirs, and we could see where these things are different and where they are the same.

Rudi: I think a lot of the people in other countries, they see only in our country what it is that our government wants them to see: that Soviet Union is a big country with very many people, and it has much richness in its land, wheat and oil and such things. But this is not only like that for our country: there are also many individuals, many different sorts of people of all kinds, poets and writers and musicians and painters, but also all kinds of ordinary people, some good, some bad. It is hard to know how to present this. And so it is true what Kira says, that the only way is to come to meet and talk with people of many different kinds.

Kira: And also now there is much talk of change in our country and how there will be more freedoms for us to go here and there, not to need so many papers for this and that. But you know, well I think a lot of this is what you should call just talk by politicians, because they think it will make them popular, and then when people ask them when is this going to happen, they reply that they should have more time. One day it will happen, not today or tomorrow but one day.

Rudi: And not next week or next month or next year, but one day. Well I think most people have heard this said all the time everywhere by all politicians and they do not believe it. So there are those who say we should go back to the old ways.

Kira: We need to learn how to think for ourselves. Not in someone else's way but in our own way for ourselves. This is how people could help us, to come to us, not to persuade us to be as they are, but to find ourselves as we are.

Slava and Julia Vadimsky*

They lived in a small two-roomed apartment on the tenth floor of a recently built tower block on an estate to the east of the city: it was a bus-ride on from the last Metro station of that section of the line. He was small and bearded; he smoked heavily, sitting at the kitchen table and drinking tea. He was fifty-eight, his wife forty-seven.

Slava: I am sorry that I could not see you last night: I had unexpectedly to go out to see a person. But I am glad you received my telephone message in time. Unfortunately again tonight I have to go in half an hour to a meeting; my wife forgot to tell you this when she telephoned you. But I will do the best I can for you in the time that is available, then afterwards she will be happy to talk with you on her own about herself or about me, or any other thing that you wish. We have no secrets from each other.

We married three years ago: for both of us it was the second time, and we knew all there was to know of each other, because we had agreed that it should be so. Julia is a very good woman and there was nothing for me to know about her that was not to her credit; but in my case it was the opposite. She already knew something about me but not all, and it was hard for me to tell her. I still find it hard to think of myself, because you see my life has been a failure.

I will say to you now the first words I will say later this evening if I stand to speak at the meeting I am going to. They are: 'My name is Slava and I am an alcoholic.' It is a meeting at the clinic which is attached to Hospital Number 21 in this area; those of us who will be there have all previously been patients resident at the hospital. It is very large, with more than two thousand beds, and is entirely for people with alcohol problems. It keeps people for treatment for periods between two months and six months, and the last occasion I myself was there in the hospital was three years and one month ago. I did not begin to attend the clinic until I think two years ago, because it was not in existence until that time.

It has been for many years the policy of our government not to admit that the problem of alcoholism is a very serious one in the Soviet Union. As a result of this, although there are many hospitals such as the one I have been speaking of, devoted only to the treatment of this disease, until recently there has been nowhere that people can go again afterwards, if they need help in not resuming to drink again. You drink, you go into hospital, you are treated with drugs, and you are discharged. If perhaps only a few months afterwards you begin to drink once more, you go back into hospital, you are treated, and so on and so on. This problem was not officially recognised, and so because of that it was officially not permitted to exist.

I was not one of them myself, but there were people such as a few doctors, and strange to say actors and writers and musicians, who wanted to alter the situation and form the kind of organisation which is known in America, and other countries too I think, as something called 'Alcoholics Anonymous'. Of course it is in fact not so strange that it should be the type of person I have mentioned, because they had in many instances travelled to America; that is how they learned of the association there, and how it functioned. Here we do not call it by the same name: it is known as 'Moscow Beginners', but it has had advice about how to bring it into being from American members of Alcoholics Anonymous. It has the name it has because it is an accurate description: in Moscow there are several million people with alcohol problems, but up to now only a few who attend the clinics. In my group for example there are twenty members; a few yards away within the hospital there are two thousand patients at one time, and six thousand a year go there; but few of them after their discharge will come to us.

The reasons for it I think are several. It has to be said that even when the government admits the size of the problem, and releases the figure that it now does, that there are 4.3 million people at present being treated for alcoholism in the Soviet Union, this does not bring any nearer a change in the public attitude towards it.

Alcoholics are regarded as scum, as people beneath contempt, not persons who have an illness. So they try to hide the fact they have been in hospital; to hide it not only from those who know them, but from themselves. Another reason, and I am sorry to say this but I have observed it myself and know it to be true, is that many of the patients in the hospital do not have a very good attitude, or one that is in any way showing knowledge of the problem and of themselves. They take their treatments, and when they are discharged believe they can then drink again as much as they like. I have even heard patients in a ward say such things as 'I am looking forward to next week when I go, because it means that then I can start to drink again.'

I may say also, that even in such a matter as trying to give information that we can exist, and hope to encourage people to join our groups, we meet resistance from magazines sometimes, in which we try to place advertisements. Some magazines will accept them for publication but others will not, saying such things as that it could not be of any interest to their readers. So you see we have to travel a long way I think.

If you wish me to, yes finally I will tell you a little of my own history. I was a teacher of chemistry at an institute here in Moscow for many years; I was married at an early age to a woman who was a teacher of music, and we had one son. He himself is married and lives in I think Odessa, but I have not seen him for several years. I began to drink quite heavily when I was thirty-five, I do not know exactly why: I could say to you that it was because my wife was unfaithful to me and had several love affairs, but I do not think now that that was sufficient reason. It came about of course that I lost my job; but I continued to drink, using up all my savings and, I am sorry to say, a large part of those of my wife also. Naturally there came the time, it was unavoidable, that she left me to live permanently with one of her lovers, taking our son with her. She cannot be blamed for this, I am sure no one would say that.

There came a divorce, and after that I can only describe my life as one of wandering and drinking. At times if you had seen me you would have thought me a beggar off the streets. Finally after several years of an existence which I would be ashamed to describe, it was my undeserved good fortune to meet, on one of my stays in hospital, a young nurse. She was more than ten years younger than myself, and I fell deeply in love with her. What was more surprising altogether was that she also should fall in love with me: a vagrant more than ten years her senior, and I assure you of no assets or virtue.

This was of course Julia. I shall be interested if she can in any way explain to you what has always been to me in every way inexplicable, which is that she should have wanted to make her future with me. You shall see, for now I regret I have to give you my apologies and go to my meeting.

She was small and slim, with thick curly brown hair beginning to go slightly grey. Her voice was quiet, but lively and cheerful.

Julia: It was when I was a nurse that I met Slava, did he tell you that? He was a nice man, gentle and kind but oh so sad. He had been a fine man once, it was easy to see; and he would sit in a chair by the window in the ward, looking out over the city and sometimes his eyes would be filled with tears. One day when he was there like that I stood beside him, and I put my hand on his shoulder gently like this. And his head, you know, he let it fall on to my hand and he cried. I too had been unhappy, so there was something at once between us, something that felt good.

He is brave, he has to be brave, it is not easy you know for those who have been drinkers that they should never drink again. Sometimes someone telephones, someone from his group of Moscow Beginners: and they say they need help immediately, they feel they are going to drink. He goes at once to sit and talk with them: he always goes without question if they need him. That was why he could not be here last night, someone needed him. I think those of us who can drink or not drink as we wish, we cannot understand that with someone who has been alcoholic you must not have any alcohol even in the house, never at all. It is too much temptation for them you know?

What I do now is I am no longer a nurse. When Slava and I were married, it is hard for me to explain: but I did not want any more to spend my time to nurse alcoholics, I wanted to be with Slava and available to him at all times. Why do I do this, tap on the table? Well we have this phrase 'knock on wood'. So far it has been always all right with Slava, and I knock on wood for luck, that it will continue.

We do not have much money, so what I do now is I go three times each week in the afternoon to Gostelradio, which is our State broadcasting organisation. I work in the radio section and I write news items and such things as announcements. I do not perform them of course, it is the ones who are trained to do so who do that. I am not happy sometimes with the things I have to write: they are of no interest to me, and I am not a good believer in the State anyway. But it is work and it earns some money, and when it is not convenient for me to go I telephone them that I come the next day instead.

On one day also each week now I am able to do some work for my church: it has to do with what is called 'Misericordia'. This is a very small organisation, it has been in existence only perhaps one year; and it is to try to help some of the old and lonely people who live as we call it 'behind the door'. In these big tower blocks on estates which you see in Moscow like this one, there are very many people who have lonely lives. They do not bother to make proper meals for themselves because of the difficulties of queuing all the time for food in the shops, they do not have their medicines, or they do not take them if they have. These are the old people who do not have families who live near and so cannot help them; Misericordia tries to do something about this.

I go in the morning early to their office, or I telephone, and they give me the names and addresses of three or perhaps four people I should visit during that day. They have themselves been told these by neighbours or by a doctor, even sometimes by a hospital where the old person has been a patient but must now go home. It is how can one say, a raindrop in a pond that is all: there are so many who need such help, and helpers are so few. It would be improved if there could be mention of this service perhaps sometimes on radio or television, and I have enquired about this at Gostelradio. But so far nothing. I think the authorities do not want to give their attention to this problem, but perhaps one day there will be more concern among people about it. I think they cannot think, you see, that perhaps it will happen one day that they also may be old and have no one to help them, and live behind the door. When you see it, you must be thankful that you are not in that situation, and you hope it will not happen ever that you will be. Once again, you see: knock on wood.

For me it is like that, but I think for Slava no, not yet, it is not the same. He has been himself you know like those he tries to help with Moscow Beginners, but I think he must always have the fear he could again become alcoholic. He does not have yet the confidence for himself, and it is very hard for him to live in this way. He cannot yet work: even to do as I do, something for two or three days only would be good for him. But I do not know that he could do it yet.

Well, we shall see. We talk often with each other about how fortunate we have been, to have found a life together. It is very small, it is very quiet, but it is more happiness perhaps than we should have expected there would be, you know?

14 Times like now

Viktor Loshak, *Moscow News*

Eugene Stolokov, Historical Monuments Preservation Society

Maxim Yallov and Ilya Valkovsky, university students

Dr Alexei Dmitriev, Physicians Against Nuclear War

Viktor Loshak
Moscow News*

From where he'd been looking down at the crowd massed on the pavement outside, he turned away from his third-floor office window and sat at his desk. A tall fair-haired man in an open-necked sports shirt and trousers, in his middle forties.

– I am glad you came on the afternoon of publication day, it allows you to see for yourself how eager people are for an independent outspoken newspaper at last. Now it is four o'clock: many of them have been here since six this morning, even on such a cold day as this, waiting for half-past five when the copies are brought out. Where we are here is our editorial offices, not our distribution centre: that is at the north of the city. But people come here because it is a more central place and you are certain to get a copy if you are in time. By tomorrow all over Moscow people will be asking at news-stands and in hotel lobbies if there are copies left, but most of them will be disappointed. It is due to the smallness of our paper allocation: our print-run is one million and a half copies, but we could sell as many as ten million I am sure. On the basis of our increasing circulation we continue to request, and slowly to receive, more newsprint; but we have very far to go before we shall approach our potential maximum of sales. There are editions in ten languages: Russian, English, German, French, Italian, Spanish, Greek, Arabic, Hungarian and Estonian, and it is difficult to estimate how many copies we should print in each. The tradition of the paper was that it was intended mainly for other countries, and it takes time for this to change; we want it to be firstly for Russia. It is needed: especially in times like now.

I will describe for you what the paper was, what it is like now, and how we hope it will become. It has existed for sixty years, and for most of that time it was written for foreign readers. Its purpose was to convince them how happily and well all Soviet people were living, and it tried to give information about aspects of Soviet life. But only the aspects which the authorities wished people in other countries to know about, not anything at all which would hint our country was not a perfect paradise. It followed the lead in mentality of Henry the Fourth of France, who said 'In my whole kingdom there is no peasant so poor that he does not have every Sunday a chicken in his pot.'

This was exactly how *Moscow News* was: for more than fifty years a piece of slavish propaganda, that is all. But then three years ago – and there is reason to believe it was at the instigation of a person whose ranking is very high in our government – a change was ordered. A new controlling board was set up to run the paper, and it was given a broad hint that it should appoint a new and different editor of a certain type: one, in short, who would exercise independence and encourage everyone who worked for him to do the same. This was not, and is not still, as easy to put into practice as it might sound. For many years Soviet journalists had been used to compliance with censorship, and to working always in that kind of atmosphere. They were taught, and they accepted it with little questioning, that a story was within sight at the end of a corridor which had in it many doors. They were all closed, and they were to be walked past at all times without being opened; the story would be obtained and brought back again without enquiry or diverting of attention.

Where to find such a person, an editor of this type who would teach journalists not to behave in that fashion at all, but to pursue any story that they wished and not be afraid to question, and question, and question yet again until they were satisfied that they had the facts? Was there even such a person left in the Soviet Union? Well the answer is fortunately, yes: a man called Yuri Yakov, and he was appointed the Chief Editor of the new-style *Moscow News*. He had only recently been dismissed from his post as Editor of a small magazine because of what were described at the time as 'divisive views'. Such a term meant in fact of course not only that he was radical and progressive, but also that he believed most strongly that all points of view should be heard, not merely those which the State agreed with. Shortly after he came he asked me to be his deputy; I had been myself a freelance, and often in trouble. In three years we have formed a strong team not only of what may be described as accurate and honest reporters of things that occur, but also of investigative journalists. By this I mean writers who work for a longer period in greater depth, on stories which are not only newsworthy, but which repay closer and more patient examination.

We knew most of all that what was needed was honest writing and honest information about a situation. So when we have decided we are going to print any story at all of this type, the facts of it have to be most carefully checked and rechecked before it appears. One error, and it would be immediately seized on as an example of our unreliability, our desire for sensation rather than fact. It would need only a small series of such errors, and our reputation would be permanently damaged. To give an example, a few months ago after most careful and lengthy enquiry we printed a report of the present situation in the area surrounding the nuclear reactor explosion four years ago at Chernobyl power station. We found that the levels of radioactivity were still much higher than the authorities would admit; that many more people were still sick as a result of the after-effects than the authorities would admit; and that the surrounding areas where it is unsafe to live are still more widespread than the authorities will admit. Before we could print these and other accusations of this same kind, we had to be absolutely sure our figures would stand up to the most rigorous critical examination which, we knew, they were certain to receive. They did: and so our criticisms and revelations of the authorities' duplicity were shown to be justified, and as a result our reputation for printing the truth became even more widely proclaimed.

We regard our purpose as being to report, to criticise where necessary, and to allow open expression of views. What we do not print in any form at all is propaganda from the State. By this I mean that when we ask for information from the government and are given it, we do not simply accept it without question. Just as we have to substantiate our own figures, so we expect from them the same in return. Up to the present, we have never been threatened with closure; but we have had sometimes reprimands from the government about comments we have made and attitudes we have expressed. Even sometimes they have suggested changes: but we have not made them. If there were no such reactions and attempts at interference, all of us who work here would now feel, I think, that we could not be doing our work properly. There are always things to criticise, everywhere, in every country; but in the USSR we have had so many years when all criticism has been suppressed, that we think it could be possible every week to fill the paper with revelations about such suppressions.

I think we have done many things which have been good, and have improved the standard of Soviet journalism and reporting. This of course could not be claimed as entirely our achievement alone, but in some important instances we have given a lead. We were for example the first newspaper or magazine in the Soviet Union to publish letters, although it had sometimes to be anonymously, from people who proclaimed themselves openly to be dissidents and firm opponents of the government, saying it was for this and this reason and for that and that. At the time when we did so, we had no idea whatsoever what would happen to us as a result. Nothing in fact happened to us at all; but it would not have surprised many people, both among those who worked for the paper and the public in general, if we had been closed down or at the least for a period suspended. So this then gave a clear signal, both to people who wanted to explain the reasons for their dissident attitudes, and to newspapers and magazines who were considering whether it would be possible to publish such letters and articles, that it could now safely be done and the consequences were no longer likely to be severe.

We have had recently another example too where we have taken the lead in publishing information and arguments about a subject which before now has not had public discussion. This is the suggestion that the Soviet Army should be made professional, with soldiers entirely those who had chosen it to be their career. And, naturally following from this, comes the demand that conscription should be abolished. It is a fact that today the Soviet Army is the biggest in the world, bigger even than that of China. So we ask the question is so large a military force needed? If it is, for what? To have so many young men wasting their time in this over-inflated and unnecessary organisation, well it is absolutely a crime. We have had a huge response of readers' letters agreeing with us, and I think without doubt before long the government will have to pay attention to this demand from so many people, in so many different sections of the community, that the Army be reduced in size.

We test opinions of our readers on such matters and many others, incidentally, not only by encouraging them to write us letters: we also actually go out frequently among those crowds who are there outside, asking people what their opinions are, what new subjects they think we should be giving prominence to in our pages? There are those now who come to outside our offices to make speeches in public, as I understand happens in your London's Hyde Park Corner. Anyone may speak, anyone may say what he wants about any subject, and anyone may argue with him. So you see slowly, very slowly, we advance towards becoming a democratic society.

It must be said as well I think however, that everyone here is agreed that the future of our newspaper is very tightly tied to this future democracy we hope to achieve. It is not impossible, and everybody knows this, that there could be such a thing as the overthrow of the government by a strong reactionary group. Another possibility would be a military coup, on perhaps the grounds that the whole country was falling into anarchy and out of control. Such possibilities do exist, and not so remotely as some people believe. If something of that nature were to occur, undoubtedly *Moscow News* would be among the very first things to disappear and be heard of no more. Or even an attempt could be made to bring it back under its same title to the thing which it was before, a disseminator merely of State propaganda. But it would then be very easy, if such a thing happened, to know it for two reasons: one would be the content of the paper, and the other the fact that no single member of today's staff had remained here.

Eugene Stolokov,

Historical Monuments Preservation Society*

A tall distinguished-looking man, with neatly brushed hair going slightly grey at the temples, he wore a lightweight suit and a striped shirt with a plain blue tie. His voice was quiet, but strong and firm; while he talked he smoked continuously, lighting one cigarette from the end of another. His office was in some old buildings behind a church, in a quiet side street.

– I am grateful you have come to see me, because although our work is widely known of here, it is very often misrepresented or sometimes ignored completely by our newspapers. Many distorted accounts of its activities and what it stands for are very often printed. We live in a time when certain views of what are sometimes described as a progressive nature are widely publicised and even encouraged, while those of people such as ourselves are not regarded as fashionable.

The full correct name of our organisation is the Old Russia Society for the Preservation and Protection of Monuments of History. It was founded in 1966 two years after the fall of Khrushchev, at the beginning of the Brezhnev era. There was already at that time a great demand that something of its kind should be brought into existence, and this came from every section of society. Khrushchev had been asked several times to allow its foundation, but he always refused, treating the idea completely negatively. It was only when he had gone and a new government had been formed that the originators of the idea were allowed once more to bring their case forward. They included many prominent cultural and creative personalities – sculptors, painters, writers, members of the Academy of Sciences, and notable persons in every sphere of activity. What is most important to be remembered however is that these people were only expressing the ideas and desires of the mass of ordinary people, speaking for them and for the one fundamental belief which all of them had in common.

This belief was, in one word, patriotism. It is difficult to understand how an ideal so simple and universal could be treated as one so insignificant and unimportant as it had been by Khrushchev. But, like all ideals, it had never been possible to eradicate it; and the demand for its recognition was so strongly presented that a special government decision was taken to recognise its worth and importance. Committees were formed, experts in the restoration not only of buildings but of valuable documents were all brought together, and there was great enthusiasm for the project everywhere. At last, after so many years, people were allowed to express their feelings.

After the Revolution of 1917, the new government had tried quite deliberately to create a different ideology of living, which it consistently put into practice and allowing nothing which opposed it to stand in its way. One of its features was a belief in evolution: I do not of course mean in a biological sense, but in a historical-political one. It preached that all which was to do with the past was unimportant and even unnecessary, with no bearing at all on the present. It should therefore be ignored, or even in certain extreme cases destroyed. If it was of the past, away with it, we are constructing a completely new society: this was the attitude which lay underneath it. Old buildings were allowed to crumble away, or even in some instances, for the creation of new roads and housing estates, were physically destroyed. Our estimates in a wide-ranging survey which we have recently made show, for example, that there are now remaining only one-fifth of the total number of buildings and monuments that were in existence before the Revolution. These are actual physical things which can be enumerated; but at the same time many other parts of our cultural and spiritual life were forgotten or deliberately overlooked also. Virtues and traditions of great value were banished from our lives.

Such an aim of the Revolutionaries, that of creating in every way a new society under the name of Communism, well to my mind – and most people now will agree with me – it rested very largely on a denial of the value of anything at all which was not in line with

Party ideology. If national traditional cultural values were opposed to that ideology, then they should be swept away and replaced with new ideas. And unquestionably, these new ideas were not ones which were part of our own heritage, but were brought into our country from outside. Many new ideas were springing up all together all the time, and people were receptive to them all without selection or criticism. They were not able to see whether they were ideas that came from our own cultural heritage or from one which was foreign. In this way, much that was of what I may call vulgar origin became dominant, and the ordinary Russian people were deceived by persons who were not even themselves of Russian nationality.

So this is our aim, to correct the harm that has been done to our true heritage in the past, and to involve people to take practical steps to save what is left. We want once more to instil into people a sense of pride in their heritage, and to express their patriotism in this way. I am aware of course that there are other groups with the same aims, who concentrate on other areas. We all keep our independence and autonomy, working separately at some times if that will be more effective, and at other times combining in projects.

An example of something we would join together to campaign about? Well recently there has been such a one, and it shows what can be done if public feeling is organised in such a way as to make its strength apparent. A decision was taken some time ago by the City Council to construct an outer ring-road for Moscow. There are already two in existence, and this third one was to be built in such a way that the destruction of a number of areas of great historical value would be necessary. The intention that this should happen – the plan for the route which the road would take – this was concealed as much as possible, and it was hoped that when the complete plan was finally revealed, by then the work would be too far advanced for it to be cancelled: nothing would be able to be done, except at unacceptable expense, to prevent it. Well fortunately this was discovered; and great protests were organised in the form of public meetings, letters to the press and such things. But demolition and construction work had already begun, and certain people took what may be called direct action to prevent it continuing. Groups lay in front of bulldozers as they were working, forcing them to a standstill; and even in some places building equipment in use at construction sites was attacked and put out of action. I can understand the feelings of those who did such things, though of course not necessarily condoning the lengths to which they went. But it gave an example of the strength of feeling among people about such matters; and a short time ago the Council took the decision not to proceed with the construction of the road. That was an achievement for us.

The patriotism to which we appeal is something which is now becoming even more widespread. There was a time especially in the year of 1960, when patriotism was a subject of fun: great mockery was made of it in newspaper cartoons, performances for members only at night clubs, and in popular stage performances by people who were anxious to gain a certain reputation for themselves for outspokenness. I think that the government allowed this to happen, in a cynical fashion, so that when visiting dignitaries from other countries came, they could be taken to see such performances as examples of the government's tolerance of criticism. Such misuse of a profound feeling is I think in every way unjustifiable: patriotism is something which every person should have, and that every person should feel proud of having. We continually stress how important it is for all Russian people to be aware of their historical heritage, and never again to allow their own culture to be swamped by influences from abroad.

Well, as you ask me a frank question, in response I will give you an equally frank reply. There are many many people in our country who are opposed to what I believe is known as Western 'rock music' and its influence on our young people. I am one such person myself. I consider that such noise – it cannot be dignified in my opinion with the name 'music' – is abominable: it should not be permitted to be performed. The result could again be, or might be, that it is replacement of our own national traditional music. It has no artistic merit, and it represents the commercial exploitation of youth by large Western business companies, who have no other principles than that of making money.

What I am saying, I am convinced, is felt also by the majority of our population. But they do not have the confidence to speak out against it in this way unless someone leads. I have spoken to dozens or even hundreds of parents: not one of them expresses anything but disdain for such a thing as this 'rock music', and the way it pervades and perverts the culture of our young people. Only very recently an announcement was made that later this year a so-called 'rock music concert' was to be staged in Red Square. Well, it is scarcely believable that such an idea could even be suggested in a country with as long a tradition of civilisation such as ours. I wrote on behalf of our society protesting at the suggestion of such a thing, and this letter was published in our newspaper *Pravda*. I said, and I think I was justifiably forthright in the words that I chose, that Red Square was in every way the centre and heart of our nation, and should be treasured as such by every person who was of sound mind. To permit its use as a place where such persons as rock musicians could perform, with their shrieks and gyrations and hideous noise, was therefore nothing less than blasphemy.

Following the letter's appearance, I understand there were more than ten thousand letters of agreement with it received both by Moscow City Council, and also by the Central Committee of the Communist Party. In the face of such an outcry the permission for the concert to be given was withdrawn: if I may say so, sanity prevailed.

This demonstrates several things to me. One is the need for vigilance against these foreign influences coming into our country; another, the huge support we have for our beliefs and principles among all right-minded people; the third the influence which public opinion can exert for good when it is properly alerted to dangers that can occur; and finally, the fundamental feelings of patriotism which exist in our people. All these things demonstrate to me that what we are doing is both necessary and correct.

I am glad to have read from time to time in our newspapers that there are similar groups to ours in your country, Britain. They also I believe are struggling to preserve your own national heritage. It was particularly satisfying to learn that a public campaign a short time ago prevented the building of a large and ugly extension to one of your great art galleries, which is located I believe in a historic setting known as Trafalgar Square. I believe that most Englishmen possess this sense of the importance of historical tradition, it is what may be described as a characteristic of them. And this campaign against the building of the alteration to the art gallery, if I am not mistaken, was led by such a person as a prince whose name is Charles who will one day be your King. This was to me a demonstration of the English people's very good attitude towards the past, and I have given it here as an example many times.

Maxim Yallov and Ilya Valkovsky,
university students

Maxim was small and sturdily built, with short fair hair and blue eyes; Ilya was taller, dark-haired and thin. Both wore blousons, open-necked shirts and jeans. They lounged in chairs at the kitchen table of Ilya's parents' apartment in a tower block, drinking tea and smoking.

Maxim: It will help us to improve our English we hope.
Ilya: We are both eighteen, we are students at Moscow University where we are in the second year of our studies. I am studying English and Maxim is studying history. This is my home, and Maxim lives on the tenth floor of the next apartment block. We have been friends with each other since we were children, small children.
Maxim: Well we have known each other all our lives, we were born together at the same time in the same maternity hospital. My mother says sometimes it is like we are twins.
Ilya: We have written down some of the things we will talk to you about. The first one, because I think it is the thing that is in the mind of every young man who is of the age we are, is what faces us in perhaps three years or two, which is when we have to go to the Army as conscripts.
Maxim: It may be that we can postpone the time before we have to go so that we can continue with our studies. But if not we shall have to go to the Army and then resume them when we return.
Ilya: We have put this the first on our list of things to say, because you see it is very important for our future.
Maxim: We think conscription is undesirable. Mostly we don't think it is necessary to serve in the Army at all, except perhaps if

there were new circumstances that arose in the world such as possibility of war.

Ilya: Two years is a long period to take from your life. There is talk now that the law may be changed and conscription will be reduced to one year only. But we think that is not right, there should not be conscription at all.

Maxim: Our country is reducing its armaments and military spending, and so the government has no argument that everyone should have conscription. It is an idiotic system.

Ilya: This law was passed that we should have it many years before we were born. I do not know if there was good reason for it, perhaps the situation in the world was not very good. But now it is different.

Maxim: You know, it is always difficult in our country for change to come. If it is the law that there should be conscription, people do not want to change the law because it has been tradition. The older people they say 'But it has always been like this in our country, every young man serves in the Army for a time in his life, why do you not want to, what is wrong with it?' There is a law which says you must go, but there is not a law which allows you to say you do not wish to go.

Ilya: If there was such a law, then people would accept that immediately.

Maxim: It might be that there were good things about serving in the Army, and then there would be no objection. If those who go were given training in something that would be of use to them when they came back from the Army, that might be something. But I do not think that peeling potatoes, or digging holes in the street for drains, these are not anything that will help you for your future life.

Ilya: Many young men now are trying to postpone their service, because they think the time must come before long when the law is changed. The most popular way to do this is to apply to become student. Then they go to the exams which are necessary, but they do not have the ability and so they are not accepted. As the applications become more in number, the waiting lists for the examinations become longer: in this way everyone is delayed, even those who are with a good chance to be accepted. All of it is very unsatisfactory.

Maxim: It is a long time to wait all together when you are trying to plan your future life for yourself. You do not know if you will pass the examinations and be accepted as student, then if you pass you do not know when you will begin, then you do not know if you will have your conscription and when it will be. So there is always worry in your mind.

Ilya: Next we will tell you what we think of the political situation in our country today. We have asked others of our student friends what they think also, so that we can hope what we say will not be the views of ourselves only, but most of our contemporaries too.

Maxim: Of course not all think the same, but what we say is what we think very many students at university of our age agree with.

Ilya: We do not like our politicians: we do not like any of them. We think those who are at the top of our government, those who are the heads of the ruling party which is the Communist Party, are not good. The Communists have had more than seventy years since the Revolution, which is two whole generations of people, to do good for the country, but they have not done this. They are all the same at heart. What they want is power only for themselves, and not first and foremost the good of the people. Therefore we distrust them and we despise them.

Maxim: They will use different words and they will use different methods. Sometimes they try to look good to the people and they use kind words and promises, and sometimes they try to look cruel to the people to make it that they are frightened of them. Whatever it is, they are all the same in their hearts.

Ilya: It is proclaimed by our leaders that what we have is socialist society, and they say what they mean by this is that everything is judged whether it is for the good of everybody, and not just for the good of some individuals more than others. And so there is no freedom for the individual, and no freedom for the mass either.

Maxim: We have no history of freedom in our society. People do not expect to have it, and many of them do not mind that they do not have it. Always the people who are at the top are saying 'Tomorrow things will be better, be patient.' But it does not happen. Each time there is tomorrow, things are not better: sometimes they are the same, and sometimes they are worse.

Ilya: If you go from Moscow, away from the city and to the countryside to see how people are living there, you would think you were walking back into the past.

Maxim: I have read many history books in my studies, and I think that you would find that the conditions for country people are like those which were in existence in for example Britain perhaps a hundred years ago. People do not have proper houses, they do not have sanitation or hot water in their homes, they have only poor food which they grow themselves and poor clothes.

Ilya: We spend money to put men into space and to make such things as rocket weapons of destruction, and in this way it is proudly said that we are technically and technological-advanced further than any other country in the world. But this is for the glorification of our politicians only, so that they may designate themselves as being important people among the world leaders.

Maxim: To us it seems as though all our people live in a dream, that they should let this continue. But nothing solves the great economic problems of the Soviet Union, and nothing that is for the benefit of its peoples has happened since the Revolution at all. The Revolution led to Stalin, then there was war; and after that as their reward, the people got Stalin again, only now no one could oppose him in any way because he was the hero who had won the war.

Ilya: As Maxim says, people live as though it was a dream for them. A friend of mine, under Stalin, his grandfather was sent to a labour camp for four years; then he came back to the village where he lived, and went on with his life as a peasant farmer. He was left alone, and so were his family. He never spoke with anyone about what had happened to him, and no one asked him what had happened to him or even why he had been sent to the labour camp. When he retired, he was given a State pension and a medal as a good revolutionary, and when he died he was honoured at his funeral: speeches were made by the local officials of the Party to say what a good life he had led. And still, even then, nothing was said about him going to the labour camp.

Maxim: It had not been a life, it had been a dream; and that is how it is with us still.

Ilya: But we have our own dream also, and we agreed that we would finally tell you about this. It will be our dream, we hope, for when we leave the university and are no longer students. It is called 'The Keepers'.

Maxim: It is a musical group. We are happy to be students at university, but when we have finished there and have to earn our living, that is how we intend to do it. There are four of us: Ilya and I and two of our friends who are also at university. We are all great friends, already we play together whenever we can, but of course our studies have to come first. It will be difficult for us to make a living, we know, because there are so many other people who want to do this. But we have the intention to make our living as a pop group, and the only way we can find out if it is possible is to try.

Ilya: We have 'The Keepers' as the name of our group because all of us are great admirers of your English author J. R. R. Tolkien. *The Lord of the Rings* is our most favourite book, and so we honour him in taking as our name the characters of his, 'The Keepers Of The Ring'.

Maxim: Why we wish to stay the four of us all together and earn our living in this way is a difficult question to answer for you. I do not know if the other three in it would agree with this, but for myself the most of all reason is that I do not wish to become part of the system. I do not know if that is the correct word for it though.

Ilya: Yes the established system, another word for it would be the establishment. I am sure what Maxim says is correct, that we all feel about it the same way as he does. We want to break away from the ways of our parents and grandparents who have let themselves lose their personalities in the system of the State.

Maxim: We want to stay as individual persons. The system can be described as a triangle like this: work, home, family. It begins for you when you end your studies and start to follow your life, and it is like that for ever – job, house, family. We do not want to begin our lives like that and we do not want to continue our lives like that.

Ilya: And for most of us especially, I think, we do not want that which involves having home and family. It is conventional for everyone in USSR that you should marry and do this, but for me I would try not to marry at all.

Maxim: It is always that if you love somebody there is no alternative for you.

Ilya: From your parents especially or your girl's parents. You cannot love unless you are registered for the future, and have permission from the authorities. We do not think it should be like that. It is why there are so many times divorce.

Maxim: You should have the freedom to decide for yourself what you want to do with your life. You should discuss it with your girl, and if you both feel you want to live together but not to be married, then this should be possible as it is in the West.

Ilya: Among our friends at the university, both male and female, there is much talk always of such things as we have been saying to you this afternoon, and I think changes will come.

Maxim: I am not as optimistic as you are, I think our society has had its spirit broken after all these years.

Dr Alexei Dmitriev,

Physicians Against Nuclear War

A tall man in a navy blue blazer and neatly pressed grey trousers, he spoke quietly and with sincerity, sitting relaxed and at ease at the end of the large horseshoe-shaped table in one of the panelled and decoratively frescoed committee-rooms at the Academy of Medical Sciences. He was forty-six.

– The latter part of 1980 was not exactly the best time that could be thought of for trying to improve Soviet–American relationships. I suppose now looking back, it could be argued that things were so bad at that time in the Cold War that, if they admitted it or not, people were really worried. People such as doctors, many of whom tend to live in a reclusive way and not think too much about the outside world, even they were stirred to try and take steps to prevent what was beginning to look like the inevitability of nuclear war. The invasion of Afghanistan, the shooting-down of the Korean airliner and other international confrontations – they were all contributing towards an atmosphere which everyone felt was going to bring war between two of the great powers. And on both sides, the attitudes of our respective governments were becoming steadily more intractable and unchangeable.

So it happened that a small group of American and Soviet doctors who had been corresponding with each other on subjects of almost entirely specialised medical interest – well, they felt they must both do something to warn their respective governments of the consequences of a war. From a medical point of view alone, if there were to be what was usually referred to as 'a nuclear exchange' – then that would be a catastrophe: not just for the two countries involved, but for a large part of the whole of the rest of the world. Therefore they arranged some private visits to one another's countries, and decided to set up an international organisation called 'Physicians Against Nuclear War'. It was to lay before their respective governments – the Americans to the American government, and the Russians to the Russian – exactly what the consequences of such an 'exchange' would be.

It was only a very small group of doctors from the two countries to begin with; but they were scientists with specialised knowledge. They felt they had an imperative moral duty to speak out and tell the truth to their own governments. One fact was, very simply, that in the event of nuclear conflict, medical help to mitigate the damage would not be available. Not only because of the extent of the damage to large areas, but because hospitals, doctors themselves, ambulances, even basic medical supplies such as bandages – none of these would escape the effects of radiation within a large radius of any actual explosion. They couldn't go or be sent into the area for weeks or months, or possibly years afterwards, because of effects of the contamination remaining there.

So it had to be made plain to the governments concerned that the use, or the threat of the use, of nuclear weapons was entirely out of the question. The two groups, small though they were, agreed that with the full weight of what authority they could command they would give an identical warning about it. Because whoever and wherever they are, doctors are in possession of certain knowledge not available to the layman, which ensures that when they speak and write, they are listened to with a degree of respect.

That was the way the organisation was born, and the reason for it coming into being. Immediately, it began work to compile cool, rational and above all factual arguments to put to the top echelons of government on both sides. What they were putting forward were only facts, and their assessments and judgements about them as professional medical men. Of course, most importantly, they were acting totally in concert with one another. Neither the American nor the Russian governments could make the accusation that doctors from 'the other side' as it were, were trying to frighten them. In a very short time the group found they were being to some extent even more successful in getting attention than they hoped. Not only were an increasing number of doctors in their own countries making enquiries from them or offering them additional information; but doctors from other countries in the world got to know about their efforts, and were asking how they could start doing the same thing in their own countries. They too were anxious to bring pressure on their own governments, not only to give up ideas of having nuclear weapons of their own, but also to get them to try to exercise influence on the big powers on the matter.

By the beginning of 1985 those who had begun as a tiny informal association of practising medical specialists realised they could no longer continue on an *ad hoc* basis. They would have to have a properly organised organisation. Forgive me, that is not very good English I think, 'have to have'. However, you will understand my meaning. Here in USSR they advertised for someone with suitable background knowledge, and with administrative experience also, to take charge. I was fortunate to be successful in my application, and that is how I come to be here now as what is known as Executive Director. It was a wonderful achievement for me personally that I should be given the position.

In my life as I've grown older, and I think and hope wiser, I have increasingly tended towards the absolute pacifist point of view. I have never believed warfare is a rational way of solving disagreements between countries who quarrel. With the coming of nuclear weapons, as I began to study them and learn about them so that I could add weight to my arguments, I start to feel all forms of warfare should be renounced. To be honest I suppose I am still not one hundred per cent certain of this: I can imagine a few circumstances, I think, in which war might be justified. But if by war is meant nuclear war, then no I cannot, it can't be justified in any way. And I say even more than that, that all nuclear weapons should be done away with by all countries. They cannot ever be used without a cataclysmic effect, not only on the countries using them but on countries which have nothing to do with the quarrelling nations involved. This was clearly demonstrated by the after-effects of the explosion at the nuclear power station at Chernobyl in the Ukraine. Countries as far afield as Sweden and Norway and the United Kingdom and Ireland – all were affected by the nuclear fall-out which followed. This was absolute proof of what our organisation has been saying all along – that you cannot control the after-effects of nuclear explosions in any way, nor can you confine them to the areas you are intending to. It should not take a war between two Arab or African countries using nuclear weapons against each other, and it to be followed by nuclear fall-out on Moscow, New York, London and Paris, before the big powers come to their senses. They should give other countries a lead in renouncing such weapons.

For the time being at least I believe firmly that whatever happens in the future, there will never again be the same tension between USSR and the West. The Cold War is over, I do believe that. So at least the danger of nuclear war between the big powers has receded. But danger is still as great, even greater than it was, of war breaking out and escalating between other countries. Therefore much work for our organisation has still to be done. We must continue to spread knowledge about nuclear war and its after-effects, and try to rid people of the insane idea that such a war could in any way be 'won'. It is necessary to try to alter the way of thinking of those in power everywhere, and make them abandon outdated concepts such as waging wars with these weapons. If any political figure of any country ever suggests such an idea, by definition the question of their sanity must arise. Consideration should be given to whether that person is a fit and proper person to be in charge of his or her country's affairs. This is not a political argument: it is a medical judgement. I would say that any person who thinks in that way has lost contact with reality.

Similarly, any person who proposes such an idea as 'nuclear deterrence' – well, they are no longer thinking rationally. You cannot have a deterrent unless ultimately, under whatever circumstances you can persuade yourself justify it, you are actually prepared to use it. So any political leader, any government's leader, who could for a moment contemplate using such a weapon – well, it has to be said they are revealing they have in them a streak of insanity. They are too dangerous to their own people, never mind to their enemies, to continue in positions of authority where they could have power to take such actions. What they are saying you see is this: for the sake of the imagined triumph of their own opinions, they will cause the deaths of thousands or millions of people, men, women and children, old and young alike, not only of their enemies but of their own people as a result of the enemy's retaliation, plus a similar untold number of deaths of other people all over the world. By any definition – medical, social, ethical, religious – this is madness, and beyond the limits of normal human thinking. Anyone who keeps nuclear weapons as a deterrent and says they will use them – well, they are announcing they are prepared to commit both genocide and national suicide.

The repeating of this at every opportunity everywhere in the world is now the principal work of our organisation. The degree of success we've had can be measured, I think, by the increasing number of requests for speakers and information we are getting daily from all over the world. Doctors, writers, concerned people of all kinds – in numerous instances even governments themselves – are asking us to send representatives to conferences, in many cases to go and organise conferences for them, and to bring in participants from as many other countries as we possibly can. We are doing this all the time. Within the past few months I have been engaged in doing such things in India, Switzerland, Italy, Egypt and Japan. The European situation, and the situation between USSR and America, have improved dramatically and rapidly within the past year. But we must never forget our country and yours and the USA, well these do not make up the whole world or even the most important part of it. And not forget either that just as situations can improve, so also can they unexpectedly go worse. Our aim is to try and ensure that people understand that even if they do, either in our part of the world or if there is trouble elsewhere, in no part of the world will they be safe if war involves the use of nuclear weapons. So we continue our work and extend it. We must not ever sit back and indulge a feeling that all danger has now passed. It most certainly has not.

My English? Well, I give many talks and speeches everywhere in the world in it. It is not good, but I hope it improves.

15 *After the disaster*

Nadia Larova, newspaper editor
Stefan Sheverenko, heating engineer
Ivan Borovich, foreman mechanic
Sonya Kornichek, stores manager
Anton Vassilievich, radiation expert

Nadia Larova,
newspaper editor*

As a member of the committee of 'The Union of Chernobyl Survivors', she had come to Moscow with some of her colleagues for a two-day visit to meet and talk with government officials. A slender dark-haired woman with a delicate-featured and fine-boned face, her manner alternated between liveliness and sudden sombre moments of near-silence when she found it hard to speak. She twisted her fingers together nervously while she talked.

– Placed together in a group, next to one another, the four reactors have the name 'Chernobyl Atomic Power Station'. But Chernobyl is the name of a region; and a small town was actually built round the power station, at first for the construction workers, then for accommodation for workers at the plant. It is called Pripyet. I went to live there when it was first built, now eight years ago, because I had been a freelance journalist: I was offered to be the Editor of the weekly newspaper to be published for the power-station workers, and given away free to them. Because I had studied the subjects of radiation and atomic power for articles I had written already for magazines, the authorities agreed I was a suitably qualified person.

I did not want the newspaper to be only for the engineers and other workers of the plant, I wanted it also to be for their families. So I began to include such things in it as items about politics, and some poetry and short stories. I wrote the first ones myself to give a lead, and encouraged the paper's readers to do so themselves. The managers of the power station became uneasy: they said such things were not suitable to be included in its newspaper. Soon after a time I had visited the site often, and talked with workers there: so I included articles which were critical of safety procedures, and pointed out shortcomings. This made the managers angry: they asked me where I had got my information from, and when I said it was from the workers themselves, they demanded to know who they were. Of course I would not tell them. Twice I was threatened with dismissal. And it was in the middle of one such time of argument and confrontation that the very warnings I had given were fulfilled, and the disaster occurred. I am now in Moscow to be questioned again about my prophecies, how it was that they were so accurate, and why it was that they were not paid attention to.

My home in Pripyet was an apartment in a newly constructed apartment block under one kilometre from the entrance to the power station. I lived there with my mother and my daughter who was then nine. My husband and I were separated and he had gone away, but we were not then divorced. Also living with us was my niece, my sister's child: she was six, and she was with us temporarily because my sister was also having some difficulty in her own life. It was quite a large apartment, everything in it new, and a pleasant home. I had even a room there where I could do my own writing, as well as my office in the power station for my work with the newspaper; so life was pleasant for me. But I had worry about the safety situation at the power station, which was concerning me increasingly.

My favourite time for my own work was late at night, when the world was still and there seemed to be no other people in it except myself. On the night of the disaster I was finishing a poem on which I had been working hard for two weeks: it was about the violinist Paganini, and how when he played music of any kind, because he was such a great genius he could make it sound as though it was not from this world, but sometimes from heaven and sometimes from hell. I had a collection of old gramophone records by him, which had been given me before he died by my father. It was perhaps midnight when finally I finished the poem, and then of course I was very excited. I knew I would not be able to sleep because my mind was still racing with the words, so before going to bed, I took a strong sleeping pill.

Because of it, in the night I heard nothing at all. The explosion happened at one-twenty-six in the morning, and my mother later told me it was not very loud. You should understand this was by no means the first explosion at the plant: such occurrences were quite common, a loud thud for example when a large amount of steam was discharged suddenly into the air. My mother herself when she heard it thought it was something of that kind, and returned to sleep.

Please, I am sorry, now for a little while I am finding it difficult to speak. Even to think of the accident, my pulse races and I feel sick. In a moment I will be able to continue again in an ordinary fashion. Forgive me.

In the morning when I woke up, I did not know something had happened until I went out of my home. My mother and daughter and niece were not there; I thought they had gone to the market in the town square as was usual for them on a Saturday morning, so after I had dressed I decided to go to join them. As soon as I went down the stairs of the apartment block and out through the door into the street, I was aware at once something was wrong. I could feel on my face a tingling as though it was raining although it was not. I felt also a taste of metal in my mouth, and my eyes began to water. I do not know why, but I sensed something had happened at the power station and I must go to it. I could not get along the street the way I usually went, because there was warning tape across it and two soldiers were there who said I could go no further. But I knew another way, through a side street and a courtyard that no one could watch over, so I took that way.

As I turned the corner which would bring me almost to the power-station entrance, I stopped. Right in front of me was a reactor, and it was on fire. Again I cannot explain this to you: but among the smoke above its roof flames were dancing, they were red and green and yellow and blue. They were not dancing wildly or with excitement, they were swaying – almost merrily, to the tune which suddenly was in my head. It was on the violin, as it had been played by Paganini, that I had been listening to the night before. It was an allegro; the flames were dancing it in a stately way, and this was terrifying to me, because it seemed I can only say quite normal, that the reactor should be doing this.

I went hurriedly back to my apartment, where I found my mother and the children had returned. They told me there had been an announcement on the radio there had been an explosion at the power station; but they had said it was not serious and there was no cause for alarm. I knew this was a lie, because I had seen the burning reactor with my own eyes: but I said nothing to my mother or the children because I did not wish them to be afraid. Then another announcement came on the radio: that in the afternoon as a precautionary measure, special buses and trains were being arranged to begin taking away anyone who lived in Pripyet and wished to go, except men who worked at the power station. My mother began to argue with me that it was not necessary, but I insisted she should take the children. I pretended for them they were going to have a holiday, and began to pack a bag for them: I got together pans and cooking utensils, cutlery, a change of clothing, and some mugs and bowls. I also remembered to tell the children to go to their room and choose for themselves a book to take with them. Then in the afternoon I went with them to the town square: buses were waiting, and when it came their turn to get on one, I tried to wave happily to them so they would still believe they were being taken by my mother on a holiday. I did not know if I would ever see any of them again. Forgive me, I am sorry, I must pause. No no, I wish to continue to speak.

I wanted to go to my office, but I was refused a special pass to get into the power station. These were for essential workers only; I was told one would not be given to me at a future time that could be estimated, and advised I should leave Pripyet. I had a friend who was an engineer at the power station, and when I was able to contact him on the telephone, he repeated it, telling me it was far more serious than was going to be admitted, and for my own safety I should leave.

There was of course everywhere confusion. I think the management themselves even, they really did not know how serious it was. I could find no one who could tell me where my mother and the children had been taken to, and so in the evening I decided I would go to Kiev and see if I could obtain information there. I thought I would go to the apartment of a friend, and see if she would give me somewhere to sleep. The distance is not much more than a hundred kilometres to Kiev: it is normally not more than a short train-journey, perhaps a little over one hour. But that night like everything else, the railway was in chaos: it took many hours, and as a result I did not get to Kiev until the early hours of the morning. As I was coming out of the railway station, there were some rough boys and they began to jeer at me and make lewd suggestions; I had no luggage and my appearance, although I did not know it then, was of someone off the streets. To be safe from them, I took my place in a taxi queue; but when it came to my turn, I could not find the paper I had written with my friend's address, and so I went to the back of the queue again, knowing at least that while I was there among others, the boys would not taunt me again. This happened perhaps four or five times, and I did not know what I could do. I was so tired, I was dirty and ragged-looking, I was afraid, and I was alone in the strange big city in the middle of the night. I stood and cried.

Then a man came up to me in the queue, a middle-aged man; he took my arm and he said 'Do not be afraid. Come with me.' He had seen me joining and rejoining the queue, but I did not know this of course, and I thought he was trying to abduct me. He spoke calmingly, telling me he would not hurt me, and finally I gave in to him, thinking it no longer mattered what happened to me. Across the street from the railway station there was a big hotel: he took me there and asked if there was a vacant room. When the reception clerk said there was, he told him he wished to book it for me for four nights, and he put down on the counter the money for it in cash. Then he told to me I should have a good rest for several days. He said he would telephone in a day or two to see how I was; then he raised his hat and wished me good-night, and he went away.

I was too tired even to thank him or to say anything at all. I went up to the room he had paid for for me, and it had a bathroom attached to it. I took off all my clothes and immersed myself in the bath which I'd filled with hot water, and then I lay there exhausted. I was not even capable of feeling amazement or even thankfulness at what had happened to me in such a strange way. I just lay in the water dozing, it seemed for all the rest of the night: warming myself, soaping myself over and over, and crying.

When finally I came to get out of the bath, I had a terrible shock. I caught sight of myself naked in a big mirror that hung behind the door. I was thirty-five, and I had the firm white body of a young woman; but on top of it my face was brown and lined with deep red like a burnt apple. Its skin was peeling, and my hair was black and coming in tufts out like this when I touched it. I cried out in horror at the sight of myself. I think then I collapsed on the bed into a deep sleep, and slept almost for twelve hours. I stayed in the room, not eating and not looking at myself, for three days.

So that is how it was for me. The man who was so kind, I have met him and his wife and his family several times since, when I go to Kiev. I can never repay him for what it was he did. My mother and the children, they have been moved to live with me in a new apartment for us in Kiev. For my children, there seem to be no after-effects. But it is not so for me: myself I am chronically sick, and how long I shall live I do not know. I was never in my life sick before; now in the last two years I have been taken into hospital fifteen times. I remember once, a long time ago, how it was that I was young and happy. Now I feel as though I am one thousand years of age, and I have lost my soul. Each year there comes again, like now, the spring: but I do not feel it is one for me.

Stefan Sheverenko,

heating engineer*

A small bald-headed man with steel-framed glasses, he wore a formal brown suit and an open-necked light green shirt. He spoke quietly and thoughtfully, with frequent long pauses in which he gathered and ordered his words before saying them. He was thirty-one.

– For me, it was the beginning of my life when I came to work at the power station. I had graduated from the University of Moscow with a diploma in heating engineering at the age of twenty-four, and at once on the recommendation of my professor I had been offered a job at Chernobyl. It was an immensely prestigious place to have the chance to work because everyone had always been told that it was the finest and most up to date atomic power station, not only in the USSR but in the whole world.

The salaries you would be paid there were higher than you could earn anywhere else in the atomic-power industry, and you were guaranteed not only that you would have your own large and newly built apartment, but that you would be given a choice from two or three different apartments. They were building them for workers there all the time, new ones were being finished every day, and if there was not one which you liked or thought suitable for yourself and your family, you would need to wait one or at the most two weeks only before others would be offered to you. The town of Pripyet which had been specially constructed for the power-station people was smart and carefully laid out with parks and lakes, and it had well-stocked shops in which were a certain amount of goods not available elsewhere.

I was not married, but I had a girl I wished to marry. I asked her if I went would she come with me as my wife and she agreed: so at once we registered our intention, and she made a special trip of five hundred kilometres to the town with her parents to look at it, and to inspect and find a suitable apartment for us. She was of course very excited by the prospects opening before us, as her parents were, and naturally as I was myself. It seemed the beginning of a dream.

We went, we married, and we had a very good three-roomed apartment on the edge of the town in a nicely wooded area. In a short period we were able to buy as well a small dacha near a lake about five kilometres to the north. Then we had our first child and, not long after it, our second. To describe it all I can only say it was an idyllic time, and apart from one small worry we were very happy. This was that sometimes my wife would suffer from bad dreams, and she would wake in the night in a very frightened state of mind. She would never tell me what these dreams concerned, saying she could not recall the details of them, but she had a sense in them that we and our children were in danger. Whether they concerned anything more specific than that, I do not know: she would not talk about it with me. These dreams of hers were not frequent: once in two or three months perhaps, no more. It is only afterwards you recall such things; at the time I was not much aware her dreams existed as regular occurrences for her. It is easy to be wise about such matters afterwards; I think now she had fears about living in Pripyet, but would not admit to them.

For myself, I had none: no fears, no doubts about going at all. After I began work I did have some doubts and anxieties about certain things, but they were not to do with safety matters: they concerned more the management and administration of the plant, and what after a time became apparent was happening in that respect. I would describe it chiefly as inefficiency, but as I say not on the technical side. There was a degree of nepotism; in an atomic power station it is not possible to give your brother-in-law a job in let us say radiation control, unless he has the necessary qualifications. But you can give him a job in the financial section or on the store-management staff without him having to be highly qualified: those are the areas where some favouritism was shown. It caused as it always does bad feeling, and in particular among the higher-level technicians such as my colleagues and myself. But it has to be repeated: such irritations and dissatisfactions as we had concerning these matters, they were entirely to do with working conditions, and not connected with safety matters.

Eventually it happened that we wrote a letter of protest to the Senior Management Committee. Much to our surprise we were invited to a meeting with them: they promised us that our complaints would be thoroughly investigated. They said where they were justified corrections would be made, and strong steps would be taken to ensure that everything wrong would be put right. The day on which this unusual meeting took place was the 21st of April, just five days before the explosion.

When it happened, I was asleep and did not hear it. It was not very loud, the power station was downwind from where we lived, and anyway like everyone else we were quite used to such noises from time to time. The next morning was a Saturday, and I had to be at the plant by seven o'clock; it was usual for all who were on the early-morning shift to gather in a large car park, and there a bus came to take us to our various destinations inside the plant. No one made any reference to the explosion during the night, which will indicate to you how much we took such things for granted.

The first unusual thing we saw was that when the bus came, its driver was wearing on his lapel a special strip of material like a piece of film negative. He said there had been some minor alarm in the night, and he had been told to report if the strip changed colour. The bus took us in through the power-station gates, and then we saw a young soldier standing by them; we all looked out through the windows of the bus and laughed at him. The reason we laughed was that he was trying to get some kind of breathing apparatus down over his head and on to his face: he was very clumsy and his hand was getting caught behind his neck in the harness. We were still laughing about this when the bus came to a halt at the entrance to a tunnel which went under one of the reactors. We were told to get out; and we did not then laugh any more, because of what happened.

We were surrounded by soldiers with automatic rifles, and all of them were wearing radiation-protection gear. We were told that only personnel above a certain level could proceed, and the rest would be permitted neither to go on or to leave, but must stay where they were. I was one of those qualified to proceed, and as I went towards the tunnel I looked to the side and upwards to the top of Reactor Number 4. Its roof had been entirely destroyed, and it was enveloped in smoke and flames. I had time to see this at a glance, then I was told to hurry forward into a building housing one of the other reactors, and go to my usual work station there in the corridor between them. When I arrived, I saw the man I was to relieve leaning against the wall and he was vomiting on to the floor. He looked up at me, and he said he thought he had eaten something in the canteen when he had come to work the night before. Then he went away, and I have never seen that man since. I am sorry, it distresses me to talk of him: we had worked together many times and he was not only a colleague of mine but my friend.

The air everywhere in the building was very hot and dry. The water supply which we used for washing, in the toilets, and from the taps to make tea or coffee, had been turned off; so also had much of the ventilation. The telephones by which we talked with each other in different parts of the complex were not working, and other signalling and communications equipment was out of action as well. One of the managers came round to talk with each one of us at our posts in turn: he said he was going to be frank with us, there had been an explosion in the night which had caused much damage. In particular he said it had interfered with the systems which operated the radiation-dosage meters. They were positioned short distances apart along every corridor wall, and he pointed out that as a result they all showed a measurement of zero radiation. But he said the system would soon be repaired and they would resume working properly again. He repeated several times that there had been no escape of radiation whatsoever. What he did not tell us was that the radiation meters had not been damaged in the accident, they had been turned off.

It was my occupation, along with those of my colleagues who were similarly qualified, to monitor the heating and ventilating systems for all the reactors. Because of this it was necessary for us to communicate; and if the telephones were not working, as they were not, then we had to move from one part of a building to another to meet and talk, or from one building to another. It soon became obvious to us during the day that we had been misled. The number of personnel at the power station when it was operational was 5,400; but on that day, the day after the explosion, those of us who were there numbered only three hundred. We were then told that we were under martial law: we would not be allowed to leave nor, when the telephone system was repaired, would we be allowed to make any calls to anyone, including our families, outside. We were also told two other things: that our families were even at that moment being evacuated to places out of the danger zone, and that it was true in fact that a severe radiation leak in the plant had occurred. No other workers would be brought in because the level of it was too high; and this of course carried with it clearly the implication that we ourselves were not expected to live.

We remained in the power station for three weeks, and we have never been told, ever since then, what radiation dosage any of us received, nor the possible extent of its effects. How it can be properly measured is still not at all understood. Some people received high doses and they died as a result; some received high doses and have been seriously ill; and some, of whom I myself am one, have received these high doses and yet afterwards have so far at least been little affected. I may tell you that my feeling about this is not at all one of thankfulness, but strange as it may sound, one almost of shame: I do not know why I should not have suffered in the same way as those who have better characters than mine have done. Now I in my turn have bad dreams about this, and wake in the night with remembrance.

My wife and children had not been present in Pripyet on the night of the explosion, and so had not been among those evacuated. She had been with them at her mother's home in Kiev, and I understand that she lives now in Moscow. We have divorced and she has remarried. I myself live now in Donetsk in the south of Ukraine, where I am a teacher at an institute. I have been offered to have work again in the nuclear-power industry, but this is something I will not do. It is necessary perhaps that we have nuclear power still, but I want to have no further connection with it, to me it was the finish of my life.

Ivan Borovich,

foreman mechanic*

A gruff-voiced stockily built man of fifty, he had short bristly fair hair and a thick bushy moustache. He wore a sports jacket and jeans and a check shirt with a silk handkerchief knotted round his throat. His manner was nervous and his watery blue eyes were sad and dull.

– I came to Pripyet just one year before the accident, with my wife and family. We have two daughters: one was then twelve and the other one ten. We lived in the city of Volvograd in the south-east of our country for ten years, and my work was at a hydroelectric power station. I was not what you could say was a man with high technical qualifications, but I was an experienced driver and operator of heavy industrial machinery such as tractors, excavators and what is called earth-moving equipment.

It had happened not long before, that I had had an accident at my work: not a serious one, but there had been damage to my leg and breakage of some small bones in my foot, and I had to be in hospital for two months while certain operations were performed. My recovery was complete, and afterwards I was sent for a recuperative holiday for two weeks to a resort on the coast of the Black Sea. I stayed at a fine hotel which was owned by the section of the union to which I belonged, and while I was there, I met another such person as myself. He also was a heavy-equipment operator who was recovering after an accident which had necessitated surgery. His place of work was the Chernobyl Atomic Power Station, and he talked very frequently about it. Anyone who worked there was like that: it was famous throughout our country as being a fine place to be, with good housing for families, better shops, and generally slightly higher wages than you could find elsewhere. It was a place of what may be called prestige, that is the way I would express it.

After some days I expressed interest to him and said that if ever such opportunity arose, I would like myself to work there. He asked me that I should write down for him full particulars of myself and my working experience, and he promised that when he returned there he would make enquiries on my behalf. Well you know, if you meet such a person on holiday and have little prospect that you should ever meet again in the future, you do not put too many of your hopes to it: you think the most likely outcome is that you should not hear from that person again.

You can imagine my surprise about three weeks after our parting when I received a letter from him, in which he said if I came to Pripyet I would not find work at all difficult to obtain. He had put my description of my work experience to his superiors; they had said if my abilities were as I had said, a position would definitely be offered to me. It is not easy in our country to change from one place of working to another: there is a great deal of unnecessary filling-in of forms and usually there are many delays. But they had said they could deal with such matters without trouble. So this was another surprise for me, that when the managers of Chernobyl Power Station wanted somebody to work for them, they could facilitate that it should happen.

I had not spoken very much with my wife on my return from holiday: you will understand that we were not, how to say, on very good terms between each other for perhaps two years already then. I had told her of meeting the man, but not of what had been said between us about work. As I have said, I thought there was little likelihood anyway of me having further communication with him. And if it should happen, frankly I had it in my mind that I would separate from my wife and go to live and work at Chernobyl on my own. But when the occasion came that on receipt of the letter I mentioned it, then there was an even further surprise for me. Instead of greeting the suggestion I should go as a solution to bring the end of our marriage difficulties, my wife eagerly spoke of it as a new opportunity for us all as a family. When I said that my thoughts had been of going on my own, and sending back money for her and our children, she cried bitterly. She said the breakdown of the marriage had been her fault, and she begged me to let her try to restore the situation.

Eventually we agreed we should compromise. I would go to Chernobyl Power Station on my own, but when I had become accustomed to my work, I would then look for suitable accommodation for us as a family. We agreed anyway that a short period of separation would enable both of us to reconsider our feelings, and after it we would meet and talk to discuss if we both still wanted the marriage to continue. If that were the case, then she and the children would come to join me.

Everyone knows it I think, that you do not truly know what your feelings are until you have in some way tested them. So it was for me. I had not been at the power station for two weeks before I was conscious every day of how much I missed my family, and in particular my daughters. It had been our arrangement that I would speak on the telephone to my family two times each week: but by the end of one month's time I was speaking almost every day. My wife and I joked about it, saying it would cost less money if I were to send them all the railway fare instead of spending so much on telephone calls. So it was, inevitably, that I was soon asking the power-station management for an apartment for myself and my family. This was quickly found, and it would be I think less than six weeks before my wife and our children came. Within that time also, my employers had recognised that my abilities as a worker were as high as I had said, or even a little higher perhaps. They marked this by giving me quick promotion to the position of foreman, and put me in charge of a section of twenty men.

So we come to the night of the explosion, Friday the 25th of April, 1986. To be exact of course, in fact it occurred in the early hours of Saturday morning April 26th, at one-twenty-six. Everyone in Pripyet has those figures engraved in their brain, I am sure you will find. Our apartment was a distance away from the power station, some two kilometres or more, and we heard nothing. Saturday for me was a day off, and I stayed in bed until the middle of the morning. My wife went with the children, to see some friends who lived in the country to the north of the town. They had taken a picnic with them to have in the woods on the way.

At about eleven o'clock a friend came, who was one of my

colleagues I worked with at the power station. He said there had been a serious accident, and we were requested to go as quickly as possible. Yet another colleague then came too, and he said the situation was very serious: the town was full of soldiers and militia, and a public declaration had been made that no one was to leave the town. He had obtained passes for the three of us, he said, to go to the power station; his car was waiting outside and we should go at once. I was able quickly to make a telephone call to the home of the friends my wife was going to see: I asked that a message should be given to her to tell her I had been summoned to work. I said she should keep herself and the children away from the centre of the town, and go quickly to stay with her brother and his wife who lived in Kiev.

At the power station the situation was such that it can hardly be described. Everywhere there was smoke and steam surrounding the reactors, no one knew whether it was all of them which had somehow exploded, or if it was only one and if so which one. Soldiers were running everywhere, shovelling debris into lorries, and bulldozers were trying to drive a way through a great mound of what appeared to be burning earth, so that firefighters could get nearer to the buildings. I was immediately given a troop of fifty-four soldiers and told to organise them to use anything they could find to assist in clearing roadways for heavy digging equipment to move along. Nobody told me, and so I could not tell the soldiers myself because I did not know, that much of the soil and debris they were being required to handle, without protective clothing of any kind, was of a highly radioactive content. I gave them orders and despatched them to carry out tasks, which I now know had fatal consequences for some of them. While I was doing this I was repeating the assurances which had been given to me, which I believed because they had been given by the highest members of the management, that although the explosion had been serious no leakage of radiation had occurred. I have since had this falsehood justified to me by some of those concerned, on the grounds that if they had told the truth the consequences would have been worse, because all the troops and other workers would have fled.

When I entered the power station that morning, I knew that I would probably be working there on a long shift. I did not know

that in fact its length was to be fifty-four days. That is the period I
stayed at the power station, until eventually I was permitted to leave
and go home to join my wife and children in Kiev. It was officially
forbidden to make telephone calls to anyone from the power station;
but as is always the case in such situations, ways can be found of
doing things that the authorities are not aware of. Naturally you
will not expect me to give any details of this.

As it came towards the end of June, finally I was permitted to go
for three days to see my wife and family. They were concerned for
my health, but at the time I saw them it seemed to be normal and I
think they were reassured. I returned to work for a further period of
five weeks, then I was allowed to have a month's leave. So it went
on in this fashion until the end of the year. There could be no
question of us or anyone else returning to live in Pripyet because by
then it had been declared a danger zone, and so my wife prevailed
on me to seek work elsewhere. That is what I did, at an industrial
plant in the Kiev region. After a short time there symptoms of
illness began to appear: I went into hospital for a period of three
months, then tried to resume work but was again ill and readmitted
to hospital. Since that time I have been pronounced to be permanently unfit for work, and receive a small sickness pension from the
State. We live now on this and my wife's small earnings as a clerical
assistant in the office of a shoe-manufacturing factory.

I am bitter that there has so far been a refusal by the power-station
authorities, abetted by the hospital doctors who have examined and
diagnosed my condition, to admit that what I have contracted can
in any way be attributed, without argument, to the radiation effects
of the power-station explosion. They point to the fact that not
everyone who was there, even for the length of time that I was, is
ill in this way; and that also many other people who have never been
within five thousand kilometres of Chernobyl have this same
disease. I am bitter too, not just for myself, but for many hundreds
and perhaps thousands of others, at the covering-up that has
followed the accident. Lies have been told, and are still being told,
about its consequences; and always, of course, they are being played
down. Many members of the medical profession, I am ashamed to
say, collaborate with the State in this, because they would lose their

positions if they were to contradict the authorities' arguments about causes.

And finally, I am most bitter of all about this: that when I went into the power station that day, and gave orders to the young boys who were soldiers to perform this task and that, and assured them there was no danger to them, I was not given full information about the radioactivity. It would have prevented me from ordering them to do things which must unquestionably have resulted for many of them in ruined health or their deaths.

Sonya Kornichek,

stores manager*

A tall strongly built woman with short fair hair and hazel eyes, she wore a plain green woollen dress and talked in a soft and tired-sounding voice that was flat and expressionless. She kept a small lace-edged handkerchief in her hand which she put to her mouth occasionally with a slight cough.

– My husband is a construction designer, and for most of his working life he has been concerned with the building of power stations. Before we went to Chernobyl he had worked on hydro-electric and coal-fired installations, but never before with atomic power. The salary that was offered to him to come was higher than average, and we were told in addition there would be a good choice of living accommodation for us. It was some years since I had worked myself: it had been as a factory storage-manager, and it was hinted that work would probably be available for me also if I wanted to work again. We had a daughter of fourteen and a son of ten, and we talked it over as a family: both my daughter and I, although we did not know very much about such things as nuclear power, we were a little worried about it, and before we came to a final decision I went to talk with an acquaintance of ours who was an official at the Ministry of Energy to ask his advice. He completely reassured me: he told me that the reactors at Chernobyl were the most advanced of anywhere in the world, and had been built to the highest standards of safety that were attainable.

Chernobyl is the name of a region; in the area around where the power station is situated, a new town called Pripyet has been built. It is at the edge of a river, and it is very nicely laid out. The apartment we were given had four rooms, it was far bigger than anything we had ever had before in our lives; and my husband's salary was sufficient for us even to be able to buy a motor car. There was a good school for the children and they liked it very much. When we went it seemed to us all, I think, that we were living in paradise: the one and a half years we spent there before the accident were the happiest time of our life. What had been said to me about work also came true, and I was soon able to take a position in the projects department at the power station. Not long afterwards I was promoted to be in charge of the construction and storage yard of Reactor Number 4, the most recently built one that was there.

On the night of the explosion I was at home; we had all gone to bed, but I was the only one who was still not asleep when it occurred. I heard it, or rather the two bangs which there were close together. The sound was not in any way different from several there had been at times previously, nor was it very loud. It did not wake my husband or the children, and not long after it I myself was also asleep.

I did not sleep very well, as a matter of fact I rarely do. I awoke in the morning at about six o'clock or perhaps a little before. It appeared to be a sunny day and not cold, and I opened the door and went from the sitting-room out on to the balcony. It did not face in the direction of the power station so I did not see anything, but there was a strange sensation in the air. At first I could not tell what it was: the air felt somehow heavy and still, a feeling of unreality. Then I was aware of something else: there was not only the stillness but a complete silence, no sound of any kind anywhere. No birds were singing, not one; and this of course was most strange at that time in the morning.

It puzzled me but it did not greatly alarm me, and I decided to dress and go to do some shopping in the early-morning market which there was every Saturday in the town's central square. I went out without waking the others, and as I came near the centre of the town I saw there were gangs of soldiers everywhere: they had hosepipes and they were washing down the streets with chemicals. I asked one of them what was happening, and why this was being done. He said he had no idea, they were simply following orders they had been given; he thought perhaps an important person from the government was visiting the town that day, and the streets were being cleaned for him. I continued to walk along, but as I came to the market I saw the roads were being closed off with tapes and soldiers put to guard them, and the market stallholders were being told they could not display their goods and should go away.

People were standing together talking with each other, and from several of them I heard there were rumours there had been an accident at the power station. I thought I would try to go there and find out, but soldiers prevented me from going in that direction; so instead I went quickly home to wake my husband and tell him what was going on. It was still early in the morning, seven o'clock perhaps, and he was half-asleep. He said 'It will be nothing, people are always talking and worrying, put on the radio to see if anything serious has happened and let me go back to sleep.'

My son had to be at his school at eight o'clock, so I woke him and made him his breakfast. While I was doing that I had a telephone call from one of my colleagues who also worked at the power station: he said there were rumours of an accident, and he thought it would be unwise if I went out in the streets. I did not tell him I had already been out, but I decided not to send my son to school. Then I looked out of the window, and I saw some of his classmates walking there: they were going to school, so I thought it must be safe for him to do the same, and sent him after all.

He returned at midday. He said they had been told at school there had been an accident at the power station but it was not a serious one, and there was no danger to anyone from radiation. By this time the same information had been given out on the radio, and my husband had gone out, saying he would find out the true situation. He had not returned, and I was very uneasy. I telephoned my aunt who lived in Kiev with whom my daughter was already staying for a few days, and said could I come to see her immediately with my son. I did not give her any reason, but of course she told me to come at once, because I think by that time she too had heard something on the radio.

I went quickly with my son to the railway station. When we got there it was crowded with people, and there was an empty train standing at the platform clearly in sight, but no one was allowed to go to it. Then suddenly there was an announcement that it was departing for Kiev; the barriers were opened, and everyone rushed to it. I was fortunate to find a place for myself on one of the bench seats in a carriage, but because there were so many people my son had to sit on my knee. After a short time the train began to move, and as it drew away from the platform those of us inside could see many hundreds of people were being left on the platform because there was no room for them. They were shouting and shaking their fists. They could not have known, how could they, that they were fortunate not to have found a place on that train.

Because the train went only a few hundred metres, and then it stopped; then a few hundred metres more, and it stopped again; then a further few hundred metres and stopped; and it went on in this way for almost half of one hour. Then it stopped yet once more; and where it was then was exactly beside the power station: no more than five or six hundred metres away from us was the blazing Reactor Number 4. My son was of course tremendously excited, as other children were: he shouted 'Let me see it, let me see it' and tried to scramble to the carriage window to look. I would not allow him to; I was angry with him, almost I fought with him to prevent him, and I forced him to lie underneath the bench I was sitting on and to stay there, and I covered him with my coat. After five minutes the train moved on again, and after that it picked up speed and we were soon in Kiev.

I had seen enough and heard enough to know that I must return immediately to Pripyet, to find my husband and to give what assistance I could in the town or at the power station. Therefore I left my son with my aunt and returned to the station: the train we had come on was still standing there, and information was given that it was returning to Pripyet. Few passengers were on it: some of them were I think like me, returning to their homes; others perhaps with only a little knowledge of what had happened were going to see relatives they were worried about.

Again the train journey was made up of stops and starts and stops. My husband was at home when I got there and was anxious because he didn't know where I was, or our son. He told me that on the following day there was to be a large-scale evacuation of women and children, and I must go. I refused, I said much help would be needed to organise it, and I would remain to take part in it. He did not argue with me.

On the next morning which was Sunday, I went to the town square and helped to organise the grouping of children and their mothers. It was necessary to list their names and addresses, and allocate them to the lines of buses of all types and ages which had been commandeered by the authorities. They were to take them to towns and villages in surrounding areas, sometimes many hundreds of kilometres away. There were many painful scenes of tears and separation. And some pictures stay in your mind. The one most of all I shall never forget, is of a group of very young children, of about the age of four; they were playing together in the square while they waited for their bus to arrive. They were picking up small pieces of paper which someone had torn up and thrown to the ground, and tossing them up into the air. As they were doing this they were laughing and calling out to each other; and what they were shouting was 'Radiation! Radiation!'

I remained doing this work for several days, until the evacuation had become more or less complete. I was then able to persuade the management authorities at the power station that I could be of value in helping them locate necessary materials or discover losses of items which had to be urgently replaced. My husband also offered his services, and both of us were allowed to go into certain buildings to carry out necessary work. The frequency with which we could go in was severely limited: we had constantly to give blood samples and undergo extensive physical examinations to make sure we did not receive too-high radiation doses. Neither of us did, nor have we suffered any subsequent after-effects.

From time to time we visited Kiev to see our children, and it was on one such occasion about three months after the explosion, that our son was suddenly taken seriously ill and rushed to hospital. After examination it was discovered that he was seriously ill with blood disease of an incurable nature, and we have been told now that we must prepare ourselves for . . . I am sorry, I am not able to talk further about this. You will remember that I told you how when we were on the train, I tried to shelter him under the bench seat I was on. I do not understand, and it is not possible to explain in any way, how it could be that I who was sitting unprotected was unaffected, while he who I was trying to protect was not. I feel that life is not really worth living if it amounts only to a lottery of that kind.

Usually I do not shed any tears; I used to, but as a rule I do not do so any longer, because they are useless. Instead I have assisted in the setting-up of an organisation which is named 'The Association of the Children of Chernobyl'. I am the Chairman of it. We give help in every way that we can to mothers whose children are ill, or dying, as a result of what happened: we offer advice, and such comfort and support as they can obtain from being brought into contact with others who are in the same situation as they are. We try also to bring pressure on to the government to accept responsibility for what illnesses have occurred, and are still occurring, as a result of that disaster. Even now four years afterwards, many women who were within a wide radius of Chernobyl are giving birth to sick and deformed children: it is at a much higher rate than can be dismissed as normal. Women who have never been in, only near Chernobyl, are being found who give birth to dead babies or grotesquely abnormal foetuses. Sometimes even it is not them but their husbands who have been within the area of radiation fall-out. We have little money: nevertheless we are commissioning a survey of people who have shown signs of having been contaminated. We now think, from early indications, that there are in the region of one hundred thousand such people. We are trying to make it possible also for all children who were there at the time of the explosion, to be medically monitored for the rest of their lives. Everything that is possible must be learned about the results of such an accident.

To be the Chairman of The Association of the Children of Chernobyl, well I do not say to you or anyone else it is something I am proud to be. It is through the neglect, the incompetence and the insane foolishness of others only, that it should be necessary for it to come into existence. But how shall we prevent such a thing ever occurring again? In only one way, I think. If we are to claim to have responsibility towards future generations, we must cease at once to tamper with things we do not understand, and turn our backs completely on so dangerous an elemental force.

Anton Vassilievich,
radiation expert*

He was a tall distinguished-looking man in a dark suit, with a white shirt and a burgundy-coloured tie. He talked quietly, fluently and authoritatively.

– I am forty-eight years in age, I am married, and my wife and I have two children. One is a boy of twenty who is a history student at Moscow University, and our daughter of sixteen, she is at school in the eleventh grade. I think it is her intention to be a chemist, I hope so, I would like that.

At the time of the disaster at Chernobyl we were living in the Gorky region, which is about five hundred kilometres to the east of Moscow. I was head of the department in a large factory which manufactures what are called dosimeters. These are precise instruments which measure the amount of radiation present in a small or large given area, depending on their type. All workers in the atomic-power industry wear such a one here on the pocket of their overall; larger ones are placed at eye-level in rooms and along corridors throughout every atomic-power plant. I am a highly qualified specialist in this subject, if I may be permitted to say so.

For the people at Chernobyl when the disaster happened, there was insufficient knowledge to know how serious it was. There was one simple reason for this: the leakage of radiation was so great there were no instruments capable of measuring it. You will hear different stories: either that the authorities did not want to admit this because they thought it would cause panic, or they themselves were incapable of imagining such a thing. They refused to believe the evidence which was in front of their own eyes. It is generally taught, you see, both within the atomic-power industry itself, and also in the information about it given to the press and other media for dissemination, that some things are so unlikely ever to happen that mention of them can be ignored. The chances against them are so high – perhaps one in one million, one in five million or ten million or whatever number is calculated – that the risks are completely negligible. It is one of the greatest dangers of those concerned with our atomic industry, that the first people they have to persuade of this are themselves: when they have done this, they can then convincingly persuade others, with less knowledge, that some such thing is unthinkable. Then if it is unthinkable, they no longer think of it; nor what to do if it should occur.

What happened at Chernobyl was such an occurrence: the unthinkable occurred. Perhaps it is true that the suppression of information about it at the beginning did, as the authorities hoped, prevent widespread public panic. They themselves were in a panic, because they did not know what to think or how to act; but they could not admit this. But among those who knew more thoroughly about the subject, information was soon making itself known. Scientists talk: they talk among themselves and with other scientists, even when they are long distances apart, by means of a scientific invention called the telephone. So it was so that soon many scientists knew. I was one of those who quickly learned what had really happened: and what I learned was that because their metering equipment could not give them enough measurement, therefore they could not know dosages of radiation and estimate what steps should be taken to give protection to their personnel.

I went at once to my superiors, and asked could I have permission to go to Chernobyl, to offer my specialised knowledge, and it was immediately given. I then talked with my wife and children, and explained to them that although the situation was one in which danger was present, I had the necessary knowledge to assist, and felt it was my duty to go. They too immediately agreed. And so within less than two weeks necessary formalities were completed, and I arrived at the power station at Pripyet at the end of May, four weeks after the explosion had occurred.

When I arrived, I have to say that the situation was in fact worse then I had imagined it to be. The whole of the town of Pripyet had been evacuated: every single person had gone who had not been detained as a worker of essential necessity. Of those who remained, few had qualifications high enough to be able to perform the task I had already defined in my mind as the first essential. This was somehow to discover the amount of radiation present everywhere in the plant, even in the smallest and least accessible areas. By calculation it had to be decided where would be safe, and where would be unsafe, and for what period of time. Of course an aspect of radiation is that it is not visible: its presence can only be detected and measured in some instances by instruments of higher sophistication than those in this day we possess. So we constantly had to make calculations which in many cases could be not more than guesses, and hope that always we were over-cautious rather than over-optimistic.

Another fact we found, but we still do not know the reason for it, was that in some places as little as two metres apart, there would be in one a dangerously high level of radioactivity, and in another no radioactivity at all. This is what causes for example the situation where two people are in close proximity to each other, and one later is found to be irradiated and the other not. We simply do not understand properly yet the behaviour of radiation. In the plant we were able, but only very slowly and gradually, to identify the radiation present at all points. It led for example to situations where notices were posted along corridors which said HERE YOU MAY WALK, and then only a few metres on would be another saying HERE YOU MUST RUN.

I worked with a team of sixteen scientifically qualified men I had selected from those made available to me: some inevitably were those whose qualifications were not perhaps as high as could have been wished. But without exception all of them were volunteers, and had to work in circumstances where it was often not known if they were dangerous, or lethal, or perfectly safe. All of them were heroes, and the same also must be said of the ordinary soldiers who worked with us, often in the most dangerous place of all. This was on what was left of the roof covering of Reactor Number 4: that was the one which had exploded and burst into flames. There still remained an extensive flat surface, and on it was lying a huge amount of smouldering debris, which it was necessary to clear, to prevent further spreading of fire which would have caused more explosions.

We were not willing to send any man, no matter what type or amount of protective clothing he was wearing, up on to the roof until we had at least an approximate idea of how radioactive it was. Among the great amount of assistance which we had received from many countries in the world, there was from Germany a highly sophisticated machine to measure levels of radioactivity. It was a robot, it was operated by remote control. This machine was lifted by crane on to the roof, where we had constructed a thick concrete bunker for shelter, and it was sent forward from there. But after a short distance it stopped: it had become embedded in debris. When eventually we retrieved it by helicopter, we found its measuring instruments had not been able to withstand the radiation level, and it had failed. We therefore had to fall back again on our own calculations. These were initially that it was not safe for a person to spend a longer period on the roof than twenty seconds. In several weeks' time the permitted period was able to be extended to sixty seconds; and then later, at its maximum, it was extended to two minutes. The longest period I myself ever spent on the roof was sixty seconds, which I did on the afternoon of Saturday 27th September at 4.30 p.m.

It was always a matter of great priority that this roof debris should be cleared. This was eventually achieved by a large team of brave soldiers and as I have said, each of them was a volunteer. Every man in turn, wearing a lead jacket and a respirator, would run out on to the roof with his shovel, fill it with debris, and run to the edge and throw it over, down to the ground. From there it was then cleared by remote-control tractors. No soldier was allowed to do this more than once, and when he returned from the roof to the ground he was then immediately tested to find the amount of radiation he had received. If it was above a certain level, he was sent instantly to hospital. So you see these were all men of very great bravery.

I remained at Pripyet from May until December, a total of 199 days. During that period I went twice back to my home to see my family, on one occasion for four days and on another for five. We did not talk about the situation, and I am grateful to my wife for that. She knew that the work had to be done, and that few other people had the knowledge of the subject which I did. She knew also, if I may say so, that because I was a professional I would approach the danger in a sensible way, and teach others to do so similarly. She accepted that it was my duty to be there, and so it was as simple as that.

After the disaster, there are many things to be reflected upon. We still do not have the full answer to its cause or causes, or what happened and why it did so. I am sorry to say I cannot assert with confidence such a thing could never occur again, either in the Soviet Union or elsewhere in the world. Indeed I would assert the contrary, that with the proliferation in number of the building of atomic-power stations, the likelihood of such a thing can only be increasing. If such an accident should again take place, I am not confident either that the necessary lessons have been learned from Chernobyl as to what actions should be taken to limit the damage. Seventy-one people died there at the time of the accident: some were workers killed in the explosion itself, some were firemen trying to control the fire, and others were members of staff who were not injured in any way but were victims of heart attacks. But this number of seventy-one in no way relates to those who died later from radiation sickness, or from radiation-induced illness such as leukaemia and other forms of cancer. It is not a matter of hundreds or thousands, but of a far greater figure; and because of the long-lasting after-effects, as we speak this figure is still increasing day by day. A total of 432 towns in surrounding areas were contaminated, and more than one million people have been evacuated from them. Undoubtedly babies yet unborn will be malformed, or will die at an early age, as a result of Chernobyl; and I mean not in Russia only, but in many other places in the world.

16 Foreigners

Richard Preston, businessman

Tom Gilman, travel agency clerk

Rupert Jenkins, foreign correspondent

Jed Miller, style editor

Richard Preston,
businessman

His office was in a modern five-storey building in a side street, off one of the main thoroughfares of the city. The best time for talking, he said, was first thing in the morning: Moscow time being three hours ahead, phone calls from London Head Office never began until midday or afterwards. He was slim, clean-shaven and quiet-voiced. From time to time a smartly dressed young Russian secretary came in, put a message on his desk for him about something he should attend to later, gave a pleasant smile, and went out again without saying anything.

– I'm the representative in Moscow of a big English financial consortium, and I've lived here now for five years. I'm single, I'm thirty-nine, and I have a small modern apartment in a block on the southern outskirts of the city. It was constructed by a group of financial and engineering companies for their management-level employees: pretty well everyone who lives there is non-Russian. It's within a kind of compound with guards on the gates, but these days they're all fairly relaxed and friendly so there's nothing very onerous about that. People who've lived there longer than me say that ten years ago they were being checked in and out every time, but that's not the impression now. I know most of the gate guards by their Christian names, and they take every chance they get to stop you; but it's only for a chat so they can practise their English. When you drive in in the evening and park your car, they ask you how you are and what sort of a day you've had, and it's all very friendly and pleasant.

How I come to be here is somewhat complicated, but I'll try and give you a simplified version. The school I went to in the north of

England was a well-known progressive one: it was a boarding
school, and I was there because my father worked abroad for a big
electronics company. Because he was often moved from one country
to another, my parents wanted me to have stability of education and
kept me in England. At this school, when you were twelve you
chose whether you wanted to be in the arts or science stream. I
chose arts, and I had to pick one additional subject from Russian,
Greek or geography. I know this sounds utterly ridiculous, but it's
the truth: I chose Russian – and for why? Because a few weeks
earlier my parents had been in England during the school holidays,
and they'd taken me to see a James Bond film called *From Russia
With Love*. I don't know whether I had idea of being some kind of
superspy surrounded by glamorous foreign ladies all the time or
what, but that was absolutely my one and only reason for making
that choice.

And I found when I got into studying the language that it
fascinated me. First I took O-level Russian, and then A-level, then I
went on to university and did it there. I took my degree in it, and
then did my Ph.D. postgraduate thesis on eastern European nation-
alism in the nineteenth century. I could very well have continued
doing research in that field for ever I think; but by the time I'd
reached twenty-six I was beginning to feel I ought to get out of the
cloistered world of academe and move on into the real world as it
were. I didn't have a clue what I wanted to do, except that I
definitely knew I didn't want to teach. He didn't work for them
himself, but my father told me he knew this company had extensive
development plans and suggested I got in touch with them. Quite
frankly I didn't see myself in the business world at all; but when I
approached them, they said they were hoping to establish themselves
in the USSR. They said with my Russian, in a few years' time there
was a possibility I might become – they actually used the words –
'their man in Moscow'. Meantime they offered to take me on as a
trainee. So for several years while they were finalising their plans for
Russia, they sent me to New York, Cairo, Stockholm and a couple
of other places, to get background experience of the company and
knowledge of its company management methods. If you were
flexible, the opportunities with them were and still are almost
endless; but of course you always have to go wherever in the world

they send you. If they think somewhere's where you'll be of most value to them, that's where you go. There's a kind of unwritten understanding they make clear to you in the early part of your career: you can refuse one posting, but one only. If you refuse a second time, they won't fire you but you'll go down on their records as being difficult, and that will affect your future with them. In my case, I didn't wait for them to ask: I made it clear I'd go anywhere in the world to work for them except one place, and that was South Africa.

When this Moscow office was finally opened and they offered it to me to take charge of, I'd slightly mixed feelings at first. I'd only been to the USSR once in my life before, and that was to Leningrad with some of the other students who were at university with me, in the time of Brezhnev. It was in the summer, and we all went to a beach one day swimming and sunbathing. There was a marvellous-looking Russian girl there, dark-eyed and exceptionally beautiful like so many Russian women are, and we got chatting. Because I could speak the language much more fluently than the others I was with, I had a great advantage over them. This girl and I met again in the evening, we went down to the beach with a bottle of champagne and so on, and it was all very pleasant indeed. The next day, by arrangement I was down on the beach to meet her again. She was there, with a group of her friends; and she totally ignored me. When I tried to talk to her she told me very rudely to go away. And I found out that evening from someone else I knew, that she'd been seen by plain-clothes men when she was with me the previous evening. So they'd had strong words with her next morning, and told her not to mix with foreigners.

That was the memory in my mind when the job offer came up; and my bosses also said that working as I was for a big international company, I was never to get myself in a position in my private life where I could be compromised in any way. The basic rule I had to follow was to have as little contact with Russian people outside work as possible. So I did have reservations about coming.

This attitude I'm glad to say has now totally vanished in the last couple of years: it doesn't exist any longer on either side. Now friendships are encouraged, and it's quite amazing the extent to which things have opened up. Perhaps because these barriers existed beforehand, now they've gone it's made people more anxious than ever to cultivate friendships. I've now got a constantly increasing circle of friends who are Russian, male and female, young and old, and I can move among them and spend time with them in perfect ease. I haven't yet met a Russian woman I'd want to marry and settle down with, but come to that I haven't met an English or any other nationality of woman either who I'd want to do that with. I'm not saying it couldn't happen, but I think as far as a Russian is concerned, anyway I feel our two different cultures would be incompatible.

For a lot of reasons. I'm sure it's a virtue in their character and a drawback in ours, but one very noticeable thing is they have an intense natural spontaneity which we don't. You'll telephone a neighbour in the evening for instance if you're cooking and ask him if you can come round and borrow some ingredient or other you've run out of. His immediate response usually will be to say at once 'We're just putting our own meal on the table, come over and eat with us.' If you don't, he'll be really hurt about it, and worry if he's said or done something recently that's upset you. Or you'll be passing a cinema with someone and you'll stop to look at the poster and the stills outside, and she'll say 'Come on, let's go in and see it.' Born and brought up like we are in England, I find it terribly difficult to respond in a simple straightforwardly natural way and say 'OK, right, let's.'

There's another problem too in relationships with women, and that's a probably very stupid but always very persistent won't-go-away thought you have all the time in your mind. It's whether a Russian girl's keen on you, or whether basically what she's keen on is getting herself a Western husband. It sounds rather a nasty thing to say, but when you've actually known English or American men who've married Russian girls and then it's all come horribly unstuck, it really does make you a bit cautious. I've known several. A western European man's a catch for a Russian girl: it gives her his nationality which means she can go out of the USSR whenever she likes, she'll have a higher standard of living and so on, and in many ways he's rather exotic. Maybe it's something personal in me, but I have to be honest about it, the feeling is there. Are they attracted to me for myself, or is it what I represent? But as I've said, I'm not yet in the marrying mode at all for a woman of any nationality, so perhaps it's some kind of basic suspicion I have about all women.

Has living in Moscow changed me? Oh yes undoubtedly it's changed me, I feel it has in many ways. Doubtless someone who knew me well would be able to tell you which were for the better and which for the worst. Fundamentally I really am very very happy living here; but then again I should say I'm conscious I'm in a privileged position, I live at a higher standard than native Muscovites because I have access to hard-currency shops. If I couldn't now and again buy occasional luxury goods in them, even basic things like toothpaste and toilet paper, without having to queue for nearly every damn thing and then only getting it in the poorest quality – well then of course I'd have much greater problems of adjustment, ones I don't know that I could cope with and go on coping with.

Yet on the other hand, when I go home for a break as I do now and again, if I go into a supermarket and see the loaded shelves, I get a kind of a feeling of I don't know what best to call it. It's a kind of irritated dissatisfaction at the way we live and everything we take for granted. I stand looking at the shelves of washing powder for instance: six different kinds, and what's the difference between them? Who on earth needs to have a choice between six different kinds of washing powder for heaven's sake? Or the insincere way people in England talk to each other: they say 'Oh are you here for a few weeks' break? Well you must come round and have a meal with us.' They don't mean it at all, and you know they don't mean it, and they know you know they don't mean it; and we carry on these sorts of paralysingly meaningless social conversations nearly half of our lives.

I often wish that when I go back to England I could really convey to my family and friends exactly what sort of people the Russians are. The lack of knowledge of them there is something I find quite frightening. I never fail to be amazed by the hospitality and kindness and depth of warm feeling which people here show to me, a foreigner, with absolute naturalness and sincerity. They have an appreciation of the simple things of life too: they've a great affinity with nature, and they'll walk or sit for hours in the woods just listening to the birds and looking at the sky. They love the different seasons – the sun and heat in the summer, and the bitter cold in the winter: they really love both, and they tell you it's all part of the pattern of life, which it is. They discuss philosophy at the drop of a hat, and tell you their deepest feelings. People just don't talk like that in England at all: they chatter, and it's all the time a way of not saying anything and not revealing their feelings.

Another thing I often think is this. I know my company will move me on, and when they do I shall miss Moscow so much it'll be extremely painful to me to leave. Wherever I go, I'll adjust I'm sure; but always part of me, a very deep and fundamental part of me, is going to stay here.

Tom Gilman,
travel agency clerk

He was slight and thin, smoked heavily and spoke in an amused self-deprecatory voice, as though expecting some critical questions. He was twenty-five.

– I'm sure a lot of people must find it strange what I've done: my parents for instance, I don't think they've got over it at all yet. And I don't know they ever will. Very conventional people, they've always been that: solid respectable working-class, they like to know where they are, where they stand with you and you with them and all the rest of it. Until he took early redundancy last year Dad was Head Technician at a northern polytechnic; Mum had been a teacher at a school for handicapped children; and my sister followed an ordinary normal career of going to teacher-training college, working in an infant school, marrying at twenty-three and having two children. All the right things; I'm not putting her down for it.

But me, well from an early age I wasn't exactly trouble but I was worrying, let's put it like that. Truanting from school a bit too much for comfort, on the edge you might say between maladjustment and delinquency. At one stage they brought in an educational psychologist to have a talk with me. What was wrong, why didn't I like school, was I unhappy at home? That was another problem: I wasn't, unhappy at home I mean, and I didn't mind school all that much, it was just I didn't think it was very interesting. When I left at sixteen I'd got a few O levels, done well for a working-class lad: my parents were quite proud of it. I remember once my mother saying 'You're all right Tom, don't let anyone tell you you're not, you're going to end up even further up the ladder than your sister.'

I thought that was a bit hard, on my sister I mean: as far as I could
tell she'd made a success of her life. At least she appeared to be
getting what she wanted out of it, and always going in the right
direction to achieve it. I didn't know what I wanted and I didn't feel
I was going in any direction.

I did some further education and was lucky enough to get a
university place at a redbrick in the Midlands. I started a language
degree course there with the vague idea I might finally come round
to the idea of a career in teaching. I was doing German and modern
German history, and French as a secondary subject. But there was a
lot about it I didn't like: the tutors, the other students, there seemed
to be too many all doing the same thing. I don't know what put me
off most, all I knew was I was getting the same feeling I'd had at
school, that it just wasn't holding my interest. Then one day in the
canteen I got talking with a couple of blokes and a girl, and I found
they were doing Russian. Up till then I'd not even known it was a
language-option that was being offered there. I thought it sounded
good, and they took me along to meet the woman course tutor,
who was a Russian herself. I told her I'd like to switch if it could be
done. She said it could, and after sixteen weeks at university
studying German, then I was suddenly doing Russian.

Everybody said the same thing: my father, my mother, my sister,
all my friends who knew me back at home. 'Russian, good God,
why Russian?' It sounded really feeble when I gave them the true
answer: 'I haven't the faintest idea.' I hadn't then and I still haven't
now. All I can say is why I made the change I don't know, but
when I did I immediately found it so fascinating I was completely
hooked. That's how it stayed for over a year; and up till then, so far
so good even if a bit erratic. I won't be immodest and say I had a
natural gift; but at long last I'd found something I really enjoyed
doing.

The next thing that then happened was I found out that in the
summer, there was a two-month intensive course for foreigners here
in Moscow at one of the language institutes. I signed up for it. It
was good, all colloquial stuff: conversation, not grammar. There
were thirty students from all over the world and we lived in a hostel;
and ten Russians of varying ages and teaching levels who took us in
groups and spoke nothing but Russian to us all day long. One of

them was a girl of nineteen, a tiny little person only this high; I won't say she was the prettiest Russian girl I'd ever set eyes on, because she's the prettiest girl of any nationality anywhere, that I've ever seen. I just took one look at her when we met, and I was absolutely sunk. She had big slanting grey eyes, long fair hair, exquisite porcelain features – well I could go on and on, but I won't, I'll just say my stomach turned over and my knees went to jelly. Even more extraordinary though was that whenever I looked at her, incredibly it was perfectly plain I was having the same effect on her. It's often said about Russian women and it was certainly perfectly true in her case, that when they look at you they convey exactly what they're thinking and feeling. That was what Natasha did and so did I, and within a week we were both so smitten we couldn't bear to be out of each other's company for a minute.

I wrote to my parents and told them about her, and I said I wasn't coming back to England for a time, I was going to stay here and marry her and try to get some kind of a job, temporary or anything I could. Like everyone else they must have thought I'd gone completely Communist, or possibly totally insane, which in their book would be more or less the same thing. Solid Conservative my parents are, with no idea anyone could ever be anything else: on the one hand there's politics which roughs and rowdies and weirdoes go in for, and on the other there's your ordinary proper decent way of life which is the Queen, Conservatives, and our dear Prime Minister. Funnily enough, I do happen to be a Tory, even more right-wing than my father I should think, but that's neither here nor there.

Anyhow, hardly had they got over the shock which that letter must have given them, when before they had a chance to reply I wrote them another three days later telling them I was fixed up with a job. Sheer fluke of course, but sometimes things happen like that. I was still in a daze with Natasha, and one evening several of us were having coffee round a table at the institute. I found myself talking with a bloke I'd never met before in my life, who was Russian and he spoke pretty good English, but he was nothing to do with the course. He told me he worked in the Moscow office of an English travel agency who did chiefly business and trade activity rather than holidays, and they'd just lost one of their staff who'd gone to work for a bigger firm. He asked me did I know either an English-speaking Russian, or a Russian-speaking English person, who'd be interested; and there'd be this bloke's apartment going with the job because he was moving to Leningrad. I said yes indeed I did know such a person, he was sitting right there next to him. He asked me to go round to his office the following morning to meet his boss, and when I did they asked me just three questions. Could I speak fairly good Russian, would I be willing to sign a contract for six months with them, and when could I start?

And that was it. Natasha and I got married as soon as we could which was two months later, she moved into the apartment, and I'm still working at the agency after fifteen months because they offered me another contract, this time for a year, when the first one ran out. The apartment's a typically Russian one, very tiny with just two rooms, in what you'd call a typically old tower block; but it's on the ground floor, it's about ten minutes' walk from the Metro station to get to work, and everything's great. I don't suppose there's another English or non-Russian person living within a mile of me: our friends all tend to be Natasha's friends meaning they're Russian, and by now I feel I'm completely assimilated into Russian life. My job doesn't pay fabulously well but I don't mind that too much, living's very cheap here with subsidised rents and staple foods and all the rest of it, so I'd say our standard of living's about the same or slightly higher than the average Russian's.

I'm more contented than I've ever been; in fact I'm more than contented, I'm perfectly happy. There's something about the Russian way of life, at least in Moscow but I don't know about anywhere else, that makes me feel at home in it. That might seem like a curious thing for an Englishman to say, and it's got nothing to do with it being a socialist system or anything like that. I'm still as much of a Conservative as I ever was, and I can see all the Russian system's faults and failings, or a lot of them I can. A Russian friend told me a joke the other night which I think hits the nail on the head absolutely. It's a riddle: 'Question: What's the difference between capitalism and socialism? Answer: Capitalism is the exploitation of man by man, and socialism is the opposite.'

Extraordinarily, I find Soviet life quite exhilarating. Like everyone else I also find it exasperating; and every morning when you wake up, you never know which it's going to be. But once you get into the swing of things, I don't know how to express it but once you accept the normality of things as they are here, it can be quite soothing. One example is queuing: it's so much a part of Russian life that you forget there's any other way. I don't mean just in the shops either, but everywhere. In the street, someone'll come along and unfold a small card table or something like it, put a suitcase on it and open the lid – and immediately a queue forms. When you see it, if you're not in a desperate hurry about something you go and join it. You say to the man in front of you 'What are we queuing for?' and he tells you potatoes or photograph-frames or light bulbs or whatever, and if you want some you stay and if you don't, you don't.

One of the things I think I enjoy the most is the book-exchange system. In a lot of bookshops they'll have a section of second-hand books which are not for sale, they're for exchange only for some specific other book. You see a copy of Sherlock Holmes stories, say, and the index card in the front says it's only in exchange for a certain anthology of Bulgarian detective stories. You remember you saw a copy of that book only a few days ago in a bookshop over the other side of the city, so off you go to get it. You buy it, you go back the next day to where the Sherlock Holmes book was – and of course by then it's gone. So you think to yourself, oh well better luck next time; but it made Saturday and Sunday two quite enjoyable days. Meantime, you're stuck with the Bulgarian book of course: but it turns out to be more interesting than it looked, and you'd never have read it otherwise.

Naturally Natasha's the key to it all for me. I wonder if I'd still be here if our meeting hadn't happened, and I doubt it. Her family have totally accepted me, they're very warm and outgoing, and they treat me like their own son. Will my family be the same towards Natasha when I take her to England for the first time is obviously the corollary to that? Well, I'm not all that hundred-per-cent sure. I hope so, but the English are so buttoned-up about showing how they really feel that obviously I worry about whether she'll think English people are cold and stand-offish. She knows there's a higher standard of living and most things are better quality than they are here. Sometimes she asks me will they think she's a peasant who's just married me for what she can get out of it. I've not hurried about taking her there because thoughts like that are worrying; nothing'll alter my love for her or hers for me, but there is a gulf and it's a wide deep one. I think I've made the crossing successfully; I just hope when the time comes that she will too.

Rupert Jenkins,
foreign correspondent

A friendly man of thirty-eight with fair curly hair, he sat on the leather-upholstered sofa of his comfortably furnished and spacious sitting room with his feet up, his hands clasped behind his head. A stereo cassette system, many of the latest English books on the shelves, children's crayon drawings, family photographs and a general air of comfort and well being.

– Help yourself to more coffee when you want it. It's a change for me being interviewed, usually it's the other way round. It'll be a salutary experience for me.

I've been working in Moscow for two years on what will probably be a three-year assignment. I live in this extremely nice modern apartment that's owned by my paper, with my wife and four children who are twelve, ten, two and a half and finally a baby of three months. All the furniture and everything else is ours, we brought it all with us when we came, and my wife's made a deliberate attempt to keep the place looking and feeling as English as possible. This is partly for the kids' benefit so it won't feel more than it has to that they're in a foreign country, and to give them some sort of continuity. It's hard for them: before I was sent here we were three years in Paris, and probably in another year or at most two, I'll find myself in Toronto or Delhi or Melbourne or wherever the powers that be think suitable.

Being sent here as an assignment I didn't expect, I must admit. I was a bit uncertain whether I'd like it or not, and I didn't speak much Russian. But as things've turned out the necessary adjustments haven't proved too difficult, at least not as far as I'm concerned. Working in one newspaper office is much like working in any other:

your job is to try and learn and send back as much information as you can, and making contacts and the news-gathering process are pretty much the same. I found, as most people who come to live in Moscow do, that the Russians are such a warm and friendly people that you never feel unwelcome wherever you go. Of course if you send back an endless series of critical and hostile accounts of everything, you won't be all that popular after a while; but I don't do that, or at least I hope I don't. I can be critical of things and I am sometimes, very, but I think what I write's regarded by the Russians as accurate and balanced, and I work for a quality newspaper, so I don't experience many great problems.

Adjustments have been much more difficult for the family. Our second child, John, is ten: when he first heard he was coming here he was very excited about it. He's mad keen on sport of all kinds – swimming, skiing, canoeing, everything – and of course he'd picked up from television how the Russians were the same, and seen pictures of all the wonderful facilities they have for absolutely everything. So he was bitterly disappointed to find when he got here that all these marvellous facilities were as a rule not available to the public as such: you had to be a member of a youth club or a sports organisation, or attend certain schools and things like that. As a result he's spent most of his time at a loose end on his own, with nothing to do in his spare time. We're thinking we might send him to boarding school back in England: he's keen on the idea himself, so I think that's what'll happen.

The eldest, Emma, things have turned out better for. She's at an Anglo-American school here and likes it, but she's very keen on learning to speak Russian and we're encouraging her to. She takes private lessons every Saturday morning and she's really working at it. Obviously we'd think very hard before we did anything drastic like moving her into a Russian school, because the prospect of staying for any length of time is limited, but we're always reviewing the situation.

The one who's had the hardest time of all without any doubt though is my wife Jennifer. Paris before here, London before that, and then suddenly she finds herself living in a place where the kind of affluence and consumerism we've always taken for granted just doesn't exist. You find if you're unexpectedly out of something, even basic things like soap or sugar or rice, you can't simply pop out to the shop round the corner and get it. Every time you go home to England on a visit, you draw up a list of things you mustn't forget to bring back: instant coffee, mosquito-bite cream, teabags of course and anything else you particularly miss. And it's easy to overdo it and get into a kind of siege mentality, and load yourself up with provisions to such an extent you've hardly any room in your cases left for clothing. Inevitably when you're home you see something like French mustard, so you bring that back because it's a thing you'd never even see here.

Like most other foreigners we make occasional excursions to the hard-currency shops where you can buy some things, a few, that Russians can't. Everything's very pricey there, and stocks are restricted because they don't deal in cheaper basics: obviously they'd sooner you spent your money on expensive French perfume rather than two tins of baked beans. But my wife hates going to them: she says every time she does, she comes out with plastic carrier bags full of tinned foods and things which the majority of people can't get, and feels she's getting black looks in the street. She probably is too. Non-Russians often find it puzzling that Russians accept this situation, where right in the middle of their own capital foreigners can buy luxuries which they never see. It's true there is this curious sort of passive acceptance in Russian people, as though they've been brought up to accept injustice as normal. I think in England, or most other European countries for that matter, people wouldn't put up with it: they'd parade up and down with protest placards, or even go as far as throw a few bricks through the window.

Another thing my wife finds irksome, and so do I, is what you might call the lack of places for any sort of casual social coming-together. There are no cafés where you can meet someone for a morning coffee, no little luncheon snack-bars or informal wine bars, there's nothing at all of that sort anywhere. In most other cities in the world where I've been, you can knock off at lunchtime just for a quarter of an hour if you're busy, and go and have a pint and a sandwich. But not here. Or if you're very very busy, you can send out for coffee and sandwiches: again though, not here. I now don't ever eat anything at all in the office at midday, because I've completely got out of the habit of it. So coming here after living in

Paris has been a sort of gastronomic inversion, and I don't think it's something we'll ever get totally used to. It might sound from the way I'm talking that I'm devoting too much time talking about the subject of food. But food has all sorts of social connotations in the western European way of life, and we miss a lot of them here. We tend to eat at home too much, Jennifer cooks English food in the English way for the family, and I think in some ways it isolates us.

It has its effect on women's way of life in general here too. The whole weight of housekeeping and queuing and cooking falls on their shoulders, to such an extent they hardly ever lead any kind of independent life of their own. They can't develop much interest in anything outside the home, politics included. It's a waste of talent for the whole of Russian society, and I think it's both sad and bad that on the Central Committee of the Politburo, for example, there are more soldiers than women.

It's the result of the Communist system, which over the years has eroded and then finally destroyed two things, one which it intended to and the other which it didn't. What it intended to destroy was a society in which the most important thing was money: the more you had the better and more important you were, and the more you could get. I don't subscribe to it myself, but there's a lot can be argued in favour of that idea. But while they were altering that, at the same time and probably without being conscious of what was happening as a result, they destroyed the value of work and the belief in the work ethic. No one would want to wish an English Anglo-Saxon Protestant work ethic on to the Soviet people, but nevertheless I think things have now gone far too far the other way. No one takes any pride in work any more. This I think is very sad, that people's main concern now seems to be how they can defeat the system, or at least how they can circumvent it: in a word, in a lot of ways, how they can cheat it. Lenin's intention of trying to build a utopian society was a great ideal; he really did try to put it into practice, and for a long time a lot of people all over the world believed he was succeeding. There's a quotation that's often attributed to Sidney Webb after he'd paid a visit to the USSR in the 1930s – but in fact I believe it'd already been said earlier, by an American named Lincoln Steffens: 'I've seen the future, and it works.' Well the fact is, he didn't see what he thought he was seeing, he only saw what he wanted to see or was shown; and it doesn't work at all, it's been economically a disaster, it's led to cruelty and oppression and the deaths of millions, and the disappointment of the hopes of idealists everywhere.

What's going to happen here in the future, and on what sort of time-scale I've really no idea. Changes are occurring so fast you simply can't keep pace with them. In one of the papers here last week there was a cartoon which I thought summed it up: a picture of God leaning forward to adjust the television he was watching and saying 'Whoops, I must have got it on fast forward.' The existence of a newspaper like *Moscow News* for example, I'd never have believed when I first came that it could happen. Every week hundreds of people stand on the pavement on publication day outside its offices, waiting to grab copies as soon as they're brought out.

It's unlike any other newspaper they've ever had before. Or us, we've nothing like it. Radical isn't in it: it exposes corruptions, lambasts bureaucracy, and criticises the government so fiercely it's beyond belief. It roots out stories the authorities would prefer people didn't know about, and in fact behaving as it does and printing what it does, it'd be constantly in danger of prosecution and suppression in England. I never miss reading it every week, even if I have to miss something else.

I think when the time does come for me to be moved on, I'll look back on being here with a certain amount of nostalgia. Like everyone else who comes into contact with them, I find the Russian people intensely warm and friendly, and I've made several real friends among them whom I'd never want to lose touch with. Those feelings won't change, and nor will my respect for the people and their country. From a professional point of view it's been fascinating to be here, particularly at a time like the present. Sometimes I've thought when the time comes, I'd be tempted to ask if I could stay for longer than the usual three years. But I have to consider the family and how things are for them. They all know, as I do, there's not much point really in putting down roots, because our future is in the hands of the people I work for. Therefore wherever we are, even if it's four years instead of three, it's still only temporary. I think I've got a great deal out of being here in terms of experience; and hope the family've found some of it rewarding too.

Jed Miller,
style editor

Strongly built and well over six feet tall, with a thick black beard and long dark hair, among Russians he'd easily have passed as one of them if he'd wished to. He spoke quietly and thoughtfully, sitting cross-legged and without shoes on the floor, leaning back against the settee.

– If you don't mind it, I'm most relaxed and can talk easiest when I sit this way. So let's see now, where'll I start, does it matter? No OK. I'm twenty-seven, I'm a New Englander, and I'm a graduate of the University of Vermont at Burlington. I have two brothers and a sister, and in my family I'm the caboose: that's the little car at the end of the train that follows the others along the lines. Only in my case I kind of did and I didn't: my sister's just gotten home from China and one of my brothers is in Thailand, so like them I like to get around, but so far none of them apart from me's been in the USSR.

I came here just about two years ago now. I'd studied the Russian language several years in the States, and as any student'll tell you, your ultimate goal is to go to the country whose language and history you're studying. I'd no particular idea which part of the Soviet Union I wanted to visit, I just kind of thought it'd be nice to come and see how things were here, so I came to summer school in Leningrad. That was nice, I liked it: they say Leningrad's one of the seven most beautiful cities in the world. I don't know what the other six are, but if they're anywhere up to Leningrad, they sure must be lovely places to be.

The only thing that struck me about Leningrad though, and I guess some people'd say this was a crazy thing to say, is that somehow I didn't feel it was quite Russian enough. Peter the Great founded it I believe with the intention of making it a window on Europe, or maybe a doorway to it, I'm not sure. Only whichever, light goes two ways through windows and people go both in and out of doors, so Leningrad is very Westernised now. I felt somehow I wanted to get nearer to what they call 'people with a Russian soul'. We had just exactly four days to spare at the end of the summer school semester, so along with a young Russian guy I'd met there who lived here, I came to Moscow.

It was while we were actually travelling overnight on the train that I suddenly had this strange idea come into my head there was a job here waiting for me if I could find it. Crazy notion, and where it came from I've no idea: it was like something that was preordinated if that's the word. But when I got here, that's just exactly how it was, and one day was all it took. I was strolling around and over the other side of the street I saw one of the offices of the big Russian press agencies. So I just kind of wandered in and said I was from the US, I was a student and did they happen to have any vacancies? A few calls from the switchboard around one or two of the offices, and then a guy comes down, shakes me by the hand, invites me up to his office, sits me down and says 'How'd you like to be a style editor?' 'Sure' I said, 'great, nothing I'd like more.' 'We've just had one walk out on us half an hour ago' he said, 'so could you start tomorrow?' 'Yes I could,' I said, 'only I don't have anywhere to live.' 'No problem,' he says, 'you can have this guy's apartment, we own it, it goes with the job.' 'What about salary?' I said. 'Don't worry' he said. 'OK that's fixed then, any more questions?' 'Well yes, just one' I said. 'What's a style editor?'

What it is is this. Normally translators work on the basis of translating out of a foreign language into their own. But in Russia there are so few English people working as translators that they have to use Russians to translate into English. This is fine, but if it's a news bulletin or a report of a speech that's going to be put out world-wide, however good a translator he is a Russian won't have a big command of colloquialisms and stuff like that, so more often than not it's going to sound rather stilted. The style editor's job is to read the translation through and put it into readable English, iron out expressions that somehow aren't right, and things like that. I really enjoy it, I work with a nice bunch of people, and we all get along together just great. They pull my leg about me writing Communist propaganda, I use a red pen for corrections and tell them it's because only red writing can be relied on, and it's a real nice atmosphere. And after a year they extended my contract for another two years, so I guess they must be fairly well satisfied with me so far. One thing's for sure and that's that I'm very satisfied with being here. My Russian of course has improved to a point it'd never have gotten to if I didn't live here too, so everything's great. I'm still as fascinated by the country and its people and their way of life as I ever was, and I'm happy to stay until the time comes, if it ever does come, when I feel I want to live someplace else. They tell me at the press agency where I work that every style editor they've ever had, American or English, has ended up marrying a Russian girl. Whether I will or not I don't know, but I've come nowhere near it yet. They're very beautiful of course, I think young Russian women must be among the most beautiful in the world; but I haven't yet fallen that hard for one.

It's hard to describe what it is about Moscow and its people that gets to me in the way it does. Around three months or so ago I went back home to the US for a visit for the first time since I've been here, to go to a family wedding. I think most of my folks thought when I did, I'd realise how much I missed Vermont and want to stay there. I wasn't so sure to be honest I wouldn't feel that way about it myself. But I didn't: not at all I didn't. What I did realise was how much different it was really living here, to what you read in the newspapers about living here, in the US. There, everyone tends to think of this as a highly political country, with everything monopolised by the Party and everyone forced to be a member of it. Well in fact Communist Party membership here is less than ten per cent of the whole population – about the same level as the Catholic Church in England. I'm not a Communist myself or anything like one, in fact I'd say I was as near not interested in politics as anyone could be. And very few of my friends here are members of the Party either: most of them are just ordinary folk getting on with their lives, being born and marrying and dying like other ordinary folk anywhere.

You'll go days and weeks without hearing a mention of the

Communist Party, except if you happen to be reading a newspaper. But right now what you won't go days or even more than a few hours without hearing about in Moscow is McDonald's. Just the other day I said to a guy at work 'Tell me something that's puzzling me: how come with all these changes that are taking place in politics and demands for democracy and everything – how come the only thing people get really excited about and talk about all the time is the opening of McDonald's?' He just looked at me, and he said 'It's because they're hungry.' Just for a minute, I guess, I thought he meant only for food, but then I realised no, he meant quite a lot more than that. And I think the guy was right.

That kind of a remark, too, it has quite a lot in it of the kind of thing about Russians which is so appealing to me. It's that word I used before, their soul. This goes right back in fact to when I was a little kid. I don't know how it came about, but when I was five or six I guess or around there, in the town where we lived there was a little old lady who used to come in and babysit me. She was a friend of the family from way back somehow, I never really knew how. She was a Russian and she was an *émigrée*, I think her parents had fled the Revolution or something of that kind. But that old lady, she always had a kind of quality about her, a sort of what you might call dignity: she seemed so wise and kind, she was like a spirit of all humanity to me, even then when I was that age. Time went on, I grew up, I don't know what happened to her but I guess she died though I don't recall being told about it. And then when I was fourteen maybe fifteen, one day at high school one of our teachers told us she was going to play some symphonic music to us on the record player by Tchaikovsky, and told us a bit about him, and how much she loved his music because he expressed everything that was essentially Russian. And it was weird: as soon as I heard it, a picture of that old lady came right back into my mind, and it felt like what I was hearing in that music was all the expression of her soul.

What's extraordinary to me here is just that what I call 'soulfulness' for want of a better word. It's right here in people all around you. It's very close to the surface, it's part of everyday life; and they talk about it and express it in a way you never hear in the West. You hear an American say 'Well that's life': it sounds, and I think it is, a kind of flippancy about something, a way of passing things off behind a slightly cynical front. But hear a Russian say 'That is life,' and it comes from down deep inside around here, and it's a philosophic observation. Yes it's life: and people savour it, the humour of it and the sadness of it, in a way that's totally different to ours. In America, if you like, the ideal is to work as hard as you can, and whoever ends up with the most toys, well he's the one who's won. People don't do that here: they pass up all that I'm-better-than-you stuff in favour of a good discussion about philosophy or a painting or a book or a piece of music. It doesn't matter who it is: they might be a cab driver or an Academician or a lathe operator in a machine-tool factory, but on subjects like that one person's opinion's as good as another's. They don't have this terrible posing about being an intellectual or a thinker or whatever. Everyone's just a human being. And I kind of like that.

Sometimes I have a hunch, I guess I haven't properly thought enough about it yet, but I have this kind of an idea that because of all their laws and restrictions and bureaucratism, to survive it they step up on to a kind of higher level when they want to be free in their minds. All that stuff about regulations and restrictions isn't important, it doesn't matter, it's not worth bothering about very seriously, you can get away from it or above it. They have this nice expression 'kitchen friends': these are the people who really matter, the friends you share all your thoughts with when you talk with them in your home in the kitchen.

I guess it sounds crazy to say this, but I feel when we talk about 'the free peoples of the world', meaning us, we shut our eyes to all the restrictions we've built for ourselves like having to succeed, having to reach targets, having to be measured by entirely material things. When I was home for the wedding, a not-very-close relative said to me 'How can you live in the Soviet Union among all those Commies?' Just for a minute I couldn't take it in, and finally I said 'I don't think I know any Commies, not in the sense you're meaning.' And he just kind of looked at me and made a little sort of disapproving cluck noise, and walked away.

Ask me some more?

17 Tea with the KGB

Igor, Boris and Vladimir

Tea with the KGB

Igor, Boris and Vladimir*

Whether they were made formally or informally, by letter or by telephone, through official channels or personal contacts, for more than seven months all requests for an interview were either ignored, or it was suggested they should be made again at some unspecified later date. Eventually an invitation came to submit questions in advance, in writing. This was declined. Then, a week before the end of my last visit to Moscow, I sent with a brief covering letter a typed draft of what I said I proposed to have as the last chapter of my book. It was entitled 'An Interview with the KGB', and consisted of three blank pages.

The next day there was a telephone call to say all arrangements had been made for a meeting, it could last as long as I wished, and would ten o'clock the following Tuesday morning (the day before my departure) be suitable? Yes? Good, well in that case I should be outside Entrance Number Four at the rear of the Lubianka building, with an interpreter, at that time. Oh yes and to make identification simpler, one of us should be carrying a folded copy of *Pravda* under his left arm.

We were met on the steps of Entrance Number Four by a tall good-looking man in his forties who was waiting for us. He was wearing a smart lightweight single-breasted beige overcoat, and a tweed sports cap set at a jaunty angle on his head. He smiled at the interpreter, shook his hand and murmured a few words to him, then gestured politely to us to follow him in through the swing doors. At the barrier immediately inside them two soldiers stood stiffly at attention, but made no move to check papers or in any way hinder our entrance.

Exchanging affable remarks in Russian about the good weather

with the interpreter, the man in the cap and overcoat led us up a
wide marble staircase and along a succession of plain wood-panelled
corridors. He stopped suddenly at a heavy oak door that appeared
in every way indistinguishable from at least a dozen others we'd
passed, opened it, and ushered us into a small outer office with a
counter. Behind it sat an elderly woman, at a desk with a typewriter
and a small telephone switchboard: she wore her grey hair in a bun
on top of her head, and a black woollen dress and horn-rimmed
glasses. When we appeared she nodded, got up and went out
through a side door, and then came back almost immediately and
nodded again curtly at the man with the cap and overcoat. He took
them off and hung them up in a cupboard, then took us round the
counter and through the open side door.

The room inside it was not very large: it had some glass-fronted
bookcases and its walls were distempered pink. Two long desks
were arranged at right-angles to each other in the form of a T, and
sitting in the middle of the one at the top was a smiling thin-faced
man with pale blue eyes and thinning hair. Also in his forties, he
wore a black suit, a striped shirt and a green silk tie. He stood,
shook hands, and said via the interpreter he was pleased to greet me
and glad that I'd been able to come. He indicated two chairs next to
each other, down one side of the leg of the T, where we should sit.
Opposite us on the other side was an older square-faced man with a
florid complexion and thick wiry hair cut close to his head. He had
a deep rumbling voice, a big smile and a frequent jovial laugh. He
was introduced as Boris, and the fair-haired man who'd brought us
in as Vladimir.

Igor did almost all of the talking, the interpreter translating my
questions to him into Russian, and his replies back into English to
me; now and again Boris interjected an amiable remark in Russian,
which was also translated. Soon the elderly secretary brought in a
large tray with glasses of tea in silver holders, and several plates of
biscuits. There was some inconsequential chat and exchanging of
cigarettes, and then the tape recorder was switched on. The atmosphere was easygoing and relaxed.

Throughout, Vladimir remained slightly apart. He sat with his
arms folded and an unchanging and slightly quizzical smile on his
face, and looked in turn at each of us as I or the interpreter spoke.

He remained totally silent throughout; until near the end of the interview.

My opening request was to ask them if they'd each please give me their names and positions in their organisation, so I could identify their voices on the tape. Igor beamed.

Igor: Mr Parker, this is we hope a completely informal and friendly occasion. So therefore we shall not be offended in any way whatsoever if you call us simply Igor, Boris, and Vladimir. As to our positions, it is best to refer to us just as employees of the KGB; though if you think it important enough to say so, I may be described as an Information Officer.

TP: Yes. Well thank you. Could I start then please by asking you just exactly what the KGB is?

Igor: Certainly. It is our State Security Committee, and the initials by which it is known are those of the Russian words which make up that title. It was as you may know first established by Lenin, when it was known as CHEKA; in later years it became GPU, after that OGPU, then NKVD, then MGB, and finally KGB.

TP: How long have you been working for it?

Igor: Myself? Twenty years. But in my present capacity now, two years only.

TP: And Boris?

Igor: Boris, how long have you been working for the KGB?

Boris: (With a laugh.) Oh a very long time indeed.

TP: Vladimir?

Vladimir: (A shrug and a slight headshake at failure of recollection.)

TP: Is it good work, do you enjoy it?

Igor: Oh yes it is very good work, I enjoy it very much. For many many years I was just an ordinary operative of a low grade, and then for a long time again after that I worked in the Department of Personnel. But you know, always I had a longing to do other and more interesting work, which would bring me more into contact with the general public. So as you can imagine, I was very pleased when I was offered this present post, and agreed immediately to take it. But I will say to you frankly that at that time I had no idea, no idea at all, how difficult it was going to be.

TP: Difficult how, in what way?

Igor: Well you see, my transfer to this position coincided with a great enlargement of the boundaries of restriction that there had been to talking about the work of the State Security Committee.

Boris: In principle.

Igor: Exactly: in principle. It could not be said that there was no openness at all about our work beforehand; but compared with what has now happened in the last two years – well, it cannot be compared at all. The extent of our present openness about our work, it is almost unbelievable. Everything we do now is no longer prohibited to be talked about under the rules of censorship. There is hardly now any censorship at all as to what information we may give about our work. If information is asked for, we provide it: it is as simple as that. But as you can imagine, this means a huge amount more work.

TP: What you're saying is that there was considerable censorship before?

Igor: Oh no not at all, please do not misunderstand me. What I am saying is this: if someone for example wished to write about us and refer to what we did, he was not encouraged or in any way helped to do so. But now if someone applies to us saying he wishes to do this, we render him assistance in every way he requires. If he requests that we check facts for him or give him information, we do so as quickly as we can; but we do not in any way interfere with what he writes, he is free to write whatever he likes without asking our permission. But well as you can imagine, so many people are now making application to us that the amount we have to do has grown immensely. Incidentally I would like to say to you at this point that this is the reason why our interview with you has taken such a long time to be arranged.

Boris: And we wish to apologise if this has in any way caused you inconvenience.

Igor: Oh yes indeed: exactly. And also I may mention that as well as freely providing information to people who wish to write about us, we are now in addition writing and publishing material on our own behalf, even before it has been requested. To give you an example, there is a popular mass-circulation magazine called *Arguments and Facts* which is published here every week. In it we have a regular column which is entitled 'The KGB Comments and Explains'. We provide a continuous stream of information in it about ourselves and our work, without restriction of any kind; except of course where matters of State security are concerned. So in this respect, I think it is possible to claim that we are now as open and unsecretive about what our State Security Service does as any other nation in the world.

TP: Is this your only concern, State security?

Igor: Yes, and all matters connected to it. The Chairman of our Controlling Committee is a member of the Supreme Soviet, and he said in a recent speech to them that our concerns were intelligence and counter-intelligence, protecting our constitutional system, and being responsible for the safety of government leaders. He made this speech, I may say, because supervision of the KGB is now the responsibility of the Supreme Soviet.

TP: It wasn't supervised by the Supreme Soviet before?

Igor: No, it was an independent organisation which was not answerable to any particular section of the government.

TP: Did it sometimes act in an unsupervised way on secret orders?

Igor: Well I am sure you will understand that by the nature of its work, any State security organisation has sometimes to engage in activities which are not spoken about. But we cannot reproach ourselves that we ever carried out operations without permission or that were illegal. Let me speak for example about KGB activities in the decade of the 1970s, against those who were known as 'the dissidents'. I will say with complete assurance that nothing was done which ever in any way breached the laws that then existed. The question may be asked whether the laws were good or bad; but whichever they are considered to be now, we always operated within them.

TP: People were very afraid of the KGB, and not only here in the USSR. And many still are. In my own country, Britain, for example – probably the four names to do with Russia which we know best are Intourist, the Bolshoi Ballet, GUM Department Store and the KGB. People usually think of the first three with pleasure; and of the last, the KGB, with fear. Are you happy about that?

Igor: No we are not. And if I may say so, we feel it is unjustified. In fact you may be interested in a specific proposal between our countries which I will tell you of. It is this: a system is now being instituted under which some of our people will go regularly to London, to have talks with members of your own intelligence services, about matters of mutual concern such as terrorism and world-wide drug-dealing, and how we may co-operate in combating them. This is being done with other countries also, including the USA. Naturally as you would expect, great publicity is not being given to this; but I believe also that such things as public lectures are under consideration. And I should again mention what was said earlier, about how much more openness is now being extended to the media of other countries.

Boris: In for example television.

Igor: Yes, in for example television. Recently we gave permission for a Japanese television unit to film and interview here in the Lubianka, for a documentary they are making which I believe will be called *One Day in the Life of the KGB.* Facilities of a similar nature have also been provided for a television company from your country. So you see great changes really are occurring, and we hope they will continue to do so and to extend.

TP: May I just revert for a moment to something I mentioned earlier? Many visitors to the Soviet Union are convinced that when they come here they're constantly under surveillance – their movements are watched, their hotel bedrooms have hidden microphones in them, their telephone conversations are listened to and so on. Are they?

Igor: You must forgive us if we smile. We know there are such beliefs among some people; but my dear Mr Parker they are entirely mistaken. Things like that truly do not occur.

TP: Did they ever?

Igor: Well, I am sure you will appreciate it when I say that any state security organisation, in any country anywhere, has far more important matters to concern itself with than trying to keep millions of tourists under surveillance. If some one particular individual was of interest for a very good reason, such as something shall we say to do with spying – yes, he might be watched, as he would be in any country he went to. But for the general mass of visitors – well, how could it be organised when there are so many of them that come? No, it has to be said that such an idea is entirely an exaggeration of the imagination. Have you yourself had any reason to suspect such a thing while you have been here?

TP: No not at all.

Boris: (With a laugh.) It makes for a little excitement on holiday perhaps, to think of it.

Igor: If you agree, shall we now pause for a few moments?

This was because the door had opened and the grey-haired secretary had reappeared with another tray of fresh glasses of tea and some small cakes. The tape recorder was switched off, she took away the empty glasses from the previous tray, and conversation turned to the mildness of the now-ending winter, and the erratic form of Moscow Dynamo, the football team which Boris supported. After ten minutes I put a new cassette in the recorder, switched it on again, and as we all settled back once more, addressed my first question direct to Vladimir on the opposite side of the desk, in English.

TP: May I ask you about something that's been intriguing me since we first met on the steps earlier on. Where did you learn to speak such perfect English?

Vladimir: (After a short pause.) You have not heard me speak English.

TP: Yes, you did to the interpreter when we arrived. I think you thought he was me, and you asked him in English did I understand Russian.

Vladimir: (Quietly.) Surprising.

TP: Your accent was perfect: in fact I'd almost say you spoke without any accent at all. Where did you learn it?

Vladimir: (Amused.) Oh I must have had very good teachers.

Igor: (Via the interpreter.) Mr Parker, may I now please ask you a question? Tell me – what do you think of our work?

I must have been as surprised as Vladimir, but less well able to conceal it. I asked the interpreter to say I didn't understand the question: did he mean since the Revolution, in the last twenty years, or what? When this was translated, Igor replied with an apologetic smile.

Igor: I am so sorry, please forgive me for not asking my question in a correct way. What I was enquiring was how you thought of the way we received you here and tried to assist you?

TP: Oh it was very good indeed thank you.

Igor: I am glad that you say this, because you see it is still in many respects a new experience for us to have visitors, and tell things and discuss them. Boris would now like to say something briefly to you.

Boris: Well first I would repeat what Igor has said; and I would like to add that we are most pleased you should give attention to us. I say this most sincerely. So we have here a souvenir of your visit that we would like to present to you. As you see, it is a book in two volumes, and it is a full and comprehensive history of the KGB covering the entire period between the year 1917 when it came into existence, and the year 1921. It is of course in Russian, but I hope when you return to your country you will be able to find someone to translate a part, or all of it, for you. Allow me to tell you a little of the background to it. When it was first issued four years ago, in an edition of a hundred thousand copies, it sold out immediately. But some of its readers then noticed that several of the documents which formed part of its contents had been shortened, or it has to be said in some cases even distorted. In fact, certain documents had been omitted altogether. Protests were made about this, and it was decided that a new and entirely complete edition would be prepared. This is an advance copy of it, and it is to be published in a short time, in an edition of one-half of a million copies. We sincerely hope you will find it of interest, and I now present it to you.

Igor: I would like also to say something else as well, which is that whenever you return to our country, if you would like us to meet again for other talks on any matters of concern to you, please telephone this number which I have written on this piece of paper for you, and ask to speak to me, Igor. I give you my personal promise that you shall have my immediate attention.

TP: Well thank you.

Igor: And finally I would like to say this also, and hope you will not think it rude of me to make such a personal request. On the occasions when you have opened your briefcase to take out a notebook or a cassette, I have noticed that you also have in it a copy of what I suspect is one of your own books that you have written. I wonder if you would consider to give it to us in return for the one we have presented to you? And would you write in it please your signature?

TP: Certainly yes of course. Would you like me to inscribe your names in it as well?

Igor: That would be a great honour for us.

TP: With pleasure. What are they?

Igor: (With a broad smile.) Mr Parker, our names are Igor – and Boris – and Vladimir.

18 Worth to stay

Dr Mikhail Mikhailov

Dr Mikhail Mikhailov

We met many times. In appearance and manner he was close to
everyone's idea of a typical Russian – wildly bushy-haired and
thickly bearded, deep-voiced, small, chubby, expansive and affectionate, and laughing from time to time with a soft rich chuckle.
His favourite clothes were baggy corduroy trousers, a faded and
darned dark blue pullover with a polo neck, and shapeless thick felt
carpet slippers; his favourite sitting position was on the low divan
serving as a settee in his apartment living-room, with a glass of
cognac in his hand and his feet pulled up under him.

– Larissa is away this evening, she gives you her love. So this is a
good time, my English friend, to make our recording. What would
you like for us to talk about? Life, fate, work, my opinions, what?
Any of them or all of them you say? This is what you call a tall
order yes? My English is very bad though, so first I have to say I
hope you will excuse it OK?

What sort of a man I am: well I will try to tell you. Happily
married is the first thing to say, that is the most important. This is
unusual these days in the Soviet Union I am afraid. Or perhaps it is
the same everywhere. But outside of my marriage, I am a little bitter
and a little sad. It is because I am fifty-six, and for most of the
middle part of my life, sixteen years of it in total, it was wasted and
I was never able to do what I wanted to. I had been professor of
history and sociology; but for that period of time that I speak of I
was employed on writing and rewriting one small section of the
Great Soviet Encyclopaedia. For sixteen years.

This is a very famous work as you will know. Every time a new
edition of it is finished, then work begins at once on the next edition.

It is like something you have in your country called I believe the Bridge of Forth: they paint at one end, and by the time they have reached the other, they have to start again once more at the beginning. My task was to write and rewrite a small section of oriental history, no bigger than this; and in all the years of course there was little alteration to it. You can imagine the continuous writing, how dull it was, and long and tiring. Your brain you know, you felt it had turned to solid; and I was not allowed to write anything else. Many occasions I was tempted to try like so many of my friends had done, to emigrate. More than one hundred of them were gone eventually: it was almost every single person I knew, one by one, all my friends. But who can tell what would have happened if I had done the same? I think often about it. If I had done so, well one thing that I know is that I would not have met Larissa, so nothing would have compensated for that.

The reason for my being put to work on the *Encyclopaedia*? It was this. I worked at the Institute of Sociological Studies, and with eight hundred of my colleagues I was a signator of a petition to Brezhnev protesting against the treatment of a well-known academic who was being persecuted. This was in 1970 and as a result I was immediately dismissed from my post, in common with everyone else who had signed it. I was told I would be allowed no other employment anywhere; but after a long struggle and with the help of a friend, I obtained the post of writer for the *Encyclopaedia*.

So it went for me, year after year. My first marriage failed, I was divorced, and there was nothing left. I was a person so to say who had no personality; and it is necessary you know to say also this – it has left a mark. If a person has been in trouble with the authorities, he is never certain he will not be so again. Even now, I am told for example now I can speak to whoever I like, and I can say to them whatever I like; it is OK now to do this. But in two years' time, three years – will it still be so? How may I tell? Fear does not entirely go away from you. You will meet many like me: it is better if you are younger, but for people who are of my age, late fifty or nearly sixty, no it is not so easy.

Enough. I will tell you about my work now. This is something completely new, and very interesting for me. It fills my mind, and therefore the present is something I enjoy to speak about. With some of my colleagues who are also historians and sociologists and statisticians, we are so to say a small team. We have been required by the Central Committee, and we are funded by the government for it, to establish what is named the 'All-Soviet-Union Centre for Research into Public Opinion'. If it had been five years ago or less even, four, and anyone had suggested that the Soviet government could ever do such a thing – want to know public opinion on matters of policy in all fields, and to take it into account – well everyone would have found themselves helpless with laughter at such an idea. They would have thought the person talking about it was having hallucinations, you know? But it has happened: it has come into being now just two years ago, and it is being developed by an assortment of people such as myself. None of us has been in the past famous, I assure you, for unquestioning loyalty to the State and the Party: so this we feel is a remarkable thing.

Our function is to design and to produce questionnaires concerning aspects of our society, and our present government's policies towards them. And we have formed a carefully composed cross-section of persons to answer, from all backgrounds, from so to say all walks of life. It is of a very large number of persons, so that it can be claimed the sample is completely representative. We put the questionnaire to them to obtain their answers; and finally by computer analyse the answers, and give this precisely accurate picture of how people feel. It is like what you call 'polls' which you have in your country, and in the United States; but if I may say so, I think it is more extensive for the numbers of people sampled, as well as I think more exact in the questions it asks.

All the time we are developing it and increasing the ways in which to use it. Recently for example there was the Congress of Peoples' Deputies here in Moscow, and for many hours each day the sessions of it were shown live on television. While this was going on, we were estimating from our sample of repliers how close public opinion was on different topics to that which Deputies claimed to be representing – or sometimes how widely it was different from it. We also measured public estimates of the performances of the different Deputies, how people felt about the way they were representing them, and so on. It was very interesting to learn the results as they were analysed – most interesting in particular to the

Deputies themselves, to discover what a cross-section of the public thought of them and what they were saying.

We have in addition questionnaires which are being made on all subjects we can think of, all the time without cease. Our results are presented three or four times a year to the government. One example would be the continuing answers to a question we ask such as 'Which problem of daily living is the most constant one in the life of you and your family?' Always fifty-five per cent or fifty-six per cent answerers say the shortage of food supplies in particular and of consumer goods in general, and the poor quality of what is available. Shortage of accommodation, poor pay and high prices – these are three other things that are also causing increasing dissatisfaction all the time. It is obvious I think that such things would be the main matters of complaint, but to be able to demonstrate it statistically to the government, well so to say it keeps up the pressure on them.

It is also interesting for us to discover something which is relating to this. If we ask let us say a different type of question, such as one that asks 'Which of our country's problems should be tackled first, if it means others will have to wait?' most people put at the top of their list environment and ecology: food shortages and poor quality consumer goods come lower down. It shows many people do not have only immediate concerns. There is also expressed strong concern on such matters as abuse of power by the government, unfair and corrupt distribution of goods and services, and of course always complaints about the too-much bureaucracy that we have.

You will understand my enthusiasm for this sort of work: it is something completely new in our country. We regularly publish in the newspapers and magazines our findings, and people are very interested in them and write us letters encouraging us to continue. It is you see a new idea here altogether that people should be told their opinions matter, and the government wants to know what they are. Though of course cynicism is widespread, because people are doubtful if the government will actually do anything in answer to all these criticisms.

I share some of their attitude myself, yes. The history of our country, you see – well it has to be said there should be understandable reasons for not being over-optimistic about the future. In the short term things might improve perhaps; but in the long term no,

I am not so sure. There have always been two faces of Russia – the cruel barbaric one, and the warm and sentimental one. It is only my personal opinion, but I think it is because of this aspect of our nature that Russia's civilisation and its way of life will never be fully reconcilable with that of the West. I feel the two societies are really fundamentally different, and we are never going to be able to understand each other properly. How can I put it more clearly, I wonder, than to say I think Western civilisation is more like a grown-up person, and Russia is an adolescent? Westerners seem to be more actively dissatisfied with conditions of life, and if conditions are not good enough they try to change them. But Russians it seems to me on the whole are more accepting, they accept that is how life is. Through all their history they have had suffering and hardships and difficulties: so to a great extent they are fatalistic. But a Western civilisation has so to say a dynamic quality, a desire for change and a belief that change can be obtained. To a Russian, what he suffers, well that is life, nothing can be done about it: he accepts it passively.

Perhaps it is a strange thing for me to say, but I feel Russians have, through their history, become so conditioned to acceptance, and what you might call almost servitude, that they really do not know why their parents, or even in some cases they themselves, were taken to prison camps. They accept that to have that happen to you, well it was one of life's dangers; so when it happened, all you could do was shrug. The tradition still exists: you accept that it happened, and in that way. But still today nobody questions *why* did it happen, what was the reason for it? And how can we make sure it happens no more? The feeling is, well there is still the chance it could happen again, no matter how much brighter the prospects look. I made it clear to you, did I not, at our conversation's beginning, that I am in no way different from this myself either? So you see I am in this way completely Russian.

The belief inside you here is that your life is not yours to do with as you wish: it is in the hands of fate, fortune, luck, whatever name you choose to give it. And believing this makes us not independent: because we feel we do not have responsibility for our lives. Fate is made a person: it is the all-powerful authority. It will decide what will happen to us: so no initiative is required. The State is authorised benefactor and authorised taker-away of benefits. The State is fate.

You can mutter, you can complain but you cannot do anything to change its power. You cannot set your own will against it, because all you will get is another and worse form of fate, which again you will be able to do nothing about.

And this is going to take not five or ten years to change, if it ever can be changed: it must take five or ten generations. I believe it will happen, but very slightly very slowly, only a little by a little. What I am doing now, the work I am involved in – all of us are doing it because we think it might contribute a little perhaps, it might influence our ways. I wish I was younger of course: then I could hope to see if things do change. It is a matter of great regret to me I lost so many years; mentally they should have been the best years of my life. But there you see, as I said I am a Russian: I shrug, and accept that it was fate.

But always still you know, at those times I have spoken of when I was thinking to emigrate, some small thing inside me here, it did not accept it fully: always at the last, sometimes at the very last, I stopped, I drew back, and I did not go. Why? I cannot say because I do not know.

I know only this. This is my country, and somehow I felt it was worth to stay; and I am glad now that I did, because now there is a feeling of, how to say it, like the weather now, of coming spring.

19 *Coda*

All those lonely people

What the stars foretell

All those lonely people

Classified advertisements from Soviet Woman, Moscow Evening News, Health Monthly *and* Country Matters

If you are as lonely as I am, please write to me and I'll be very glad to answer your letter. I live in the Moscow region, I am female, 46 and single, and I have a university diploma. In what? Write and find out, and I'll tell you more about myself.   No. 4265.

Young male computer specialist would like to meet an attractive girl who has relatives or friends in England, or in English-speaking countries. I am not yet 30.   No. 5656.

I am looking for a broad-minded female model under 25. Photo is essential, and I will send you mine.   No. 2143.

I am a man who needs a companion to talk to in the Moscow area. She must be unattached, be interested in a wide range of subjects, and have lots of spare time in the afternoons.   Reply A/466.

I am a male of 36, Jewish, 5′ 9″ in height, with a higher-education diploma. I live in the countryside north of Moscow, and would like to meet an attractive woman, not above 39, who will share with me a love of nature.   No. TS/223.

A bachelor, 6′ 0″ tall, aged 40, with an engineering diploma and an apartment of his own, would like to meet a quiet unpretentious girl who is under 28 and who would be interested in having a family. Nationality and education are of absolutely no importance. No. 5320.

Wanted, a female partner for playing tennis, mountain skiing, and skating.   Reply C/334.

Father and son who are both professional engineers, seek a mother and her daughter to come and live with them in Moscow, in their apartment with a telephone.   No. TS/461.

A young female companion is invited for a motoring trip to the Black Sea coast. All expenses paid. Send photo.   No. 7522.

Young female Muscovite, aged 22, 5′ 5″ tall, who likes knitting, cooking, theatre, cinema, literature and sport, wants to meet a genuine young man under 32 who is ready to set up house on a basis of mutual understanding and respect.   No. MM/414.

I seek a female helper of pre-retirement age, for living together in Moscow. Further details from CM/1078.

A female will be happy to meet a kind and intelligent male under 60, optimistic and with a sense of humour, and without drinking habits. As for myself, I am 51, Tartar, 5′ 3″ in height, with an education diploma, slightly overweight but young-looking, and what you would call nice. A letter with a photo would be appreciated.   A/327.

I invite a cultured male to assist me in setting up house and bringing up a boy 9 years of age. Exchange photos and references.   No. FG/2778.

A male of 40 seeks a graduate of the music Conservatoire for help around the house. Send telephone number.   No. 4392.

A photographer is looking for a young female assistant to join him in interesting and varied work, which could develop into something more.   No. 6768.

A family of two men, one 50 and the other 18 years old, living in a two-roomed apartment, are looking for a female housekeeper who will care for them. Lots of free time. In return, security is offered. No. FH/6012.

An honest, punctual and not very talkative male of 35, with secondary education and without children, doesn't think highly of his appearance, and lives with his parents in Moscow. He likes modern music, fishing, jogging, photography and gardening at the family dacha. He would like to meet a slim, sociable, kind and practical woman of 28–35 who is without children and would share his interests. His housing is in the Moscow region.   Box 4683.

A male in the Moscow region, I am 44 years of age and a professional in the field of creative activity, securely well-off and with no housing problem. I am 5′ 6″ tall, and I would like to meet a sportswoman of 28–35 who would become a friend and help in creative activity. My drawbacks are uprightness, straightforwardness, and smoking. No. 5114.

A young man is searching for a young attractive Muscovite, preferably one with her own plot of land or dacha.   RD/654.

My name is Nadia. I am 32 and 5′ 7″ tall, a slim and energetic medical doctor, materially secure and with my own apartment. I have never been married and would like to meet a compatible male under the age of 45. I will answer any letter with a photograph. No. 3231.

A woman with an adopted son, living in Moscow region, seeks a friend of 44–55 years of age who would like to join her in setting up a family home for orphans and abandoned children. Would consider having another child of her own. I shall take care of all financial expenses.   BT/8844.

A female divorcee of 42, Jewish, 5′ 5″ in height and with a secondary education, would like to meet a male from Moscow or Leningrad with a view to having a family.   Box 1475.

Male, 52, at present living near Odessa, has a diploma of higher education. Tall, he seeks a female with broad interests including the arts. Children would not be a problem and absence of housing would be immaterial. Let us exchange letters and photographs. No. 2394.

A female of 40 invites a well-educated and interesting male companion to tour historical buildings with her. DF/333.

A male of 62, 5' 5" in height, a higher-education graduate, likes an active way of life which promotes longevity, and is still working. He would like to become acquainted with a female who lives in Moscow, under 50, not tall and not inclined to corpulence. No. 8790.

I am an attractive blonde of 40, 5' 7" tall, and a technical-school graduate who is bringing up a 3-year-old son. I am a resident of the city of Moscow, and have normal living conditions. I would like to meet a kind, reliable and good-natured man, without any bad habits and who is aged under 48. I believe I would make a faithful and loyal friend and a good housewife. I will ignore all letters written only out of curiosity. TD/564.

A fit attractive male doctor of 30, 5' 10" in height, Armenian and with high moral beliefs, would like to meet a slim and intelligent young lady of 20–27 who is also Armenian. Box 6652.

Life is full of unexpected things, is it not? I am not yet losing hope that I may before long meet a respectable male under 40 who is kind and modest, without bad habits, and with serious views on family life. I am 33, 5' 8" tall, of prepossessing appearance and benevolent character, divorced, bringing up a son. I live with my parents and wear glasses. TM/287.

Woman with university education, 48, German, 5' 4" in height, has an apartment of her own and three grown-up children. She likes music, is mainly cheerful, and has still not lost hope of having an active and eventful life. She is of an optimistic nature, with a liking for all kinds of leisure activity, and is told she easily adapts to any new situation. She would like to meet a man aged 55–60 who would appreciate these qualities, and who is himself active, modest, and intelligent.   Box 3030.

I would like to hear from a tender and easygoing female. I appreciate humour, kindness, and reliability in human relations. I am 52, Jewish, and with a university diploma. I have average weight and height, and am indifferent to alcohol. Looks are not important, but I would appreciate a photograph which would be returned if requested.   No. 6542.

A woman of 30 seeks male companionship.   MC/651.

Woman, aged 57, 5′ 3″ in height, with passions for sport, music and art, would like to meet a cultured man aged 55–65, who would have a sense of humour and mutual understanding, values such qualities as kindness, and cannot stand cigarette smoke and strong drink. I would like us to spend a golden autumn together.   No. 4843.

Young woman aged 22, height 5′ 1″, lives in Moscow and is quite pretty but very shy. Likes classical music. Needs kind young man to escort her and help her become more at ease. Marriage is a possibility.   DS/956.

Man, 24, working in Moscow for next three months, wants to meet older woman for uncomplicated relationship.   No. 9232.

This is my second-time advertisement. I had no replies to my first. If you are as lonely as I am, please write to me and I'll be very glad to answer your letter. I live in the Moscow region, I am female, 46 and single, and I have a university diploma in philology. If you write I will tell you more about myself. What is there to lose?   No. 6765.

(Translations by Galina Fadeyeva)

What the stars foretell

from Commersant, *a weekly journal of the USSR Alliance of Co-operatives*

What the stars hold in store for you this week. (*Astra inclinant, non necessitant.*)

Monday looks good for those wanting to begin court proceedings and put things straight with law-enforcement officers and social workers – but only if you are seeking justice in earnest. It will also be an auspicious day to contact business partners and arrange conferences and consultations, where you will most probably have a chance to obtain useful and desirable information. But do not try to get it in ways which are not entirely in keeping with universal moral principles, or else your acquisitions may entail a high price.

Tuesday will be a good day to make personal and business contacts with the opposite sex, and the best time to do so is after four o'clock in the afternoon. Mental efforts will hardly produce any tangible results on this day, and neither will contemplation of pending decisions. But today may bring luck to factory managers, co-op chiefs and other bosses, except those concerned with the production of freezers and refrigerators.

Wednesday is going to be good for any business undertaking from contract-signing to marginal domestic innovations. But entrepreneurs in agricultural business or environmental projects would be best advised to finish their working day before nine o'clock in the evening.

Thursday is perhaps the worst day of the week, so don't venture into anything serious, especially if you make or sell products for the ladies or run a dating agency. On this day be careful also to mind your health problems: diet if possible, and avoid any extreme situations.

Neither is Friday a promising day for anything of any kind at all: any new undertaking is likely to end in failure. But luck may come to science workers and those involved in high technology. Also on this day, you may encounter legal problems, up to and including conflicts with law-enforcement officers, so be wise and avoid all contact with them. However, if this is impossible, try to arrange any examinations of yourself in the afternoon, preferably after four o'clock. If on this day you unavoidably need to make an important decision, do not follow the advice of people you usually keep in high esteem but use your own intuition instead.

Saturday will bring a smile to the face of those who work for companies associated with the defence sector – armaments, medicine (surgery), water and underwater operations including fisheries, and also to those politicians and people who are public figures at present in opposition to those in power. The latter will be best advised to start their working day not before nine in the morning, and to postpone all weekend plans until Sunday. Charity activities are not advisable for anyone, and for leisure and recreation intellectual games will be best.

Sunday is likely to be better for everyone. Even if you don't feel very well, there is no reason to worry. Just try to devote this last day of the week to rest and leisure, domestic chores, or going to see next of kin or friends. It may pay to remember that today Lady Luck will be a more frequent visitor to men than to the representatives of the fairer sex.

(*Please note.* This horoscope applies to Moscow, Leningrad, Kiev, Tallin, Riga, Vilnius, Minsk, Kishinev, Kharkov, Sevastopol, Murmansk and adjacent areas sharing the same solar time zone only.)

from Moscow Evening News

In this horoscope compiled for the coming week, the Astrologer advises all born under the sign of CAPRICORN (December 22–January 20) that they should be more confident in themselves and their own strength. Don't be afraid of opponents and your enemies – they won't do you any damage, says the Astrologer. He warns married Capricorns that they may have some family difficulties. He also recommends all born under this sign to be more careful in spending money between March 19 and 21. If you have not yet introduced a regime of economy, you had better do so as soon as possible.

Those who are AQUARIANS are advised by the Astrologer to keep away from politics. It is very likely that this week will be the best time for them to concentrate on their job, and to put any innovative ideas they have into practice. It is even likely they may change the profile of their job, though it could be without immediate results.

Those born under PISCES (February 22–March 20) will feel anxiety this week. Judging by the disposition of the stars, any enterprising initiative will be unsuccessful at this time. Success in family life is equally unlikely. The Astrologer feels sorry for married Pisceans – they may have to part from their spouses. Let's hope though that it will be because of just another quarrel, or even for a usual business trip. Bad news is also in waiting for all Pisceans this week. Such a forecast will no doubt not add to their optimism, but there is always possibility of alternatives. Astrology after all is not an exact science.

For those whose sign is ARIES (born March 21–April 20) there is something frightening in the offing, and it's most likely it will come on Sunday. But during bad moments, those who are men will find great support and comfort from women. As for women under this sign, there is nothing whatever to be afraid of: if there were, the Astrologer would certainly have known and been able to tell them where they should look for support.

Changes for the better await those whose sign is TAURUS (April 21–May 21). There will be good prospects for those in business. Children will bring a lot of joy to those with families. But life will not be a total idyll. There might be some slight worries, most likely about complete trifles, between March 19 and 21.

For those born under GEMINI (May 22–June 21), if they have intelligence and fresh ideas, they will be highly praised by their chiefs. Though the two things are not in any way directly connected, they are likely to find themselves taking a deeper interest in religion. In the middle of the week they may find themselves in a difficult situation, but as usual will be able to find an excellent way out of it.

It would be a good thing for anyone who is a CANCERIAN (born June 22–July 23) to take more care of his health. Overwork should be avoided on these days, and you should not get too involved in business. Family difficulties may also occur, and there is the possibility of an unpleasant talk with your boss.

Those born July 24–August 23 under the sign of LEO will have to forget totally any idea of rest. Even trifling matters will require strenuous effort. The Astrologer makes no secret of the fact that the coming week is very far from being a good one for those under this sign.

VIRGO (August 24–September 23). If this is your sign, you are advised to give your special attention to family relationships. A row may break out at any time, so it is advisable to try and anticipate events and resolve disputes before they can arise. All that is needed is understanding and love. Keep an eye on your children if you have any, otherwise they may escape from your control.

LIBRANS (September 24–October 23) are likely this week to lose the balance which is so characteristic of them, and this will leave its imprint on their mood and behaviour. There may be disagreements with relatives. Librans who are in any way connected with building will find themselves facing serious difficulties. But if they are men, apart from in business matters they will enjoy the favours of women, and this will help them partially to restore their confidence.

The mental abilities of those born under the sign of SCORPIO (October 24–November 22) will experience some sort of crisis, and despite all their efforts they will be unable to solve certain problems facing them. In difficult situations they will find their friends come to their help. And if they are out of favour at work, in the long run things will improve but not immediately.

For SAGITTARIANS who are having children, this week will be the most favourable time, with Thursday the best day of all. But do not let it negatively affect your work. In business or finance on the other hand, do not anticipate success: it will come in time, so do not worry about it.

(*Translation by Galina Fadeyeva*)

Acknowledgments

A book such as this takes a long time to prepare, a longer time to gather the material for, and an even longer time still to write. In all, this occupied me for just over two years, and during that time so many different people helped me in some or all of the three different processes that it's difficult for me to thank every one of them adequately and properly. Apart from those I've mentioned at the beginning – David Godwin my editor at Jonathan Cape, my friend and agent Gill Coleridge of Rogers Coleridge & White, and Barbara Laird of East-West Reach – both the Society of Authors and the Writers' Guild of Great Britain should be thanked for giving me initial and most helpful letters of introduction to the Union of Soviet Writers in Moscow. There as I've said Vladimir Stabnikov opened not only doors but windows for me as well, providing a great deal of patient and valuable advice as well as almost limitless assistance. I am profoundly indebted to him: certainly without his help I should have had to face many more obstructions and difficulties than I did. Also at the Writers' Union in Moscow, the Head of Receptions, Natalia Kokhanovsckaya, and the Chairman of the Foreign Commission, Oleg Severgin, both at all times extended most generous hospitality and did many favours for me. I thank them warmly, as I do for the same reasons Yakov Aksyuta, Head of the International Department of the Writers' Union of Ukraine, and his colleagues.

Additionally in Moscow, literally dozens of individuals helped me in a private capacity, introducing me to their friends and families and associates, and frequently acting as interpreters for me, often in obscure and distant places, and at considerable inconvenience to themselves. None of them would ever accept any payment for their skills, or so much as reimbursement for their expenses. Often I felt that in the Soviet Union friendliness and generosity towards foreigners seemed to be a natural part of everyday life. I'm greatly indebted too of course to all who gave so freely both time and hospitality to me when we talked. I'm conscious there are many mistakes and inaccuracies in the text: wherever they occur the fault is entirely mine, due to my lack of knowledge of the Russian language and the inability to grasp properly what was being said.

Some people – quite a number, unhappily – asked me not to name them, and so I cannot. But of those I can, I give special thanks to Alexander Fadeyev and Nina Pavlova in particular: and also to Paul Pozner, Arthur Raffe, Leonid Sedov, Tatiana and Sasha Pavlova, Alexei Dmitriev, Vladimir Popov, Oleg Alyakrinsky, Marina Moskvina, Irena Maximova, P. Tchaikovsky and D. Shostakovitch.

Additionally in Moscow, Stephen and Eve McEnelly at the British Embassy did many kindnesses which I shall always appreciate; and I am very grateful also to Chris Perry, Stuart Seaman, and Peter Formhals, who all gave me great assistance and much most useful advice.

In England, a large number of people helped me as well. I thank Andrew Nurnberg for his advice and generous practical assistance; as always, John Studd of Barclays Bank for contacts and financial arrangements; and, again, Louise Castro of Hogg Robinson for handling complicated travel arrangements and alterations to them with her usual efficiency and good humour. I thank especially too Dr John Barber of King's College Cambridge, Lyn Smith of The Imperial War Museum, Peter Jarman of Quaker Peace and Service, Brenda Ferris of Babel Translations in Norwich, and Richard Humphries of Halesworth Adshop; and also Madge Pickard, Harvey Pilcher, Roy Ridgway, Gale Carruthers, Marian Johnson, and my daughter Kristen Buchan. Linda Ginn typed and retyped many notes and drafts, as well as the final version of the manuscript, with dedication, speed and consummate skill; and as befits the best copy editor that there is, Vicki Harris yet again brought enjoyment to meticulousness with a firm hand and a light touch.

My wife Margery was a companion on all my visits to the USSR. As always she faced domestic difficulties and upheavals with either calmness or enthusiasm, whichever was appropriate and whenever it was. She spent long hours walking great distances in Moscow in the summer's heat and the winter's slush and cold, searching for such things as notebooks, tomatoes, toothpaste and tin plates when they were required: and even longer hours still in cramped and uncomfortable dimly lit places transcribing recorded tapes of interviews. Her stamina was limitless and her steady helpfulness unfailing: every writer needs such support, and I can't imagine how anyone could survive without it. I couldn't, I know.

I've briefly referred already in the Introduction to Galena Fadeyeva, my assistant, researcher, and principal interpreter. But what I've written there in no way at all properly indicates or describes the full amount or extent of how much she helped me. In each of the intervals between my visits to Moscow she worked ceaselessly and assiduously: telephoning, writing letters, going to see people and explaining to them what I was trying to do and how, and making appointments in advance for me before my returns. She did it so carefully and thoroughly, and arranged it every time so faultlessly, that I often completely lost sight of the fact, when I went to talk to someone, that she herself had usually seen them three or four times previously to prepare the way. 'We feel we know you very well already,' was a frequent warm and friendly greeting to me: and it came of course entirely as a result of her preparations. I have never had so close and rewarding a relationship before with someone I was working with, and in every sense it made this book possible. It is dedicated to her for that reason, because in so many ways it is not only mine but hers.

Tony Parker
Westleton, Suffolk